REFORMING EDUCATION

Mortimer J. Adler

REFORMING EDUCATION

THE OPENING OF THE
AMERICAN MIND

Edited by Geraldine Van Doren

MACMILLAN PUBLISHING COMPANY

NEW YORK

COLLIER MACMILLAN PUBLISHERS

LONDON

Macmillan Publishing Company
866 Third Avenue, New York, NY 10022
Collier Macmillan Canada, Inc.

Library of Congress Cataloging-in-Publication Data
Adler, Mortimer Jerome, 1902–
    Reforming education.
    Bibliography: p.
    1. Education—United States—History.
2. Education—Philosophy.   I. Van Doren, Geraldine.
II. Title.
LA212.A37   1988   370'.973   88-8339
ISBN 0-02-500551-0

Macmillan books are available at special discounts for bulk purchases
for sales promotions, premiums, fund-raising, or educational use.
For details, contact:

Special Sales Director
Macmillan Publishing Company
866 Third Avenue
New York, NY 10022

10 9 8 7 6 5 4 3 2 1

Designed by Jack Meserole

PRINTED IN THE UNITED STATES OF AMERICA

PERMISSIONS

Chapter 16, "What Is an Idea?" by Mortimer J. Adler, first appeared in *Saturday Review of Literature*, November 22, 1958. Copyright © 1958 by Mortimer J. Adler. Reprinted by permission of the author.

Chapter 19, "A Sound Moral Philosophy" (1982) by Mortimer J. Adler, first appeared in *The Great Ideas Today, 1982* and is reprinted by permission of Encyclopaedia Britannica, Inc.

Chapter 20, "Ethics: Fourth Century B.C. and Twentieth Century A.D." (1988) by Mortimer J. Adler, first appeared in *The Great Ideas Today, 1988* and is reprinted by permission of Encyclopaedia Britannica, Inc.

Chapter 21, "Reconstituting the Schools" (1983) by Mortimer J. Adler, first appeared in *The Center Magazine*, September/October 1983, and is reprinted by permission.

Chapter 22, "The Three Columns Revisited" (1987) by Mortimer J. Adler, first appeared in *The Paideia Bulletin*, May 1987, Special Edition, and is reprinted by permission.

Chapter 23, "A Declaration of Principles by the Paideia Associates" (1988) by Mortimer J. Adler, first appeared in *The Paideia Bulletin*, October 1988, Special Edition, and is reprinted by permission.

Let us engage in the serious business of conducting our discussion rationally and logically, to discover the truth about points on which we differ.

CONTENTS

PART THREE
Teaching and Learning

PART FOUR
Thinking About Moral Values

PART FIVE
Paideia: Its Inception and Development

EDITOR'S PREFACE

"Can anything be done about American education?" Mortimer Adler posed that question in 1940 ("This Prewar Generation"). His answer was, "I doubt it." Nevertheless, reforming education has been at the center of his life and thought for more than half a century. While they are not arranged chronologically, these essays record his progress in pursuit of that task from 1939 to 1989, the task of formulating and presenting his ideas about what should be done to improve education in America, and why it should be done. The essays respond to questions about schooling, the curriculum, teaching, learning, and more—questions that are both perennial and contemporary.

What should be taught? How? In what order? To what purpose? And to whom—to everyone, or just to a select few? What does democracy require? What about happiness? The philosopher looks at education and asks; the teacher explains what we should know and the skills we need for learning because we are human beings and because we live as free citizens in a modern democracy.

Paideia is a subject common to all of the essays. Adler defines the word:

> PAIDEIA (py-dee-a) from the Greek *pais, paidos*: the upbringing of a child. (Related to pedagogy and pediatrics.) In an extended sense, the equivalent of the Latin *humanitas* (from which "the humanities"), signifying the general learning that should be the possession of all human beings (*The Paideia Proposal*, Macmillan 1982).

What constitutes paideia, the substance of a general education, and who should have access to it have always been matters of controversy. Whether there is any such thing any longer, in the modern world, is a new question that compounds the controversy. Paideia is what we need to know and know how to do in order to enable us to earn a living, to perform the duties of citizenship, to live decent lives, and to improve ourselves and our lives. Our schools and colleges are not delivering it, not even for a few, much less for all American children.

Controversy about what should be done to improve American education continues. Adler is still in the thick of it. In his prologue to this book, written in 1988, he informs us that Allan Bloom, among others, has recently noted some deficiencies in American education. But Bloom, says Adler, has failed to see what they really are, in particular, with regard to the obligation of American education to democracy, and to equal educational opportunity. In the prologue, and throughout these essays, Adler tells us precisely what those deficiencies are, how and when they originated, and how we can begin to remedy them.

With Bloom and others declaiming on one side about what a general education should be and who should have it, and with the students at Stanford, Duke, and other colleges and universities complaining on the other side about the texts that would give them access to it—texts which they would prefer to replace with more works by women, African, and Eastern authors—one would think that neither democracy nor education can long survive.

A curse on both their houses is Adler's position. He proclaims them both wrong. Adler takes a stand against both the elitists and the relativists, and dares to speak about universal values and truth. Once the ultimate goal of philosophy, of education, and of the humblest of human lives as well, now even the word "truth" has been all but banned on college campuses. To mention it suggests the charlatan, the crackpot, the dogmatist. But our preoccupation with the truth of scientifically verifiable findings as the only existing truth, Adler regards as the source of the impoverishment of mind and soul that Bloom and others lament.

In his prologue Adler also tells the story of his own career and that of the great books movement, which he helped found and with which he has been so intimately involved both on and off college campuses. Adler's autobiography, *Philosopher at Large* (Macmillan 1977), can fill in a few of the gaps. A footnote for those skeptics who think Adler invented the great books as a modern publicity stunt is that the course he describes, which was taught by his teacher, John Erskine, at Columbia University, beginning in 1921, was modeled on an older course of reading and tutorials at Oxford University called Ancient and Modern Greats. Erskine called his course Classics of the Western World. The title "Great Books of the Western World" comes from both of those courses. It is the title of the set of books Robert Hutchins and Mortimer Adler edited for William Benton, owner and publisher of Encyclopaedia Britannica, Inc., and vice president of the University of Chicago, that would serve as the material for seminars in the college of the University of Chicago and for adult seminars outside the university. Their use in those seminars, as Adler tells us, was not to teach Western civilization, but "how to read critically and to think reflectively about basic ideas and issues."

What should be taught and, just as important, how it should be taught are the subject of all of these essays. Both are considered as means to ends. The goals of schooling and of education after schooling rule all of the discussions. Those goals are considered singly in some of the essays. They come together at the end in the Paideia program.

Paideia is the culmination of Adler's lifelong, intense, loving, and often brutal struggle against the forces of utilitarianism, elitism, scientism, specialism, and any other dogma infesting American education. Accused of dogmatism by those who know no other way of thinking, he has pursued a dialectical approach to all ideas and issues, including the ideas and issues most closely concerned with education. In the essays that were written before the Paideia project was begun in 1979, the reforms he proposed clearly anticipate Paideia and the solutions it presents.

Adler warns us that if we approve them, the Paideia reforms will still take a long time to be realized. They will entail work and cooperation from within the schools and from the outside. They will require some humility on the part of school administrators and teachers, and some courage as well. Paideia comes, however, with a kind of guarantee: Wherever the program has been tried, on however small or large a scale, the changes it has brought about for students and for teachers as well have been for the better. If that is an irresistible incentive, then Adler's efforts may be rewarded.

Whatever success it may enjoy, Paideia is also the offspring of defeat in the battle which began after the First World War and in which Adler and many other eminent educators participated to reinstate liberal education in the colleges and universities. It was a battle that was lost, and the defeat now seems permanent for many reasons. Some of them have to do with the elective system, which gave another meaning to general education; with the unavoidable specialization of the sciences and the avoidable, but fashionable, specialization in other fields; with the fact that the Ph.D., the badge of the specialist, is required for a successful academic career; and that publication of research, which usually further narrows one's specialty, is necessary for advancement in such a career.

Young teachers understandably are not happy serving the aims of Paideia, or general education, and they often do it poorly because they have little experience in dialectical discussion and maieutic teaching. That is the heart of the Paideia program, the seminars which are conducted by the Socratic method, using questions to increase understanding.

The Paideia program offers a number of solutions for those who lament the loss of general education and for those students who find some of the texts not to their liking. They are all in these essays, which bring us full circle to the epilogue and, as always, to the great books, the material of and means to a liberal education.

In "Epilogue: Great Books, Past and Present," Adler returns to the great books to discuss their role in continuing education for adults, thereby completing the discussion of them begun in the prologue. The occasion for the first part of the epilogue was a speech given at the auditorium of The Fair Store in September 1948. It was one of several events of Great Books Week in Chicago, which was proclaimed by Mayor Kennelly to acknowledge the contribution of the great books to adult education. Adler informed his audience about the aims of the great books movement and of its widespread acceptance and success. In the second part of the essay, which was written in 1988, he provides some answers to the question of what makes a book a great book, and he gives us a list of great books dating from Homer to the twentieth century. Finally, in the third part, he talks about what works can be called great books in this century, and he gives us his own nominations for that list. This discussion first appeared in *The Center Magazine* (May/June 1977), a publication of the Center for the Study of Democratic Institutions.

Of his own experience in teaching great books seminars, Adler said in his autobiography, "Most of the things I have learned from teaching—as well as about teaching itself—I have learned from leading great books discussions, not only in colleges and universities, but also with adult groups all over the country." With the advent of Paideia, that statement must be emended to include groups of high school and elementary school students as well. It stands as testimony to the author's belief that the best teachers are those who continue learning, from their students and from their fellow teachers. To the many students in and out of schools who have known Mortimer Adler as their seminar leader, and to his colleagues who have worked with him on the Paideia program and elsewhere, the agility and accessibility of his mind make him one of the greats among teachers.

He has written scores of books, delivered hundreds of lectures, conducted thousands of seminars, and coedited *Great Books of the Western World*. He has also, with the help of hundreds of editors, writers, and scholars, transformed the *Encyclopaedia Britannica* from a gigantic compendium of knowledge into more than a reference work—a syllabus of general education—with the addition of the *Propaedia*, an outline of knowledge.

And he has had a few other good ideas—about how to read a book (more than one way); about how to teach a great book (dialectically and not dogmatically); about how to teach (three ways and not just didactically).

The essays in this volume range over a half century—from 1939 to 1988—and were chosen from both published and unpublished material, the latter most often lectures. Nothing has been included and no changes have been made without the author's approval. Considering the length of time over which they were composed, they display a remarkable degree of coherence and consistency in their basic views. However, here and there careful readers will discover minor inconsistencies in thought and in terminology, but they themselves will be able to take account of these by observing the dates and circumstances of the essays in which such inconsistencies occur. The headnotes introducing each essay are mine, and the numbered footnotes in chapters five and fourteen will be found at the end of the book.

GERALDINE VAN DOREN
June 1988

Great Books, Democracy, and Truth

1

Because of its title, *The Closing of the American Mind*, by Allan Bloom, sold widely, probably much more widely than it was read. Its misleading but attention-grabbing subtitle, *How Higher Education Has Failed Democracy and Impoverished the Souls of Today's Students*, lamented the failure of our colleges to serve our democratic society, but paid little attention to the dismal deficiencies of basic schooling in the United States, which are much more important as far as serving democracy is concerned.

With regard to the academic malaise that Mr. Bloom describes, but mistakenly regards as recent, his analysis of its causes is both inaccurate and inadequate. Worse, his slight effort to propose a cure falls far short of what must be done to make our schools responsive to democracy's needs and to enable our colleges to open the minds of their students to the truth.

These are serious indictments. But for me the book's most glaring defect is with regard to the undergraduate use of the great books over the last sixty years, and the more recent introduction of them into basic schooling by the Paideia program. Allan Bloom either has no knowledge of these facts or is gravely at fault for neglecting to report them. There is but one reference in *The Closing of the American Mind* to the "good old great books approach." Nevertheless, he proposes that approach as a remedy for the reform of our colleges.

Before Allan Bloom was born, I was a student in the first great books seminar that John Erskine taught at Columbia University in 1921. From 1923 to 1929, with Mark Van Doren, I taught great books seminars at Columbia University. At the invitation of Robert M. Hutchins, President of the University of Chicago, I brought the great books educational program to Chicago in 1930, and Hutchins and I taught the great books there long before Allan Bloom arrived on the scene. We continued teaching them while he was a young student at the University of Chicago.

Allan Bloom either is ignorant of the work that had been done at Columbia and at the University of Chicago; or worse, he intentionally ignored it in order to foster the impression that his recommendation— that the great books be read by college students—was his own educational innovation. However, this interpretation of his failure to tip his hat to his many predecessors, especially those at his own university, is partly negated by the fact that he refers to "the good *old* great books approach" (italics added). Hence, one might conclude that his recommendation of the "great books approach" is qualified by the condition that they be read and taught in the style that he, Allan Bloom, and his teacher, Leo Strauss, have read and taught them.

That is most certainly not the way that John Erskine, Mark Van Doren, Robert Hutchins, Stringfellow Barr, Scott Buchanan, Jacques Barzun, Lionel Trilling, Otto Bird (the last three of whom were students of mine), and many others taught them long before Allan Bloom arrived at the University of Chicago. When I come to the consideration of the great books in relation to philosophical truth, I will try to explain why the dialectical rather than the doctrinal style of reading and teaching the great books is much to be preferred in the education of the young.

2

Erskine's great innovation was the undergraduate seminar in which students and teacher sat around a table and engaged in critical conversation about the ideas in an assigned text. Erskine developed the first list of some sixty great books to be read by college juniors and seniors. Nothing like it ever existed before in undergraduate instruction. Seminars, in the German style, had been conducted, but they were only for Ph.D. candidates and for the consideration of their doctoral researches.

Erskine's original reading list has been considerably revised and expanded since the early 1920s—at Columbia itself, at the University of Chicago, at St. John's College, and at other institutions (Notre Dame, St. Mary's College) that adopted the great books seminars—but all subsequent lists of great books have retained about 85 percent of Erskine's original list.

In 1928 a grant from the Carnegie Corporation enabled Scott Buchanan (who later became Dean of St. John's College in Annapolis) and me to organize fifteen great books seminars for adults in New York City. This, so far as I know, was the first attempt to employ the reading and discussion of great books as a major form of continued learning for adults, later to become a national program under the auspices of the Great Books Foundation. There were two leaders for each of these seminars.

Before Hutchins went to Chicago, he and I discussed the Erskine list of great books that I had been teaching at Columbia. Hutchins confessed that in his undergraduate years at Yale, he had not read more than three or four of those books. Hutchins knew that his duties as president of the University of Chicago would get in the way of his own education unless he himself taught a course in which he had to read the books he had not read in college. He asked me to come to Chicago mainly for the purpose of teaching a great books seminar for entering freshmen that he and I would conduct as Mark Van Doren and I had done at Columbia. We did so from 1930 until 1948. From that, many other achievements followed.

In 1936, Hutchins established a Committee on the Liberal Arts. He invited Stringfellow Barr and Scott Buchanan of the University of Virginia to join us in planning an ideal, completely required curriculum for a liberal arts college. The reading and seminar discussion of great books for four years were central to that curriculum. This resulted in a greatly expanded list of great books, including works in mathematics and the natural sciences that had been for the most part absent from the original Erskine list. It also resulted, in 1937, in the establishment of the completely required New Program at St. John's College, the fiftieth anniversary of which has recently been celebrated. The renown of St. John's College, which was generally known as "the great books college," led other institutions around the middle of the century, such as Notre Dame and St. Mary's, to adopt modified versions of the program.

There were other, even more far-reaching results of what had been started at Columbia and Chicago.

In 1940, I published *How to Read a Book*, which should have been

entitled *How to Read a Great Book*. That volume contained in its
appendix a list of the great books, which enlarged Erskine's original list
and the one in use at the University of Chicago and at St. John's College.
It was a best-seller in 1940 and has been in print ever since. It has been
used by many high schools and colleges in English courses as an instrument for cultivating skills in reading, and was revised in 1974 by
Charles Van Doren and me.

In the 1940s, Hutchins and I also established the Great Books
Foundation for the purpose of promoting great books seminars for adults
all across the country. In that connection, I developed the first manual
of instruction for the guidance of ordinary lay persons in the conduct
of great books seminars. I also trained the first generation of seminar
leaders in Chicago.

During that same period, Hutchins and I conducted a great books
seminar for Chicago's civic leaders, many of whom were trustees of the
University of Chicago. Begun in 1943, it continues to this day, although
its membership has changed considerably.

There were still other significant developments of the great books
movement. The University of Chicago operated extension courses for
adults in University College, which was then called "the downtown
college." With the enthusiastic endorsement of Cyril Houle, dean of
that college, I outlined another modification of the St. John's program.
It was called "The Basic Program of Liberal Education for Adults" and
began its long and successful career in the late 1940s. Allan Bloom and
other students of Leo Strauss at the University of Chicago were among
the young men who were enlisted to teach the great books in that
program. It was his first teaching job.

In the great books seminars that Hutchins and I conducted for
Chicago's civic leaders at the University Club were Walter and Elizabeth
Paepcke. Their growing interest in the great books as an educational
instrument for adults led in 1950 to the establishment of the Aspen
Institute for Humanistic Studies. Starting out with just great books
seminars, the Aspen seminars, especially the Executive Seminars, developed in other directions, but a handful of great books has always
been at the core of the reading lists.

Another by-product of the great books seminars that Hutchins and
I conducted at the University Club was the publication in 1952 by
Encyclopaedia Britannica, Inc., of *Great Books of the Western World*.

William Benton, then a vice president of the University of Chicago, was a participant in that University Club seminar. When in 1943, he became owner and publisher of Encyclopaedia Britannica, Inc., he asked Hutchins and me to edit a set of great books for it to publish. We worked hard on that project for eight years, during which time I invented and produced the *Syntopicon* of the great ideas to accompany the set.

Then, on a grant from the Ford Foundation, the Institute for Philosophical Research was established to undertake a dialectical examination of the great ideas. Since then, it has published a series of books, beginning with a two-volume work, entitled *The Idea of Freedom*. Finally, in 1982, after three years' work with a group of eminent associates, I wrote and published *The Paideia Proposal*, an educational manifesto that called for a radical reform of basic schooling (kindergarten through twelfth grade) in the United States, and outlined a completely required curriculum that involved great books seminars in elementary and secondary schools.

I mention all this as background because *The Closing of the American Mind* and the reviews of it—both adverse and favorable—have made me realize that it is necessary to retell the story of the great books movement for the present academic generation, whose memories do not go further back than the 1960s, or at most, the end of the Second World War. It is also necessary to restate as clearly as possible the fundamental notions that underlie the selection of the great books, the proper way to discuss them in seminars, their use in a truly democratic system of education, and their relation to the pursuit of truth.

I would like, first, to discuss the ideal of a truly democratic system of education, which does not yet exist in this country and which Bloom's book nowhere considers. Second, I think it necessary to examine truth and error in the great books, and their bearing on the proper way to conduct discussions of them, which is the dialectical method, not the doctrinal style employed by Allan Bloom and his teacher, Leo Strauss. Third, I must deal with a problem that deeply concerns Allan Bloom —the prevalent skepticism about moral philosophy and the prevalence of subjectivism and relativism about values among students and professors—the causes of which Mr. Bloom inaccurately diagnoses. Finally, here and in the epilogue, I will set forth the fundamental notions and principles of the great books movement.

3

Many readers today think of democracy in twentieth-century terms as constitutional government with universal suffrage and the securing of natural, human rights. The other two quite different senses of democracy are the senses in which Plato and Aristotle in antiquity and Rousseau in the eighteenth century used the word: either for mob rule or for a constitutional government with citizenship restricted to men of property. In our terms, they used the word "democracy" to signify an oligarchy that conferred citizenship on men of small property instead of restricting it to those having large estates. *

Neither for them nor for Allan Bloom, who admires the political philosophy of these oligarchs, does the word "democracy" stand for the political ideal—the only perfectly just form of government. That use of the word makes its first appearance in 1861 in John Stuart Mill's *Representative Government*. Mill was the first great political philosopher who spoke for universal suffrage, extending it to women and to the laboring classes. He thought that justice required securing political liberty and equality for all, with few exceptions. But in 1861 Mill was a reluctant democrat who feared the unenlightened self-interest of the working-class majority, and so advocated plural votes for the upper classes to help them defeat majority rule.

All of Mill's predecessors in Western political theory thought that democracy, in *their* sense of the term, was either the worst form of bad government or the least desirable of the good forms of government, and none had even the slightest conception or even conjecture of democracy, in the twentieth-century sense of the term, as a political ideal to be realized in the future.

Bloom's readers have to guess in which of these radically different senses of democracy he uses the word. On the one hand, he could not be complaining about the failure of our educational institutions to serve democracy if he did not think of it as a desirable form of government. On the other hand, can any reader of *The Closing of the American Mind* fail to detect the strong strain of elitism in Bloom's own thinking, as evidenced by his devotion to Plato, Rousseau, and Nietzsche, and

---

*In Athens, at its most "democratic" extreme under Pericles, there were only 30,000 citizens in a population of 120,000. Excluded were women, slaves, and artisans.

by his advocacy of reading the great books by relatively few in the student population, certainly not by all?

The recency of constitutional democracy in this country explains and may even justify our not yet having a truly democratic system of public schooling or institutions of higher learning that are concerned with making good citizens of those who attend our colleges.

In 1817, Thomas Jefferson, as much an oligarch as John Adams, James Madison, Alexander Hamilton, and all the rest of our founding fathers, called upon the Virginia legislature to give three years of common schooling to all the children of the state. After three years, he advocated dividing the children into those destined for labor and those destined for leisure and learning (and citizenship and public office), and sending only the latter to college.

In our twentieth-century understanding of the term "democracy," Jefferson's educational program was thoroughly antidemocratic, but it still exists in the United States today. Though virtually all the children in our schools are now destined to become citizens, we still divide them into the college-bound and those not going from high school to college. The quality of schooling given the noncollege-bound does not prepare them for citizenship or for a life enriched by continued learning; nor, I should add, does the quality of education given the college-bound when they get to college. It is still a fundamentally antidemocratic system of schooling with a sharp differentiation between two tracks, one for those of inferior ability and one for their betters.

The first real departure from Jefferson's antidemocratic policy (dominating American education from 1817 to the present day) occurred in this century with startling pronouncements by John Dewey and Robert Hutchins. *The Paideia Proposal* in 1982 was dedicated to them because of their commitment to a democratic system of education.

In 1900, John Dewey said that the kind of schooling that the best and wisest parents would want for their own children is precisely the kind of schooling that the community should want for all its children. Any other policy if acted upon, he said, would defeat democracy.

In his epoch-making book, *Democracy and Education* (1916), Dewey enunciated a position the opposite of Jefferson's. He said all the children in our nation, now that it was on its way to becoming democratic, had the same destiny—to lead lives in which they would earn a living, act as intelligent citizens of the republic, and make an effort to lead a decent and enriched human life.

Bloom's book does not manifest the slightest commitment to a program for giving *all* the children the same quality of schooling to enable them to fulfill their common destiny. Nor does it give its readers any indication that the most grievous failure of our schools and colleges to serve democracy, now that democracy has at last come into existence, lies in the early differentiation of students, with different tracks for different students.

In the early 1930s President Hutchins was asked whether great books seminars, then open only to a picked handful of students, should be accessible to all the students in our colleges. His brief reply was crisp and clear. He said that the best education for the best was the best education for all. Great books seminars in our public schools and in our colleges should be available to all the students there, not only to the few who elect to take them or who are specially selected. That is not the answer to be found in Allan Bloom's book.

4

Some basic truths are to be found in the great books, but many more errors will also be found there, because a plurality of errors is always to be found for every single truth. One way of discovering this is to detect the contradictions that can be found in the books of every great author. Being human works, they are seldom free from contradictions. Skill in reading and thinking is required to find them. But, given that skill, finding contradictions in a book puts one on the highroad in the pursuit of truth. The truth must lie on one or the other side of every contradiction. It is there for us to detect when we are able to resolve the contradiction in favor of one side or the other.

More important is the fact that the great books contradict one another on many points in the various fields of discourse in which they engage. Once again, it must be said that the relation between truth and error is a one-many relationship: if the truth on a given point is thought to be in one or several of the great books, contradictions on that same point are likely to be found in many more great books.

In any case, it is clear that, if the great books contradict one another on many points, it must follow that many errors as well as some truths are to be found there. That is why the great books are such useful instruments in the pursuit of truth. For every truth, understanding all the errors it refutes is indispensable.

What I have just said holds particularly for the philosophical and theological works that belong in any comprehensive list of great books —the writings of Plato, Aristotle, Epictetus, Marcus Aurelius, Augustine, Aquinas, Calvin, Hobbes, Descartes, Locke, Hume, Rousseau, Kant, Hegel, Nietzsche, Mill, William James. Since Bloom and his teacher, Leo Strauss, are specialists in the field of moral and political philosophy, I will draw my examples from that field of discourse.

If Aristotle's political philosophy is thought to contain a number of fundamental truths, then errors must be found in Plato, Hobbes, Locke, Rousseau, Kant, and Hegel. If J. S. Mill's political philosophy is thought to contain some truths not found elsewhere, then on these points errors must be found in Aristotle. If Aristotle's *Nicomachean Ethics* is thought to contain a number of basic truths in moral philosophy, then on these points serious errors must be found in Plato, Epictetus, Kant, Hegel, and Nietzsche.

Though the same can be said for works in other branches of philosophy—metaphysics, the philosophy of mind, and the theory of knowledge—the examples I have given from the field of moral and political philosophy will suffice to enable me to distinguish between the right and wrong way to teach the great books, if the aim in using them is to teach students how to think and how to pursue the truth. Since the kind of teaching done by Leo Strauss and by his students, among them Allan Bloom, represents in my judgment the wrong way to teach the great books in our public schools and in our undergraduate colleges, let me describe the difference between what I consider to be the right and wrong way to read the great books.

The difference between Strauss's method of reading and teaching the great books and the method that Hutchins and I had adopted (the method also used by Erskine and Van Doren at Columbia, and by Barr and Buchanan at St. John's College) lies in the distinction between a doctrinal and a dialectical approach. The doctrinal method is an attempt to read as much truth as possible (and no errors) into the work of a particular author, usually devising a special interpretation, or by discovering the special secret of an author's intentions. This method may have some merit in the graduate school where students aim to acquire narrowly specialized scholarship about a particular author. But it is the opposite of the right method to be used in conducting great books seminars in schools and colleges where the aim is learning to think and the pursuit of truth.

When in the late 1940s Leo Strauss came to the University of Chicago and we were both on the faculty teaching great books, President Hutchins suggested that I get to know him. We met several times and discussed our reading of Plato and Aristotle. I soon learned that Strauss read these great authors as if they were devoid of any serious errors, in spite of the fact that on many points they appeared to contradict one another. I also learned that for Strauss the radical changes in our social and political institutions that have occurred since antiquity had no bearing on the likelihood that Aristotle made grave errors about natural slavery and about the natural inferiority of women. In his view, these were not errors. After a few conversations, I told Hutchins that I found talking to Strauss about philosophical books and problems thoroughly unprofitable from the point of view of leading great books seminars in the college.

The word "disciple" stresses the difference between the doctrinal and the dialectical teaching of the great books. Leo Strauss was preeminently the kind of doctrinal teacher who made disciples out of his students, disciples who followed in his footsteps and repeated again and again what they learned from him. The doctrinal teaching of disciples enables them to learn what the master thinks. The dialectical teaching of students enables them to think for themselves. I would go further and say that the doctrinal method *indoctrinates*, and only the dialectical method *teaches*.

Those of us who teach the great books dialectically exert an influence on our students, but only so far as a good use of their minds is concerned. We never make disciples of them. Strauss's use of the doctrinal method resulted in students learning what the master thought about the work under consideration. I would even go so far as to say that the doctrinal method is most appropriate in reading a sacred book. It is like the orthodox Hassidic approach to reading the Talmud. But it is totally inappropriate in liberal education at the college level or in our public schools.

5

I come now to the skepticism about moral values that prevails among college students and their teachers. I will treat this matter briefly because I have written many essays that bear on the subject. One in particular was written for *Harper's Magazine* under the title "This Prewar Generation" (1940). As the title indicates, the college students of that time generally held the view that judgments about moral values were matters of subjective opinion, different for different persons, and relative to the circumstances of time and place.

Before I go on, let me say what is meant by the distinction between subjective and objective and between relative and absolute. The subjective is that which differs for you, for me, and for other individuals. The objective is that which is the same for all of us. The relative is that which varies with the circumstances of time and place. The absolute is that which is invariant always and everywhere.

In "This Prewar Generation," I pointed out that subjectivism and relativism about value judgments on the part of students emanated from the same stance on the part of their teachers, especially their professors in philosophy and in the social sciences. At that time, the reign of philosophical positivism among Anglo-American professors gave rise to the doctrine of noncognitive ethics. This meant that moral philosophy was not knowledge, not a body of valid truths. Some went so far as to say that judgments that contained the words "ought" and "ought not" were neither true nor false. There were no prescriptive truths.

At the same time, what was known to sociologists and cultural anthropologists—that the tribal or ethnic mores differed from tribe to tribe, from culture to culture, and from time to time—led them to the dogmatic denial that there are any objectively valid moral judgments. As the positivists among the philosophers dismissed ethics as noncognitive, so the social scientists denied ethics objectivity and universality by putting the members of one tribe, culture, or ethnic group into what they called "the ethnocentric predicament." This meant that they were unable to make objective judgments about the values espoused in other tribes and cultures.

Is there any wonder that subjectivism and relativism should have been prevalent among college students exposed to such indoctrination by their professors in the 1930s and 1940s? That indoctrination has continued right down to the present. The moral skepticism among the students is the same as it was then and its cause is the same, though the vocabulary in which it is expressed may have changed in detail.

More recently I have returned to the defense of objective and absolute truth in moral philosophy by reviewing books by two eminent

professors of philosophy—Alasdair MacIntyre's *After Virtue* and a book
by Bernard Williams entitled *Ethics and the Limits of Philosophy.* Both
books concede the dismal failure of philosophy since the seventeenth
century to develop an ethics that can claim to have objective truth.
Both books, the first more explicitly than the second, give Nietzsche
credit for exposing the failures of modern thinkers to develop a sound
moral philosophy. Both books concede that Aristotle's *Ethics* was sound
in Greek antiquity. MacIntyre, however, called for its revision to make
it acceptable to us today, and Williams rejected it as no longer tenable.
The critiques I wrote of these two books argued that Aristotle's *Ethics*,
without the revision proposed by MacIntyre, is just as sound in the
twentieth century as it was in the fourth century B.C.

Against the background of what I have just said, I have only two
points to make about the mistakes of Allan Bloom in dealing with the
impoverishment of student souls in the late 1960s and continuing until
the present day. If by "impoverishment" he is referring to their lack of
firm dedication to objective and absolute moral truths, then that impoverishment existed as well in the 1930s, 1940s, and 1950s. He is
simply wrong as a matter of historical fact.

The other mistake made by Bloom concerns the causes that generated the result he deplores and wishes he knew how to remedy.
Ascribing contemporary skepticism about moral values to the influence
of Nietzsche's nihilism is wide of the mark. The two causes were those
already mentioned—philosophical positivism and the relativism of sociology and cultural anthropology. Nietzsche was not at all in the picture
when these began to influence American thought; and if that has changed
recently and his influence has become evident, it is still a minor cause
as compared with the others that I mentioned.

6

The great books, read and discussed with an eye out for the basic
truths and the equally basic errors or mistakes to be found in them,
should be a part of everyone's general, liberal, and humanistic education. This program should begin with what might be called "junior
great books" in the early grades, continued throughout basic schooling
with more and more difficult books, and be pursued on an even higher
level in college. It would still be everyone's obligation to read many of
these books again in the course of adult learning, for the greatest among

them cannot ever be plumbed to their full depths. They are inexhaustibly rereadable for pleasure and profit.

A genuine great books program does not aim at historical knowledge of cultural antiquities or at achieving a thin veneer of cultural literacy. On the contrary, it aims only at the general enlightenment of its participants, an essential ingredient in their initial liberal education and something to be continued throughout a lifetime of learning. Its objective is to develop basic intellectual skills—the skills of critical reading, attentive listening, precise speech, and, above all, reflective thought. Through the use of these skills, the reading and seminar discussion of the great books seeks to help students pass from less to greater understanding of the basic ideas in the Western intellectual tradition and of the controversial issues with which those great ideas abound.

Let me repeat: the controlling purpose behind this recommendation is twofold. First, only through reading and discussing books that are over one's head can the skills of critical reading and reflective thought be developed. Second, of the three educational objectives—acquisition of knowledge, development of intellectual skills, and increase of understanding of basic ideas and issues—the third is by far the most important, and cannot be achieved without seminar discussions of truly great or almost-great books.

Finally, the earlier the reading and discussions begin and the more persistently they are continued in college and in the learning of adults, involving as it must the oft-repeated reading and discussion of the same books, the better anyone will be enabled to reach his or her ultimate goal in the later years of life—that of becoming a generally educated human.

No one ever becomes a generally educated person in school, college, or university, for youth itself is an insuperable obstacle to becoming generally educated. That is why the very best thing that our educational institutions can do, so far as general education is concerned (not the training of specialists), is to afford preparation for continued learning by their students after they leave these institutions behind them. That cannot be done unless the skills of learning are cultivated in school and unless, in schools and colleges, the students are initiated into the understanding of great ideas and issues and are motivated to continue to seek an ever-increasing understanding of them.

It is necessary here to distinguish, sharply and clearly, the reading and seminar discussion of great books as a lifelong educational program from the current misuse of the phrase "great books" in connection with courses in Western civilization that college students are required to take as part of a core curriculum.

Until the end of the eighteenth century, there were no great books of Western civilization that were not of European origin. Until the nineteenth century, all were written by white males. Hence if one were to read all or almost all of the great books of Western civilization, most of them would, perforce, be written by white, male Europeans.

It is certainly arguable that under the radically changed circumstances of the twentieth century, college students should be required to study global civilization, both Eastern and Western, not just Western or European. It is also arguable that many books written in this or the last century, books which are clearly not great, should be studied for their relevance to the most pressing problems of our age. But all such arguments have nothing whatsoever to do with the educational program associated with a list of great Western books, most of which were written by white European males.

The educational purpose of the great books program is not to study Western civilization. Its aim is not to acquire knowledge of historical facts. It is rather to understand the great ideas. Its objective is not to become acquainted with the variety of conflicting cultures and groups that engender the problems that confront us in the contemporary world. Its controlling purposes, as I have already pointed out, are solely to learn how to read critically and to think reflectively about basic ideas and issues, not just in school and college but throughout one's life.

For that purpose, the minimum list of great books to be read would include at least the works of 60 authors. A more intensive program would extend that number to 125. At the college level, the minimal program should include seminars once a week for two years; at the maximum, it should include two seminars a week for four years. At the level of basic schooling, it would involve seminars once a week for at least nine years—from grade three to grade twelve.

I mention these numbers lest it be thought that a required single semester or a one-year college course in the history of civilization, Western or global, with twelve or fifteen traditionally recognized Western classics in the list of required readings, is even, in small part, a great books program. Such survey courses are mainly history courses, conducted primarily by lectures. They may be supplemented by small group discussions that only faintly resemble great books seminars.

To recapitulate: A true great books program is not a course in the history of Western civilization, nor is it devoted to the scholarly study of the books read. It is concerned primarily with the discussion of the great ideas and issues to be found in those books. It may, therefore, be asked why the works read should consist entirely of works written by Westerners, both European and American, and not by authors who belong to one of the four or five major cultural traditions of the Far East.

The answer is simply that the basic ideas and issues of our *one* Western intellectual tradition are *not* the basic ideas and issues in the *four* or *five* intellectual traditions of the Far East. In the distant future there may be a single, worldwide cultural community with one set of common basic ideas and issues; but until that comes into existence, becoming a generally educated human being in the West involves understanding the basic ideas and issues that abound in the intellectual tradition to which one is heir either by the place of one's birth or by immigration to the West.

PART ONE

Education in America—

Problems and Principles

1

This Prewar Generation

(1940)

"This Prewar Generation," published in Harper's Magazine *(October 1940), continues a discussion Adler began in the prologue to this book. There he addressed "the skepticism about moral values that prevails among college students and their teachers . . . the view that judgments about moral values [are] matters of subjective opinion, different for different persons, and relative to the circumstances of time and place." Adler views this skepticism as one of the most fundamental failures of education in this century.*

The causes of this skepticism, he says, are twofold: the claims of science that the only knowledge we can have concerning human nature comes to us from the laboratory or the clinic, and the emphasis of the social sciences upon the diversity of mores, allowing no moral judgments outside of the assumptions of a given culture—no universal principles. One effect of these doctrines is that by denying the existence of moral knowledge they pose a continued and constant danger to democracy and the principles on which democracy rests.

Written under the threat of the Second World War and the fascist assault against democratic principles, "This Prewar Generation" was more than a philosophical exercise. Struggling to counter the subjectivism and relativism avowed by his students and colleagues, Adler also wrote, in the summer of 1940, A Dialectic of Morals: Towards the Foundation of Political Philosophy *(University of Notre Dame 1941). There, in a conversation with an imaginary student, Adler posed questions about moral knowledge—what it is, how to seek it, and why that search is important. He argued for the objectivity and universality of moral stan-*

3

dards and against those who say that moral judgments are entirely matters of opinion, which in the sphere of politics commutes into might makes right.

In A Dialectic of Morals Adler established a foothold for political as well as ethical standards. Thirty years later, in The Time of Our Lives (1970), and more recently in the essays in Part IV of this book, he continues the effort to come to terms with the difficult questions moral philosophy presents.

G . V . D .

1

THE FIRST WORLD WAR produced a postwar generation. Its young men won a fight but lost what they were fighting for. Their lives had been interrupted, their purposes undermined, and their eyes opened. They were self-conscious of their disillusionment and demoralization, and their spokesmen—the artists and journalists among them—publicized their cynicism so successfully that it came to be regarded as the mood of a whole decade.

The Second World War finds us with a prewar generation. It consists of the youngsters still in college and the graduates of the past ten years. Considering their state of mind, one is tempted to say that the fathers have tasted war and the children's teeth are set on edge. Archibald MacLeish has in fact suggested that the temper of the postwar generation communicated itself and formed the temperament of youth today.

The facts of resemblance must not lead us, however, to a hasty conclusion about causes, for there is one remarkable difference between the two generations. The veterans of the last war had had "illusions"; they had pledged themselves in the name of "ideals." They were a lost generation because they had lost something. But it would be incorrect to speak of the present generation as disillusioned or demoralized. They seem to have grown up without any allegiances that could be betrayed, without a moral philosophy to renounce. They talk like calloused realists, though their actual experience of life cannot account for their imperviousness to traditional appeals.

This prewar generation has obviously not been produced by the present conflict in Europe nor by the threat of America's involvement. It existed five years ago, ten years ago, but it took the dire calamities of May 1940 to make us generally aware of the characteristics of our college-bred youth. The commencement orators last June spoke with an amazing uniformity on this one point. Whatever type of foreign policy they favored, they all recognized a danger sign in the disaffection of youth, its distrust of any cause which spoke the language of principles. In address after address the country over, college presidents or their surrogates appealed for a revival of idealism; tried to persuade the young that there are things worth living, and hence dying, for; pleaded for courage and self-sacrifice in devotion to the common good. They argued against what they called the prevalent materialism, the single-minded self-interest of the college graduate's aim—to take care of himself and let the rest go hang, to get ahead in the world by beating his neighbor. And most tragically significant of all, they begged the youth of the country "to have faith in democracy."

In most cases the commencement orators were thinking of preparedness, of national defense or active participation in the war. They asked for faith in democracy with an ulterior purpose. Congressional appropriations for armament are not enough, nor even the armaments themselves, built at any speed and in any quantity. Wars, especially modern, total wars, are waged with the energy of youth. Though it seldom became explicit, the speeches last June evoked the contrasting images of Hitler's youth and ours. Of course Hitler's youth were regimented and hop-fed, but they had some "virtues" after all. They were loyal and resolute. If only we could generate overnight a faith in democracy that would equal the faith in fascism, with its spirit of self-sacrificing devotion to a cause!

The educators or leaders who spoke to America's young men last June were so anxious about the immediate consequences of their audience's mood that they did not stop to inquire into its causes. Obsessed with the urgent need for change, they forgot that only by altering causes can one control effects. In their impatience, however sincere, they committed a basic error in rhetoric. They did not even ask themselves why all their words would fall upon deaf ears, why stirring phrases would not stir, why not even the loftiest visions would inspire.

2

What are the causes? How did this prewar generation come to be what it is? Since no one can pretend to know the etiology of a whole generation, I claim no more for what I have to say than that it is a guess based on more than fifteen years of classroom experience with the disease I am trying to diagnose. But before I tell my story let me consider some of the other guesses which have recently been aired.

In his now famous address on postwar writers and prewar readers, Mr. MacLeish claimed that the one had contaminated the other, that literature was the avenue of infection, especially the novels of such men as Latzko, Dos Passos, Hemingway, Remarque, and Aldington. I do not know whether MacLeish had the parallel in mind, but he was repeating Plato's charge that the poets, the storytellers, the tellers of half-truths, were the corrupters of youth. I have never thought that Plato was right about the poets. His characterization of them was right, but not his judgment of their influence. They are storytellers; they are men of imagination rather than of thought; they certainly cannot be relied upon to give youth sound moral and political instruction; but they are not important as compared with other educational influences, much less so in our day than in earlier times.

The writers themselves seem to agree with me on this point. Mr. Robert Sherwood said: "Archibald MacLeish is right in his conclusions, but he exaggerates the influence exerted by writers of our generation. By far the most successful of antiwar books, *All Quiet on the Western Front*, failed to convert young Germans to pacifism." Mr. Richard Aldington dismissed the notion that authors really affect the national state of mind as a typical highbrow delusion: "most people in America have never heard of the writers MacLeish mentions and could not have been influenced by them." I am sure that most college students have not read these novels. Even allowing for the influence they may have worked through the movies, or by indirect communication, I cannot agree that they are the major cause.

The writers who commented on MacLeish's speech had guesses of their own to offer. Again I quote Mr. Sherwood, who felt that youth considered "democracy a decadent mess—and no wonder, in view of the environment in which they grew up: the jazz age of the early 20s, the hypocrisy and crime of prohibition, the drunken sailorism of the Coolidge boom, and the wailing defeatism of depression." Another author placed the blame on young men's doubts about their economic or spiritual stake in American democracy. And still another said that they had "lost faith in democracy. It is up to democracy to show it is worth fighting for."

There is some truth in all these remarks, but I do not think they go to the root of the trouble. There is no question that the spectacle of democracy malpracticed may have killed some youthful enthusiasm for its cause, no question that the go-getting materialism of the American environment has corrupted youth more than novelists ever could, no question that the young have felt themselves betrayed by their elders. But it is not the failure of democracy to solve its economic problems, nor the shallowness and stupidity of its political leadership which has caused the disaffection.

The real trouble is that our college students and recent graduates do not take *any* moral issues seriously, whether about their personal affairs or the economic and political problems of the nation. Their only principle is that there are no moral principles at all, their only slogan that all statements of policy, all appeals to standards, are nothing but slogans, and hence frauds and deceptions. They are sophists in the most invidious sense of that term which connotes an unqualified skepticism about all moral judgments. Such skepticism leads naturally to *realpolitik*: in the game of power politics—and there is no other—only force and propaganda count. The issue between fascism and democracy cannot be argued as if there were a right and wrong to it. Whoever wins is right; whatever works is good. Our college students today, like Thrasymachus of old, regard justice as nothing but the will of the stronger; but unlike the ancient sophist, they cannot make the point as clearly or defend it as well.

What, then, is the difference between our youth and Hitler's? Even if ours have not read *Mein Kampf* or been inoculated with the revolutionary spirit of nihilism, they have become "realists" of the same sort, believing only in the tangible rewards of success—money, fame, and power. Unlike Hitler's youth, however, they mean by success their own personal advancement, not nationalistic aggrandizement. Hitler's young men, through a mystical identification of personal with national success, work for Germany. Our young men work for themselves, and they will continue to suffer democracy—which, remember, they do not think can be *proved* to be intrinsically better than fascism—only so long as it works for them. True, at the present moment, they *feel* that Hitler is a bad man and say they don't *like* totalitarianism; but if pressed for reasons they will repeat phrases such as "civil liberties" or "human rights," the meaning of which they cannot explain, the justification for which they cannot give. They can readily be pushed to admit that these too are only opinions, which happen to be theirs by the accident of birthplace.

Here precisely lies the danger. The present generation has been immunized against anyone who might really try to argue for democracy in terms of justice, but not against the attractions of success and security. The only slogans they have learned to suspect are those which claim the approval of reason; and the thing which seems most like propaganda to them is what "pretends" to offer rational arguments for a course of action—as right rather than expedient. They have no sales resistance against the appeal of promises to gain for them the things every animal wants. They will even have "faith" in democracy if such promises can be made in its name. They are ready to have faith in any program which does not insist that it is right by reason. Let America cease to be the land of opportunity for individual success, let another and much worse depression increase the number who are hopelessly insecure, and our young men may find a leader who can change their "faith." They are democrats now only by feeling and opinion. Feelings and opinions are easily changed by force of circumstances and by rhetoric which mocks at reason, as Hitler's did. If some form of fascism offers immediate fruits, they who have forsaken the way of principles and reasoning will not see that democracy is better in principle, despite abuses which impair its beneficence in practice.

Mr. MacLeish diagnosed the disease correctly but he failed to trace its causes to their roots. John Chamberlain had observed that the younger generation "needs none of Mr. Stuart Chase's semantic discipline. The boys and girls tend to distrust all slogans, all tags—even all words." Agreeing to this, MacLeish went further. He saw that their basic distrust is of "all statements of principle and conviction, all declarations of moral purpose"—for it is only such statements and declarations that they regard as slogans. But he merely scratched the surface when he supposed that it was the literature of our period that "was disastrous as education for a generation which would be obliged to face the threat of fascism in its adult years." The education of this prewar generation has been disastrous indeed; but the calamity has been caused by our schools and colleges, not by our novelists. Even if the First World War had never happened, even if there had been no postwar generation to spread its disillusionment, even if such phrases as "making the world safe for democracy" had not come to symbolize how men can mistake empty slogans for sacred shibboleths, the present generation would be as full of sophistry and skepticism. For the past forty years there have been forces at work in American education which had to culminate in this result.

3

The factors operating in the current situation have been prepared by centuries of cultural change. What has been happening in American education since 1900, what has finally achieved its full effect in the present generation, flows with tragic inevitability from the seeds of modern culture as they have developed in the past three hundred years. The very things which constituted the cultural departure that we call modern times have eventuated, not only in the perverted education of American youth today, but also in the crises they are unprepared to face. That fascism should have reached its stride in Europe at the same time that pseudo-liberalism—the kind Lewis Mumford denounces as corrupt, pragmatic liberalism—has demoralized us, is a historic accident. Only the timing is a coincidence, however, for both the European and the American maladies arise from the same causes. They are both the last fruitions of modern man's exclusive trust in science and his gradual disavowal of whatever lies beyond the field of science as irrational prejudice, as opinion emotionally held.

I do not wish to make science itself the villain of my piece. It is the *misuse* of science, intellectually as well as practically, which is to blame. We do not blame science for the murderous tools it has enabled men to make; neither should we blame science, or for that matter scientists, for the destructive doctrines men have made in its name, men who are for the most part philosophers and educators, not scientists. All these doctrines have a common center—positively, the exclusive adoration of science; negatively, the denial that philosophy or theology can have any independent authority. We can regard this intellectual misuse of science as another one of the false modern religions—the religion of science, closely related to the religion of the state. We can group all these doctrines together and call them by names which have become current: *positivism* and *scientism*. And again we can see a deep irony in the historic coincidence that just when the practical misuse of science has armed men for wholesale slaughter, scientism—the intellectual misuse of science—has all but disarmed them morally.

Let me see if I can explain the mind of this prewar generation by the scientism which dominates American education. I am also concerned to show how the semanticism, which Messrs. Chamberlain and MacLeish noted in the youthful distrust of all language, is a closely related phenomenon. Just as scientism is a misuse of science, in itself good, so semanticism names the excessive exploitation of semantics, which in itself is a good discipline concerned with the criteria for determining the significance of words.

An American college student who, under the elective system, samples courses in the natural and social sciences, in history, philosophy, and the humanities gradually accumulates the following notions: (1) that the only valid knowledge of the nature of the world and man is obtained by the methods of experimentation or empirical research; (2) that questions which cannot be answered by the methods of the natural and social sciences cannot be answered at all in any trustworthy or convincing way; or, in other words, answers to such questions are only arbitrary and unfounded opinions; (3) that the great achievement of the modern era is not simply the accumulation of scientific knowledge, but, more radically, the recognition of the scientific method (of research and experimentation) as the *only* dependable way to solve problems; and, in consequence of this, that modern times have seen man's emancipation from the superstitions of religion, the dogmatisms of theology, and the armchair speculations of philosophers; (4) that the study of social phenomena became scientific when research divorced itself entirely from normative considerations, when economists and students of politics no longer asked about the justice of social arrangements, but only who gets what, when, and how.

A bright college student will readily draw certain inferences from these few basic notions that get dinned into him from every source of his education. He will see for himself that moral questions, questions of good and bad, right and wrong, cannot be answered by the methods of natural or social science. He will conclude that "value judgments" cannot be made, except of course as expressions of personal prejudice. He will extend this conclusion to cover not only decisions about his own conduct but also moral judgments about economic systems and political programs. He will accept without question the complete divorce of economics from ethics and, in discipleship to Machiavelli, he will become as much a realist in politics as Hitler and Mussolini. If, in addition to being bright, he is proud of his modernity, he will regard anyone who talks about standards of goodness, principles of justice, moral virtues as an unregenerate old fogy; and he will express his aversion for such outmoded opinions by the *ad hominem* use of epithets like "medieval" or "scholastic" or "mystic."

Even those who are not bright enough to draw their own conclusions from the main tenets of a college education get them ready-made in certain courses. They are told by the teachers of social science that all "systems of morality" reduce to tribal mores, conventional taboos and prescriptions which govern the culture of a given time and place. They learn, as a result of this complete moral relativism, that they must respect their "ethnocentric predicament," which simply means that they, who belong to a given culture or system, cannot judge the right and wrong of any other without begging the question, without taking their own point of view for granted, though it is neither better nor worse than the contrary assumptions of those whom they judge. They are told, in so many words, that anyone who proceeds otherwise is an absolutist. To suppose that all men living at any time or place are subject to the same fundamental canons of right and wrong, however diverse their manners or mores; to suppose that all men, precisely because they are all men, sharing equally the same human nature, should be motivated by the same ideals of truth and goodness—that is the demon of absolutism which every social science course in the curriculum tries to exorcise. When they succeed, as they usually do by sheer weight of unopposed prestige, the college student who has been thus indoctrinated even dislikes using such words as "truth" and "goodness" because they sound like "absolute values."

I said a moment ago that the teaching pronounced in unison by the social scientists is unopposed. You may think that opposition must come from at least one quarter of the campus—obviously from the philosophy department. But, paradox of paradoxes, if the student is not already thoroughly debunked, rid of all "medieval superstitions" and "absolutisms," he gets the finishing touches of his modern education in the philosophy courses. While it is not unanimously accepted, the doctrine of scientism is certainly the dominant dogma of American philosophy today. The degenerative tendency of modern philosophy to move in this direction reached its culmination in American pragmatism and all its sequelae—the numerous varieties of positivism. All the varieties agree on one point: that only science gives us valid knowledge of reality. Hence philosophy, at its best, can be nothing more than a sort of commentary on the findings of science; and at its worst, when it refuses to acknowledge the exclusive right of scientific method to marshal evidence and draw conclusions therefrom, philosophy is either mere opinion or nonsensical verbiage. The history of philosophy, especially in the primitive times before the scientific era, is told as a history of guesses, some bright, some wild, but all equally unworthy of modern credence.

Far from opposing the social scientists, their colleagues in the philosophy department support the derogation of "systems of morality" as so many ways of rationalizing emotional fixations and cultural complexes. (Ethics becomes a sort of psychoanalysis.) It is in the philosophy course that the student really learns how to argue like a sophist against all "values" as subjective and relative. Far from being the last bulwark against the scientism professed or insinuated by every other part of the curriculum, the philosophy courses reinforce the *negativism* of this doctrine by inspiring disrespect for any philosophy which claims to be independent knowledge. And, to complete the job, the ancient sophistries which our philosophy departments have revived are implemented by semanticism. The student learns to suspect all words, especially abstract words. Statements which cannot be scientifically verified are meaningless. The abstract words which enter into moral judgments—such words as "justice" and "right" or even "liberty" and "happiness" —have only rhetorical meaning. Denuded of deceptive verbiage, all such judgments can be reduced to statements of what I like or what displeases me. There is no "should" or "ought."

Concerning the intellectual character of this generation, there appears to be agreement. Certainly the most plausible explanation of that character is in terms of the education youth has received. If I have fairly summarized the impact of a college education have I not accounted for the state of mind which seemed to worry the commencement orators last June, and which Mr. MacLeish attributed to the insidious effects of postwar novels?

Whether or not they go to war, irreparable damage has been done to the young men of this generation. They have been misled by their teachers into giving up their birthright. Education has failed democracy as well. When men no longer have confidence that right decisions in moral and political matters can be rationally arrived at, when they no longer regard themselves as rational animals, but as rationalizing brutes, the institutions of democracy are the walls of an empty house which will collapse under pressure from without because of the vacuum within.

4

There are two misconceptions I wish to avoid. The picture I have painted is black enough but it is not utterly so. It must be qualified in the first place, by recognizing that there are a few teachers on every campus who take their stand against the tide; and in the second place, by acknowledging that most college students are at heart good boys and girls. (So, may I add, were Hitler's boys and girls.) It is sometimes difficult to decide whether they think sophistically or only talk that way, but it is easy to discover that their sophisticated speech masks a kind of natural goodness. Let me report some of my own experiences to illustrate these points.

For some years now at the University of Chicago President Hutchins and I have been teaching courses in which the students are asked to read great works in ethics, economics, and politics. They have already had enough education to be suspicious of Plato and Aristotle, St. Thomas Aquinas and John Locke. They react at once against these, or any other authors, who write as if truth could be reached in moral matters, as if the mind could be convinced by reasoning from principles, as if there were self-evident precepts about good and bad. They tell us, emphatically and almost unanimously, that "there is no right and wrong," that "moral values are private opinions," that "everything is relative."

This is not the picture of one class, but of many. What is impressive is the uniformity of our experience during the past ten years in teaching high school students, college students of all classes, graduate students drawn from various divisions of the university. We have found the same thing in trying to teach the philosophy of law to future lawyers and the philosophy of education to future teachers. Nor should it be thought that the reaction is elicited by the books we assign, that it merely signifies the students' suspicion that we are doctrinaire Aristotelians or Thomists, or something equally bad. It happens as readily in reading Rousseau, who tries to prove republicanism from the rights of man; or in reading *The Federalist Papers*, along with the Declaration of Independence and the Constitution; for those fellows also talked about self-evident truths and used such words as "liberty" and "happiness" as if they had some meaning. And for those who suppose that American colleges are hotbeds of radicalism, let me say that the same thing happened when we asked them to read Karl Marx's *Capital*. We tried to show them how Marx had proved the injustices inherent in the historic processes of capitalism. They resisted, not because they could answer Marx's arguments, but because they initially rejected the very notion that a moral judgment about capitalism, or anything else, can be proved.

Yet, I say, these same boys and girls are good at heart. We revealed their hypocrisy to them one day when they accidentally displayed their devotion to ideals. The subject was education in relation to the state. For the sake of clarifying a point in Aristotle's *Politics* on the statesman's use of education, Mr. Hutchins took the position that education cannot *improve* the community, that education will never serve the cause of social progress. He argued that the aims of education are always determined by *existing* moral and political standards, and hence one cannot hope for educational change to raise the general morale. Apart from the merits of the argument, the interesting fact is that the students were plainly shocked by such pessimism. They *hoped* that education could make men better and uplift society. This hope, we pointed out, was inconsistent with everything else they had been saying. They who had been denying objectivity to the distinction between better and worse were now affirming the possibility of progress, of human betterment. They had been taken off guard by Mr. Hutchins's apparent turnabout and, for the moment, betrayed a strain of natural aspiration. Deep down in their hearts they still wished to believe there was some meaning to "better" by which progress in human affairs could be measured. But when faced with the implications of such belief, they refused, albeit with some embarrassment, to concede that reason could require all men to acknowledge such things to be true. Here was a new hypocrisy. The old-fashioned hypocrite paid lip service to moral maxims which his conduct flouted. These youngsters appeared to have some love for the good; they might even act accordingly; but except in unguarded moments, their sophisticated minds prevented them from speaking accordingly.

Whoever says that it makes no difference what people think or how they speak so long as their hearts are in the right place, commits a dangerous fallacy. One hypocrisy is as bad as the other; if anything, this one is worse because, when right feelings are not supported by right thinking, good men can be insensibly corrupted. Men of good will are not just sweet-tempered animals, but beings whose desires aim at a good they rationally apprehend as such. When the mind refuses to *see* the good and the bad of things, repudiating any moral quality in things and actions to see, the will is blind, and blindly attaches itself to this or that through natural instinct, waywardness, or caprice. Not rooted in reason, such attachments are impermanent. They can be easily uprooted by those who are skilled in playing Pied Piper to the passions. That is why I dread the instability of a generation which, at best, will only have "faith" in democracy—but no sure reasons for upholding it as *objectively* the best form of political community. If their "faith" in democracy amounts to nothing more than well-disposed feelings at the moment, change of circumstances may alter the direction of their sentiments and they may find themselves with a faith in fascism or the same thing by another name.

Let me illustrate the inconsistencies and confusions which result from the divorce of head and heart, by a few tales out of school about my colleagues, the teachers of this prewar generation. On one occasion last spring an eminent professor of history at the university took the position in after-dinner conversation that, while he didn't *like* Hitler, no one could *prove* that he was wrong. I tried to argue that I could demonstrate—demonstrate as certainly as Euclid could a theorem in geometry—that totalitarianism is intrinsically unjust; but in vain, for the professor of history replied that any demonstration I might make would be valid only in terms of its premises, and, obviously, my premises would be *my* arbitrary assumptions. Hitler need not grant them; he could make others, and prove the opposite case as well. Nondemocratic political systems could be just as valid as non-Euclidean geometries. I did not succeed in convincing him that moral thinking, unlike geometry, does not rest on postulates, but commands assent to its conclusions because they are drawn from self-evident first principles—traditionally known as the natural moral law. The historian denied self-evident truths; what looked like them were just verbal tautologies, word magic. He smiled at the notion of a natural moral law; there were just primitive urges which could be rationalized in different ways. My historian was a democrat "by faith"—by the way he felt at the time. It is easy enough to imagine how a change of heart might be forced on him; his mind would present no obstacle to such change.

On a later occasion I was dining with the local authority on international law and a professor of medicine. It was shortly after the Nazi invasion of the Low Countries. Both my colleagues were hot under the collar about American isolationism. They wanted immediate action in support of the Allied cause. What was that cause? I asked. It was the cause of democracy, our cause, and we must act at once. At the time those were my sentiments too, but I soon discovered that I could not make common cause with my colleagues. After dinner I reported the conversation I had had with the professor of history, and again I said that I thought the political truth of democracy could be demonstrated. *No such thing!* Democracy could be saved by force of arms but it could not be proved by weight of reason. The professor of international law told me that his "preference" for democracy was simply a cultural bias, arising from "postulates" which could not themselves be examined for truth or falsity. That we Anglo-Saxons accepted them, that Italians and Germans rejected them, was simply an inscrutable fact, a historic accident. The professor of medicine spoke similarly: outside the domain of natural science there is only opinion; each man systematizes his opinions in a certain conceptual frame of reference, there is the democratic frame of reference, the Nazi frame of reference, and so on. I knew the impossibility of plumbing this argument to its depths. That would mean challenging the scientism which made my colleagues skeptical about morality. I simply said that I might be willing to fight for democracy as a political good I could rationally apprehend, but that I wouldn't move an inch to make the world safe for a cultural bias, a set of postulates, or a frame of reference.

This prewar generation has been made what it is by its teachers— these colleagues of mine, justifiably respected in their special fields, yet undermining all the merits of their teaching by a false philosophy, the destructive doctrine of positivism. But the blame should not fall entirely on the colleges and universities. The corruption begins at the lower levels, long before the student becomes sophisticated in semantics or learns about the ethnocentric predicament. The public school system of the country, at both elementary and secondary levels, whether explicitly "progressive" in program or not, is Deweyized in its leadership. I use the name of Dewey to symbolize what Lewis Mumford describes as pragmatic liberalism—a liberalism "so completely deflated and debunked" that it forsakes all the "essential principles of ideal liberalism: justice, freedom, truth" and hence disavows a rationally articulated moral philosophy; supposing instead that " 'science,' which confessedly despises norms, would eventually supply all the guidance necessary for human conduct." Public education in the United States is run by men and women who have been inoculated with pragmatic liberalism at the leading schools of education (Columbia, Chicago, Harvard, California) where fundamental policies are formed. Mr. Mumford has done yeoman's work in castigating his old friends on the *New Republic* and *Nation*, but it is much more important to change the mind behind the school system of the country than the minds of the readers of the so-called liberal weeklies.

Mr. Hutchins and I discovered what that mind was like when we taught a course in the philosophy of education last year. It was taken by men and women who were candidates for the Ph.D. in education, many of whom were already in responsible teaching or administrative positions. We began with this definition: "Education is the process whereby the powers of human nature become developed by *good* habits." I have italicized the word "good" because that, as usual, was the stumbling block. The class objected to the definition as normative; the *science* of education must be objective. Some of them said there was nothing good or bad about education, and others shocked us even more by suggesting that education might just as well be a development of bad habits. The argument went on for days, requiring us to get down to fundamentals. In the course of it we discovered that these professionals in education had been thoroughly indoctrinated with scientism and positivism. The mark of indoctrination was that they really couldn't defend their position; the marks of the doctrine they had swallowed were the familiar denials—of the objectivity of moral standards, of the rationality of men, of any method for answering questions except that of empirical science.

If the teachers of the country, and more than the teachers, their higher-ups, are in this state of mind, can we expect the present generation to be otherwise? Mr. MacLeish may think that those who write a country's novels are more influential than those who make its laws. I think that those who teach its youth are more, immeasurably more influential than either.

5

Can anything be done about American education? I doubt it. The college presidents who expressed such deep concern about American youth last June do not, for the most part, see educational failure itself as the major cause of their condition. If they remember their commencement addresses they may open college with a renewed effort to inspire "faith in democracy," to appeal for a purely emotional loyalty to the nation in time of stress. As the emergency increases there may be talk of military training and similar expedients for immediate preparedness. But of that long-term preparedness which consists in fundamental educational reform there will be nothing. College presidents will not try to fight the enemy in their midst—the destructive doctrines which dominate American education today—because they do not recognize this enemy, or worse, they belong in his camp. President Conant, for example, has been one of the most vocal exponents of intervention. He urges us to fight for democracy. But he has never affirmed—and being a scientist, is not likely to see the need for—an independent metaphysics, without which ethics and politics have no rational foundation. In consequence, his educational policy involves no challenge to scientism and positivism in all corners of the Harvard curriculum.

One college president has issued that challenge again and again. He too spoke about preparedness last June. But he was thinking of a basic intellectual reform as indispensable to safeguarding democracy from dissolution, as well as from attack by force. He said:

> In order to believe in democracy we must believe that there is a difference between truth and falsity, good and bad, right and wrong, and that truth, goodness, and right are objective standards even though they cannot be experimentally verified. They are not whims, prejudices, rationalization, or Sunday school tags. We must believe that man can discover truth, goodness, and right by the exercise of his reason, and that he may do so even as to those problems which, in the nature of the case, science can never solve. . . . Political organization must be tested by conformity to ideals. Its basis is moral. Its end is the good for man. Only democracy has this basis. If we do not believe in this basis or this end, we do not believe in democracy. These are the principles which we must defend if we are to defend democracy.
>
> Are we prepared to defend these principles? Of course not. For forty years and more our intellectual leaders have been telling us they are not true. They have been telling us in fact that nothing is true which cannot be subject to experimental verification. In the whole realm of social thought there can, therefore, be nothing but opinion. Since there is nothing but opinion, everybody is entitled to his own opinion. . . . If everything is a matter of opinion, force becomes the only way of settling differences of opinion. And, of course, if success is the test of rightness, right is on the side of the heavier battalions.

But President Hutchins will not succeed in changing education at Chicago for the same reason that it will not be changed in most of our institutions. The faculties, by and large, see the other way. They are (and perhaps no one else can be) the ultimate guardians of the curriculum, the oracles of its content. That being so, I doubt if anything short of a major cataclysm or a miracle could work the transformation.

We have some reason to be wryly optimistic about the cataclysm. If we are forced to fight, we will; in that eventuality young men will join the colors or be drafted. But we may be forced to defend democracy without the violence of arms, and to defend it against interior decay and boring from within. Even if we fight, or perhaps because we do, we may be faced with the necessity of resuscitating democracy from the almost lethal dose of wartime measures. Even if we win a defensive war, fascism may still reign among our enemies, and we shall be too morally and spiritually weakened to combat their success story, the triumphant march of totalitarian ideologies. In any of the possibilities I can foresee, our greatest need is the clearest understanding of what democracy means, the most patient rational articulation of its principles. And I do not mean that this should be a rare secret, possessed by the favored few who have written books on the subject. I mean it should belong to the masses whom democracy educates—certainly all those who enjoy the opportunities of college education. That, as I have tried to show, cannot happen until the colleges make their students philosophers instead of sophists.

Last June, while the commencement orators were calling for renewed faith in democracy, a student at Williams College wrote a guest editorial in the college paper which bluntly said fascism is a better object of faith than democracy. It has more to offer, positively and constructively. Democracy is decadent and dying. It does nothing but repeat old shibboleths, out of step with the times. Fascism does things, and does them in terms of contemporary realities. "The English government and the French government," he wrote, "offer no twentieth-century set of aims and principles in which the poor soldiers in Flanders can put their faith as the German boys put their faith in Hitler." We of the democracies are fighting for next to nothing. "It is we, rather than they, who are nihilists."

Thus the cataclysm may overtake us like a summer cloud, without our special wonderment. War or no war, victory or defeat, we may wake up some morning to find that a good many boys feel as the writer of the Williams editorial. Whether it is a prewar or postwar generation will make no difference so long as it is a generation which has been educated in the manner of the past forty years. They will pass from a faith in democracy to a faith in fascism simply because outward circumstances will have sufficiently attenuated the one and strengthened the other. As President Hutchins pointed out, our present intellectual position is "much closer to Hitler than we may care to admit. . . . Such principles as we have are not different enough from those of Hitler to make us very rugged in defending ours in preference to his. And second, we are not united and clear about such principles as we have. We are losing our moral principles. But the vestiges of them remain to bother us and to interfere with a thoroughgoing commitment to amoral principles. Hence we are like confused, divided, ineffective Hitlers." The payoff is indicated: "In a contest between Hitler and people who are wondering why they shouldn't be Hitlers, the finished product is bound to win."

This may sound like a counsel of despair. But it is defeatism in the schoolroom, not on the battlefield. Strangely enough, it is much easier to solicit preparedness for war than preparedness for peace. Men can be energized into action, even radical reforms, when the issues are urgent enough, and the ends not much beyond their noses. The long-term objectives are seldom achieved by the purposeful planning of man or the concerted action of nations. They are reached, slowly and painfully, through the inscrutable windings of history. Education will not shake off its typical modern faults until history is ready for the end of modern times and the birth of a new cultural epoch. The impending cataclysm foreshadows the event. I know I may be looking for miracles, but I cherish the hope that if democracy dies it will be reborn in a better culture than that of the modern world.

2

The Chicago School

(1941)

"The Chicago School" was written on the occasion of the fiftieth anniversary of the University of Chicago. Published in Harper's Magazine (September 1941), it documents the strange and wonderful achievements of the university. The occasion called for praise, and Adler gave it. But uncritical praise is for politicians, not philosophers. So Adler improved the occasion by exposing the defects as well as the virtues of the university. They are also the defects of American thought and education, which the University of Chicago so profoundly influenced in this century.

Like "This Prewar Generation," "The Chicago School" was written under the threat of the Second World War and the possible destruction of American values and institutions. But like the earlier article, it too affirmed that the greater threat to American democracy and values was from within the very culture and institutions we fought to preserve. That threat seems to increase with time.

Although many changes have occurred in American culture and education since 1941, the weaknesses exposed here, and the conditions for their existence, persist. Adler's observations are therefore of more than historical interest. One of them is that we continue to seek information for its own sake and lack the principles needed to use it well. Another observation concerns a failure of communication, the failure that is now loudly lamented as the disease of every American institution from the family to the federal government. Adler's diagnosis traces the disease to its historical and philosophical roots. Like all good doctors, he offers the cure. It will be proposed again and again in this collection of essays. It is the Hutchins-Adler cure: restore a truly liberal education to American schools. In our present situation the same problems call for the same cure.

Once in a while a voice rises in support of the Hutchins-Adler program. In April 1976 The Chronicle of Higher Education *published a convincing plea to bring Robert Hutchins back to serve as a college president so that his influence once more might be brought to bear on higher education in America. Hutchins's influence was unfortunately not as far-reaching as that writer would like to think it was, so Adler informs us—and neither was his. Little has changed. Yet, there may still be time.*

G.V.D.

1

I HAVE the duty on Monday of reporting at a "philosophical conference" on the Chicago School of Thought. Chicago University has during the past six months given birth to the fruit of its ten years of gestation under John Dewey. The result is wonderful—a *real school*, and *real Thought*. Important thought too! Did you ever hear of such a city or such a university? Here we have thought, but no school. At Yale, a school, but no thought. Chicago has both. . . ."

So wrote William James to Mrs. Henry Whitman in October 1903. We have no record of the report he gave to his colleagues at Harvard, but the general tenor of his remarks can be gathered from a review he wrote shortly thereafter of philosophical papers by Dewey, Mead, Angell, and others, reprinted from the first series of Decennial Publications. "The rest of the world," he began, "has made merry over the Chicago man's legendary saying that 'Chicago hasn't had time to get round to culture yet, but when she does strike her, she'll make her hum!' Already the prophecy is fulfilling itself in a dazzling manner. Chicago has a School of Thought!—a school of thought which, it is safe to predict, will figure in literature as the School of Chicago for twenty-five years to come." And he went on to say that the work of Dewey and his disciples presented "a view of the world, both theoretical and practical, which is so simple, massive, and positive that, in spite of the fact that many parts of it yet need to be worked out, it deserves the title of a new system of philosophy."

This September the University of Chicago celebrates its fiftieth anniversary. This September the world may not have time or patience to give much attention to an academic celebration—to its learned symposia, its recital of degrees *honoris causa*, its ritual of eulogy. But if there is still any time left for us to think about what we are doing we might well use a little of it to consider the institution and development of a university which, more than any other, reflects the temper of *our* culture. Universities in general may symbolize the achievement of European civilization—the endurance of which now seems to depend upon soldiers, not gentlemen or scholars; but the University of Chicago, like the city in which it was founded, is almost 100 percent American.

When Chicago got around to culture she was not content to make it hum. She turned out an American brand. It was not merely a "new system of philosophy"—the pragmatism or humanism which William James applauded—but a new orientation of the higher learning itself. President Harper accepted the definition of a university as "an agency recognized by the people for resolving the problems of civilization"; but from the beginning, and increasingly ever since, Chicago's university applied this maxim by doing the sort of work which took its bearings from, and exerted influence upon, the main directions of American life. The pragmatic philosophy of Dewey and others simply made articulate the principles of this new departure—a higher learning indigenous to America, the birth of a typically American university.

The University of Chicago is popularly thought of as one of America's youngest institutions. In truth it is one of the oldest, if we discriminate between an undergraduate college and a university, a place for graduate study and research. Harper's Chicago is preceded only by Gilman's Johns Hopkins (1876) and by G. Stanley Hall's Clark (1888). Before these institutions there was only sporadic and casual graduate work at Harvard and Columbia, Yale and Cornell. There was neither a formal program for graduate study nor a faculty to give full-time instruction to graduate students. At Yale, in 1871, there was only one full-time graduate professor. Americans went to Europe, especially to the universities of Germany, to complete the studies for which an A.B. degree was supposed to prepare. After Johns Hopkins and Chicago led the way some of the older colleges on the eastern seaboard quickly transformed themselves into universities by collecting professional schools and organizing graduate faculties. Harvard and Columbia, under Lowell and Butler, became universities; but Chicago was founded as one, at once exceeding even Johns Hopkins and Clark in the degree to which it realized the ideal which had motivated Gilman and Hall.

Gilman started with forty graduate students and a small faculty; Hall also had a handful of students doing work in five divisions of graduate study. But when Harper opened Chicago's doors it was prepared to offer instruction and conduct research in twenty-seven departments; it had a staff of 120, divided into two faculties (of arts and literature, and of science); and in the very first quarter of the university's operation these men taught 594 students, about half of whom came to do postgraduate work.

Harper vigorously fought the American college system which, in his view, impeded the intellectual growth of able men by giving them heavy programs of undergraduate teaching. Teaching loads at Chicago were light, and promotion depended on successful research rather than on meritorious teaching. This, more than anything else, set the academic style and nourished what William James was later to call "the Ph.D. octopus." In part, Harper's intention seems to have miscarried, for his emphasis on research sacrificed many promising young men to the coils of the octopus, crushing (if not killing) them as much as a heavy burden of sophomores. But this must not lead us to neglect another point from which to view his intention, and its execution by Chicago's faculty. In 1895 he said:

> It is not enough that instructors in a university should merely do the class and lecture work assigned them. This is important, but the university will in no sense deserve the name, if time and labor are not also expended in the work of producing that which will directly or indirectly influence thought and life outside the University. . . . The true university is the center of thought on every problem connected with human life and work, and the first obligation resting upon the individual members who compose it is that of research and investigation.

Steadfast devotion to and brilliant performance of this mission brought Chicago fair renown in the first ten years of its existence.

Just four years ago Harvard celebrated its tercentenary. At that time, when peace still encouraged us to think of the future's promise, Professor Whitehead congratulated Harvard on having completed its process of growth. "About twenty-five for a man," he wrote, "and about three hundred years for a university are the periods required for the attainment of mature stature." Once full-grown, the measure of a university is "in terms of its effectiveness." After three hundred years of growing up, Oxford and Cambridge played their part effectively in what Whitehead regards as "*the* brilliant period of European civilization," the seventeenth and eighteenth centuries.

It did not take Chicago three hundred years. Chicago sprang full-grown from Harper's head. In ten years it had become a dominantly effective force in "American civilization," as the testimony of William James suggests. It is easy to make light of this achievement by saying that the delivery was well oiled by Rockefeller millions, by saying that rapid growth and quick cash returns simply expressed the American way of doing everything in the industrial nineties. Of course it is true that money talked, then as now. Harper bought whatever he thought was needed to start right off in a big way. During the preliminary negotiations Harper wrote to Goodspeed: "Naturally we ought to be willing to begin small and grow, but in these days when things are done so rapidly, it seems a great pity to wait for growth when we might be born full-fledged." He bought the best professors, paying the unheard-of top salary of $7,000, and taking as many as twelve from Stanley Hall's sixteen carefully selected scientists. He disregarded deficits. That was a problem for "the Founder." His problem was to waste no time in using money, in pocket or promised, to create the superlative university. To that end he not only collected the best staff of men, but also managed, under forced draft, to get them to publish a tremendous body of completed research within the first ten years.

But the twenty-eight volumes of the Decennial Publications, containing the work of eighty-one contributors, and costing the university $50,000 which it did not have, expressed more than Harper's ability to do big things in a hurry by pyramiding with money. They expressed, in more ways than William James realized, *a school of thought*. It was neither the eminent qualities of its individual professors nor the great quantities of research done in various fields which made Chicago the leading, the most typical, American university within a decade. Money bought professors for Chicago; it could buy them back for eastern institutions, as the competition for triple-starred names during the last half century reveals. Harvard, for example, has always had a larger endowment than Chicago and could usually procure the services of academic leaders. The fact that Chicago and Harvard have been for some time now closely tied in the ranking of American universities according to the number of "eminent names" on their faculties, or according to the number of "eminent departments" (as measured by productivity), is not the important fact about Chicago—except perhaps in the eyes of those who think Harvard provides the absolute standard for comparison. The important fact about Chicago—the fact so distinguishing that in this respect Chicago escapes comparison—is the intellectual life it has cultivated, and the influence which this has exerted, educationally and culturally, upon the rest of the country.

In 1904 "the Chicago School" meant one thing; in 1936 it meant another; but at both times it signified the existence there of an extraordinary intellectual ferment, a leaven which worked from there outward to raise the whole cultural mass. During this month of celebration on the Midway academic orators may praise Chicago for many things, but the main point will be missed if Chicago's peculiar vitality is not analyzed. Unfortunately the main point cannot be made as a paean of unalloyed praise. Chicago has defects peculiar to its special virtues, and the defects, as well as the virtues, are characteristic of American life during the past fifty years. The contribution of Chicago in the first and in the last decade of that period calls for criticism, not eulogy.

2

When I was a student at Columbia in the early twenties the return of John Dewey from China, to resume his professorial duties at the university, was a long-awaited event. At last I was going to find out about that "Chicago school of thought." Even though John Dewey made his hegira from Chicago in 1904, even though William James had published a book called *Pragmatism* (1908) which successfully popularized some of the notions that had been much more technically expounded in *Studies in Logical Theory*, anyone who was interested in the pragmatic philosophy still turned in the twenties toward Chicago as toward Mecca. Though Dewey had been at Columbia for many years, and though James had left some disciples to carry on his teaching at Harvard, neither the Columbia nor the Harvard philosophy department could claim to be the seat of orthodoxy. Only at Chicago was there a homogeneous body of men who worked together with apparent understanding of a common doctrine. Some of these men, Tufts and Mead and Ames, had been at Chicago from the beginning; they had collaborated with Dewey in the early publications of the Chicago School.

But to think of the Chicago School entirely in terms of a doctrine called "pragmatism," or to restrict it to the "thought" of its philosophy department, misses the forest for the trees. The homogeneity which could be found in the philosophy department in 1904 or in 1924 (in fact, almost until the arrival of Hutchins) characterized the whole university. Whether it was an extraordinary accident, or whether Harper's feeling for the *zeitgeist* was so strong that he intuitively picked men in every field who uniformly reflected the same spirit, the remarkable fact remains that the University of Chicago had a central point of view which dominated most of its departments and united its faculty in a common enterprise. With few exceptions—notably Paul Shorey, the Platonist—the Chicago faculty consisted of men who saw eye to eye on fundamentals, whether they were professors of geology or economics, of physiology or religion, of education or sociology.

I do not mean to imply that various departments always collaborated in research—although more of that has occurred at Chicago than anywhere else—but I do say that the large round tables of the faculty club could usually assemble a diversity of specialists who really understood what the other fellow's research was driving at because it was a common objective they all shared. If a university should be a *community* of scholars, if it should sustain a *universe* of discourse, then the pre-Hutchins Chicago almost (I say "almost") rang the bell. Paradoxically, Hutchins was attacked by the Old Guard at Chicago for wishing to "unify" the university by "imposing" a fundamental point of view (loosely called "a metaphysics"), when, in fact, his efforts to introduce new elements were restricted by a faculty trying to maintain its unity. The issue in the past ten years has not been a fight of schismatics against a unifier (if anything Hutchins and his group were the schismatics) but a conflict of basic doctrines.

That, however, is another story which I shall presently tell. Here I am concerned to define the unity of the earlier Chicago.

The general line of Chicago's pragmatism is too well known to need discussion beyond pointing out that much of its case rested on "the new science of psychology." According to Dewey's own report, it was James's *Principles of Psychology* which had awakened him from his dogmatic slumbers in the bower of Hegelianism. That book was radical in its chapters on instinct, habit, and emotion, in its attempt to give a physiological diagram for every aspect of behavior, in its view of man as an animal—whether rational or not. Although Aristotle had known

long before about man's animality, this fact had been obscured or
forgotten by the psychologists of the early nineteenth century who dealt
almost exclusively in "states of consciousness" or "the association of
ideas." But when the old truth was rediscovered it packed a new punch
because the human animal, like every other, was now primarily viewed
as engaged in the struggle for existence by adaptation to environment.

It was not merely discoveries in neurology, but Darwinism that
altered the conception of man as a knowing or a desiring animal, as
political or artistic. This "evolutionary" conception of man as a system
of reflexes which could be conditioned, as a bundle of drives which
impelled him to adapt, gave rise to the new logic and the new ethics
—both pragmatic in the sense that the ultimate criterion of the true
or the good was successful adjustment, in thinking or action, to a
changing world or a changing society. But most important of all was
the emphasis on change itself. Darwin had shattered the illusion of a
static universe. Evolution made a mockery of the quest for certainty.
Everything, including truth, is in flux. Creative intelligence must look
to the contingent future. Novelty should be prized rather than feared;
for with the aid of Science the Savior man could be optimistic about
winning the struggle for existence under the most adverse and unfore-
seen circumstances.

William James epitomized this new view of things when he wrote,
in *The Nation* (1904):

> Not only has the doctrine of Evolution weaned us from fixities and inflex-
> ibilities in general, and given us a world all plastic, but it has made us ready
> to imagine almost all our functions, even the intellectual ones, as "adaptations,"
> and possibly transient adaptations, to practical human needs. The enormous
> growth of the sciences in the past fifty years has reconciled us to the idea that
> *Not quite true is as near as we can ever get.* [Italics are mine.] For investigating
> minds there is no sanctity in any theory, and "laws of nature" absolutely
> expressible by us are the idols of the popular-science level of education exclu-
> sively. Up-to-date logicians, mathematicians, physicists, and chemists vie with
> one another as to who will break down most barriers, efface most outlines,
> supersede most current definitions and conceptions.

This may not be a fair summary of pragmatism or, as James called it,
humanism (because human needs were the ultimate measure). But it
does define the point of view which unified Chicago, and made the
university a single school of thought. One has only to recall a few of

the famous names on the early faculty to see how this way of looking at things prevailed on all sides.

In biology there was Jacques Loeb, who pushed mechanism to its limits by trying to interpret even human adjustments to environment as physicochemical tropisms. In psychology there was James Rowland Angell, who, as a follower of William James, developed "functionalism," and this ultimately became, in the hands of John B. Watson, his student, radical behaviorism. In the social sciences there was Thorstein Veblen, whose iconoclasms demolished conventional views of the human enterprise, social and political, as well as economic; there were Albion Small and W. I. Thomas, who instituted data collecting to make sociology descriptive and scientific instead of normative and moralistic, and used biological and evolutionary principles to account for social facts. In theology, or shall we say "religion," there were President Harper, himself completely modernist (not without cause did the Baptists question his orthodoxy), Shailer Matthews, Shirley Jackson Case, and others, who not only made Chicago famous for "higher criticism" but also introduced "social service" into the divinity school and turned the emphasis from dogmatic theology to comparative religion, studying the varieties of religious experience as psychological phenomena, creeds as ethnic by-products, and religion itself as part of man's struggle for existence. In education there were again Harper and Dewey, who agreed perfectly that educational institutions must serve, to use Harper's words, as "the Messiah of democracy, its to-be-expected deliverer." To this end, Harper, as president, started university extension work and called research from the ivory tower to the street; Dewey, as founder and head of the first school of education, started, with the help of Ella Flagg Young, reforms in the Chicago school system, which spread nationwide as "progressivism."

All of this paints a picture of an institution resourcefully carrying out the impetus originally given it by such men as Harper and Dewey, zealously devoted to putting a new line of thought to work in every academic field, its members united in what might be called the religion of militant modernism.

But though it stands in the foreground, the University of Chicago must not be allowed to occupy the whole picture, for its School of Thought soon dominated the work of other institutions (in philosophy and education, in biology, social science, and religion); and when the background is completely envisaged we see the outlines of American culture itself during the past half century. Even if, in part, Chicago merely went with the tide, its clear formulation of principles and policies, its energetic application of them in practice cannot be denied profound influence upon the whole contemporary scene. More than the Academy of Plato (a real ivory tower so far as the main currents of Greek life were concerned), more than the medieval University of Paris (which never achieved sufficient unity of doctrine to maintain a "school of thought"), Chicago had, in its first long period, both homogeneity in itself and affinity with the general trend of American culture. It was the larger community in microcosm.

Why should anyone have wished to reform the University of Chicago? Was it not everything a university should be, doing everything a university should do? The answer is simply that its unity had been achieved too quickly and at too great a cost. The price must be measured in terms of the things which Chicago, and American culture generally, had been willing to give up, had, in fact, renounced as outmoded. At its very center, exercising centrifugal force, was a hard core of negations and exclusions. The denial of metaphysics and theology as independent of empirical science, the denial of stability in the universe and certainty in human knowledge, the denial of moral values transcending adaptation to environment and escaping relativity to time and place, the denial of intellectual discipline in education and of the light shed by an abiding tradition of learning, the denial of a personal God, self-revealed, and of a Divine Providence concerned with man's supernatural salvation—these kept the ball rolling, and gave it its terrific impact on American life.

It would be difficult to enumerate a set of propositions, codifying the Chicago School of Thought, which did not convey, explicitly or with merely verbal concealment, these profound negations. There were positive points of course, and therein lies the truth of pragmatism, of a functional psychology, of progressivism in education, of empirical methods in social science. Professor Barzun to the contrary, Darwin's discoveries were momentous, and the concept of evolution legitimately changed men's fundamental views. The misfortune, for which Chicago, not Darwin, can be blamed, arises from the overemphasis, the exclusions, the "nothing-but" fallacy, in the drawing of the implications.

The "nothing-but" fallacy is a common human failing. We do not seem able to appreciate a new departure in thought which occurs by way of *addition* to the old. Novelty by itself does not stir us; it must be proclaimed as dispensing us from former allegiances. We are not content to say "This too is true"; we must revolutionize thought by saying "Nothing but this is true." If the positive points in the Chicago movement had been temperately affirmed, truth might have been increased, even transformed, by their addition; but there would probably be no record today of any Chicago School of Thought. Given a sharp, negative twist, they not only created a school of thought but unified its members in a crusading movement against the old and supposedly outworn. Once remove the negations and make the contrary supposition—that the old is not outworn, but must be integrated with the new—and you will see how hollow at its center was Chicago's unity before Hutchins came along.

What Hutchins attempted to establish at Chicago was not a new school of thought, just as exclusive in its own way as its predecessor. The faculty misinterpreted him in terms of their own extremism. They charged him with wanting "nothing but Thomism," "nothing but principles," or "nothing but the past" where before there had been "nothing but pragmatism," "nothing but facts," or "nothing but the present." On the contrary, Hutchins's aim was synthesis—to relate science, philosophy, and theology harmoniously without sacrificing the autonomy of each, to be contemporary and American in education without promoting militant modernism or cultural isolationism. It was not merely the university that Hutchins sought to reform. He wished to free American education and culture from the negations and provincialism which Chicago typified.

3

In 1936, a little more than thirty years after William James had reviewed some of the Decennial Publications, under the title "The Chicago School," another review appeared bearing that same title. But this time the book was President Hutchins's *No Friendly Voice*, and the reviewer was a later-day follower of John Dewey—Professor T. V. Smith. Had the title been truly deserved, its compact irony would have summarized a remarkable shift in the winds of doctrine at Chicago. William James had predicted that Chicago's School of Thought would be known as such "for twenty-five years to come." The time had run, the prediction had been verified; but despite Professor Smith's suggestion to the contrary, the first Chicago School has not been displaced by a second and opposite intellectual movement, under the leadership of Hutchins.

It takes more than one man or a few to make a school of thought in the sense in which Harper's Chicago deserved that description. In the past ten years there have been numerous references to "the neo-scholastic movement at Chicago," "Chicago Thomism," "Aristoteli-anism on the Midway," "the revival of classicism," "the return to the Middle Ages"—all suggestive of the fact that Chicago had become the center of another orthodoxy, the seat of an opposite school of thought. That, however, is simply not the fact; and, surprising as this statement will seem to some of his opponents, I do not believe that Hutchins ever wished it to be. It was merely that he and his associates in reform were vastly outnumbered by the dissident voices on the faculty—more than an echo of the old Chicago spirit, which John Chamberlain neatly caught in Anton J. Carlson's reiterated "Vat iss the ef-fidence?" The truth is rather that Hutchins fought the old school not to replace it by another, but to place its positive contributions, shorn of their "nothing-but" exaggerations, in the perspective of the whole European tradition. Justice could be done to modernity without throwing ancient wisdom out of court.

The Editor of *The Christian Century*, commenting on the change from Harper to Hutchins, saw this truth when he wrote:

The essential distinction of this [the first Chicago] school which charac-terized its departure from orthodox metaphysics was its adoption of the scientific method as the true method for the discovery not only of scientific truth but of metaphysical truth as well. . . . When President Hutchins came upon the scene the first phase of this development had run its course. This phase had been characterized by what is now generally regarded as a too narrow conception of scientific method. Especially in the philosophical disciplines, it has come to be recognized that its procedure, copying too closely the procedure of the physical scientists, has left on one side large portions of reality, and the most important portions, which now clamor for attention. The new President voiced this insistent demand. He spoke not for himself alone, but for a wide body of disillusionment with regard to the sufficiency of science.

There is here the additional point that, just as Harper's Chicago reflected and formulated the "religion of science" which dominated American culture from the nineties to the thirties, so Hutchins's Chicago, in the past ten years, has focused attention upon—more than that, has become the leading forum for—the crucial issue of our day: *whether science is enough, theoretically or practically*; whether a culture can be healthy, whether democracy can be defended, if theology and metaphysics, ethics and politics are either despised or, what is the same, degraded to topics about which laboratory scientists pontificate after they have won the Nobel Prize or are called to the Gifford Lectureship.

Chicago's leadership in American education and its formative influence upon American thought are just as clear in the Hutchins era as they were under Harper. But it would be a mistake to suppose that Hutchins has succeeded in the sense in which Harper did. Harper built a school of thought which lasted for almost forty years, and during that time was the generator of educational movements and intellectual trends that spread over the country, east and west. Hutchins has neither built a school of thought nor been able to transmute the heat of the controversies he generated into the light of resolutions. But those controversies, which have gradually come to be recognized as the leading issues of our day, have been more heatedly agitated at Chicago than anywhere else in the country. Where there is so much heat there is always hope, at least, for the emergence of light.

The Chicago Fight now plays the role in American culture once played by the Chicago School. The university which, in its first period, mirrored the prevailing ideology in its own solidarity of doctrine, still functions as the cultural microcosm. For the past ten years it has been the arena in the spotlight. The heavyweights in its ring have staged a fight for a nationwide audience—an audience drawn not by their lust for blood, but by their genuine concern with the points in issue. Chicago did not make the issues important. They had gradually risen, by nature's demands, to the forefront of popular consciousness. But Chicago was willing to see the fight through, wherever the chips fell. It did not run away from trouble by insisting upon academic dignity, by hiding behind the false face of academic politeness. Dispensing with kid gloves and Queensberry rules, the discussion turned into something of a public brawl, with all sorts of kibitzers on the sidelines mixing in. But, however lamentable some aspects of the controversy now seem, the Chicago Fight, like the Chicago School, performed the type of service which a university owes to the community.

Before we consider the defect which mars the virtue of Hutchins's Chicago, let me be sure that the reader understands what I mean by the exceptional character of Chicago's intellectual vitality. Unless he has lived through the past ten years at Chicago he will probably not believe me when I say that there has been more real tangling over basic issues at Chicago than has occurred at a dozen other places during the same time, or at some during their whole existence. I have taught elsewhere, visited a great many institutions, and know about many more from intimate report. Their faculties may harbor differences of opinion about fundamentals, but you would never know it by listening to the talk at the faculty club, reading the student papers, or detecting signs of strife in administrative decisions. From this usual state of affairs, Chicago differs almost in kind, not degree. The campus has been a seething ferment these past ten years, and everybody has been involved from the president to the janitors—the students as well as the faculty. I shall make no effort to explain this extraordinary phenomenon: it may be the Middle West; it may be the lawless Windy City; it may be a sulphurous vapor exuded by the Midway or animal spirits blown from the stockyards. Whatever the cause, the fact remains that the university is incomparably alive and kicking.

A few stories may help to gain credence for this fact. In December 1933, President Hutchins delivered a convocation address entitled "The Issue in the Higher Learning." Negatively, he criticized aimless gadgeteering on the part of laboratory scientists, and the social scientists' propensity to collect facts for their own sake. Positively, he urged that research of every sort be directed by leading principles, be illuminated by ideas. "We have confused science with information," he said, "ideas with facts, and knowledge with miscellaneous data. . . . I am far from denying the accomplishments of modern empirical science. Its record has been a grand one. . . . But as the Renaissance could accuse the Middle Ages of being rich in principles and poor in facts, we are now entitled to inquire whether we are not rich in facts and poor in principles. . . . Our bewilderment has resulted from our notion that salvation depends on information. The remedy may be a return to the processes of rational thought."

Hell broke loose shortly thereafter. "Facts *vs.* ideas" became fighting words. On Hutchins's side the *Daily Maroon's* student editor ran articles which got students and faculty engaged with each other in all sorts of alliances and oppositions. There was a running feud between Editor Barden and Professor Gideonse, now president of Brooklyn College, in which Gideonse posted his answers on a faculty bulletin board, answers that later formed the substance of his reply to Hutchins in a pamphlet called *The Higher Learning in a Democracy*. In that same year the *Maroon* published four long criticisms of the faculty's syllabi for the basic courses, written by pro-Hutchins youngsters, and based on the December proclamation. Other students rose in defense of their teachers. The feeling between student groups ran so high that it spilled over into sports: the Aristotelians crossed bats with the Social Scientists in baseball!

But the high point of the year came when the old warhorse "Ajax" Carlson stopped his researches on thirst and hunger long enough to challenge the opposition to a public debate. It was arranged at first to take place in a laboratory theater before graduate students in biology. But the demand for tickets was so great that the scene shifted to Mandel Hall, the University's largest auditorium. The tickets were free, but at such a premium that some students trafficked in them, selling them for as much as a dollar apiece. The faculty, by departmental groups, bought boxes in the horseshoe circle to defray the expenses of the hall. On the day of the event every chair that could be squeezed into the hall or onto the platform was added to accommodate the overflow. I know what the audience looked and sounded like, the intensity of its feeling, the thunderclap of its partisan applause whenever a punch landed on either side. I know how heating, if not enlightening, Chicago polemic can become, for I was the other man in that debate.

The story of the Chicago Fight in 1933 has its mate in almost every other year of the Hutchins regime. There have been other debates, one between Hutchins and Dean Melby of Northwestern, sponsored by the *Daily Maroon*; one between Hutchins and Chancellor Carmichael of Vanderbilt, sponsored by the Alumni Council. The alumni have been drawn into the controversy by attacks and replies printed in the alumni magazine, some by the faculty and some by the old grads themselves. But one more story will suffice to show that students and faculty never miss an opportunity for intellectual fisticuffs, and the extent to which local wrangling has national repercussions.

Last year I delivered a paper at a Conference on Science, Philosophy, and Religion, held in New York City. Its title was "God and the Professors." Its argument bore directly on the controversy between Hutchins and his academic opponents. When, by way of the Hearst papers, which published my speech in full, or by way of *The New Republic*, which published Professor Sidney Hook's attack on it, the Chicago boys got wind of this off-campus dispute they were soon "r'aring" to go. The *Maroon* at first reprinted my piece and Hook's, and editorialized on the pros and cons. But the faculty, and other students, had to have their say. Columns were filled with attacks and replies, mostly attacks; until finally, the *Maroon* issued a special six-page supplement which contained the gems of the occasion. The astonishing fact is that this supplement sold 5,000 copies. Requests for copies in small and large lots came from colleges all over the country long after none were left. Nor was the controversy confined to the *Maroon*: it raged in classrooms and drawing rooms, both in Chicago and elsewhere—wherever, in fact, the Chicago Fight had gained adherents to its sides.

The ultimate comment on all this, revealing the trouble with Chicago in the past decade, was contained in the title of Milton Mayer's contribution to the *Maroon* Supplement. He, speaking for the innocent bystander, headed his piece: "I Can't Hear Myself Think." Despite the amazing vitality which Chicago has exhibited in seeing the fight through, it has never seen through the issues, nor clarified them sufficiently, for itself or for the public, to permit a sober resolution. The issues have been the same for the past ten years. Each year, when the shouting dies and the smoke lifts, prejudice and passion are left mumbling and smoldering until the bell rings for the next round.

4

First, unity without diversity! Then, conflict without community! The defects of Chicago in its first and last decades are equally symptomatic of our cultural malaise. The causal connections here are manifold. A healthy unity requires the harmony of differences. But when, in the university or in our culture, other elements began to claim a place along with science, the weak unity, which had been maintained by negations and exclusions, gave way to discord rather than to the harmony of ordered differences. Nevertheless, the shift from the Chicago School to the Chicago Fight is a small step toward the ideal of civilization, the ideal of a university, which Whitehead, writing of Harvard's future, defined as "the possible harmony of diverse things." It is, he said, "the peculiar function of a university to be an agent of unification. This does not mean the suppression of all but one." From a negative unity to a warring diversity is change from a false peace to a significant conflict. From the conflict of violent extremes to a reconciliation of differences would be motion toward that genuine peace which still lies ahead. This is the university's future. There is more chance of its happening at Chicago than elsewhere, because at Chicago the opponents at least try to talk to one another.

What is needed to bring this about? Last September a conference of scholars was called not merely for the purpose of assembling leading representatives of science, philosophy, and religion, but *supposedly* to have them understand one another's role in the development of culture. Those who called this meeting felt that unless philosophy and religion are genuinely acknowledged—that is, given their *proper* place *above*, not just *along with*, science—democracy is threatened from within culturally, perhaps even more seriously than from without by force.

Anyone who had been through the Chicago Fight could have predicted the outcome of this Conference on Science, Philosophy, and Religion. It would fail. Though it meets this September in a second session, and next year again, the prediction remains unchanged, because what happened last year will continue to occur until the causes for such frustration are overcome. The failure I refer to is failure of communication. When there is no communication between reconcilable elements they appear to be irreconcilable extremes. Ten years' experience at Chicago indicates what one might expect from a gathering of scientists, philosophers, and theologians, who have no common universe of discourse. Nor can such community be achieved, in a university or at a conference, simply by bringing the diverse elements together and having them read papers at one another. The obstacle to be surmounted first, the most difficult task to discharge, is teaching the specialists *how* to talk to one another.

As a matter of fact, conferences of this sort should not be necessary to achieve the end in view. That should be the main business of our universities. Their greatness should not be measured by the number of eminent scholars on their faculty lists, or by the holding of symposia at which learned papers are read, as at Harvard four years ago and at Chicago this September. A university's greatness consists in its being the intellectual forum of the community, the place where the basic issues of its culture are fruitfully debated. Chicago's greatness lies in the *partial* performance of this service. For ten years it has debated the issues which the Conference on Science, Philosophy, and Religion met to consider—made necessary only by the fact that such debate has not occurred at other universities, as at Chicago. But the point still remains that the debate has not been fruitful. What is needed to make it so?

What must happen before Chicago can perform *completely* a university's function, before it can fulfill the promise of light which its career of intellectual ferment perhaps portends?

The extremes to be avoided are easy to point out. A university must avoid, on the one hand, the "peace" of sleep, resulting either from conventional academic politeness or from the hollow unity achieved by "the suppression of all but one"; and, on the other hand, it must avoid the violence of fruitless polemic. It must not commit the "nothing-but" fallacy which exaggerates the claims of any indispensable part at the expense of excluding others equally indispensable; nor should it be satisfied with an armistice, instead of real peace, by compromising issues rather than resolving them. Neither domination by one exclusive extreme nor suspended hostilities among many is desirable. Both counterfeit the ideal of true unity won from diversity by right order.

What is desirable is that peace of understanding which enables intelligent discussion to work progressively toward agreement—an end which may never be fully realized but which, nevertheless, gives discussion its highest meaning, if not its only justification. Unless controversy is to be as inconsequential as Ping-Pong, those who join issue in debate must aim at, and hope for, an ultimate resolution of the issues. But agreement, which is the concurrence of minds in the truth about things, cannot be reached, cannot even be aimed at by discussion, until there is understanding—the communication of minds through shared meanings in a single universe of discourse. The liberal arts and a common intellectual tradition are, therefore, indispensable prerequisites for the work of a university—the one giving men the technic of communication, the other rooting them all in the same cultural soil. Lack of liberal discipline has made our debates a babel of jargons, incurable by the logical esperanto of the semanticists. Lack of a common tradition has turned our universities into a jungle of predatory growths, impenetrable by special conferences or academic symposia.

The disease itself indicates the therapy. The cure will come only by a fundamental educational reform below the level of the university. The great tragedy of American education is that our universities were founded just at the time when genuinely liberal colleges were ceasing to exist. In fact it was the developing university which, imposing the elective system, helped to kill the liberal arts curriculum of the colleges. The other wound came from below, from the defection of the elementary and secondary schools. Crushed from above by a burden of specialization, which insisted upon departmental autonomy at the college level, its underpinnings removed by failures in preparatory education, the college gave up the ghost of its liberal arts curriculum, retaining only the name of the degree.

The great difference between the medieval and the modern university is not that the former reached its apex in theology, and the latter laid its foundation in science; rather it is that the members of the medieval university, its students and faculty, were truly bachelors of liberal arts. They had learned how to communicate before engaging in the disputations which made the medieval universities the vital forums of their day. Embraced in a common tradition of learning, they could at least understand one another when they did not agree. The medieval universalism, of which Etienne Gilson spoke at the Harvard tercentenary, did not derive from the universality of Latin as the learned tongue, nor from the catholicism of the Christian faith; for this universalism included the Jews and Arabs, many languages and many faiths. The European community of culture flowered because of excellence in liberal education—the cultivation of its arts, the possession of a common heritage of learning.

Walter Lippmann did not exaggerate when he said that "the prevailing education is destined, if it continues, to destroy Western civilization, and is in fact destroying it." He might just as well have said that we shall not have genuine universities again until all the preparatory stages of education are radically reformed, until the college, above all, is restored to its liberal function. The fate of Western civilization, as a cultural community, cannot be separated from the state of its educational institutions. Only one college in this country, St. John's at Annapolis, is working for the revival of a liberal curriculum. Only the University of Chicago has throughout its history manifested devotion to the true functions of a university—formation of fundamental doctrines, debate of the most serious issues. If the performance of these functions could be elevated by liberal education the doctrines might be moderated to the sanity of truth, the debate might become fruitful of sober resolutions. If in some way the spiritual union of St. John's and Chicago could be consummated, we might hope for the blessed event of a cultural rebirth.

3

Liberalism and Liberal Education

(1939)

In "Liberalism and Liberal Education," Adler attacks another problem of education in America. He proposes that the essential questions concerning education and the individual, and education and the state, are all normative. The answers, he says, are therefore not likely to be found in science. The questions are, rather, ethical and political and have already found their solutions in practical philosophy. But the general truths of practical philosophy have been obscured by a false liberalism that has become prevalent in American thought. The article was published in The Educational Record (July 1939). What Adler said then, he is saying still: "American education has failed to achieve liberal ends by liberal means—and is still moving in the wrong direction."

Since then "liberalism" has become even more nearly synonymous with license, synonymous with freedom without authority or discipline, and therefore odious. True freedom has thereby been lost as the aim of education; and false liberalism, the worst enemy of true freedom, is still destroying liberal education.

G.V.D.

THE BASIC PROBLEMS of education are normative. This means, positively, that they are problems in moral and political philosophy; and, negatively, that they cannot, they have not and never will be, solved by the methods of empirical science, by what is called educational research. The reason for the unalterable inadequacy of science is not far to seek. Science can measure and observe, can collect facts of all sorts and generalize from such collections, but neither the facts nor the generalizations can by themselves answer questions about what *should* be done in education. Such questions require us to consider what is good and bad, to define the ideals or norms of human life and human society, and this is the work of the moral and political philosopher.

The ultimate questions involved in the problem of emotions and the educative process are all moral. They cannot be answered by science. It must be said to the credit of the researchers that they acknowledged the impasse at which they arrived when they realized that ethical criteria could not be avoided. But, unfortunately, it must also be said that they manifested the prevalent positivism by supposing that the impasse was due merely to the present limitations of scientific knowledge which further research may remedy. Until then, they regret, "philosophy must continue to play a large part in determining the objectives of education with regard to the training of affective behavior." They *regret* because they think that ethical criteria are relative and subjective, culturally determined or matters of individual opinion. If that were true, they would have reached an impasse, indeed, for then the problems of education would be forever insoluble, because there is no justification whatsoever for the optimism that science will some day answer normative questions.

May I take issue with the investigators on this crucial point? Not only are the major problems of education—whether in relation to the individual or to the state—soluble, but they have already been solved, for their solution does not depend on scientific research. Scientific research is relevant only in a minor connection, namely, the application of universal principles to local and contemporary circumstances. To hold, as I do, that the major problems of education are already solved, is, of course, to hold that we possess a body of settled truths in the sphere of practical problems, the problems of human conduct and association.

In the light of all that we know about man, without the aid of scientific research, it is demonstrably true that man's well-being depends upon the regulation of his emotional life by reason, what the ancients called the discipline and moderation of the passions. This discipline can be accomplished only by the formation of good habits of action and passion, and these good habits are the moral virtues. To whatever extent the school as an educational institution must deal with the emotions of the young, its aim must be the same as that of the church and of the home, namely, the development of the moral virtues. There are difficult questions here about the division of responsibility among the several cooperating agencies, such as school, church, and home, but there is no unsolved problem about the end which they must all serve. That the cardinal virtues are prudence, justice, temperance, and fortitude is as certain a truth as any theorem in geometry, and as universal and objective, independent of the mores of the tribe and of your and my private prejudices.

I am not saying that the human race has solved the problem of how to train its young, how to cultivate the virtues, but I see no evidence that scientific research has substantially improved our position in this regard. At best, we have learned a little about the pathology of the passions and that may, in turn, have made us realize anew how patient and persistent our efforts must be if, as educators, we share in the responsibility for making children into good men and women.

I have said all this illustratively to explain my approach to the problem of general education and the state. I would not be speaking honestly if I pretended that I was going to express my opinions or the opinions of others. There is no room for opinion in philosophy. This applies to practical as well as theoretic philosophy, and to the philosophy of education as a chapter in ethics and politics. I do not mean, of course, that all men agree, but only that their disagreements are not to be regarded as an affair of obstinate prejudices on their part. These are arguable matters, and argument is both empty and vicious unless it is undertaken on the supposition that there is attainable truth which, when attained by reason in the light of all the relevant evidence, resolves the original issues. Moreover, to claim truth for what one is saying is not to be intolerant of others who may differ, for we can try to speak the truth "with malice toward none and charity for all," but not unless we have "firmness in the right as God gives us to see the right." And, as a contemporary writer has pointed out, if liberalism forbids such firmness, then liberalism has chosen the path toward doctrinal suicide.

The problem of the individual and education—of which the problem about emotions is a part—is a moral problem. The major principles needed for its solution are to be found in the analysis of the virtues, both moral and intellectual. The problem of education and the state is a political problem. Here the major principle is the most general of all political truths, namely, the distinction between good and bad states, just and unjust governments. The ancients formulated this principle by saying that the criterion of justice resides in the end which the government serves. A government consists of men who, in one way or another, have come to occupy the offices of ruling their fellows. Either they perform the task of ruling for the sake of the common good, for the well-being of the community, or instead of seeking to serve the common interests of the governed, they misuse their offices to further their own private interests. Furthermore, the common good is not an end in itself; the well-being of the community is a good because it contributes to the happiness of the citizens. The tyrant—and tyranny can be taken as the name for any unjust rule—not only misuses his office by considering only his own advantage, but usually tries to conceal his violence by identifying his own fortunes with the state itself, and then making the success of the state the paramount good which all men must serve, though they perish spiritually as well as physically in the process.

The contemporary world, I almost regret to say, has not allowed us to forget this ancient truth. We in America have come to cherish our good institutions with renewed vigor because of the contrast that is afforded by the obviously bad societies in the world today. We regard our institutions as good because they respect the integrity, the sanctity, of human beings, and aim to help them achieve good lives. And by the same principle we regard the various totalitarian regimes as bad because they have made the state itself an absolute end. They have deified the state and have sacrificed men upon a false altar. Whenever men are treated as if they were mere means, they are misused. The totalitarian myth that the state as such is supreme always results in such misuse.

On the contrary, government itself is an instrument for achieving the common good, and the community thus well maintained is a means toward the perfection of men. When I speak of human happiness as identical with the perfection of human nature, I am not thinking in terms of the utilitarian formula of "the greatest good for the greatest number." I am distinguishing between the individual, whose private and idiosyncratic interests are always subordinate to the common good, and the person, constituted by that essential and spiritual nature in which all men equally share. It is not *my* private interests as opposed to *yours* which the community must serve, but only my personal, or essentially human, well-being, and that is, in every respect, the same as yours.

These general truths of political philosophy determine the proper role of public education as a political institution. Along with law enforcement agencies, public health service, military forces, the educational system is one of the instrumentalities of government, and in a sense the most important because it is entirely positive and constructive in its operations. All of these implements of government are well employed only if they are directed to the ends which government must itself serve, in order to be just, namely, the common good immediately, and the happiness of men ultimately.

The question "What is a good education?" can be answered in two ways: either in terms of what is good for men at any time and place because they are men, or in terms of what is good for men considered only as members of a particular social and political order. My thesis is that the best society is the one in which the two answers are the same; and that one society is better than another in so far as it approximates this ideal. The totalitarian regimes misuse education because they misuse men. They must use education, as they use other pressures and propaganda, secret police and concentration camps, to make men into political puppets. Such bad societies, vicious in principle as well as ruthless in execution, cannot afford to consider education as a means for perfecting men and making them happy.

We must condemn the fascist educational program for the same reasons that we condemn fascist government and fascist international policy. All of these condemnations are justified by the same fundamental principle, according to which we distinguish good and bad in the political and social order. If there is anyone who would say that this principle is merely a matter of opinion—and, *a fortiori*, that there are no objective and universal political truths—that person, whether he knows it or not, is as vicious as his fascist adversary, for he is ultimately reduced to the same position, that only might makes right. This is the suicide of the false liberal, to which I previously referred.

It is a basic tenet of American democracy that men have sacred rights above the state. While admitting that its present forms and operations may be far from perfect, we are, nevertheless, compelled to honor the institutions and practices of our government as abiding by the principle of justice. The corollary which would seem to follow is that American education is fundamentally sound, because we seek to solve the problem of education in our democracy only by determining what is good education for all men everywhere. Unfortunately, that is not clearly the case.

Education as it exists in this country today—and I am thinking primarily of our schools and colleges which perform the function of general education, and not universities and professional schools—has been distorted by some of its leading practitioners in almost the same way that it is misused in the totalitarian countries. The distortion is plainly manifest in a recent publication of the John Dewey Society, a book called *Democracy and the Curriculum.* The educators who have written this book—and they represent an important faction in our teachers colleges—are so anxious to save democracy that they are willing to make the educational process serve no other end than the perpetuation of a form of government. Their fundamental error is not lessened by the fact that the government they seek to support is relatively just, as compared to others; for they have misconceived the nature of democracy as a good government if they fail to see that citizenship—intelligent participation in government—is only one, and not the exclusive or primary, aim of good education. Public education in a democracy serves the state not simply by making children into faithful democrats, but primarily through serving the welfare of its citizens, not merely as subjects of the state, but as free men. In fact, unless education makes men free it cannot serve democracy at all.

It is not just a play on words to say that the aim of liberal education is to make men free, and for this reason democracy must sustain and extend liberal education or perish, since democracy is the society of free men. There may be a play on words in the motto of St. John's College—*Facio liberos ex liberis libris libraque*—but the punning on the Latin stem for the word "free" is deeply significant, because to state the purpose of a liberal college as making free men out of children by means of books and balances not only proclaims the end but specifies the means—the liberal arts and the tradition of learning.

The trouble with American education today is not merely that in many quarters the end of liberal education has been forgotten or mistaken, but that the means have been corrupted or deformed. These are related occurrences, for when educators bend their efforts toward making school and college a training camp for citizenship—insisting even that the organization and administration of the school be a miniature democracy so that the pupil can get inoculated with small doses—they also turn the curriculum, if they retain that odious thing at all, into a scheme of indoctrination. But if democratic citizens must be free men, they must have free minds, and minds cannot be made free except by being disciplined to recognize only one authority, the authority of reason. That discipline is accomplished only when the intelligence is trained to work critically on all matters; only when every human doctrine or policy, even that of democracy itself, is submitted to the examination of reason; only when, furthermore, the mind is freed from all local prejudices and current exigencies through being elevated by those universal truths to which the whole human tradition bears witness.

When I say that American education has failed to achieve liberal ends by liberal means—and is still moving in the wrong direction—I appeal for support to the obvious facts with which we are all acquainted. Scientific measurements of the educational product of the schools of New York and Pennsylvania show not merely a failure to master the ordinary subject matters of instruction but, what is much more dismal, the inadequacy of the schools with respect to the basic operations of critical intelligence as these occur in reading and writing. Not only are distressingly large numbers of high school graduates unable to read and write to that minimum degree which must be possessed by free minds participating in a democratic community, but the evidence further shows that after graduation they have neither appetite nor capacity for reading anything better than the local newspaper or mediocre fiction. Some of these many high school graduates have terminated their schooling. For them we can have little hope. School has given them neither the equipment nor the impulse to continue their education out of school. Their intelligence, of whatever degree, has been so untrained and so uncultivated, that they will be ready to follow the first demagogue who seeks to beguile them.

If, as Thomas Hobbes observes, a democracy tends to degenerate into an oligarchy of orators, and even sometimes, as we have recently seen abroad, into the tyranny of the leading orator of the land, then education in this country, as judged by its high school products, is inimical to democracy. Nor is the remedy the one proposed by the spokesmen for the John Dewey Society, who would inoculate and indoctrinate the students with democratic notions and practices in the school. That is demagogic rather than democratic education. The person who has not learned to think critically, who has not come to respect reason as the only arbiter of truth in human generalizations, who has not been lifted out of the blind alleys of local and contemporary jargons and shibboleths, will not be saved by the orator of the classroom from later succumbing to the orator of the platform and the press.

Of course, we must remember that some high school graduates go to college, and among these, perhaps, are a few who have profited from their schooling. But we can derive little consolation from this thought because here, too, the facts prevent us. Though they are even more obliged by their historic mission to perform the work of liberal education, the liberal arts colleges fail on their level as badly, if not worse, than the high schools do on theirs. Our colleges produce undisciplined and hence unliberated minds, minds which are cultivated only by a superficial literacy. Almost worse is that they produce skeptics about reason and knowledge, relativists about morals, sophists in political matters, in short, liberals in that worst sense of the word in which liberalism is suicidal because it is unable to give a rational defense of its sentimental protestations without contradicting itself. Since liberals of this sort are comfortable in the presence of contradiction, it will not be implausible if I add that these same college graduates who are skeptics and sophists are also deeply indoctrinated with the local prejudices of their teachers, especially the scientists, natural and social, who dominate the college curriculum. The college graduate is neither a liberal artist nor a liberated mind. When college has affected him most "spiritually," it has made him into a "liberal," by which I mean that monomania for freedom in which the mind abhors discipline and does not acknowledge the authority of reason.

I am, of course, using the words "liberal" and "liberalism" in a dyslogistic sense. These words can also be used as terms of the highest praise, and then it would be true to say that a liberal education serves democracy by making men liberal. The distinction here between the contrary senses of "liberal" and "liberalism" turns upon a true and a false conception of the nature and place of liberty in human life. The liberalism I have been attacking as false is false because it misconceives the role and extent of liberty in human affairs. It is this false liberalism which is as much a part of our eighteenth-century heritage as the good democratic institutions which we have preserved and developed. The founding fathers did not speak a pure political truth, a truth unmixed with error; they were inspired by Locke and Voltaire and Rousseau, but they were also misled by them.

The tradition of American democracy is a great blessing in the modern world, but it is not without its blemishes, chief among which is the false liberalism that was present at the beginning and has more recently been augmented by the positivism, the skepticism, the anti-rationalism, which are so many noxious weeds that seem to attend the flowering of science in a culture. There is no intrinsic and necessary connection between the principles of democracy and this false liberalism; on the contrary, democracy will become mature only through the cure of this infantile disorder. The fact remains, however, that at the present moment we are not only a democratic people but one which has not yet rectified its liberalism.

The false liberalism of which I speak is nowhere more dominant than among our professional educators, our teachers colleges, and our college faculties. The vicious circle of reciprocal causality is nowhere more manifest than in our educational system. Our educators are themselves the products of our schools and colleges and their liberalism signifies the extent to which our institutions have failed to accomplish liberal education. And their liberalism, on the other hand, is of paramount importance in sustaining the present deplorable state of affairs, in some cases going even further in the wrong direction, in others acting to oppose reforms which seek to institute a truly liberal education.

I do not mean to say that false liberalism, on the part of our educators or the public generally, is the only cause of what is wrong with American education today; but it is certainly among the principal causes. I have singled it out for discussion because we are here considering the relation of general education to the state. My point is that although American education can be good because it exists in a democratic country and need not, therefore, be misused, it is at present bad. It is bad largely with respect to the means we employ and the obliqueness of the way in which we direct them to the right end. This we do because of a false liberalism, historically associated with our democratic principles, and rampant today in the texture of our national life.

Let me illustrate this by citing again the authors of *Democracy and the Curriculum*. They want freedom to such an extent that they wish to be rid of a curriculum as a prescribed course of study. Because it is prescribed, because it expresses the authority of teachers imposed upon students, because it makes teacher and student unequal, it is regarded as undemocratic—as if democracy did not depend, as does every good social order, on leaders and followers, rulers with authority and subjects, not submissive, but well ruled. Throughout their writings they confuse authority, which is nothing more than the voice of reason, with autocracy, which is the violent imposition of a will by force; they confuse discipline with regimentation; they convert the equality of human beings as persons, sharing in a common nature and a common end, into an equality of individuals, despite the differences in their capacities and their merits. This is not the liberty and equality which constitute democracy as the social order in which popular sovereignty is most fully realized because, through the discipline of reason, men have the authority to govern themselves and use the freedom of self-government. This is the romantic libertinism and egalitarianism of Rousseau.

I am willing to admit that I have chosen an extreme example in using this book to make my case; maybe the rank and file of American educators would not accept so preposterous a position. Yet false liberalism is generally prevalent among them, though perhaps not so blatantly, and the falsity is manifested by the same confusions. As President Barr of St. John's College recently said:

> The day's news suggests that liberal democracies are paralyzed. If they are, it is because we twentieth-century liberals have missed the point of our faith. We have slithered into the belief that liberty meant being left alone, and nothing else. We have come to assume that liberalism is the absence of authority because we can no longer distinguish between authority and tyranny. We have forgotten that the mind that denies the authority of reason falls under the tyranny of caprice. We have forgotten that he who will not answer to the rudder must answer to the rock. We have therefore allowed totalitarian dictators to take out a copyright on words like authority and discipline, although their tyranny is a caricature of authority and their terrorism is a caricature of discipline.

It is appropriate, indeed, that these words should be spoken by the president of St. John's, because it is the only college in the country which is making a proportionate effort to adapt and devise means that may succeed in achieving the ends of liberal education. The venture is still too new to be judged by its products, but in aim and spirit it has already overcome false liberalism. Liberty is prized at St. John's, but with such discrimination and moderation that authority and discipline are not sacrificed. The elective system has been entirely abolished. The students become free men at St. John's through liberal disciplines, not through the repeated exercise of unprincipled choices.

This is not the place, nor is there time, to give an adequate analysis of the philosophical errors which underlie false liberalism. But I would like to point out a few of its misleading notions. As we have seen, liberalism is confused in so far as it confuses authority and tyranny, discipline and regimentation. These confusions discover for us the roots of error. In the first place, the confused liberal has a false conception of human liberty because for him it is both a negative and infinite value. It is always "freedom from" and not "freedom for," freedom as a condition of positive accomplishment. Following the major trend of modern thought, the confused liberal denies man's natural freedom, which is the freedom of man's will in acts of choice, and substitutes for natural freedom in this sense, the freedom from government which man possesses in a hypothetical state of nature. This hypothetical freedom man surrenders when, by social contract or otherwise, he enters with his fellows into society and submits to government. Government as such is an evil which must be suffered because life in a state of nature is worse—according to Hobbes, nasty, brutish and short. Hence, we get such eighteenth-century maxims as the one that that government governs best which governs least. And individual, civil liberty, freedom from being regulated or restricted in any way, becomes an unlimited and absolute good. It is a good in itself and we cannot get enough of it. There are, of course, numerous contradictions in this sequence of notions, but that does not prevent many men from taking the false position which exaggerates the value of liberty beyond everything else.

If, on the contrary, we begin by affirming man's natural freedom as his God-given power of free choice, we see that this freedom is, in itself, neither good nor evil *morally*, since it is equally the condition under which men perform good and bad acts. Freedom is morally good only when it is well used. That is why St. Augustine defined the moral virtues as the proper use of our freedom. It follows, furthermore, that civil liberty is good only to the extent that it comports with justice. Not that government which governs least or most is best, but only the one which governs most justly. Civil liberty is justified only by justice; anything else in excess or defect is license or oppression. In short, a man should have neither more civil liberty than he is able to use justly, nor less than he needs to lead a good life. Totalitarianism, at one extreme, commits the error of defect; false liberalism, at the opposite extreme, commits the error of excess.

The foregoing insight, that civil liberty is not incompatible with government, that, on the contrary, just government augments rather than diminishes one's freedom, leads us to the second point. Man's will is responsive either to the judgments of reason or to the movement of his passions. Only when reason rules the will, however, is a man fully free in his acts. It is not any sort of voluntary conduct which constitutes human freedom, for animals behave voluntarily and so do men under the impulse of their animal passions. Though freedom is in the will, its root or principle is in reason, as a power of deliberation and judgment. Here, again, we see that freedom, far from being the absence of all rule, is rather the submission to a right rule. We are free, in society or in our own acts, when we are properly governed. And this explains the meaning of authority within the human sphere. Authority is reason and nothing else.

Now, here, the confused liberal makes an amazing, a paradoxical, error. Although he usually denies man's free will, he is almost always at the same time a voluntarist, by which I mean that he affirms, by implication at least, the absolute primacy and inviolability of the will. Making the mistake of supposing that law is an expression of the sovereign will, rather than a command of reason, he must necessarily regard government as an organization of force, an imposition which violates his sacred will. For whereas another can speak to me with authority in so far as I can discern therein reason's commands, a voice that proclaims nothing but another's will speaks only in the language of force, and I must either oppose or submit my will according to our relative mights. Furthermore, voluntarism, in subordinating reason, tends to merge the will and the passions, so that the ruling principle in society or the individual is merely the force of desire *as such*, and everyone seeks a maximum freedom to follow his own inclinations.

There is still a further consequence of the voluntarism which is part of the liberal's confusion. The liberal exaggerates the province of the will in thought as well as in action. Whereas, in truth, the intellect moves necessarily within the sphere of its proper objects, so that men are not free to affirm what is self-evidently false, or to deny conclusions which are validly demonstrated by true premises, the liberal makes everything a matter of the will to believe. Thinking is not only voluntary as the exercise of our rational power, but it is voluntary in all its acts, so far as what is affirmed or denied is concerned. It follows, therefore, that just as in the realm of politics, the primacy of will identifies authority with force, so in the realm of thought the primacy of will reduces everything to arbitrary opinions or academic conventions. There are no first truths, but only postulates, demands of the will that something be taken for granted. In some sense, all knowledge rests on acts of faith, though the only principle of such faith is one's private predilections. Liberalism in the realm of thought has gone so far as to regard even mathematical truths as mere conventions, and the rules of logic itself as a set of postulated canons which have only pragmatic significance.

I hope I have said enough to indicate why I think false liberalism is the enemy of liberal education, and why a truly liberal education is needed in this country to correct the confusions of this widely prevalent liberalism. I know I have not said enough to demonstrate the errors of false liberalism, for that would be a work of extended analysis. Suffice it if I have intimated the demonstration by revealing the multiple con-tradictions with which false liberalism abounds. The task of correction is hopeless in so far as the liberal is not bothered by contradictions. The only hope is in the young, for if they are truly liberally educated they will become sensitive to contradictions, and if, in addition, they come to understand and respect the authority of reason in human affairs, they may be saved from the confusions of false liberalism. Our hope must be for a better education, *an education which democracy not only makes possible but needs,* for in the rectification of liberalism itself, in the school and in the state, lies the promise of maturity for American democracy.

4

Are There Absolute and Universal Principles on Which Education Should Be Founded?

(1941)

"Are there absolute and universal principles on which education should be founded?" was on two occasions the question for debate, or rather disputation, between Mortimer Adler and an adversary. The essay presented here is from the debate with Paul A. Schilpp in Cahn Auditorium, Northwestern University, 6 March 1941. Two months earlier Adler had engaged with Bertrand Russell to debate the same question. Dr. Adler was shocked and even a little outraged by Lord Russell's performance on that occasion . . . but he tells the story better than anyone.

The debate with Schilpp was published in Educational Trends (July/ August 1941). Only Adler's argument is included here as appropriate to this collection. If that seems unfair, the injustice may be mitigated by the view that any consideration of the question is almost as important as its answer, or who "won" the debate, since this question governs all other questions about the problems of education. The occurrence of the debate was therefore of great importance, for unless issues are joined, as Adler hoped they would be on this occasion, no educational problems— or any other problems—will be adequately understood, much less solved.

G.V.D.

53

MAY I BEGIN this evening by telling you not only that I am
happy to be here participating with Professor Schilpp in this
discussion, but also how it is that I happen to be here—
considering that major athletic relations between Chicago and Northwestern have been broken off.

In January of this year, I undertook to debate with Bertrand Russell
the question whether there are absolute and universal principles on
which education should be founded. Then, as now, I proposed to prove
the affirmative answer. And when I say "prove" I mean *prove*, for I
take philosophical discussion seriously. Unless a philosopher can fully
demonstrate the conclusions he holds to be true, he is no better than
a man of *mere opinion*, and has no special claim upon your time or
attention. It follows, of course, that if a philosopher denies a conclusion,
or holds it to be false, he must demonstrate its falsity. This is what I
expected Lord Russell to do, for I had somehow supposed that he was
a philosopher.

I cannot tell you how disappointed and shocked I was by Lord
Russell's performance, disappointed because his early writings—mostly
before 1910—led me to regard him as a philosopher, and shocked to
find that a man, whom most people still suppose to be a great philosopher, should be willing to make such a fool of himself in public. Lord
Russell made no attempt to demonstrate the falsity of the conclusion I
had tried to prove to be true. For the most part he was not even relevant
to the issue. He made no effort to understand the issue, nor did he
hesitate to misquote my statements to gain a cheap advantage. I did
not win that debate, but Lord Russell certainly lost it in the estimation
of every critical member of that audience, whose intelligence he insulted
by clowning on the platform instead of taking the whole matter seriously
enough to try to argue.

I was, therefore, delighted to receive a letter from Dr. Schilpp in
which he proposed the present occasion. In that letter he said: "I happen
to have been one of the people in the audience who heard you debate
Lord Russell. Let me say, frankly, that I didn't think Professor Russell
did justice to your arguments. Despite the fact that Lord Russell is a
personal friend of mine, I must say that I was quite disappointed with
his presentation. In my judgment, he did not make any great attempt
to meet your arguments at all. And this (meeting your arguments logically) I should try my level best to do, if you would do me and others
here the courtesy of accepting me as your opponent in debate."

That is the kind of challenge one philosopher likes to receive from another. I accepted at once. But I proposed one change in the proceedings. I suggested that we make this a disputation rather than a debate. A debate has come to be what people like Lord Russell have made it—a travesty on intellectual discussion and serious argument, a game of wits in which neither party pays much attention to the reasoning of the other. In sharp contrast to the modern degraded notion of debating, the medieval disputation was a public discussion in which a thesis was seriously defended and seriously attacked. I suggested to Dr. Schilpp that we make this a disputation, in which I would defend the thesis, and he would attack it in a numbered series of objections, each of which concluded by saying that thus it has been shown that the thesis is false. The defender is then obliged to rebut each separate objection to his original constructive argument, in which he sets forth the reasons for affirming the thesis.

In his most recent letter to me, Dr. Schilpp said he thought he had abided by the spirit, if not the letter, of our arrangements, in so far as he had made "a serious attempt by really meeting the major contentions of your propositions (something which I felt Lord Russell had neglected to do) and which, moreover, it seemed to me not only eminently worthwhile to do, but rather important that it *should* be done."

I say all this, by way of introduction, for two reasons: first, to acquaint you with the background of this affair, but second, and more importantly, to point out that Dr. Schilpp *appears* to agree with me concerning the function of intellectual discussion. He obviously does not think we should try to amuse you by clowning or joking. He obviously does think that it is worthwhile to meet arguments with counterarguments. He goes further, and says most emphatically that this *should be done*. It is this last fact which I wish to interpret for you—so that you will be able to tell whether Dr. Schilpp only *appears* to, but does not *really*, agree with me about the purpose of this discussion.

I take it, in the first place, that Dr. Schilpp accepts the logical principle of contradiction, which requires us both to acknowledge that one and the same thesis cannot be both true and false. And, in the second place, since Dr. Schilpp proposes to refute what I propose to prove, he must regard as false the thesis I hold to be true. This means that we both cannot be right; further, if the issue has been well drawn, this means that both of us cannot be wrong—one must be right, and the other wrong. Hence, if Dr. Schilpp succeeds, not only must you all agree with him, but so must I; whereas if I succeed, he as well as you must agree with me.

Dr. Schilpp must be aiming to convince me, as I am aiming to convince him, and that means we are both aiming at the same ultimate result—agreement in the truth of the thesis or in its falsity, that is, the truth of its contradictory. Unless that is the case, I have completely misunderstood Dr. Schilpp's protestations about being intellectually serious, in contrast to the buffoonery of Lord Russell; unless that is the case, I regard this whole affair as a waste of my time and yours. Finally, let me say that you must distinguish between real disagreement and apparent disagreement. There can be real disagreement between Dr. Schilpp and myself only if we fully understand each other's words. Unless Dr. Schilpp fully understands my thesis, and the argument supporting it, it really makes no difference whether he agrees or disagrees—for issue has not been joined.

These preliminaries accomplished, I shall proceed at once to the matters at hand. First, let me analyze the question itself, so that we know what we are arguing about; and then, let me try to state the arguments on my side as briefly as possible.

The question is: Are there absolute and universal principles on which education should be founded?

To explain the question, and to sharpen the issue, let me comment on the significance of its basic words. Education, like government and medicine, is a practical affair. Just as medicine is an art of using knowledge about the body to prevent and cure disease, to sustain and improve health, so education is an art of using knowledge about the nature of man to prevent and cure ignorance, to sustain and improve what one might call mental or spiritual health. To say, then, that the problems of education are practical, or artistic, is to say that they are questions about what men *should* do in educating themselves or others. Notice here the word "should." The history of education answers the purely theoretical questions about what men have done; the philosophy of education is practical, not theoretic, precisely because it answers a different sort of question: what men should do.

In the solution of every practical problem, the basic terms are ends and means. The end of medicine is health; the means are the various procedures of prevention and therapy. We solve a practical problem, so far as thinking goes, by determining the ends to be achieved and the most efficient means for achieving them. (To solve a practical problem completely, we have to put our thinking into action, but tonight we are on the level of thinking, not acting.) Now since the means are to be chosen and used for the sake of the ends to be reached, the ends are the first things we must think about in the order of practical thinking, even though they are the last things we reach in the order of action itself.

Hence, the principles on which educational policy should be founded are the ends which should be aimed at by anyone undertaking any educational responsibilities, for himself or others.

Now I take it there can be no disagreements so far: for anyone who is intelligently going somewhere must know where he is going. Anyone who starts out to educate himself or others, must, if he is to proceed intelligently, have some goals in mind. Whatever any man's goals are, they can be regarded as, for him, his basic educational principles.

But the question is whether everyone should have the same goals, whether in education, as in life, everyone should be going to the same place. We know, as a matter of fact, that men appear to be going every which way, in life as in education. Clearly men do not have the same educational goals or principles. But should they? *That is the question.* If you answer Yes, then you are saying that there are absolute and universal principles of education—the same ends which all men should be seeking. If you answer No, then you are denying, not that there are educational principles, but that they are absolute and universal.

The issue, therefore, reduces to this one point. It is made by the words "absolute" and "universal" in the question. If they had been omitted, what the argument would have been about I do not know. They were put into the question quite purposely—to make the issue. Now let me finally focus your attention on this issue by telling you what I, as the affirmative, must affirm and prove. And the burden of proof is on me, though Dr. Schilpp has the complementary burden of denying and disproving.

I say that the ends of education, the ends men should seek, are always and everywhere the same. They are absolute in the sense that they are not relative to time and place, to individual differences and the variety of cultures. They are universal in the sense that they are invariable and without exception.

To say this is to hold, as I do, that to the basic question about the ends of education, there can be only one true answer. This means that there are not many philosophies of education, among which men can choose according to their tastes and temperaments, but only one which all men must agree to just as they must all agree to the well-established truths of natural science, according to the weight of the evidence and the dictates of reason.

But let me be sure to avoid one misunderstanding. Though the right ends may be always and everywhere the same, and though the universal means for achieving these ends may be similarly absolute because universal, it does not follow at all that the particular means are absolute. On the contrary, just because they are particular, they are relative and variable—relative to different cultures and different individuals, and hence variable according to the varying circumstances of the time and place at which the universal and absolute principles must be applied.

This point is of the greatest importance. That there is only one true educational philosophy does not mean that actual educational practices must be everywhere the same. On the contrary, they should be different, for an intelligent application of practical principles requires that they be adapted to the particular circumstances. (The same is true of medicine and law.)

Anyone who fails to understand this point will suppose I am trying to prove more than can ever be proved. That more is simply not true. And if you do understand this point, you will, I hope, see at once that the great variability in actual educational practices, which we know from history and anthropology, is in no way inconsistent with the position that the universal principles, the ends in general, are absolute and invariable.

If I can now assume that the issue is understood, I can proceed to the proof.

My first and basic proposition is that human nature is everywhere the same. The universality and constancy of human nature, the same throughout history, the same in various cultures, the same in different individuals, is the source of the universal and absolute principles of education.

By human nature I mean the nature a human offspring has at birth—whatever it is that makes that offspring something capable of growing into a man rather than a flea or a pig.

And the aspect of human nature, which all human offspring have, that I wish to emphasize is its potentialities or capacities for growth and development. My point simply is that the offspring of papa and mama flea, or papa and mama pig, does not have the capacities for becoming a man. Trying to make a baby pig into an adult man is one miracle no educator has ever attempted, though some have tried, and almost succeeded, in making a man-child into an adult pig.

When I speak of the constancy and universality of human nature, I mean precisely what a biologist means when he speaks of the uniformity in procreation of any animal or plant species. There is a human species. Maybe it has evolved from other species; maybe it hasn't; maybe other species will evolve from it, maybe not. But all this is beside the point—so long as the human species endures on earth, all members of that species will have the same specific nature, and it is that same specific nature which I say is everywhere the same.

My second proposition is a definition of education itself. Human nature, as we have seen, is something which is not fully developed at birth. Man can change as he lives and grows, precisely because his nature at birth has potentialities or capacities which can be developed. In the light of these facts, I say that education is the process whereby a man helps himself or another to become what he can be. The definition as just stated is not complete. Mere change is not enough: it can be either for better or worse, as all of us know. And a man can be either a good man or a bad one. Hence education must be defined as the process whereby a man is changed for the better, whereby a man helps himself or another to become a good man, which is something he can be, though perhaps not as readily as being a bad man.

Now, it may be asked why education has to be defined as a process of human betterment? Why can it not just as well be defined as a process of human corruption? I have two answers to that question.

In the first place, the definition must express what everyone understands education to be, and I say that, as a matter of fact, education is everywhere and always regarded as a process of betterment or improvement. You might just as well ask why medical therapy aims at restoring or improving health rather than at spreading disease.

In the second place, I can support my statement that, as a matter of fact, education is regarded as a process of betterment, of causing a change for the better. For if this were not the fact, how could we justify compulsory education? The fact that we all approve, as just and wise, the laws requiring every potential citizen to submit to a certain minimum of education, and the fact, furthermore, that most of us would like to increase that minimum a great deal, these facts, I say, indicate that we think that education is good for men (just as we think health is good for them, and so make certain hygienic observances compulsory). But how could we think that education was good for men, if it did not aim at making men better rather than worse? We call a drug poison when, in certain doses, it injures men; we call a drug medicine when, in certain doses, it helps them toward health. In the same way, I say, only that which helps a child or man to become a better human being do we call *education*.

My third and final proposition follows from the first two. In the light of the constancy and universality of specific nature, especially as a set of capacities for development; and in the light of the definition of education as a process of developing those capacities to their best realization; I can now say that the ends of education are twofold: proximate and ultimate. The proximate ends of education are the moral and intellectual virtues. (If Dr. Schilpp or anyone else is irritated by that word "virtue," let him substitute the strictly equivalent phrase "good habit.") The ultimate end of education is happiness or a good human life, a life enriched by the possession of every kind of good, by the enjoyment of every type of satisfaction.

The reason for this distinction between the proximate ends and the ultimate end of education is as follows: more than good habits are required for happiness, even though they are indispensable. The educator is as educator not responsible for providing all the conditions indispensable to happiness, but only some, and those are the virtues, or good habits. That is why we speak of the virtues or good habits as the proximate ends of education, and we mention happiness as the ultimate end, because it would be wrong to suppose that the virtues were ends in themselves—they are ends, but they are also means—means to happiness.

The proximate ends of education are the virtues. It is necessary to add one more distinction now—between two kinds of virtue—moral and intellectual, or good habits of knowing and thinking, which are the intellectual virtues, and good habits of desiring and acting, which are the moral virtues.

Hence we can say that the ends of intellectual education are the intellectual virtues; and the ends of moral training are the moral virtues.

One more step remains to complete the proof. I have so far only given you what might be regarded as my private opinion, my personal conception, of the ends of education. But I am obliged to do more than that. I must show you that the ends I have named must be the ends which education always and everywhere should aim at—that these ends are the absolute and universal principles upon which education should be founded. I shall proceed at once to show you that.

If specific human nature is everywhere and at all times the same in all men, then all men have the same powers or capacities to be developed—though, as individuals, they differ in the degree or extent to which they possess these capacities.

If the powers or capacities just referred to are parts of human nature, they are natural capacities, and as natural each has a nature—a determinate character, by which it tends naturally toward a certain kind of development.

Therefore, habits, as developments of powers or fulfillments of capacities, can be said to be good if they conform to the natural tendency of the power or capacity which they develop. Let me illustrate this: the power of knowing, shared by all men, is perfected by habits of knowledge, not by habits of error or by that privation of knowledge which we call ignorance. Similarly, the power of thinking, shared by all men, is perfected by habits of thinking well, by the arts of thinking; it is not perfected, but rather wasted or ruined, by habits of thinking poorly or inartistically.

Hence I say that we call a habit good when it perfects a power, when it develops a capacity in the direction toward which that capacity naturally tends.

And in the light of all this I conclude that the virtues, or good habits, are the same for all men, because their nature and their natural capacities are the same. (And it almost goes without saying, I might add, that happiness is the same for all men, for the same reason: the constancy and universality of human nature.)

The proof is thus completed. Let me summarize it for you in the following formulation: If education must aim at the betterment of men by forming good habits in them, and if the virtues, or good habits, are the same for all men because their natural capacities are the same and tend naturally toward the same developments, then it follows that the virtues, or good habits, as the ends of education, are absolute and universal principles on which education should be founded.

The conclusion follows logically: but it is true only if the premises—the two *ifs*—are true.

The truth of these two premises is guaranteed by two propositions

which I think cannot be denied by anyone: my first proposition about
the constancy of specific human nature, and my second proposition,
i.e., the definition of education as a process of betterment.

I have thus indicated to you, and to Dr. Schilpp, what must be
attacked by anyone who tries to avoid agreeing with my conclusion. If
my premises are in fact true, and if my reasoning is valid, the conclusion
is inescapable.

Although I have now completed the constructive part of my argument, I am going to do one thing more. As in my argument against
Lord Russell, I am now going to try to show you that Dr. Schilpp really
agrees to one of my major contentions, in part at least, even though
he himself thinks he does not. This can be done by using the form of
argument known as a *reductio ad absurdum*. When you use this form
of argument against your opponent in an issue, you proceed as follows:
you try to show that if your opponent denies something you have said,
he is forced to conclusions he is himself unwilling to accept; hence to
avoid these conclusions, he must agree to your premises. In this particular case what I am going to try to show is that Dr. Schilpp must
agree with my contention that there are intellectual and moral
virtues—the same for all men everywhere at all times—because he
himself wishes to affirm certain things, which affirmations are strictly
incompatible with the denial of my point about intellectual and moral
virtues.

You have already seen how crucial to my whole argument is the
proposition that the intellectual and moral virtues are the same for all
men, for if they are, they constitute the proximate ends of human
education, and hence its absolute and universal principles. I think I
have already proved this proposition, but Dr. Schilpp may not think
so. Hence what I am now going to do to show him, in terms of his
own beliefs, why he must think so. I cannot do this for every intellectual
and every moral virtue, but it will suffice if I do this for some of the
intellectual virtues, and some of the moral virtues. If Dr. Schilpp is
forced to admit that there is a single intellectual virtue which is good
for all men at all times, or a single moral virtue, then he is in a tight
corner, out of which I hope he won't even try to squirm, because to
do so will involve him in self-contradiction.

Let me show you, first, that Dr. Schilpp thinks there is some intellectual virtue. I am going to show this in two ways: first, that Dr.
Schilpp thinks there is objective truth, the possession of which by our

minds is the intellectual virtue of knowledge; then, that Dr. Schilpp thinks there are the intellectual virtues known as the liberal arts, the possession of which makes one mind better than another.

As I pointed out in the beginning, Dr. Schilpp in his various letters to me admitted that intellectual argument should be carried on seriously. He bemoaned the fact that Lord Russell did not try to refute my thesis, and he offered to do this himself. In a few moments he is going to try to do just that. But if a man seriously tries to refute a thesis, it must be because he honestly thinks it to be false—not merely false for him, but false for anyone, false in fact. There would be no point in his standing here and telling us that what I have to say may be true-for-me, though it is false-for-him. I am not interested, nor can I see why you should be, in his private and personal opinions. We are all interested in what Dr. Schilpp has to say, because he offers to refute a falsehood and thereby show us that its contradictory is true—true because it agrees with the facts, with the way things are. I say, therefore, that Dr. Schilpp admits that real knowledge is possible, as opposed to ignorance and error. I say, moreover, that Dr. Schilpp himself believes it is better for a man to know the way things are, than to be ignorant, or to harbor false notions about them. And this holds for all men everywhere, and not just for us here and now. Hence Dr. Schilpp agrees that the possession of knowledge is a good habit of the mind, an intellectual virtue which education should always aim at. I am not saying that what is supposed to be knowledge is always the same, but that the distinction between knowledge and ignorance or error is always the same. Dr. Schilpp is thus faced with this paradox: if he disagrees with me because he thinks that I am really wrong, objectively in error, then he must agree with me that there is a real distinction between having knowledge and being in error. And if he agrees to this, he agrees that there is some intellectual virtue, which was to be proved.

I can also show you that Dr. Schilpp agrees to other intellectual virtues, the liberal arts, which are the arts of right thinking and correct speech. I will do this hypothetically in advance of Dr. Schilpp's presentation. If Dr. Schilpp, in the course of his speech, points out to you that I commit fallacies in reasoning, then he must be admitting that fallacies are flaws in thinking, and that a person who habitually avoids fallacies is a better thinker than one who habitually commits them. There are, in short, rules of good thinking which should not be violated by anyone who wishes to use his mind as an instrument for knowing the truth about things. A logically trained mind is, other things equal, better than one which lacks such training. Hence I say to you, and I warn Dr. Schilpp, that if he even tries to appeal to logical principles of sound reasoning in showing that I am wrong, he is by that very fact agreeing to one of my major points—namely, that a mind which possesses logical art has an intellectual virtue which is the same for all men. Certainly Dr. Schilpp cannot say that the fallacies he points to in my reasoning are just fallacies in *my* reasoning. They are fallacies into which any human mind can fall at any time or place, and which should, therefore, be always and everywhere avoided. Furthermore, if Dr. Schilpp should point out that some of my statements are meaningless, then he is applying semantic criteria for distinguishing between meaningless and significant utterances. I accept these criteria, for I, too, think that there are grammatical or linguistic rules which must be followed by any man who wishes to speak significantly. Whether I have violated these criteria is not the point here. The whole point is that if Dr. Schilpp employs such criteria, he is agreeing to the grammatical or semantic art as another intellectual virtue, which all men should possess, and which education should always and everywhere aim at.

Finally, I wish to show that Dr. Schilpp believes in at least one moral virtue—the virtue of justice, a justice which is the same for all men everywhere, which it should always be the aim of moral education to cultivate. Again I shall proceed hypothetically, by calling your attention in advance to what Dr. Schilpp may fall into. If—I say *if*— Dr. Schilpp appears to say that democracy is good, or at least better than totalitarianism—not for us Americans alone, but for any human being—then he is agreeing with me that there are certain principles of justice which are ideals every society should approximate. If he appears to say that a just society is one in which there is freedom of thought and freedom of speech, I agree with him; but then he also agrees with me that in the regulation of human affairs, justice is objectively better than injustice. And any educational system which trains men to be just in their dealings with other men is objectively better than one which prepares some men for slavery and others to use them as their tools.

You, the audience, will be able to judge whether Dr. Schilpp reduces himself to absurdity. Dr. Schilpp must, therefore, either agree with me that there are some intellectual and moral virtues, the same for all men everywhere and always the ends of education, or, if he wishes to avoid agreeing with this major point in my argument, he must make no appeals whatsoever to logic and grammar as canons of sound thinking and correct speech, he must be willing to violate the law of contradiction, and he must be willing to tell you that there is no such thing as justice, that there is nothing wrong with tyranny and slavery, with medieval inquisitions or modern gestapos, and that anyone who says democracy is the best form of government is talking through his hat.

My cards are on the table. It is now Dr. Schilpp's turn to play. I have done my best to warn him where the trumps lie.

Tradition and
Progress in Education

(1939)

Like Horace, Adler advises his readers to seek the mean between extremes. In this case the extremes are the excesses of classicism and of progressivism. In "Tradition and Progress in Education" Adler clarifies the role and order of both traditional and progressive studies in the curriculum and exposes the myths that support extremism in educational theory. The issues are decisive ones.

This essay is adapted from two articles, "The Crisis in Contemporary Education" in The Social Frontier *(February 1939) and "Tradition and Novelty in Education" in* Better Schools *(June 1939). While much has changed for the better, the conditions of education have not, and neither, one is sorry to note, has the intellectual climate that dominates education in America. It remains as stubbornly constant as human nature itself. Adler's pessimism on that score was well founded and has been justified.*

G.V.D.

A BADLY STATED ISSUE calls for false or extreme solutions. It is important, therefore, to correct the impression that the issue in American education today is between classicism and pro-gressivism. Both of these names signify undesirable extremes which have exaggerated and distorted some sound elements of educational policy. Classicism names the arid and empty formalism which domi-nated education at the end of the last century. It emphasized the study of the classics for historical or philological reasons. It was interested in the past for the past's sake. It mistook drill for discipline. Against such classicism, the reaction which took place was genuinely motivated and sound in principle. Unhappily, as always the reaction went too far.

We have reached an extreme in the swing of the pendulum, an equally unfortunate extreme that, in its many forms, is called progressive education. Progressivism has become as preposterous as classicism was arid. It is so absorbed with the study of the contemporary world that it forgets human culture has traditional roots. It has substituted information for understanding, and science for wisdom. It has mistaken license for liberty, for that is what freedom is when it is unaccompanied by discipline. Professor Dewey himself has scored the excesses of some of his would-be followers.

What is obviously indicated, to avoid a false issue which offers a choice between undesirable extremes, is a moderate position, one which would agree with progressivism in correcting the abuses of the classical program but which would rectify progressivism itself by retaining whatever was essentially right in the classical approach. If one sets out to remedy abuses, one should remember that one is doing so because something good has been spoiled. The trouble with most reforms is that they start out to remove flaws and end by throwing the good away with the bad. We must eliminate the present excesses of progressive education without discarding the basic insights which motivated the movement.

William Whewell, master of Trinity College, Cambridge, made a distinction between permanent and progressive studies. The permanent studies, he said, are those which remain the same in every period of human culture, because they respond to the permanent needs of human nature, which education should aim to cultivate. Human nature—by which I mean the powers and needs of men—is constant in the sense in which man as a biological species has a constant specific nature. We are not here concerned about individual differences because education should evoke our humanity, and not develop our individuality.

The permanent studies, then, are those which cultivate the humanity of each student by disciplining his reason, that power in him which distinguishes him from all other animals. Such discipline is accomplished by the liberal arts, the arts of reading, writing, and reckoning—the three Rs. And since wisdom does not change from generation to generation, or even from epoch to epoch, the permanent studies include the funded wisdom of European culture as that reposes in its great works, its great books, its masterpieces of liberal art.

The progressive studies, on the other hand, are those which change from time to time, almost from generation to generation. Such are all the natural and social sciences which have a changing content of knowledge. So, too, are all courses which are nothing but disguised surveys of current events.

The permanent and progressive studies represent the elements of tradition and novelty in the educational curriculum. Both are needed, but the permanent studies must come first, both because they are more fundamental educationally, and because they are a necessary preparation for good work in the fields of progressive knowledge. Classicism not only ignored the progressive studies, but presented the permanent ones in a degraded and sterile form. Progressivism, in its turn, has almost entirely excluded the permanent studies or, at best, has put them in the wrong place, at the end of the educational process rather than the beginning.

Since the reform of contemporary education must be accomplished by curing the defects of progressivism, I shall dwell on these in greater detail, in the hope that no one will suppose I want to return to the kind of classicism we are well rid of. I would call the right educational program Traditionalism. *Traditionalism* indicates that tradition, as well as progress and novelty, is a factor in education.

If that name could be taken to signify the moderate position which combines both tradition and novelty in the right way, it describes the reform which is required and has been outlined by President Hutchins of Chicago in his *Higher Learning in America*. It is partly in operation at St. John's College in Annapolis, Maryland.

That the Hutchins proposals and the St. John's program have been generally attacked and disapproved by the vested interests ruling American education, both administratively and through teachers colleges, on the one hand, and generally applauded by parents and college graduates who remember the emptiness of their own schooling, on the other, is *prima facie* evidence of the accuracy of the diagnosis. But the case need not rest there. The various objections must and can be answered. The issue must be clarified of all irrelevancies and misunderstandings.

There are two basic issues which divide President Hutchins and his opponents. Both are philosophical. The first has to do with the *nature of knowledge* and the distinction between science and philosophy, as different kinds of knowledge having different histories and different utilities. The second has to do with the *nature of man*, whether he is merely an animal whose biological destiny is adjustment in the struggle for existence, or, though an animal, also rational and having a uniquely human destiny of self-perfection. The educational consequences of affirming that man is a rational animal, different in kind and not merely in degree of intelligence, and that philosophy is more eminently knowledge than science, having a validity which is independent of scientific findings, and a utility superior to that of science—these determine the main points in the Hutchins program. The errors of progressive education are similarly determined by the educational consequences of the opposing denials.

It would be naive to suppose that these issues could be adequately argued in short scope. Even in a fairly long book, I have failed to argue these matters with rhetorical effectiveness.[1] Not only does the resolution of these issues rest upon profound and extensive considerations, but the mere statement of the affirmative theses arouses so many and such violent prejudices in minds which have suffered the kind of education which their denial has sanctioned, that it is almost impossible to get a hearing, even from persons who call themselves liberal. It almost seems that being educated under the Hutchins program is a necessary prerequisite for understanding the educational philosophy on which it turns. Similarly, the educational philosophy of our teachers colleges is received as the obvious truth by those who have been educated under its auspices. *But unless everything is just a matter of opinion, and the might of the majority makes right, these issues are genuine, and the truth lies only on one side.* Furthermore, philosophic truth is not a private intuition. It is capable of such explication and demonstration that it becomes the public property of all minds free enough from prejudice to be convinced by evidence and reasons.

Since adequate argument is not possible here, I must content myself with trying to sharpen the issues themselves. I choose to do this in a frankly polemic manner—for there is no point in concealing an adherence to the truth as one sees it—by defining the philosophical errors which underlie progressive education. I shall discuss, first, the twin myths of progress and utility which are the misleading notions of pragmatic positivism; second, the false educational psychology which denies or ignores man's rationality; and, finally, the way in which the progressive program has been determined by these errors.

It is no play on words to say that *the myth of universal progress, progress in all things, lies at the heart of progressive education.* This myth of progress is a nineteenth-century notion, due partly to positivism and partly to illicit extensions of the doctrine of evolution.[2] Progress differs from change in that it is change in a definite direction and is measured by standards which evaluate stages in a process as better and worse. The growth of a plant or animal is a progress from infancy to maturity, to the point where the organism reaches its biological perfection. But everywhere in nature growth is followed by decline, maturity by senescence. The one possible exception to the rule that natural progress is not interminable is that which the panorama of evolution appears to present. But even here, taking the facts as they are usually told in the story of evolution, it is only by a questionable extrapolation of the curve that one could conclude that there is interminable progress in the development of forms of life. Yet it was just this uncritically reached conclusion which propagated the notion that the law of progress rules all things, and that as we move into the future we go endlessly from worse to better, from lower to higher.

The other source of this myth of progress was a view of cultural history, dictated by positivism. If one supposes, as the positivists do, that science is the only form of valid, general knowledge about the world, and that the technical application of science to the control of things is the only kind of utility which knowledge has, then there appears to be uninterrupted and interminable progress in human affairs as well as in nature. For does not Auguste Comte tell us that there are three stages in human history—the superstitious or religious; the speculative, conjectural, or philosophical; and the stage of positive knowledge, or the scientific—and is this not progress? In the era of science itself does not every century see the ever-increasing scope of scientific knowledge and the ever-enlarging domain of technology? As the years roll by, we have more and better knowledge, bigger and better inventions or utilities. The positivists are so enraptured by this picture of progress and by the dreams of the future it generates that they are somehow able to forget that in our moral and political affairs a Hitler and a Mussolini and their followers are not much of an improvement upon a Nero or a Caligula and the gangs they led. But this flaw in the picture must not be forgotten, for it is the clue to one of the two great exceptions to the law of progress in human affairs which make the notion of universal and perpetual progress a deceptive illusion.

The first exception is human nature itself. If we can discriminate between nature and nurture, we can understand the sense in which human nature is constant throughout all the variations of culture and all the transformations of history. Man is a biological species, and if a species means anything it means a constant nature which is transmitted from generation to generation. When that constancy fails, when another specific nature is generated, we have, whether by mutation or otherwise, the origin of a new species. It must follow, then, that so long as what is generated remains specifically man, human nature remains constant from generation to generation. By human nature I mean the native abilities and the organic needs which everywhere constitute the same animal, known as man.[3]

The second exception is more difficult to discuss, for it turns on the essential difference between philosophy and science. The positivists cannot accept biological science and deny the specific constancy of man; they can remain positivists and still recognize how the unchanging character of human nature explains the failure of progress in social and political affairs. But they cannot remain positivists and agree that philosophy is knowledge which is not only nonscientific in its method but also independent in its validity of all the ever changing findings and formulations of research. Since I cannot argue the point here, I shall try only to indicate how affirming philosophy affects our view of cultural history.

As I have said elsewhere,[4] the positivist is right in his effort to deontologize science, to define science as knowledge of phenomenal relationships, generalizing the correlation of diverse sensibles and being totally unconcerned with substances and causes. He is wrong only when he is a negativist, that is, when he denies philosophy, which is ontological knowledge, which is concerned with substances and causes, and which seeks to penetrate beneath the sensible to the intelligible. There is a clear distinction here between the formal objects or noetic aims of science and philosophy; and that distinction is accompanied by a distinction in method. All human knowledge arises from sense experience, but the activity of the senses alone can account for no generalizations of the sort which distinguish both science and philosophy from history. Intelligence or reason must work reflectively, analytically, inductively over the materials of sense experience. These two factors, sense and reason, observation and reflection, experience and thought, are common to both science and philosophy. The difference in their methods lies in the fact that science requires special experience, the data achieved by all kinds of research, investigation whether experimental or otherwise; whereas philosophy arises from reflection about the common experience of mankind, the experience which all men have everywhere and at all times as a result of the noninvestigative use of their senses, and which is always the same because the sensitive powers of man are as constant as his nature and the natural world on which they operate is the same.

From this distinction in object and method arises a basic difference in the historical careers of science and philosophy. Science is progressive, and interminably so, as long as men are ingenious and industrious in their efforts at research. There are no apparent limitations to the progress in scientific knowledge except the width, breadth, and depth of the world to be investigated. But philosophy does not grow with an enlargement of experience. Its data are always the same. It grows only by a refinement in the intellectual process itself, by profounder insight, by better analysis. Its development is restricted by the limitations of man's intellectual powers; and if our ancestors have accumulated philosophic wisdom, we can improve little on their work. I am saying no more here than what Whitehead means when he says that the history of European philosophy is nothing but a series of footnotes to Plato.[5] I cannot resist adding that Aristotle wrote most of the footnotes.

In short, there is perpetual progress in scientific knowledge because of the nature of science itself, the contingency of its conclusions as relative to the available data; but there is no such progress in philosophy or wisdom because its conclusions are not contingent, and the *relevant* experience is always the same. The historical movement of science is a straight line ever upward. The historical movement of philosophy is a deepening spiral, in every turn of which the same truths and the same errors reappear. Professor Gilson has magnificently demonstrated this in his William James Lectures on "The Unity of Philosophical Experience."[6]

The essential difference between science and philosophy bears not only on the myth of progress, but also on the utility myth. The positivist, regarding only science as knowledge, thinks that the only utility knowledge can have is to give man control over the operable things of nature. But the things which we can control are utilities only in the sense of means. None of them is an end in itself. Clearly the difference between intelligent and unintelligent operation lies in referring means to ends. Furthermore, everyone can see that science is the kind of knowledge which can be used for evil purposes as well as good, according as the means it provides us with are ordered to the right or the wrong ends. But what determines the ordering of means to ends, and what provides the criteria for judging ends as good and bad? Either this is mere opinion, and again might makes right, or it is knowledge. But it is clearly not scientific knowledge, for otherwise science could protect itself and all mankind from the misuses to which it is so readily put. It is philosophical knowledge, which in the practical order is called morals and politics, that must direct us in intelligent operation toward the right ends. The utility of philosophy is thus superior to that of science, and what is even more obvious, science without moral wisdom—a command of utilities without right direction—is a dangerous thing. The more science we have, the more we are in need of wisdom to prevent its misuse. *The imminent tragedy of the contemporary world is written in the fact that positivistic modern culture has magnified science and almost completely emancipated itself from wisdom.*

One further point must be added. Philosophy's independence of science holds in the practical as well as the theoretical sphere. We have not progressed in moral wisdom. All the advances in science have not changed the moral and political problems which men face, except to make them more difficult because men have more implements at hand to gain their ends.

I turn now to the psychological error concerning man's nature. So-called scientific psychology, which has its roots in the physiological laboratory and its ideology from the evolutionary speculations of nine-teenth-century materialism, regards man as an animal different from others only in degree of intelligence or in such accidental matters as erect posture. Man is a bundle of reflexes which can be conditioned, as in other animals, by the positive and negative stimuli of pleasure and pain; he learns as other animals do, by trial and error—or if he has insight, as the gestaltists claim, so do all other animals; his habits are all sensory-motor coordinations, the archetype of which is the reflex arc. When to the experimental literature are added views which have their origin in the clinic or on the psychoanalytical couch, man's rationality, if admitted at all, is reduced to the craft whereby his ego is forced by his id to rationalize the basic instinctive drives which get him into social conflicts. His behavior originates with and is controlled by his visceral urges, and intelligence is their servant, reason their cunning.

It should be apparent, though it is seldom seen, that such a conception of human nature makes it impossible to explain how man can be a scientist, not to mention a philosopher. Scientific truth, which man possesses, and the scientific method which he employs, cannot be accounted for in terms of conditioned reflexes or sensory-motor coordinations, except by the most obvious verbal legerdemain. The very ideal of science—that the truth, to whatever extent it is achieved, is objective and independent of our passions and urges—must be an illusion, if reason operates only in the service of the gut and under its dictation. With the scientific ideal goes all the rest of morality, for all ideals become illusions which thinly conceal man's brutishness. The paradox still remains, however, that man is the only animal that finds it necessary to fool himself with ideals.

The opposite view, which makes the issue, can be simply stated, though not here argued. Man is a rational animal, and in possessing rationality, which is not just animal intelligence to a higher degree, he is essentially, that is, specifically, different from brutes. Man has all the powers possessed by brute animals: he has vegetative powers, he has sensitive, appetitive, and locomotive powers. But in addition he has an intellect, and this power, the power of understanding, of abstracting, judging, reasoning, no other animal has.[7] It is by the exercise of this power that man is an artist, a scientist, a philosopher; that he lives socially by conventions determined by himself rather than instinctively as other social animals do; that he has a syntactical language for the communication of knowledge and commands; that he is able freely to choose the means by which he attains the end he desires because he understands it to be good.

Opposite educational consequences follow from choosing opposite sides in these two issues.

If man is a rational animal, constant in nature throughout history, then there must be certain constant features in every sound educational program, regardless of culture or epoch. The basic education of a rational animal is the discipline of his rational powers and the cultivation of his intellect. This discipline is achieved by the liberal arts, the arts of reading and listening, of writing and speaking, and, perforce, of thinking, since man is a social animal as well as a rational one and his intellectual life is lived in a community which can exist only through the communication of men. The three Rs, which always signified the formal disciplines, are the essence of liberal or general education. They cannot be inculcated by college courses in logic or mathematics or classical languages. That was the error of classical education, which the progressivists rightly condemned. One learns to write and read only by performing these acts, but since reading and writing are intellectual arts, the habits must be formed under the discipline of rules of art; moreover, intellectual habits cannot be formed intelligently unless the rules themselves are understood. The program of liberal education consists of the liberal arts, acquired as habits through performance under intelligible disciplines. In short, the A.B. degree should be awarded for competence in reading, writing, and reckoning.

But one cannot learn to read and write without subject matter. The reason is trained in its proper operations by these arts, but the intellect is not cultivated by them. That can be accomplished only through furnishing it with knowledge and wisdom, by acquainting it with truth, by giving it a mastery of ideas. At this point, the other basic feature of liberal education appears, namely, the great books, the master productions in all fields, philosophy, science, history, and belles lettres. They are not only the material which must be used to teach students how to read and write, but they constitute the cultural tradition by which the intellects of each generation must first be cultivated.

Note, here, how the myth of progress is denied. If there is philosophical wisdom as well as scientific knowledge, if the former consists of insights and ideas that change little from time to time, and if even the latter has many abiding concepts and a relatively constant method, if the great works of literature as well as of philosophy touch upon the permanent moral problems of mankind and express the universal convictions of men involved in moral conflict—if these things are so, then the great books of ancient and medieval as well as modern times are a repository of knowledge and wisdom, a tradition of culture which must initiate each new generation. The reading of these books is not for antiquarian purposes; the interest is not archaeological or philological. That was the type of interest which dominated the humanistic course in the German *gymnasium,* and was "classical education" at its worst. Rather the books are to be read because they are as contemporary today as when they were written, and that because *the problems they deal with and the ideas they present are not subject to the law of perpetual and interminable progress.* The fact that the ancients and medievals were wrong in many matters of scientific knowledge, the fact that even Newton and Galileo were wrong in their turn, makes no difference to the philosophical accomplishments of these periods, nor even to the insights and procedures of the great masters of science.

There is not space here to expound fully the curriculum for liberal education which President Hutchins has proposed and which is in operation in St. John's College in Annapolis.[8] I am merely indicating how the emphasis upon the liberal arts and the great books follows from and is justified by the fundamental theses that distinguish his educational philosophy. If the educational system were properly divided into three parts—elementary, secondary or collegiate, and university—what I have here called liberal or general education would occur at the second level. At the lowest level, elementary education would inculcate the fundamental routines of language and mathematics and stimulate the imagination and the talents for fine arts, thus preparing for college in a manner quite unlike that determined by college board examinations. At the university level, which might begin at what is now the junior year of college, if the A.B. were advanced as the degree for secondary education, would come all the specialized and professional studies. A man can be well trained as a chemist or a historian, a lawyer or a physician, only after he has been fundamentally educated, after he has learned to read and write and has some ideas. If general education emphasizes the permanent studies—the liberal arts and the cultural tradition—specialized education, at the university level, is the place for the progressive studies, the studies in which novelty and invention predominate.

If one examines the education which now prevails from the elementary school through to the university, one discovers that the opposite theses are at work. Influenced by the myths of progress and utility, failing to recognize the constancy of human nature, and denying, implicitly or explicitly, man's distinctive rationality, the existing system has completely discarded the permanent studies or, what is almost as bad, put them in the university where they are out of place. In terms of a false educational psychology which misinterpreted experiments on the transfer of training as showing there is no point to formal discipline, not enough effort is made to teach students how to read and write. If man has an intellect it can be disciplined, despite all the findings on the limited transferability of training from one set of sensory-motor coordinations to another. In terms of pragmatic positivism, the cultural tradition is ignored because there is nothing worth knowing except the most recent results of scientific research. Any book older than yesterday is hardly worth reading, for by the law of progress we must have advanced to a new and better stage of knowledge. We must teach students how to face contemporary problems, and each generation must pull itself up by its own bootstraps, for the problems are ever changing and the past can afford no help at all.

Because man is viewed as having only an animal career and not a human destiny, interest and adjustment have taken the place of discipline and cultivation as the watchwords of educational policy. The whole aim of education changes, for adjustment leads to the cult of success, the "ideal" of getting ahead by beating your neighbor. The emphasis on the interests of the student makes him a buyer instead of a patient, and the teacher becomes a salesman rather than a doctor prescribing the cure for ignorance and incompetence. It is the student who is the master under the elective system, which was invented because of the excessive proliferation of scientific courses in the curriculum, and has been perpetuated by the perversion of educational policy which makes the young, i.e., the relatively ignorant and incompetent, choose their own road to learning, according to the fickle interests of their immaturity. Extracurricular activities originated in response to interests that were tangential to the main business of education, but in many schools they have become the curriculum, and the substantial studies have been thrown out. They are not even extracurricular. Many college curriculums offer courses from A to Z without discrimination; and the university, instead of being a hierarchy of studies and a community of scholars, is a collection of specialties, together only in geographical proximity.

Elementary education is devoid of discipline. The basic routines in language and mathematics have been dropped or corrupted. Memory is not cultivated. Social studies, current events, manual arts, and games occupy the major time. Secondary or collegiate education fails even more, though in part the failure is due to the inadequate preparation given in the elementary schools. Our bachelors of arts cannot read, write, or speak their own language well; neither they nor, for that matter, our masters of arts, are acquainted with the liberal arts. They cannot read and they have not read the great books in all fields. They do not possess the leading ideas or understand the basic problems which are permanently human. They have been fed for years on textbooks and lecture courses which hand out predigested materials; and, as a result, they are chaotically informed and viciously indoctrinated with the local prejudices of professors and their textbooks.[9] As a final consequence, education at the graduate and professional level has been necessarily debased. Law schools must teach reading; graduate schools struggle to get Ph.D. candidates to write simple, clear English.

The reasons for this deplorable situation are many: the violent reaction against a bad classicism; the curricular chaos produced by the elective system; the false notion that the teacher should be guided by the pupil's interests rather than the pupil disciplined by the teacher's science and art; all of the fads and fancies of a superficial educational psychology, such as the overemphasis on individual differences, and the discarding of all formal disciplines by irrelevant research on transfer of training; the shallow pragmatism, which conceives utility in terms of biological adjustment and success rather than in terms of the perfection of man; and last, but not least, the fact that our teachers themselves have been badly educated and thoroughly misdirected by the requirements of the existing school system and under the leadership of our teachers colleges.

I conclude with the question: What are the chances of this deplorable situation being remedied? What chance is there of the Hutchins reform being effected? I ask this question, of course, on the assumption that the truth lies on his side of the basic issues, and with the insight that his program is the moderate one between the extremes of a dead classicism and a progressivism run amuck. Even granted this, I must confess that I am pessimistic, for a number of reasons.

First and foremost, there is the inertia of vested interests, which perpetuate existing human institutions. *Organized education is one of the largest rackets in this country, and the teachers colleges, especially such influential ones as those at Columbia, Chicago, and California, are the gangs that control what goes on,* in ways that do not always meet the eye and would not stand inspection. To call education a *racket* is, of course, to speak metaphorically, but the comparison has point. Reforming education will have to use racket-busting techniques or it will not succeed.

In the second place, there is the vicious circle in the teaching profession itself. The teachers of today were taught by the teachers of yesterday and teach the teachers of tomorrow. When this vicious circle, which has always existed, gets standardized by schools of education, in which a philosophy of education becomes an official program imposed upon the profession and the system by various accrediting agencies, degrees, requirements for promotion, and so forth, the circle becomes almost impregnable. Even if the great mass of teachers were to feel that there is something wrong with education, they could do nothing about it. They have been subjugated; worse than that, they have been indoctrinated by the reigning philosophy so that they no longer have enough free judgment to be critical; but worst of all, they themselves have been so inadequately educated that they would be hindered from understanding the principles or taking part in the execution of the reform being proposed.

For the most part, the members of the teaching profession are overtrained and undereducated. Teaching is an art and a teacher must be trained, but since the technique is one of communicating knowledge and inculcating discipline, it is not educational psychology and courses in method and pedagogy which train a teacher, but the liberal arts. A good teacher must be a liberal artist. Further, a teacher should have a cultivated mind, generally cultivated regardless of his field of special interest, for he must be the visible and moving representative of the cultural tradition to his students. But how can he be this if he has no acquaintance with the cultural heritage, if he cannot read well, and if he is not well-read?

Finally, there is the even deeper vicious circle in which *an educational system and the society in which it flourishes are reciprocal. You cannot improve a society without changing its education; but you cannot lift the educational system above the level of the society in which it exists.* We probably have as good an educational program today in this country as we deserve, according to our cultural attainments and aspirations. If my pessimism encounters objection on the grounds that the movement which John Dewey led succeeded in changing American education, I must answer that that change moved with the tide of American life and expressed its own dominant values and interests. The reform in which I am interested must work against the tide, challenging the worst, and also the most obdurate, features of our national ethos—our materialism, our pragmatism, our modernism.

But pessimism must not lead to despair, for much is at stake that makes it imperative to keep working for reform so long as a chance remains. There are many signs that the modern world is headed for a drastic cultural eclipse. In this country, democracy and liberal institutions are at stake, for these can be sustained and developed only by a truly liberal education. Failing to develop critical minds, failing to liberate the mind by discipline, contemporary education makes the way easy for demagogues of all sorts. Education which does not build on wisdom or respect reason above all else, leads to the frustration of the individual and the brutal conflict of social forces. For whenever reason does not rule, the mind must yield to the sheer weight of opinion propagated by pressure: only might remains and none dares say it is not right.

6

Education and
the Pursuit of Happiness

(1976)

This analysis of the relation between education and the pursuit of happiness will surprise some readers and delight some too. Adler makes a distinction between two conceptions of happiness—one psychological and nonmoral, the other ethical. He concludes that the role of education in the attainment of happiness is limited but vital.

Adler also affirms here that the essential problems of happiness, like those of education, have valid solutions in moral philosophy and not in psychology alone. That there are right and wrong desires is not a strange idea even for those brought up in the permissive era of child rearing. But that right desires are determined solely by what is good for a person, that the good is universal, and that it defines happiness will be a revelation to some. The notion that there are right and wrong desires has almost disappeared from modern education because it sounds too authoritarian. But for the reader who keeps in mind Adler's definition that "authority is reason and nothing else" (see chapter 3, "Liberalism and Liberal Education"), the concepts of happiness, freedom, and human rights are restored to their full measure of strength, and the education required to secure them follows. What also becomes apparent from Adler's discussion is that the various negative reports about the relation between college education and income published in recent years miss the point. So does much of what passes for education.

"Education and the Pursuit of Happiness" was the commencement address at the University of Denver, 29 May 1976. The analysis of

81

happiness in relation to needs and wants is more fully developed in
× *Adler's book on ethics,* The Time of Our Lives. *There he demonstrates*
⤸ *the indefeasible relations between happiness, leisure, and education.*

G. V. D.

T HE FACT that your graduation from the University of Denver coincides with the bicentennial anniversary of the Declaration of Independence dictates the theme of this commencement address.

We are all endowed, the Declaration tells us, with certain unalienable rights. Among these are life, liberty, and the pursuit of happiness. It seems to me fitting, on this occasion, for us to consider how the education you have so far received has prepared you for the pursuit of happiness in the years ahead. To answer that question, it is necessary, first, to consider the meaning of happiness in order to discover the sense in which it is true to say that a just government is one that secures for all its people the rights and conditions that facilitate the pursuit of happiness.

On the conception of happiness which is most prevalent in the modern world, and which, I fear, you yourselves may hold, that proposition is not true. In fact, it would be impossible for a government to do anything to aid and abet the pursuit of happiness on the conception of happiness that is current in the world today. That is possible only when happiness is understood in the sense in which it was conceived in antiquity—in the *Ethics* of Aristotle.

After I have clarified the difference between these two conceptions and have persuaded you, I hope, that we must adopt the ancient view of happiness not only to make sense of the Declaration of Independence but also to give significance to your education, I will try briefly to indicate how your education should serve you in the pursuit of happiness.

Let me turn at once to the two main conceptions of happiness in the tradition of Western thought. In both conceptions, happiness is an ultimate objective or end. It is something sought for its own sake, not as a means to some further good beyond itself. In both conceptions, a man is happy who has everything that he desires; the happy man is one who desires nothing more. But in one of the two conceptions, the one that predominates in modern times, happiness as an ultimate goal is a terminal end. This means that happiness is a goal that can be reached and enjoyed at one or another moment in the course of a life. The individual is deemed happy whenever, at a given time, he has satisfied all the desires that he happens to have at that time. Accordingly, he may enjoy or experience happiness at one moment, be unhappy at some later moment when his desires at that time are frustrated or unfulfilled, and again become happy at a still later moment.

In the other conception of happiness, which prevailed in antiquity and the Middle Ages but has little currency in our time, happiness as an ultimate objective is not a terminal goal, but only a normative end. This means that happiness is conceived as the goodness of a whole human life and, therefore, as something which cannot be experienced or enjoyed at any moment during the course of a lifetime. A good life is one enriched by the possession or enjoyment of all the things that are really good for a human being to have. A good life as the end that human beings should seek is normative in the sense that it sets the norm or standard by which the individual's actions should be judged morally according as they promote or impede the individual's achievement of the end.

The introduction of the words "good" and "should seek" calls attention to another, and even more fundamental, difference between these two conceptions of happiness. There is no reference to "good" or "ought" in the modern conception of happiness. It conceives happiness in purely psychological or nonmoral terms. It involves no distinction between good and bad desires, right and wrong desires. It involves no distinction between what men do in fact desire and what they ought to desire. Happy is the man who, at any given moment, has all that he desires regardless of what his desires may be—good or bad, right or wrong.

In sharp contrast, the ancient conception of happiness is not psychological at all; it is a purely ethical conception—a conception of the good life, and therefore one that involves the distinction between good and bad desires or right and wrong desires. As St. Augustine puts it, happy is the man who, in the course of a lifetime, has satisfied all his desires, *provided he desire nothing amiss*—provided that the things he has desired are things really good for him and, therefore, are things rightly desired. We find in Aristotle a statement that dovetails with Augustine's. Aristotle said that a good life is one that is lived in accordance with moral virtue. Moral virtue consists in the habitual disposition to desire nothing amiss—to act on right desires, and to avoid acting on wrong ones.

You are probably wondering what is meant by right and wrong desires. To answer that question as briefly as possible, I must call your attention to the distinction between needs and wants. By needs, I mean those desires which are inherent in human nature and which, therefore, are the same for all human beings everywhere and at all times. By wants, I mean those desires which arise in individuals as a result of the particular circumstances of their own lives. Hence one individual's wants are likely to differ from another's, and the differences in their wants are likely to bring them into conflict with one another.

If you consider for a moment how you ordinarily use these two words, you will realize not only that you do understand the distinction between needs and wants, but also that the distinction enables us to understand the difference between right and wrong desires.

Needs, as Lord Keynes astutely observed, are desires so basic that they exist without regard to what is offered in the marketplace and without an individual's comparing his own condition or possessions with those of others; whereas, in contrast, wants are desires that are induced by what is offered in the marketplace and are augmented and intensified by an individual's comparing what he has with the possessions of others. Needs are absolute; wants, relative.

Needs are desires that may or may not be consciously felt, whereas wants are always consciously felt desires.

It is impossible for anyone to be mistaken about what he or she wants, but it is quite possible for an individual to make the mistake of thinking that he needs something when, in fact, he only wants it because someone else has it.

Almost all of us want things we do not need, and fail to want things that we do need.

Needs are always right desires; there can be no wrong or misguided needs, as there can be wrong or misguided wants. What we want may be something either rightly or wrongly desired, whereas anything we need is something rightly desired.

A man never needs anything that is not really good for him to have, but he certainly can and often does want something that is not really good for him.

The truth of Augustine's observation that happiness consists in having everything that one desires, provided that one desires nothing amiss, can now be seen to mean that happiness consists in having all the real goods that are rightly desired because they are things every human being needs to lead a good life. To desire nothing amiss is to seek the satis-faction of only such wants as do not impede or frustrate the satisfaction either of one's own needs or of the needs of others. Such wants are benign or innocuous. All other wants are injurious or malignant. Moral virtue, as the habit of desiring nothing amiss, directs our choices among goods so that we seek all the real goods we need for our happiness and avoid satisfying any wants except those for apparent goods which are benign or innocuous.

Which conception of happiness must be read into the Declaration of Independence in order to make what it asserts true rather than false?

If happiness consisted in each individual getting what he wanted, it would be impossible for any government to secure rights that enabled each individual to strive for happiness, since one individual's wants may and often do conflict with the wants of others.

On the psychological conception of happiness, desires are morally neutral; there is no consideration of whether they are right or wrong desires. To secure the rights that implement the pursuit of happiness on this conception would therefore involve a government in facilitating the satisfaction of wrong desires as well as right desires, without any differentiation between them.

Only on the ethical conception of happiness is it possible for the government of a society to attempt to provide all its human members with the external conditions or enabling means which they require in order to make good lives for themselves. Only on this conception of happiness, which involves an understanding of natural rights as rights to the real goods that each of us needs in order to make good lives for ourselves, is it possible for a government to implement the pursuit of happiness by all.

The attainment of happiness, the achievement of a good life, is beyond the power of government to provide. It involves factors, such as moral and intellectual virtue, which are internal and within the power of the individual to acquire for himself. Yet even here external circumstances may facilitate or impede. Here, therefore, is where the influence of your training and schooling comes in.

What do you need to succeed in making a happy or good life for yourself, and how has your training and schooling aided and abetted your efforts in this direction?

The real goods you need can be summarized under seven headings. (1) You need the goods of the body—physical health, bodily vigor, and the pleasures of sense. (2) You need economic goods, such as a decent supply of the means of subsistence, living and working conditions conducive to health, and opportunities for access to the pleasures of sense, the pleasures of play, and esthetic pleasures. (3) You need political goods, such as civil peace and political liberty, together with the protection of individual freedom by the prevention of violence, aggression, coercion, and intimidation. (4) You need social goods, such as equality of status and of treatment in all matters affecting the dignity of the human person. (5) You need the goods of personal association, such as family relationships, friendships, and loves. (6) You need the goods of the mind, such intellectual virtues as knowledge, understanding, a modicum of wisdom, both practical and speculative, together with such goods of the mind's activity as the liberal arts—the skills of inquiry and of learning, the habits of critical judgment and creative production. (7) You need the goods of character, such moral virtues as temperance, fortitude, and justice, all of which are firm habits of not yielding to wants that will get in the way of your acquiring the goods you need.

The training and care you received at home, together with the education and direction you received at school, have made some contribution to your acquirement of at least five of the seven classes of goods that I have just enumerated. Some of these goods—I have in mind particularly the economic, political, and social goods—we all owe to the good fortune of living in a technologically advanced constitutional democracy which, while still far from being a perfectly just society, has achieved a greater measure of justice for its people than almost any other society in the world. Our possession of some of these goods, such as the goods of the body and the goods of personal association, we owe to the blessings of good fortune. While we have some control over our acquisition of them, they are, initially at least, put at our disposal by favorable circumstances.

With regard to the acquisition of wealth in all its forms, you may be tempted to think that your schooling was intended and designed to play a major role; you may even think that the primary reason for going to college and getting an education is that it will help you not just to earn a living, but to forge to the front in the race for the accumulation of worldly goods. This, I think, is an egregious error made by too many Americans today—among them, educators and parents, as well as students in our colleges.

There is, as you know, a great deal of talk about the relative inutility of a college education because it does not guarantee that its graduates will become worldly successes in monetary terms. There is also a great deal of talk about remedying this deficiency by substituting one or another form of narrow, specialized vocational training for a liberal course of study, broad and general in its outlines. All of this talk is, in my judgment, profoundly misguided, for the following reasons.

In the first place, success in the pursuit of happiness cannot be equated with success in the accumulation of a vast amount of worldly goods. All that a man needs to lead a good life is a moderate amount of wealth. To have more than one needs is to have an excess that puts a great strain upon one's moral virtue, for it permits one to gratify wants that may not be innocuous and so may interfere with one's attainment of the real goods that one needs.

In any case, the least important of all the reasons for going to college and trying to get an education is that it will help one to earn a living. While earning a living may be indispensable, it is at best only a necessary, but hardly a sufficient, condition of leading a good life. The most important reason is that it will help one to lead a better life than one might otherwise have been able to achieve. It can do that only to the extent that it contributes to the formation of the moral and the intellectual virtues.

There may be other reasons for going to college, but unless the chief reason is to learn what needs to be learned in order to live well, in order to lead a decent human life, then one might have been better off, perhaps, not to have gone to college at all.

As I have just indicated, the principal contribution that institutions of higher learning can make to the pursuit of happiness is in the sphere of the virtues—those interior goods of character and of intellect which are regulative of the way in which you conduct your life and act with respect to all other goods. I must add at once that even here the contribution that can be made by higher education is mainly limited to the sphere of the intellectual virtues. For better or worse, good and bad moral habits—virtues and vices—are formed at an earlier age. Whether or not the individual forms good habits of choice and of action depends largely upon the influence of family and of friends. Try as they may, colleges and universities can do little to confirm good habits or alter bad ones; nor, since they are educational institutions, should this be held against them. The ancient Greeks were correct in their insight that the moral virtues, unlike the arts and sciences, cannot be taught in schools or be inculcated by teachers.

We are left, therefore, with the formation of the intellectual virtues as the main contribution that institutions of higher education can make to the attainment of happiness by those whom they graduate. However, of the intellectual virtues, one—wisdom—is beyond the province or power of any school to cultivate. Wisdom cannot be attained in youth or during the prolonged immaturity of those who remain students under institutional auspices. Wisdom is the ultimate intellectual good that comes only with years of experience and after a lifetime of learning.

The rudiments of another intellectual virtue—understanding—may be attained in school, but its development in depth is, like wisdom, a product of mature years and of sustained inquiry. It is, therefore, mainly with respect to the arts and sciences that colleges and universities can be expected to make their chief contribution to the individual's pursuit of happiness. While some acquisition of knowledge in the sciences and other fields of scholarship can be achieved in college and university, more must be acquired after graduation if the individual is to become truly learned in any particular field.

Since, for anyone to become an educated person, it is necessary for his or her learning to continue throughout the lifetime that follows graduation from college or university, the most crucial contribution that these institutions can make is in the field of the arts—the liberal arts, which are the arts of learning and the arts which discipline our creative powers. If your education so far has given you a superficial introduction to the whole world of learning, if it has given you the skills you need to go on learning, skills that also help you to use your mind creatively, and if it has inspired you with a zest to use these skills to the utmost of your ability, then it has done for you as much as you have any right to expect.

Whether, in the years ahead, you take advantage of the education you have received depends entirely on you. It will depend on the choices you make with regard to the activities or occupations that fill the free hours of your life. The chief ingredients of a life well lived are the activities of learning and of creative production. These two things—learning and creativity—constitute leisure, in sharp contradistinction to play, recreation, and idling as other ways in which human beings fill their free time. A good human life is one that is enriched by as much leisure as one can cram into it.

The education you have so far received, which I hope you will enlarge by further learning, aids and abets your pursuit of happiness by providing you with the resources you need for filling your life with the highest leisure activities of which you are capable. If you do that and if, in addition, you are blessed by good fortune in other respects, then there is a reasonable chance that when you graduate from this world at the end of your life, it can be said that your life was a happy one.

PART
TWO

Liberal Education

and Schooling

7

Labor, Leisure, and Liberal Education

(1951)

A concern with the ends of a liberal education begins the discussions in this section. Adler's analysis of the relations between labor, leisure, and liberal education leads to some compelling conclusions about the parts of life, their order in terms of ends, and the role of liberal education. The central concepts in this essay—work, play, leisure, rest—are more clearly defined and articulated in a book that Adler wrote almost twenty years later, The Time of Our Lives (1970), and also in chapter 1 of an even later book, A Vision of the Future (1984).

This essay is a corollary to "Education and the Pursuit of Happiness." It continues to explore concepts developed there and, at the same time, it establishes terms for understanding the discussions that follow it.

The question here is essentially one of definition. The broadest definition, Adler says, with which he thinks no one can disagree, is that education is a process which aims at the betterment of men. What constitutes betterment, however, is a subject of controversy. To that point, Adler offers a choice between two distinct views of education. The article was first published in The Journal of General Education (October 1951). Liberal education will never again be a vague, loose, or empty term for anyone who reads it.

G.V.D.

ALTHOUGH the title of this essay is "Labor, Leisure, and Liberal Education" and although it begins and ends with a consideration of liberal education, its main concern is with the distinction

93

between labor and leisure. This is so because I have found it almost impossible, in my own thinking about the subject, to understand liberal education except in terms of what its *end* is. And the end of liberal education, it seems to me, lies in the use we make of our leisure, in the activities with which we occupy our leisure time.

In support of this thesis, that liberal education is to be understood in terms of leisure, I should like to proceed in the following order: first, to make some approximations to a definition of liberal education in terms of leisure; second, to try to reach a deeper understanding of the significance of this definition by examining more closely the distinctions between work or labor, on the one hand (I shall use the words "work" and "labor" interchangeably), and leisure, on the other; and, third, to draw from this analysis some implications or consequences for the place of liberal education in an industrial democracy like ours.

Let me begin where anyone has to begin—with a tentative definition of education. Education is a practical activity. It is concerned with means to be employed or devised for the achievement of an end. The broadest definition with which no one, I think, can disagree is that education is a process which aims at the improvement or betterment of men, in themselves and in relation to society. Few will quarrel with this definition because most people are willing to say that education is good; and its being good requires it to do something that is good for men. The definition says precisely this: that education improves men or makes them better.

All the quarrels that exist in educational philosophy exist because men have different conceptions of what the good life is, of what is good for man, of the conditions under which man is improved or bettered. Within that large area of controversy about education, there is one fundamental distinction to which I should like to call to your attention.

There seem to be two ways in which men can be bettered or improved: first, with respect to special functions or talents and, second, with respect to the capacities and functions that are common to all men. Let me explain. In civilized societies, and even in primitive societies, there is always a rudimentary, and often a very complex, division of labor. Society exists through a diversity of occupations, through different groups of men performing different functions. In addition to the division of labor and the consequent diversity of functions, there is the simple natural fact of individual differences. So one view of education is that which takes these individual and functional *differ-*

ences into consideration and says that men are made better by adjusting them to their occupations, by making them better carpenters or better dentists or better bricklayers, by improving them, in other words, in the direction of their own special talents.

The other view differs from this, in that it makes the primary aim of education the betterment of men not with respect to their differences but with respect to the *similarities* which all men have. According to this theory, if there are certain things that all men *can* do, or certain things that all men *must* do, it is with these that education is chiefly concerned.

This simple distinction leads us to differentiate between specialized education and general education. There is some ground for identifying specialized education with vocational education, largely because specialization has some reference to the division of labor and the diversity of occupations, and for identifying general education with liberal education because the efforts of general education are directed toward the liberal training of man *as man*.

There is still another way of differentiating education in terms of its ends. Aristotle often talks about the difference between the useful and the honorable. What he means by the "useful" and the "honorable" can sometimes be translated into extrinsic and intrinsic ends. An educational process has an *intrinsic* end if its result lies entirely within the *person* being educated, an excellence or perfection of his person, an improvement built right into his nature as a good habit is part of the nature of the person in whom a power is habituated. An *extrinsic* end of education, on the other hand, lies in the goodness of an *operation*, not as reflecting the goodness of the operator but rather the perfection of something else as a result of the operation being performed well.

Thus, for example, there can be two reasons for learning carpentry. One might wish to learn carpentry simply to acquire the skill or art of using tools to fabricate things out of wood, an art or skill that anyone is better for having. Or one might wish to learn carpentry in order to make good tables and chairs, not as works of art which reflect the excellence of the artist, but as commodities to sell. This distinction between the two reasons for learning carpentry is connected in my mind with the difference or distinction between liberal and vocational education. This carpentry is the same in both cases, but the first reason for learning carpentry is liberal, the second vocational.

All of this, I think, leads directly to the heart of the matter: that vocational training is training for work or labor; it is specialized rather than general; it is for an extrinsic end; and ultimately it is the education of slaves or workers. And from my point of view it makes no difference whether you say slaves or workers, for you mean that the worker is a man who does nothing but work—a state of affairs which has obtained, by the way, during the whole industrial period, from its beginning *almost* to our day.

Liberal education is education for leisure; it is general in character; it is for an intrinsic and not an extrinsic end; and, as compared with vocational training, which is the education of slaves or workers, liberal education is the education of free men.

I would like, however, to add one basic qualification at this point. According to this definition or conception of liberal education, it is not restricted in any way to training in the liberal arts. We often too narrowly identify liberal education with those arts which are genuinely the liberal arts—grammar, rhetoric, and logic and the mathematical disciplines—because that is one of the traditional meanings of liberal education. But, as I am using the term "liberal" here, in contradistinction to "vocational," I am not confining liberal education to intellectual education or to the cultivation of the mind. On the contrary, as I am using the phrase, liberal education has three large departments, according to the division of human excellences or modes of perfection. Physical training, or gymnastics in the Platonic sense, if its aim is to produce a good coordination of the body, is liberal education. So also is moral training, if its aim is to produce moral perfections, good moral habits or virtues; and so also is intellectual training, if its aim is the production of good intellectual habits or virtues. All three are liberal as distinguished from vocational. This is not, in a sense, a deviation from the conception of liberal education as being concerned only with the mind, for in all three of these the mind plays a role. All bodily skills are arts; all moral habits involve prudence; so the mind is not left out of the picture even when one is talking about moral and physical training.

After this purely preliminary statement, I should like to discuss the problem of what labor is, and what leisure is, and how these two things are related. For as understanding of these two terms becomes clearer, I think understanding of liberal education and of the problem of liberal education in our society will become clearer.

Let me begin by considering the parts of a human life—and by "the parts of a human life" I mean the division of the twenty-four hours of each day in the succession of days that make up the weeks, months, and years of our lives. The lives of all of us today are divided roughly into thirds. This was not always the case. The lives of the slaves of antiquity and, until recently, the wage slaves of our modern industrial society were divided into two parts, not three. We are, however, accustomed to think of our lives as having three parts.

One-third is sleep. I include with sleep—because they belong to the same category, and I shall use "sleep" as a symbol of all such things—*eating* (in so far as it is not liberal, in so far as it is quite apart from conversation, eating just to sustain the body); the acts of *washing* and *cleansing* the body; and even *exercise*, in so far as it is indispensable for physical fitness. These things are like sleep because they maintain the body as a biological mechanism.

Sleep, then, is one-third; work or labor, one-third; and one-third is free time or spare time. I am defining the latter negatively now, as time not spent in sleep or work, time free from work or biological necessities. Now I say this threefold division of the parts of a day (and, therefore, of a human life) into sleep and the adjuncts of sleep, work or labor, and free or spare time is not entirely satisfactory. A further division is required. Free time, it is clear, may be used in two ways when it is not used, as some people use it, for sleep and other biological necessities. One of the two ways in which free time can be used is play—and by "play" I mean recreation, amusement, diversion, pastime, and, roughly, all ways of killing time. The other use of free or spare time I should like to denominate roughly for the moment—I will analyze it more carefully later—engagement in leisure activities. If you say, "What do you mean by leisure activities?" I answer, "Such things as thinking or learning, reading or writing, conversation or correspondence, love and acts of friendship, political activity, domestic activity, artistic and esthetic activity." Just think of that list of things. They are not work, and they are not, or they seem not to be, play. Here is a group of activities which occupy time free from sleep and work and which are distinct from recreation or amusement. But the line of distinction is not clear, nor is the definition of the class of activities.

Before I push the analysis further, let me ask another question. Do these four things—sleep, work or labor, play, and leisure activities—exhaust the parts of a human life? I have two answers to the question. If you look at a human life on the purely natural plane, I think these consume all its time. But I think there is a fifth part of life not reducible to any of these four, though I cannot fully account for it on the purely natural plane. That fifth part I call "rest." Now you might think that rest is identical with sleep, or with recreation by which one is "rested" from fatigue. But I do not mean that when I use the word. I mean by "rest" something that is quite distinct from sleep, an activity that is specifically human. No animal could possibly rest in the sense which I intend when I use the word. An animal sleeps. I mean rest in a sense quite distinct from play or recreation or refreshment, for all these things are for the sake of work, and rest is not for the sake of work at all.

The only way I can begin to convey what I mean by "rest" is to say the most obvious thing: that it is to be understood philosophically, as the opposite of motion. The easiest way to understand the connotation of the term "rest" is to consider the phrase "heavenly rest" and to ask whether there is any rest on earth. I think there is none because by "rest" I mean not merely a terminal activity, one which is done for its own sake, but also a nonrepetitive or an exhaustive activity, one that does not require repetition because it in itself exhausts the need for activity. But I must then add immediately that, as I understand rest, its meaning is supernatural. It is the sense in which God rested on the seventh day, the sense in which the commandments of God bid us observe the Sabbath day and keep it holy as a day of rest. It is in terms of this conception of rest that I distinguish between contemplation and thinking. Thinking, it seems to me, is a leisure activity; contemplation, an activity of rest. Accordingly, if rest exists at all in this earthly life, it exists only, I think, in religious activity, only in prayer and worship and in the contemplation practiced by religious orders. From this point of view, all human life is either work or rest. Everything I have subdivided into sleep, play, work, and leisure becomes work, as compared with rest, though there are distinctions on the natural plane that make work just one of four parts.

Leaving rest aside for a moment, let me see if I can explain the differences of work, play, and leisure activity. Certain criteria, which are often used to distinguish work, play, and leisure, fail, I think, to define these three things. For example, persons often use the criterion of pleasure and pain, somehow thinking of work as painful and play or leisure as pleasant. It is immediately apparent, I think, that this is incorrect. Play can be quite painful. What does one mean by speaking of a "grueling" match of tennis, if one does not mean that there is often physical pain in playing a long, fast tennis match? Work certainly can be pleasant. There is actual pleasure in a skilled performance, even if the performance is part of a laborious activity. And leisure activities, if I am right in thinking that learning is a typical leisure activity, certainly can be quite painful. Note, moreover, a very common phrase, one used in school, namely, *school work* or *home work*. Though schoolwork and homework are study and are therefore a part of learning and belong to leisure activity, we call them "work." Why? Because there is some pain involved? I think not. I think we call them "work," as I shall try to show you subsequently, not because pain is involved in them but because we do them under some obligation, under some compulsion. This is the first indication that the meaning of "work" somehow involves the compulsory.

Fatigue is a second criterion that is often used to distinguish work, play, and leisure. All forms of activity can be tiring, and all forms of activity which involve both the mind and the body call for sleep to wash away fatigue. Nor is it true to say that work is difficult and play and leisure are easy, for play and leisure activities can be difficult, too. Nor do I think that the Thomistic division of the good into the useful, the pleasant, and the virtuous will by itself (although I think it comes near to it) perfectly distinguish between work as the useful, play as the pleasant, and leisure as the virtuous. Unless those terms are more sharply restricted, I think one could regard work as pleasant or even virtuous in a sense; play as useful in so far as it is recreative and performs a biological function; and leisure activities, although they may be intrinsically virtuous, as useful and pleasant. Let me therefore offer a criterion which I think will succeed in drawing the line between labor and leisure and will take care of play as well.

Though it may not perfectly account for play, I would like to propose that the distinction between labor or work, on the one hand, and leisure activities, on the other, is to be made in terms of what is biologically necessary or compulsory and what is rationally or humanly desirable or free. Let me see if I can explain this criterion by applying it. Labor, I say, is an economically necessary activity. It is something you do to produce the means of subsistence. It makes no difference at all whether the worker gets consumable goods immediately by his laboring activity or wages wherewith to buy consumable goods. Let us think of this for a moment in the following way. Let consumable goods—either direct consumables or money—be the compensation of the laborer; and, further, let us assume for the moment that no man gets his subsistence, in the form of either consumable goods or money, without labor. Then the definition of work or labor is: that activity which is required, is compulsory, for all men in order for them to live or subsist and which therefore must be extrinsically compensated, that is, the laborer must earn by his labor the means of his subsistence.

Let us test this. Men who have ample and secure means of subsistence have no need to labor. This is the historical meaning of the leisure class. Provide any man or group of men with ample and secure means of subsistence, and they will not work. I do not mean that they will not be active, that they will not be productive, that they will not be creative. But they will not work. They will not labor in the sense in which I tried to define that term sharply. Anything they will do will have to have for them some *intrinsic compensation*. Strictly, the word "compensation" is here wrongly used. The activities in which they engage will have to be *intrinsically rewarding*. What they do will somehow be done for its own sake, since they are provided with the means of subsistence.

Let us consider what I regard as the great experimental station for all thinking about man, namely, the Garden of Eden, peopled by men who have not sinned. Suppose the race of man had continued to live in the Garden of Eden. Not having sinned, man would not have inherited labor, disease, and death as punishments of sin. Man would have had no *need* to labor; he could have lived on the fruits of the trees and the grains of the earth. He would not have played, and neither would he have slept. In other words, life in the Garden of Eden would have consisted entirely of leisure activities. Because the body of sinless man would have been quite different from the human body as it is in the world, there would have been none of the peculiar divisions of life that exist in the world.

Leisure activities, in sharp distinction from labor or work, consist of those things that men do because they are desirable for their own sake. They are self-rewarding, not externally compensated, and they are freely engaged in. They may be morally necessary, but they are not biologically compulsory. You can see the trouble with this definition as soon as you say it. You may ask at once, What is play? Is not play self-rewarding? Is not play distinguished from labor by the negative distinction that it is something you do not have to do? Something that you freely choose to do?

I think we can get some light on how to sharpen the definition of leisure, and keep it distinct from play, by etymological considerations. I must confess to being genuinely fascinated by the background of the word "leisure." The word which in Greek means "leisure" is *scole*. Notice that our English word "school" comes from *scole*.

Now the Greek word *scole* has two meanings, just as the English word "pastime" has two meanings. In the dictionary the first meaning of "pastime" refers to the time itself, to *spare* time. The second meaning of "pastime" refers to what is done with such time, namely, *play*. It is this second meaning that we usually intend by our use of the word. So the first meaning of *scole* refers to the time; the second, to the content or use of the time. The first is leisure in the merely negative sense of the time *free from* labor, or spare time; but the second meaning, which appears very early in Greek literature, refers to what men should *do* with this time, namely, learn and discuss. It is the second meaning— what one does with time free from labor—which permits *scole* to become the root of the word "school." This, it seems to me, throws a fascinating light on a phrase that was used frequently in my youth when boys of sixteen faced, with their parents, the question, "Shall I go to *work* or shall I go to *school*?" Making this a choice of opposites is quite right, because work is one thing and school is another. *It is the difference between labor and leisure.*

When we look for the Latin equivalent of the Greek word *scole*, more light is thrown on the subject. The first meaning, time free from work or labor, appears in the Latin word *otium*. *Otium* is the root of the word *negotium*, which means "negotiation" or "business." *Otium* is the very opposite of *negotium* or "business"; it simply means time *free from* work. What is wonderful here is that the English word "otiose" is not a very complimentary word—it means "unemployed, idle, sterile, futile, useless." The second meaning of *scole* is translated by the Latin *schola*. This again is a source of "school." Finally, the first meaning of *otium* has a synonym in Latin, *vacatio*, from which we get the word "vacation" and also, interestingly enough, "vacancy."

The English word "leisure" comes down a totally different line. It comes from the French *loisir*, and from the Latin *licere*; it has the root meaning of the permissible and the free. The Latin *licere* is also the root of "liberty" and "license," in addition to "leisure." I think it is extraordinary to see these three words related in that one Latin root.

In the light of this etymology, I think we can distinguish leisure from play as two quite different uses of free or spare time, that is, *not-working time*. Play may be one of two things. It may be biologically useful like sleep, just as vacations and recreational activities are biologically useful. Just as sleep is a way of washing away fatigue, so a certain amount of play or vacation or recreation has the same kind of biological utility in the recuperation of the body. Play may be, however, something beyond this. Obviously, children do not play just to refresh themselves. And I often wonder whether this does not have a bearing on the role of play in adult life, that is, whether or not the role of play in adult life is not always a temporary regression to childhood.

One can admit, I think, that life involves two kinds of play: play for the sake of work, when it serves the same purpose as sleep, and play for its own sake. Sensual pleasure is admittedly a part of human life, but only in a limited quantity. Beyond that you have licentiousness; so, too, licentious play is a misuse of leisure.

Certainly, no quality attaches to useless play other than pleasure. I, for one, can see no perfection, no improvement, resulting from it. But leisure consists of those intrinsically good activities which are both self-rewarding and meaningful beyond themselves. They need not be confined to themselves. They can be both good things to do and good in their results, as, for example, political activities, the activities of a citizen, are both good in themselves and good in their results. This does not mean that leisure activities are never terminal, never without ends *beyond* themselves; it means only that they must be good *in themselves*, things worth doing even if there were no need for them to be done.

The results of leisure activity are two sorts of human excellence or perfection: those private excellences by which a man perfects his own nature and those public excellences which can be translated into the performance of his moral or political duty—the excellence of a man in relation to other men and to society. Hence I would define leisure activities as those activities desirable for their own sake (and so uncompensated and not compulsory) and also for the sake of the excellences, private and public, to which they give rise.

Suppose I try now to do a little of what I have just suggested. Suppose we draw a line between economically or biologically useful activities and those which are morally or humanly good, what Aristotle calls the "honorable" or "noble" activities. What results from making this separation? We get a threefold division: from the biologically necessary, we get sleep, work, and play (in so far as these serve to recuperate the body or to remove fatigue); from the humanly, morally good, the noble or honorable, we get all leisure activities; and from the superfluous, the otiose, we again get play, but here we mean play as it consists entirely in killing or wasting time, however pleasant that may be.

We see, furthermore, that the very same activities can be either labor or leisure, according to the conditions under which they are performed. Let us take manual work again—for instance, carpentry. Manual work can be leisure if it is work done for the sake of the art that is involved and for the cultivation of an artist. It is labor if it is done for compensation. That example may be too obvious, but we can see the same thing in teaching or painting, composing music, or political action of any sort. Any one of these can be labor as well as leisure, if a person does it in order to earn his subsistence. For if, to begin with, one accepts the proposition that no man shall get food or clothing or shelter, no man shall get the means of subsistence, without earning them, then some activities which would otherwise be leisure must be done by some persons for compensation. This makes them no less intrinsically rewarding but gives them an additional character. This double character causes certain activities to be labor, looked at one way, and leisure, looked at another.

This accounts for the fact that in professors' lives or statesmen's lives the line between labor and leisure is almost impossible to draw. In the *Protagoras*, the *Meno*, and the *Apology* Socrates was horrified at the notion that anyone would take pay for teaching. That the Sophists took pay for teaching aroused a moral repugnance in Socrates. This is not a minor matter. It was the first time anyone had done so, and it raised a very serious moral problem. For the first time an essentially leisure activity, like teaching, was compensated.

Not only can the same activity be both leisure and work; but even play, or things that I would call play, can be work for some people. Professional football is work to those who play it. Think also of all the persons whose working lives are spent in the amusement business.

This leads to further interesting points about the kinds of work. I would like to abstract this discussion from the distinction between manual and mental work, and particularly mental work as preparatory for, or directed toward, manual work. Taking both manual and mental work into consideration together, I would like to make the distinction between productive and nonproductive labor. I would say that work or labor is productive when it is economically useful, that is, when it produces means of subsistence in one form or another.

Here it is proper for the mode of compensation to consist of wages (or, as they are called more politely, "salaries"), with some basis for what we call a fair wage in a relation of equivalence between the amount of labor and the product of labor. Nonproductive labors, on the other hand, are activities which may be called work only in the sense that they are compensated—such things as teaching, artistic creation, the professional work of medicine and law, and the activities of statesmen. Here it is wrong to use the words "wages" or "salary"; and it is interesting to note that the language contains other words. We speak of an "honorarium" or "fee"; but the word I like best is the word "living" in the sense in which a priest gets, not wages or a salary, but a *living*. He is *given* his subsistence. He has not earned it by *production*. He has done something which it is good to do, but he also has to live; and there is a sense in which he can be said to have "earned his living." Here there can be no calculations of fair compensation. When one talks about fees or honoraria, the only thing one can talk about is the amount of time spent. Lawyers very often set their fees entirely in terms of time.

I would like to make a second distinction—between servile and liberal work. I think it is difficult to draw the line between these two, except in extreme cases, because many kinds of labor or work are *partly servile* and *partly liberal*. But the extreme cases are quite clear; and it is important at least to recognize the mixed cases or the shadowy ones that lie between.

By "servile work" I mean work done only because it is economically necessary and done only for compensation—work that no one would do if the means of subsistence were otherwise provided. "Liberal work" is work or activity which, though sometimes done for compensation, would be done even if no compensation were involved, because the work itself is self-rewarding. In other words, liberal work contains, at its very heart, activities that are essentially leisure activities, things that would be done for their own sake, even though subsistence were otherwise secured. The consequence of this is that the man who is a liberal worker—a teacher, lawyer, statesman, or creative artist—may, and usually does, work many more hours than are required for his compensation. He does more than is necessary to do a fair job for the person who is compensating him, because he cannot determine the point at which his activity passes into strictly leisure activity, though some part of it earns his compensation. I think examples of the research scientist, the teacher, or the statesman make this perfectly clear.

Finally, in terms of these distinctions, there is at least the beginning of an order for the parts of life. It would seem to me that, by the very nature of the terms themselves, sleep and its adjunct activities and play as recreation must be for the sake of work; and work must be for the sake of leisure. Earning a living, in short, and keeping alive must be for the sake of living well. Many of the obvious disorders of human life result from improper understanding of the order of these parts—for example, sleeping for its own sake, which is at least neurotic and at worst suicidal; working as an end in itself, which is a complete perversion of human life; working for the sake of play, which is certainly a misconception of leisure; or free time as time to kill in pleasure seeking. Play for its own sake, in order to kill time or escape boredom, is as neurotic as sleep for its own sake. And perhaps I should add the error, which many of us make, of confusing leisure with rest. Among those who share this confusion are persons who think that Sunday is a day to be spent in aesthetic, speculative, or liberal activity or that going to the theater or a concert or indulging in some form of sport is the proper observance of the day. I am not trying to preach the doctrines of a strict Sabbatarian—that is not the purpose of this lecture—but, nevertheless, I keep asking myself, "What can be the meaning of the admonition 'Remember the Sabbath day, to keep it holy'?" A day of rest cannot be identified with a day of play; and a day of rest, just as clearly, I think, cannot be identified with a day of leisure, for leisure activities are not rest.

In terms of this very brief and sketchy analysis of the parts of life, and of these distinctions between work, play, and leisure activities, we now can see clearly the difference between vocational training and liberal education. Vocational training is learning for the sake of earning. I hope I step on nobody's toes too hard when I say, as I must say, that therefore it is an absolute misuse of school to include any vocational training at all. School is a place of learning for the sake of learning, not for the sake of earning. It is as simple as that. Please understand that I do not mean vocational training can be totally dispensed with; I mean only that it should be done on the job. It should be done as preparatory to work; and as preparatory to work, it should be compensated. No one should have to take vocational training without compensation, because it is not self-rewarding. To include vocational training in school *without compensation* is to suppose that it is education, which it is not at all. In contrast to vocational training, liberal education is learning for its own sake or for the sake of further education. It is learning for the sake of all those self-rewarding activities which include the political, aesthetic, and speculative.

There are three further comments I should like to make on this distinction. First, professional education can be both vocational and liberal, because the kind of work for which it is the preliminary training is essentially liberal work. The work of a lawyer is liberal, not servile, work. In Greece free men who were citizens were all lawyers; there education for legal practice was liberal education. Professional education is vocational only in so far as this kind of leisure activity happens to be a way that some men, in our division of labor, earn their compensation.

Second, liberal education can involve work simply because we find it necessary to compel children to begin, and for some years to continue, their educations. Whenever you find an adult, a chronological adult, who thinks that learning or study is work, let me say that you have met a child. One sign that you are grown up, that you are no longer a child, is that you never regard any part of study or learning as work. As long as learning or study has anything compulsory about it, you are still in the condition of childhood. The mark of truly adult learning is that it is done with no thought of labor or work at all, with no sense of the compulsory. It is entirely voluntary. Liberal education at the adult level can, therefore, be superior to liberal education in school, where learning is identified with work.

Third, if schooling is equivalent to the proper use of leisure time in youth, then the proper use of leisure time in adult life should obviously include the continuation of schooling—without teachers, without compulsion, without assignments—the kind of learning that adults do outside school, the kind they do in conversations and discussions, in reading and study.

Finally, we may ask the place of liberal education in an industrial democracy. We can do this quickly by considering two basic errors or fallacies peculiar to our society: the first I would call the aristocratic error; the second, the industrial fallacy.

The aristocratic error is simply the error of dividing men into free men and slaves or workers, into a leisure class and a working class, instead of dividing the time of each human life into working time and leisure time. Karl Marx's *Capital* and, quite apart from the theory of surplus value—Marx's special notion of capitalist production—is filled with the horrible facts about the life of the laboring classes until almost our own day. We must face the fact that, until very recently, the working classes did nothing but *sleep and work*. When we realize that children started to work at the age of seven; that whole families worked—men, women, and children; that the hours of working time were often twelve and fourteen hours a day, sometimes seven days a week, then we realize that the distinction between the leisure class and the working class is something you and I no longer can appreciate because it has disappeared from our society. It does not exist in the world today, at least not in the United States. But, if we consider the past, in which workers were like slaves, the aristocratic error consisted in the division of mankind into two classes, a leisure class and a working class.

To correct this error, we must say not only that all men are free but also that all men must work for their subsistence (which is nothing but a democratic or socialist variant on the biblical admonition that man must eat by the sweat of his brow). You will see the educational consequences of this fallacy when you stop to think how little point there would have been in talking about liberal education for all men in the eighteenth and nineteenth centuries, when much more than half the population had no time for education. It would have been just as meaningless for them to have been given a liberal education, doomed as they were to lead lives of work and sleep.

The second fallacy arises from the fact that industrial production has created an abundance of leisure time for all. I do not mean that the working classes today have as much leisure time as the leisure classes of other centuries. I mean simply that more leisure exists today, *per capita*, than ever existed before. Though industrial production has produced this abundance of leisure, industrialism as such has made all men servants of productivity; and, when productivity itself is regarded as the highest good, leisure is debased to the level of play or idleness, which can be justified only as recreation. The man of leisure is regarded by industrialists, interested solely in productivity, as either a playboy or a dilettante. Leisure loses its meaning when industrial society reduces it to an incidental by-product of productivity.

If these two fallacies are corrected, we reach, I think, the obvious conclusion that in a rightly conceived industrial democracy, liberal education *should be* and *can be* for all men. It should be because they are all equal as persons, as citizens, from a democratic point of view.

It can be because industrialism can emancipate all men from slavery and because workers in our day need not spend their entire lives earning their livings. Liberal education in the future of democracy should be and should do for all men what it once was and did for the few in the aristocracies of the past. It should be part of the lives of all men.

But I may be asked whether I have forgotten about individual differences. Even if all men are citizens, even if they are emancipated from the complete drudgery of labor, it still is not true that all men are equally endowed with talent or have an equal capacity to lead the good life. Let me give you an un-Aristotelian answer to this objection, because I cannot help feeling that Aristotle's opinions on such matters were affected, to some extent at least, by the fact that he lived in a slave society.

The good or happy life is a life lived in the cultivation of virtue. Another way of saying this is that the good life or the happy life is concerned with leisure. The good life *depends on labor*, but it *consists of leisure*. Labor and all conditions that go with labor are the antecedent means of happiness. They are external goods, that is, *wealth*. Leisure activities are the ends for which wealth is the means. Leisure activities are the constituents of happiness. Leisure activities constitute not mere living but living well. They are what Aristotle calls "virtuous activities" or the "goods of the soul."

Happiness so conceived is open to all men, *when all men are both workers and free men*. As regards both work and leisure, each man should do the best work and participate in the best sort of leisure activities of which he is capable, the highest for which his talents equip him. So conceived, happiness is the same for all men, though it differs in actual content, in degree of intensity, according to the individual differences of men.

It is clear, I think, that liberal education is absolutely necessary for human happiness, for living a good human life. The most prevalent of all human ills are these two: a man's discontent with the work he does and the necessity of having to kill time. Both these ills can be, in part, cured by liberal education. Liberal schooling prepares for a life of learning and for the leisure activities of a whole lifetime. Adult liberal education is an indispensable part of the life of leisure, which is a life of learning.

As a final word, let me tell you the most infallible sign of the liberally educated man. Aristotle said that the mark of a happy man is that he wants for nothing. I say that the mark of the happy man is also the sure sign that he is liberally educated, namely, that you never find him trying to kill time.

8

Liberal Education—
Theory and Practice

(1945)

Adler explains why and how the goal of a liberal education for all should and could be reached. He tells us that educational practices unfortunately were never very successful, but in the past, at least theory was sound. Practices, Adler says, continue to be largely unsuccessful, but in addition, the idea of a liberal education, which once informed the American dream, is now misunderstood by most educators and is shunned by colleges in favor of career training. The practical suggestions in this article, which follow from Adler's thesis, will sound like heresy to many. The article was published in the University of Chicago Magazine *(March 1945), and in the* Vassar Alumnae Magazine *(November 1945).*

G.V.D.

DESPITE considerable evidence to the contrary, I still cling to the notion that everyone understands what it means to be a liberally educated man or woman. The marks of a liberally educated person are not wealth or recognition, success in business or marriage, emotional stability, social poise or adaptation to environment, good manners, or even a good moral character. Each of these things is worth having, not in itself or for itself, but for its contribution to the fullness of a happy life. But none is the direct result of liberal education, though we may hope that liberal education does not oppose the acquisition and possession of some, if not all, of them. The direct product of liberal education is a good mind, well disciplined in its processes of

109

inquiring and judging, knowing and understanding, and well furnished with knowledge, well cultivated by ideas.

In any roomful of people, we would pick out the liberally educated man or woman as the one who manifests all the goods which belong to the intellect. These goods—the truth and various ways of getting at the truth—contribute to a happy life; they may even be indispensable, as is good moral character and some amount of wealth; but by themselves they do not make a man happy. A liberally educated man, lacking the goods which liberal education does not provide, can be more miserable than those who have these other goods without the benefit of liberal education. Liberal education is a perilous asset unless other and independent factors cooperate in the molding of a person. It is an asset, nevertheless, both because of what it contributes—a good mind, which everyone would enjoy having—and because a good mind is useful, though never by itself sufficient, for the acquisition of all other goods.

Anyone who thus understands the point of liberal education should recognize three corollaries. (1) Since every normal being is born with an intelligence that can be disciplined and cultivated—with some degree of capacity for developing a good mind—everyone can be and should be given a liberal education to an extent that equals his capacity. (2) No one can be given a completed liberal education in school, college, or university, for unlike the body, the mind's capacity for growth does not terminate with youth; on the contrary, the mature mind is more educable than the immature; therefore, adult education must take up where the schools leave off and continue the process through all the years of adult life. (3) Schools and colleges may concern themselves with other goods than a good mind—in a defective society this may be necessary—but if they do, they do so at the expense of time and energy taken away from liberal education.

Now the chief difference between ourselves and our ancestors, considering even those who lived as late as the end of the nineteenth century, is *not* that their educational institutions succeeded in the work of liberal education while ours so plainly fail. The sad fact seems to be that at no time in European history—neither in classical antiquity nor at the height of the Middle Ages, neither in the Renaissance nor in the eighteenth and nineteenth centuries—did schools and colleges, teachers and administrators, do a good job for most of the children submitted to their care; and until very recently adults were always left to shift for themselves. In every generation a small number of persons managed to get liberally educated, even as today a few can, in spite of bad schools and teachers. Learning has always been hard; thinking always painful; and the flesh always weak, weak in the teacher as well as the student.

The chief difference between ourselves and our ancestors is that they, for the most part, talked sense about liberal education, whereas we for the most part—I mean our leading educators—do not. Since I have admitted that our ancestors did not succeed in practice despite their sound conceptions, does it matter, then, that our institutions are dominated by misconceptions and confused theories of what liberal education should be?

I think it does matter because I still have hope that the difficulties in practice can be overcome, that education can achieve a greater measure of success in fact than history has yet evidenced. To make this hope come true, we must think as soundly about liberal education as our ancestors, and beyond that we must remedy their deficiencies or rectify their errors in practice. But unless we start by setting ourselves straight on the level of theory, we shall certainly go backward rather than forward on the level of practice.

It seems to me that our ancestors were able to think more soundly about liberal education because (1) they were not democrats and hence *wrongly* failed to recognize that every human being deserves the maximum educational opportunity proportionate to his ability; (2) the consequences of an industrial economy did not make themselves fully felt until the middle of the nineteenth century; and (3) until that time, the wonders of technology had not created the religion of science, with the consequent exaggeration of the place of scientific studies in the curriculum.

The third of these factors was responsible for the elective system. The second generated vocationalism. The first led us to suppose that the liberal education which our ancestors advocated was essentially aristocratic in theory as well as in practice, and so prompted the false conclusion that there must be some other theory of liberal education more appropriate to a democratic society.

It is undoubtedly easier to think soundly about liberal education if you are preparing to give it only to the few who are favored in natural endowments or economic position. But democracy is right and we must solve the problem of giving to everyone the sort of college education that is most readily given to the favored few.

The industrial economy is here to stay, for better or for worse, and we must somehow free the colleges from the burden of vocationalism by having other social agencies do whatever may be necessary to fit people into jobs. (What I am saying here about earning a living applies equally to all the other goods, such as emotional stability or moral character, which cannot be achieved by liberal education, and therefore should be taken care of by other social agencies; or if by colleges, *at least outside the curriculum.*)

Finally, scientific method, knowledge, and ideas deserve a proper place in the curriculum, together with, but not out of proportion to, poetry, philosophy, history, mathematics, theology, for all these differently exemplify the liberal arts; and though we now see that the traditional "classical" curriculum was too exclusively "humanistic" in a narrow sense of that term, the problem is obviously not solved by throwing away or corrupting what should have been amplified and thereby invigorated.

The practical suggestions I have to offer as therapy follow from the foregoing diagnosis of the illness of our colleges. We must so reform the curriculum, methods of teaching, and examinations, that we do not mistake the B.A. degree as signifying either a completed liberal education or adequate preparation for earning a living or living a happy life. It should signify only decent preparation for the continuing task of adult education.

A liberal curriculum should, therefore, include no vocational instruction; nor should it permit any subject-matter specialization. In a liberal college there should be no departmental divisions, no electives, no separate course in which grades are given for "covering" a specified amount of "ground," no textbooks or manuals which set forth what students must memorize to pass true-false examinations. The faculty should comprise teachers all of whom are responsible for understanding and administering the whole curriculum; lectures should be kept to a minimum and they should be of such generality that they can be given to the whole student body without distinction of year; the basic precept of pedagogy should be the direction of the mind by questions and the methods of answering them, not the stuffing of it with answers; oral examinations must be used to separate facile verbalizers and memorizers from those in whom genuine intellectual skills are beginning to develop and whose minds have become hospitable to ideas. No student should be dropped from college because he fails to measure up to an arbitrary standard determined by a percentage of mastery of a subject matter or skill; he should be kept in college as long as he manifests any development of his own capacities, and lack of such evidence should be interpreted as a failure on the part of the college, not the student.

These recommendations are, I know, either negative or formal. They do not positively or materially prescribe the course of study which should be in the curriculum of a liberal college. But if they were all followed, and if a faculty understood the purpose of liberal education, I would trust them to devise a curriculum worthy of the B.A. degree —aiming to do what little can be done in college toward the production of a good mind.

That would still leave us with four unsolved problems: how to overcome the weakness of the flesh on the part of both teachers and students; how to make what must be essentially the same college curriculum work for every level of intelligence and every diversity of talent; how to institute the sort of schooling which properly prepares all children to go to a liberal college; and how to organize and execute a program of continuing adult liberal education to carry ever further what the colleges begin—the motion toward that unreachable goal, the ideal of the good mind which would be attained by each individual only if we could exhaust his capacity for knowing the truth and how to get it.

9

The Schooling of a People

(1957; 1958; 1976)

This essay, like the problem it attacks, is in every sense at the heart of Reforming Education. *Equal education for all is the problem, and after many years of thinking, lecturing, and writing about it, Adler gives his most complete formulation of it in "The Schooling of a People." (His solution to the problem will come later, in the Paideia Program.) Adler departs here from his usual practice and takes pains to establish the historical as well as the philosophical context for understanding the problem. While emphasizing the limits of schooling as the beginning of education, Adler argues for what should be done and why.*

The introduction, which gives some background for this discussion, is taken from a lecture given in San Francisco in April 1957 called "Liberal Education in an Industrial Democracy." It was the third of three lectures in a series entitled "Major Issues of Our Time," sponsored by the Industrial Indemnity Company. Another very small portion of the essay was adapted from material gathered for a seminar in 1951 sponsored by the Fund for Adult Education and the Fund for the Advancement of Education, some of which was published in The Revolution in Education, *by Mortimer J. Adler and Milton Mayer (Chicago: University of Chicago Press, 1958). But the largest part of the essay appeared under the same title in* The Americans: 1976 (Critical Choices for Americans, vol. 2), *edited by Irving Kristol and Paul H. Weaver (Lexington, Mass.: D.C. Heath & Co., 1976).*

G . V . D .

THE DEMOCRATIC and capitalist revolutions confront our society with an educational problem that exceeds, in magnitude and difficulty, the educational problems which past societies have faced and solved.

We have not solved the educational problem that confronts us. Nor have we yet turned our efforts toward trying to solve it. Most Americans do not know the shape this problem takes; and it would almost seem as if most American educators have deliberately tried to avoid recognizing it. Yet the problem is one of the most serious that our society faces; and with the changes that lie ahead, it will become even more so. If it remains unsolved, it will become the most serious threat to the future of our society—its safety, its sanity, its prosperity.

With few exceptions, American educators tend to be satisfied with the accomplishments of American education in the last fifty years. This is the clearest and surest indication that they do not understand the problem our country is called upon to solve; for if they did, they could not possibly deceive themselves about what has so far been achieved.

They would know that everything we have done in building the largest school system the world has ever seen amounts to no more than a bare first step toward the solution of the problem of giving liberal education, the best conceivable, to all the children whom that school system is intended to accommodate. They would frankly admit that no one at present knows how to solve this problem. They would recognize that the problem is so difficult that it may take us the next hundred years to solve. Above all, they would see that, until the problem is understood in all its difficulties and accepted as the most serious problem we face, the intelligence, energy, and wealth required to solve it will not be applied to the task.

With the advent of democratic institutions in the twentieth century, universal suffrage was established for the first time, and the distinction between a ruling and a subject class was abolished. With the maturation of industrial production in the last hundred years, human life and energy has at last been emancipated from grinding toil, and the distinction between a working class and a leisure class has been effaced. If the capitalist revolution in the next fifty years completes what the industrial revolution began, we can look forward to the first truly classless society in history—a politically classless society in which all men are citizens and members of the ruling class; and an economically classless society in which all men are capitalists and members of the leisure class.

It is the extraordinary difference between such a classless society, emerging now for the first time in history, and all the class-structured societies of the past, which helps us to understand why an industrial and truly capitalist democracy is confronted by a novel educational problem and one it will find so difficult to solve. This contrast between the classless society of the future and all the class-structured societies of the past also helps us to understand the nature and difficulty of that problem.

1

If we were to survey the history of educational thought and practice from its beginning to the middle or end of the nineteenth century, we would not find the answers to the major problems of education in our day and in our society.

The best answers we could find—answers to the perennial questions about education, answers on which substantial agreement had been reached across the centuries—would not lead us to the solution of those problems which are peculiarly our own. On the contrary, they would intensify our sense of the difficulty of the problems we face. The better grasp we had of the wisdom about education gained during the preceding twenty-five centuries, the more appalled we should be by the magnitude of the problems that have arisen in the last hundred years. The double impact of democracy and industrialization has created problems both new and difficult.

It may be thought that every age, with pardonable exaggeration, feels this way about its own problems. The practical problems of education are always relative to the society and epoch in which they arise. They are conditioned by the political institutions, the economic system, the social arrangements, and the general culture of a particular society at a particular stage of historic development. Granting this, the difficulties of the problem confronting us can hardly be exaggerated, nor would they be diminished by the most sympathetic appreciation of the difficulties faced by our ancestors in their own day.

From our point of view, the history of education in the West falls into two parts, one very long and one very short, and both important.

Before the last hundred years, the two most serious crises in Western education occurred with the transition from Greco-Roman antiquity to medieval Christendom, and with the widespread changes effected by the Protestant Reformation. What is common to both can be briefly summarized in terms of issues concerning the relation of church and state, the place of religion in human life and in the formation of society, and the emphasis in education upon temporal or eternal goals. These two crises in Western education have left us with a legacy of problems, even though, with the progressive secularization of our society and culture, we have moved further and further in the direction taken at the Reformation and with the Renaissance.

That direction, as the spirit of the Renaissance suggests, was in part a return to and revival of classical learning, and with it an establishment of secular education according to one version of classical forms and principles. From the fifteenth to the middle of the nineteenth century, the main course of European and later of American education represents a continuity rather than a break with the education of antiquity. That continuity was not interrupted by the religiously oriented education of medieval Christendom. The Middle Ages saved and incorporated whatever of the secular learning of pagan antiquity they could Christianize, and erected a Christian educational structure upon ancient foundations.

Only with a sense of that continuity of Western education from the Greeks to the nineteenth century can we fully appreciate the sharpness of the break that has occurred since 1850. During the whole preceding period, education had certain common aims and methods, not unrelated to the fact that it was always restricted to the few. No society up to that time was concerned with the schooling—much less the education—of all its people. Thomas Jefferson's proposal to the Virginia legislature in 1817 (not adopted at the time it was made) that *all* the children should be given three years of common schooling at the public expense marks the emergence, in our country at least, of the central problem that our kind of society faces and that it has not yet solved in any satisfactory manner.

The American republic in Jefferson's day resembled the Greek republics in the time of Plato and Aristotle in two fundamental respects: (1) economically, it was a nonindustrial society; (2) politically, all men were not admitted to citizenship. Hence for Jefferson, as for Plato and Aristotle and almost all educators in between, anything except the barest beginning of education was for the few who belonged to the ruling class destined for a life of leisure and learning, not for the working mass, destined for a life of labor, necessary to support a society in which machines had not yet replaced the productive power of human muscle.

In a letter to Peter Carr in 1814, Jefferson outlined the basis of a Bill for Establishing a System of Public Education, which he submitted to the legislature in 1817. He wrote:

The mass of our citizens may be divided into two classes—the laboring and the learned. . . . At the discharging of the pupils from the elementary schools [after three years of schooling] the two classes separate—those destined for labor will engage in the business of agriculture or enter into apprenticeship to such handicraft art as may be their choice; their companions destined to the pursuit of science, will proceed to the College.

The suggestion that *all* children, even those destined for labor rather than for the arts and sciences as pursuits of leisure, should be given at least three years of schooling is the beginning of the democratic revolution in this country. But the explosive force of that revolutionary idea could not spread until the economic and political barriers to universal public schooling had been removed. Two basic changes—in the constitution of government and in the production of wealth—had to take place before society was fully confronted with the problem of how to produce an *educated people*, not just a *small class of educated men*. The two changes, dynamically interactive at every point, were the extension of the franchise toward the democratic ideal of universal suffrage and the substitution of machines for muscles in the production of wealth.

An industrial democracy, such as we have in America today, is a brand-new kind of society. It represents the most radical transformation of the conditions of human life that has happened so far. Hence it should not be surprising that the problems of education in an industrial democracy are startlingly new problems and much more difficult than any that our ancestors faced.

The novelty and difficulty of our problems cannot be accounted for solely in terms of the quantitative expansion of education from the schooling of a relatively small portion of the population to that of the people as a whole. It is also necessary to consider a profound qualitative change in our culture. This change, in preparation since the seventeenth century, has reached its peak only in the last fifty years. We live in an age of science fully matured, an age of specialized research, dominated by the centrality of the scientific method and by the promises or threats of technology. Our educational problems are what they are—both in novelty and difficulty—because of the interplay of these two sets of factors: the quantitative extension of schooling to the whole population and the qualitative alterations in the content of schooling demanded by science and technology.

2

To understand the difficulty of our problems, it may be useful to consider briefly why the educational wisdom of our ancestors, developed in undemocratic societies, in nonindustrial economies, and in eras not dominated by science and technology, does not solve our problems for us. On the contrary, it appears to accentuate the difficulties we face in trying to solve them.

It is not necessary to pretend that there was perfect unanimity among educators and philosophers of education in the twenty-five centuries prior to our day, in order to summarize the basic insights and convictions that they shared. The institutions and practices of education have changed, of course, with successive epochs in Western history. In addition, the great contributors to educational theory have differed and disputed on many points. One need only mention the names of Plato, Aristotle, Cicero, Quintilian, Augustine, Bonaventure, Aquinas, Montaigne, Erasmus, Francis Bacon, Comenius, Locke, Rousseau, Kant, J. S. Mill, and Cardinal Newman to have some notion of the controversial questions. Nevertheless, with few exceptions, the differences of opinion tend to be more concerned with particular policies and practices than with general principles. The prevalence of common practices throughout the whole period during which schooling and education were restricted to the few, together with the sharing of basic theoretical insights, indicates a substantial agreement about general principles.

That measure of agreement can be summarized in the following six statements. As we consider each of these statements, let us ask ourselves three questions. *First,* can we still affirm the truth of what is being said when our concern is with the schooling and education of the people as a whole rather than a small portion of the population? *Second,* if we do affirm the truth of what is being said as still applicable to the conditions of life in an industrial democracy and in a culture dominated by science and technology, do we know how to apply that truth to the schooling and education of the people as a whole? *Third,* if we must reject what is being said as no longer applicable, at least not without substantial modifications or qualifications, then how shall we formulate the principles that must replace the ones we have rejected?

1. The aim of education is to cultivate the individual's capacities for mental growth and moral development; to help him acquire the intellectual and moral virtues requisite for a good human life, spent publicly in political action or service and privately in a noble or honorable use of free time for the creative pursuits of leisure, among which continued learning throughout life is preeminent.

2. Guided by the aim of education just stated, basic schooling must be liberal in character; that is, a preparation for liberty or a life of freedom—the political freedom enjoyed by citizens (or the ruling class in society) and the economic freedom of time free for the pursuits of leisure, time free from labor in the production of wealth and time free for political activity and intellectual or artistic pursuits. Such basic schooling, in method and content, should be the same for all, involving little or no specialization. It does not include the specialized training of workers in the skills required for earning a living. Specialized schooling may be required beyond basic schooling; it is the schooling needed to impart the knowledge and skills required for vocations that are essentially liberal in character—the learned professions and the professions of learning.

3. Basic schooling, even when followed by professional schooling, does not complete the education of a man. The satisfactory completion of school requirements merely certifies that the individual is equipped to carry on learning by himself in any sphere of knowledge or skill. Education cannot be completed in school because of the limitations intrinsic to youth or immaturity and the inherent limitations on any course of study that is appropriate for youth. One of the essential forms of leisure activity is the continuation of learning after school, for which schooling at its best is only a preparation. The pursuit of understanding and wisdom involves the effort of a lifetime. It cannot be accomplished in youth, nor can the obligation to go on learning be fully discharged while any capacity for learning remains.

4. Society's interest in the schooling and education of human beings is twofold. On the one hand, it seeks to enhance its own welfare by deriving from well-educated persons the contribution they can make in the service of society. On the other hand, it seeks to put the resources

of society at the service of the individual by contributing through schooling and education to his own pursuit of happiness or a good human
life. So far as it is agreed that society and the state exist for the perfection
of human life, and that the individual human being, while under an
obligation to act for the social welfare, has ends beyond that which are
paramount, society's concern with schooling and education cannot be
limited to their utility for its own welfare. On the contrary, that interest
must be pursued in a manner that does not conflict with or detract
from society's obligation to facilitate and enhance the education of the
individual for the sake of his own development as a human being.

5. The profession of teaching is both a learned profession and a profession of learning, and so it involves knowledge and skill beyond basic
schooling. Since the liberal arts are the arts of learning and teaching,
the preparation of teachers involves, in addition to basic liberal schooling, special training in the liberal arts. The teacher must know what
to teach as well as how to teach. Hence the best teachers are those who
not only perfect their teaching through practice of its arts, but who also
deepen their grasp of the subjects they are teaching by further study of
those subjects.

6. Not all who teach or study may be able to contribute to the advancement of learning, but the vitality of education in any society
depends upon the efforts of those who augment learning as well as upon
the efforts of those who disseminate or acquire it. Such efforts normally
prosper through the cooperation of scholars. The advancement of learning, therefore, depends upon the condition requisite for such cooperation—a community of scholars which exists only to whatever extent
scholars can and do communicate with one another across all the
specialized fields of learning.

In the context of the questions that must be asked about them, the
foregoing six propositions raise more problems than can be discussed
within the confines of this essay. I will, therefore, concentrate on the
problems raised by the first four and, even so, I will try further to narrow
them down to what I regard as the most important and far-reaching
critical choices that confront us in the field of public education. Before
I attempt to define the alternatives that challenge us, I would like to
review briefly the American commitment to public education; and,
following that, to indicate the altered circumstances which have altered
the nature of that commitment.

3

Beginning with the earliest days of the republic, and even before that in the years of its formation, the commentators on the genius of its institutions called attention to the education of its citizens as a prime requisite not only for the preservation of their liberties, but also for the effectiveness of their engagement in public affairs. The institution of public schools, Noah Webster wrote in 1785, "is the necessary consequence of the genius of our governments; at the same time, it forms the firmest security of our liberties. It is scarcely possible to reduce an enlightened people to civil or ecclesiastical tyranny." Two years later, in 1787, Benjamin Rush told an audience in Philadelphia on the eve of the Constitutional Convention, that "to conform the principles, morals, and manners of our citizens to our republican forms of government, it is absolutely necessary that knowledge of every kind should be disseminated through every part of the United States."

In his inaugural address as president of Cumberland College in Tennessee in 1825, Philip Lindsley began by saying that "a free government like ours cannot be maintained except by an enlightened and virtuous people. It is not enough that there be a few individuals of sufficient information to manage public affairs. To the people, our rulers are immediately responsible for the faithful discharge of their official duties. But if the people be incapable of judging correctly of their conduct and measures, what security can they have for their liberties a single hour?" Elementary schooling, for the poor as well as for the rich, is not enough for this purpose, Lindsley argued. Colleges must be provided, not only to make better citizens but also to enable those citizens to lead better lives. Against the view that "superior learning is necessary only for a few particular professions," Lindsley maintained that "every individual who wishes to rise above the level of a mere laborer at taskwork ought to endeavor to obtain a liberal education."

In a somewhat similar vein, William Seward, in a speech delivered at Auburn, New York, in 1835, observed that elementary instruction in reading and writing was not enough. "Without some higher cultivation of the mind," we become "the sport of demagogues, and the slaves of popular passion, caprice, and excitement. . . . To discharge the duty of electors, we should understand some of the principles of political economy, of the philosophy of the human mind, and, above all, of moral and religious science." For the preservation of our free institutions and for their conduct to the maximum advantage of all, he urged that "the minds of all the people should be thus instructed."

In contrast to those who advocated enlarging the scope of public education for the political benefits it can confer, John H. Vincent, in a speech about the Chautauqua Movement in Boston in 1886, insisted that "education, once the peculiar privilege of the few, must in our best earthly estate become the valued possession of the many. It is a natural and inalienable right of human souls. The gift of imagination, of memory, of reason, of invention, of constructive and executive power, carries with it both prerogative and obligation. . . . No man has a right to neglect his personal education, whether he be prince or playboy, broker or hod carrier." If a just society is one that secures human rights, it is obliged to do all that it can to provide human beings with such schooling as will facilitate the exercise of their right to an education and, through it, their personal development.

These themes are echoed again and again, changing slightly as we pass to later generations. In *The Promise of American Life*, published in 1909, Herbert Croly declared that "democracy must stand or fall on a platform of possible human perfectibility. If human nature cannot be improved by institutions, democracy is at best a more than usually safe form of organization." But for democracy to prosper as well as to endure, Croly looked to the benefits of education. "It is by education that the American is trained for such democracy as he possesses; and it is by better education that he proposes to better his democracy. . . . It helps to give the individual himself those qualities without which no institutions, however excellent, are of any use." Thirty years later, James B. Conant, in his charter day address at the University of California in 1940, pointed out that the three fundamentals of the Jeffersonian tradition were "freedom of mind, social mobility through education, [and] universal schooling." These, he said, have represented "the aspirations and desires of a free people embarked on a new experiment, the perpetuation of a casteless nation." Though his theme on this occasion was education for a classless society, Conant concluded his address by insisting that "extreme differentiation of school programs seems essential," in support of which he referred to Jefferson's differentiation between the schooling of those destined for labor and the schooling of those destined for leisure and further learning.

Two other themes make their appearance in the historic record of the American concern with public education. One is the educational significance of vocational training in the public schools. Jane Addams and John Dewey, who defended such instruction when it was first introduced into the curriculum, did not do so on the ground that vocational training served the purpose of preparing the young to obtain jobs and earn their living. They would not have espoused it for that reason. On the contrary, they argued for its educational value as contributing to an understanding of "the social meaning of work," in Jane Addams's words; or, as John Dewey put it, "scientific insight into natural materials and processes, points of departure whence children shall be led out into a realization of the historic development of man. . . . When occupations in the school are conceived in this broad and generous way, I can only stand lost in wonder at the objections so often heard that such occupations are out of place in the school because they are materialistic, utilitarian, or even menial in their tendency."

The other theme is the role that public education plays in promoting the equality of conditions that constitutes a democratic and supposedly classless society. Horace Mann was one of the most eloquent spokesmen for education as the great equalizer. In a report to the Massachusetts legislature in 1842, he asserted that "individuals who, without the aid of knowledge, would have been condemned to perpetual inferiority of condition and subjected to all the evils of want and poverty, rise to competence and independence by the uplifting power of education." Six years later in another report to the legislature, Horace Mann summed up his conviction on this point by saying "education, then, beyond all other devices of human origin, is the great equalizer of the conditions of men, the balance wheel of the social machinery. . . . It gives each man the independence and the means by which he can resist the selfishness of other men. It does better then to disarm the poor of their hostility towards the rich; it prevents being poor."

As we pass from the last century into the present one, the hope that Horace Mann held out came to be looked upon as illusory. Writing in 1892, President Eliot of Harvard reported "serious and general disappointment at the results of popular education up to this point. . . . Skeptical observers complain that people in general, taken in masses with proper exclusion of exceptional individuals, are hardly more reasonable in the conduct of life than they were before free schools, popular colleges, and the cheap printing press existed. They point out that when the vulgar learn to read they want to read trivial or degrading literature. . . . Is it not the common school and the arts of cheap illustration, they say, which have made obscene books, photographs and pictures, low novels, and all the literature which incites to vice and crime, profitable, and therefore abundant and dangerous to society?"

After citing a long list of similar complaints, all of which might be made in the present decade as well as in the 1890s, President Eliot pointed out that the laboring classes "complain that in spite of universal elementary education, society does not tend toward a greater equality of condition; that the distinctions between rich and poor are not diminished but intensified, and that elementary education does not necessarily procure for the wage earner any exemption from incessant and exhausting toil." In addition, they allege that education "has not made the modern rich man less selfish and luxurious than his predecessor in earlier centuries who could barely sign his name . . . [and] also that the education of the employer and the employed has not made the conditions of employment more humane and comfortable."

The question, which President Eliot did not answer, was whether the fault lay with defects in the educational system itself, defects which might be remedied to produce the opposite results, or whether universal public schooling, even with all its defects removed, should never have been regarded as the equalizer of conditions that Horace Mann claimed it would be. Both answers have been given in this century. George Sylvester Counts of Teachers College, Columbia, and an educational reformer in the line of John Dewey, claimed in 1922 that the selective character of American secondary education made it, in effect, anti-democratic—a major factor in the perpetuation of class differences. Much more recently, the Coleman report on equality of educational opportunity, published in 1966, and the book by Christopher Jencks and his associates, *Inequality, A Reassessment of the Effect of Family and Schooling in America* (1972), tend in the opposite direction to point out that no improvement in the system of public education by itself can produce either an equality of educational opportunity or an equality of social and economic conditions.

4

The statements quoted and the views reported in the foregoing brief survey of the American commitment to universal public schooling are submitted as a sketchy sampling of opinion from the beginning of the republic to the present day. They should not be read as accurately reflecting the facts about the school system, much less as giving us reliable appraisals of its effectiveness or accomplishments. They may generate the impression that, almost from the beginning, this country was dedicated to the schooling of all its children at the public expense, both for the perpetuation of our free institutions and for their own fulfillment as human beings, but not until the present century—in fact, not until very recently—have the number of children in our schools and colleges and the duration of their attendance at these institutions come near to approximating a system of universal public education that looks as if it might be serving the aims which our ancestors had in mind.

Even if, before this century, all or most or a majority of the children had the benefit of primary or elementary schooling, that could not be expected to achieve more than a rudimentary literacy and numeracy. It was certainly not adequate to the task of producing an educated people—a citizenry or electorate capable of exercising a free and critical judgment on public issues and on the performance of public officials and a society of cultivated human beings, each of whom schooling had helped to realize his capacity for learning, each in a measure proportionate to the degree of his native endownment. Not until this century does the extension of schooling, both in the number of children it accommodates and in the number of years it provides instruction for them, reach a quantitative scope that warrants us in saying that we are now engaged in the schooling of a whole people. Unfortunately, no one who has any acquaintance with how the system works would feel warranted in saying that the qualitative level attained by the products of our educational institutions, taken in aggregate, remotely resemble what we have in mind when we contemplate the ideal of an educated people.

This striking discrepancy between the quantitative and the qualitative measures of educational achievement underlies the alternatives which, I submit, constitute the single most important—the central or focal—critical choice that confronts America in the field of public education. How we decide it will determine how we approach all the other options that are open to us. It is important to remember that the choices we face have never been faced by any society before this century, and are being faced in this century only by societies like our own in their political and economic arrangements. Remembering this, we should not be surprised by our failure so far to create a system of public education that is qualitatively as well as quantitatively adequate to the task of producing an educated people. The novelty and the difficulty of the problems involved may extenuate our failure to solve them, but they do not excuse failure on our part to open our eyes and see clearly the magnitude of the problems themselves.

Let us remind ourselves once more of the changes that have brought us to our present plight, and also of the realities of contemporary society and culture—the circumstances which have generated problems so novel and difficult that the traditional principles and practices of Western educational theory, *even if they were completely valid*, would not solve.

In 1850, 5 percent of our productive power was supplied by machines, the rest by human and animal muscle. In 1950, 84 percent was supplied by machines, the rest by muscle; and a quarter of a century later the percentage differences are even more striking. In 1850, more than half the human population of this country was disfranchised; less than half exercised the suffrage that is indispensable to political liberty and participation in self-government. By 1950, the franchise had been extended to include the whole population, and a quarter of a century later steps had been taken to insure that all those who possessed suffrage could freely exercise it.

The revolution in education has followed in the wake of industrialization and democratization. In 1850, a very small percentage of the children who went to school went beyond the elementary school, and not all went to school. In 1900, less than 10 percent of the children of eligible high school age were in high school. By 1950, over 85 percent of the children of high school age were in high school, and twenty-five years later that figure has increased substantially.

With universal suffrage, all normal children are destined to become citizens—members of the ruling class. In line with the democratic conception of citizenship, the basic schooling of future citizens, both elementary and secondary, is necessary and is, therefore, made compulsory. Under conditions of industrial production, it is economically possible and, perhaps, even economically desirable for compulsory basic schooling to be lengthened to twelve years, and for another two or four years of schooling at the public expense to be added on a voluntary basis.

Along with the abolition of slavery and the attenuation of economic servitude in all its myriad forms, the industrial economy has either abolished or blurred the separation between a leisure and a laboring class. All human beings are citizens with suffrage and, with exceptions that are rapidly becoming anomalous, all are also both workers and persons with sufficient free time at their disposal to be engaged in the pursuits of leisure (over and above the time that is devoted to recreations and amusements). The division between labor and leisure is no longer a division of society into distinct classes; it is now a division of the time of citizens into distinct activities—the activities of labor, on the one hand, and the activities of leisure as well as play (which is quite distinct from leisure), on the other.

With the shortening of the work week, the increase in the time available for leisure pursuits has made the continuation of learning in adult life possible for all workers; and since basic schooling by itself, even at its best, could not possibly suffice either for their proper functioning as citizens or for their personal fulfillment as human beings, continued learning in adult life would seem to be necessary for all, if our educational aim is to produce an educated people. Furthermore, with the lengthening of the period of compulsory basic schooling for all, there is less and less need for adults to go back to school to make up for insufficient schooling in childhood; adult education can become the kind of education which continues and sustains learning after sufficient schooling has been completed.

The great increase in the number of students in school and in the number of adults who can and should be helped to go on with learning places an enormous burden on society with respect to the housing and expenses of education and the preparation and support of school teachers and of leaders in adult education.

The number of learned professions, or of vocations requiring specialized schooling beyond basic schooling, has increased with the intensified division of labor in an industrial society, with the demands of its technology, and with the social ambitions of occupational groups. The advancement of learning in a culture dominated by science and technology calls for more and more intense specialization in both study and research; and this has not only affected the organization of our higher institutions of learning, but has also tended to influence the content of the curriculum in the years of basic schooling.

5

To state the central critical choice that a society such as ours faces, it is necessary to make certain underlying assumptions explicit. They all rest on the proposition declared self-evident in the Declaration of Independence; namely, that all men are by nature equal (if human equality is to be self-evident, "by nature" must be substituted for "created"). The equality affirmed is the equality of all persons belonging to the same species, having the same specific human nature and the species-specific properties and powers appertaining thereto. Such equality of all human beings as persons is quite compatible with all the inequalities which differentiate them as individuals—inequalities in the degree to which they possess the same specific endowments and inequalities in the degree of their attainments through the development and exercise of their native gifts. In fact, the only respect in which all human beings are by nature equal is the respect in which they are all persons, all human, all members of the same species. In all other respects, they tend to be unequal as individuals

Against this, consider the ancient doctrine that some men are by nature free and some are by nature slaves—some destined from birth to the free life of a citizen engaged in self-government and in the pursuit of human happiness, and some destined by their meager native endowments to be subjected to rule by others and to serve by their labor the pursuit of happiness by others. While it may be true that this doctrine is no longer espoused by anyone in the harsh form which would justify the ownership and use of human beings as chattel, it is far from clear that a softened form of the doctrine has no exponents in modern times or in contemporary society. Until the twentieth century, there were many who held the view that only some human beings were fortunately endowed with native capacities that made them genuinely educable. It would be folly to try to educate the rest; suffice it, in their case, to train them for the tasks they would have to perform, tasks that did not include the duties of enfranchised citizenship or the pursuits of leisure. Even in the present century, there have been some distinguished educators who have held similar views.

For example, less than forty years ago, President Darden of the University of Virginia recommended that compulsory education beyond grammar school should be abandoned. He urged a return to Jefferson's dictum that we are obliged to teach every child only to read and write. After that, Darden said, "it is our obligation, as Jefferson visualized it, to provide a really fine education beyond reading and writing for the students who show talent and interest." Albert Jay Nock went further in urging a return to the aristocratic notions of the past. "The philosophical doctrine of equality," he wrote,

gives no more ground for the assumption that all men are educable than it does for the assumption that all men are six feet tall. We see at once that it is not the philosophical doctrine of equality, but an utterly untenable popular perversion of it, that we find at the basis of our educational system.

Nock accepts the philosophical doctrine of equality only to the extent that it calls for the abolition of chattel slavery. He does not think that the doctrine calls for universal suffrage or for equality of educational opportunity. While he endorses a minimum of compulsory schooling for all, he thinks that it should be directed toward training "to the best advantage a vast number of ineducable persons." To require the public school to provide, over and above their function as training schools, forms of education that are appropriate only for the gifted few is to impose upon them an obligation that they cannot possibly discharge.

In stating what I regard as the central critical choice confronting us today in the field of education, I am proceeding on an assumption diametrically opposed to that implicit in Nock's theory of education. I call it an assumption only because, within the confines of this essay, I cannot fully present the reasons that would show it to be true, and so something that must be postulated without argument. From the self-evident truth that all human beings are by nature equal (or from the truth of what Nock calls "the philosophical doctrine of equality"), I think it can be shown not only that chattel slavery cannot be justified, but also that all human beings are by nature fit to lead free lives—the lives of self-governing citizens with suffrage and lives enriched by engagement in the pursuits of leisure, preeminent among which is learning in all its many forms. If that can be shown, it must follow that all human beings are educable, though in different degrees proportionate to differences in their native endowments. Without spelling out in detail the reasoning involved, suffice it to say that we live in a society which has assumed that these things are true—that all human beings have the right to be politically free, to be citizens with suffrage, to have enough free time and other economic goods to be able to engage in the pursuits of leisure; and assuming these things to be true, our society has committed itself to two consequent propositions—that all human beings are educable and that all should be given, through public institutions, equal opportunity to become educated.

On these assumptions, the central critical choice we face can be stated as a decision between the following alternatives: on the one hand, (a) differentiated basic schooling, such as now exists in this country; on the other hand, (b) undifferentiated basic schooling which would require a radical reform of the present system. Each of these alternatives needs a word of further explanation in order to make the issue clear.

Differentiated basic schooling. By basic schooling is meant the whole sequence of years in which schooling is compulsory—either ten or twelve years from the first grade through the tenth or twelfth. Beyond that, if the young do not elect to leave school, they can voluntarily go on to further schooling, either to senior high school or to two or four-year colleges. For reasons that I will give later, let me proceed as if basic schooling extended over a period of twelve years and was divided into two levels—primary (the first six grades) and secondary (junior and senior high school)—each taking six years. Now, such basic schooling is *differentiated* when its aim and curriculum are the *same only at the primary level*, and when, beyond that, at the secondary level, students are shunted into different courses of study which are motivated by quite different educational aims, such as vocational training, on the one hand, and what is called "college preparatory training," on the other. The situation is not greatly altered if the differentiation occurs after eight years of elementary school and the children pass on to quite different kinds of high school.

Undifferentiated basic schooling. On this alternative, it is requisite that the period of basic schooling cover at least twelve years, six years of primary or elementary and six years of secondary schooling. Such schooling is *undifferentiated* when its aim and curriculum are the *same for the whole period of compulsory attendance at school*—at the secondary as well as the primary level. The curriculum may include the study of vocations or occupations, but not, as John Dewey pointed out, for the sake of training the young for jobs, which is the training of slaves, but rather as one aspect of their introduction to the world in which they will live. Furthermore, while the curriculum is such that it would prepare for further schooling, in college or university, that is not its essential aim, because all thus schooled will not necessarily go on to higher institutions of learning. Rather the aim of undifferentiated basic schooling is to make the young competent as learners and to prepare as well as inspire them to engage in further learning whether that takes place in higher institutions of learning or in the course of noninstitutionalized study through a variety of facilities or means.

Exponents of both alternatives subscribe to the proposition that all should be given equal educational opportunity, but they interpret this proposition differently. Exponents of differentiated basic schooling think that such equality of opportunity is provided if all the children attend school for the same period of years, even though during some portion of that time the schooling they receive is different in content and motivated by different aims. Exponents of undifferentiated basic schooling think that equality of educational opportunity is provided only if the quality as well as the quantity of basic schooling is the same for all; and they mean by this that the curriculum and method of basic schooling as a whole should be directed toward the same goal for all—their preparation for a life of learning and for responsible participation in public affairs.

There is one other fundamental difference in the views of those who defend differentiated basic schooling as it exists today and those who advocate the reform of present institutions and practices to make basic schooling undifferentiated. The former hold to the ideal of the educated man conceived in terms which makes it unrealistic for all human beings to aspire to some measure of fulfillment of that ideal. The latter so conceive the ideal that it is within the reach of all, with the qualification, of course, that its attainment will vary, from person to person, in a manner proportionate to their initial differences in endowment and their subsequent use of their abilities. It is this difference which leads the exponents of differentiated basic schooling to reject undifferentiated basic schooling as unrealistic: a realistic appraisal of the human potentiality for education, they maintain, supports the conclusion that one portion of the population, the larger portion, perhaps, should be treated differently at the secondary level, because they are not truly educable in the same way and toward the same end as the other and smaller portion. If we call them the realists, and their opponents the idealists, we must also acknowledge that both are, in their different ways, democratic rather than aristocratic in their views of public education, for both adhere to the tenet of equal educational opportunity and both regard that as an inescapable corollary of the truth that all men are by nature equal and endowed with the same inherently human powers and rights.

If it is within the purview of this essay to go beyond a statement of the alternatives and to argue that the decision should be made in one direction rather than the other, I would like to spend a moment more saying why I favor undifferentiated basic schooling. The rudimentary literacy and numeracy, which is a large part of what can be achieved in the primary grades, is certainly not adequate as preparation either for discharging the duties of responsible citizenship or for engagement in the pursuits of leisure. Six more years of schooling at the secondary level should be devoted to those ends—for all, not just for some, since all will be admitted to citizenship with suffrage and all will have ample free time for further learning and other pursuits of leisure. The realistic democrat is inconsistent in thinking, on the one hand, that all normal children have enough innate intelligence to justify their right to suffrage and free time, and enough intelligence to exercise these rights for their own and for the public good, but also thinking, on the other hand, that all do not have enough intelligence to receive the same educational treatment at the secondary level. At this level, some, probably a majority, must be separated from the minority among their fellows who are educable in a different way and with a different purpose in view.

Having gone this far, it is also incumbent upon me as an idealistic democrat, to answer the objection that the realists raise against the alternative that I favor. It has two prongs. One is the point that the wide range of individual differences in educational aptitude calls for differentiation in educational treatment when we pass beyond the primary level of instruction. Great inequalities in intelligence and other native endowments must be acknowledged; but to acknowledge them does not require us to adopt different aims in the schooling of the less gifted and in the schooling of the more gifted. A pint receptable and a quart or gallon receptacle cannot hold the same quantity of liquid; but, while differing in the size of their capacity, they can all be filled to the brim; and if, furthermore, the very nature of their capacity craves the same kind of filling, then they are treated equally only when each is filled to the brim and each is filled with the same kind of substance, not the smaller receptacles with dirty water or skimmed milk and the larger receptacles with whole milk or rich cream.

The other prong of the objection is that, while we have for many centuries known how to help the large receptacles imbibe whole milk or cream, we have *not yet* been able to discover ways of helping the smaller receptacles get their proportionate share of the same substance. The operative words here are "not yet," and the answer to the objection is that we have not yet given sufficient time, energy, and creative ingenuity to inventing the means for doing what has never been done before. If whole milk or rich cream is too thick and viscous a substance easily to enter the narrow apertures at the top of the smaller receptacles, then we must invent the funnels needed for the infusion. Until a sustained and massive effort is made to discover the devices and methods that must be employed to give all children the same kind of treatment in school, motivated by the same aim and arising from a conviction that they are all educable in the same way, though not to the same degree, it is presumptuously dogmatic to assert that it cannot be done. All that can be said, in truth, is that it has not yet been done.

In the light of evidence recently amassed, it may be further objected than an attempt to carry out the mandate of equal educational opportunity by undifferentiated schooling is doomed to defeat by differences in the children's economic, social, and ethnic backgrounds and especially differences in the homes from which they come—differences which affect their educability and which cannot be overcome by the invention of new educational devices and methods as, perhaps, their differences in innate endowment can be. Does this require us to abandon the effort to carry out the educational mandate of a democratic society, or does it require a democratic society to undertake economic and social as well as educational reforms to facilitate carrying out that mandate?

6

I have dismissed without discussion an issue that is antecedent to the choice between differentiated and undifferentiated compulsory schooling. The question whether compulsory schooling should be abolished or maintained has been much agitated of late, but I do not think it presents us with a genuine option. In a recent essay on the subject, "The Great Anti-School Campaign," Robert M. Hutchins reviewed the various attacks on compulsory education and the proposed substitutes for it, and he argued persuasively to the conclusion that what is needed is not a substitute for the system of compulsory schooling but rather radical improvements in the organization, aims, and methods of the schools that constitute the system.

However, I would like to deal briefly in these concluding pages with another set of alternatives which, in my judgment, do present us with a genuine option and a critical choice that I think we shall have to make in the years immediately ahead. The choice is between (a) retaining the present organization of our system of educational institutions and (b) substituting for it a quite different scheme of organization. Let me make this choice clear by describing the alternatives.

The present organization. It consists of twelve years of schooling beginning at age six and normally ending at age eighteen, and usually divided, as we have seen, either into eight years of elementary school and four years of high school or into six years of primary school, three of junior high school and three of senior high school. The period during which school attendance is compulsory may, under certain circumstances and in certain states, be less than twelve years; but, in any case, schooling at the public expense is open to all during this period. Beyond secondary or high school, the system includes two-year municipal or junior colleges, four-year colleges, and universities; and many of these institutions, especially the municipal or junior colleges, provide further schooling at the public expense, and beyond that, attendance at state colleges and universities involves the payment of only nominal fees. On the principle of "open admissions" which has become widespread in recent years, nothing more than a certificate of graduation from high school is required for admission to our so-called institutions of higher learning. Schooling at the public expense has thus been extended from twelve years to sixteen, and even more if graduate instruction at the university is involved; it is, moreover, open to all, though it is not compulsory but voluntary at whatever age the law allows the young to leave school without being truants.

The proposed reorganization. In place of the existing sequence of three or four levels of continuous schooling at the public expense, it is proposed that the system be divided into two main parts, quite different in their aims and character and not continuous in sequence.

The first part would be twelve years of basic schooling, beginning at age four rather than age six in order to terminate at age sixteen instead of age eighteen. This would be compulsory for all. It might, for convenience, be subdivided into a primary and secondary level, but this would have little educational significance if this whole period involved *undifferentiated schooling* for all. Since the aim of such basic schooling would be to inculcate the arts of learning and to introduce the young to the world of learning—to make them competent learners, in short, rather to try to make them genuinely learned (which is impossible for the young)—it would be appropriate to award the bachelor of arts degree at the completion of such basic schooling. Doing so would return that degree to its original educational significance as certifying competence in the liberal arts, which are the arts or skills of learning in all fields of subject matter. Basic schooling, thus conceived, might be terminal schooling for some and preparatory schooling for others—terminal schooling for those who would engage in self-education in adult life without further formal attendance at higher institutions of learning for the purpose of getting advanced degrees; preparatory schooling for others who would attend higher institutions and seek advanced degrees. In one sense, basic schooling would be preparatory schooling for all, in that it would prepare all for continued learning in later years whether that occurred in educational institutions or by other means and facilities.

The second part of the system proposed would consist of what I shall call *advanced* schooling in contrast to *basic* schooling; it would be voluntary rather than compulsory schooling. Though attendance at higher institutions of learning would be at the public expense or involve only nominal fees, it would not be open to all who had completed their basic schooling, but only to those who qualified by criteria of aptitude, competence, and inclination. Advanced schooling would include both further general education and also specialized training in all the learned professions and in all vocations requiring technical proficiency, as well as specialized training for the profession of learning itself—all the forms of scholarship and research involved in the advancement of learning. Certain aspects of what is now collegiate education would be integrated with the final two years of basic schooling, and certain aspects of it would be reserved for the first two years of advanced schooling; but, in either case, the curricular elements would be retained only in so far as they constitute general not specialized education. Differentiated and specialized education, of whatever sort, would begin only after undifferentiated and general education had been completed.

The proposed reorganization of the educational system involves one further innovation which, in my judgment, is an essential ingredient of the plan. It consists in the introduction of a scholastic hiatus, either for two years or four, between the completion of basic schooling and the beginning of advanced schooling in institutions of higher learning. With graduation from high school at age sixteen, and with nonattendance at school made compulsory with few if any exceptions, advanced schooling would begin for those tested and qualified at age eighteen or twenty. For those going on to institutions of higher learning, the period of the enforced hiatus would be spent in remunerated work either in the private or public sector of the economy.

The hiatus is designed to serve a threefold purpose: (1) to interrupt the continuity of schooling and save the young from the scholastic ennui that results from too many successive years of sitting in classrooms and doing their lessons; (2) to counteract the delayed maturity induced by too many years of continuous schooling and thus to remedy some of the disorders of adolescence; and (3) to populate our institutions of higher learning with students who have gained a certain degree of maturity through the experiences afforded them by nonscholastic employments, as well as with students who return to educational institutions for further schooling because they have a genuine desire for further formal study and an aptitude for it, instead of students who occupy space in our higher institutions as the result of social pressures or because to continue on with more schooling is following the path of least resistance.

In the course of describing these alternatives, I have made no attempt to conceal my partisanship in favor of the proposed reorganization. The reasons why I favor it should also be sufficiently apparent not to need further comment. However, I might add two observations.

One is that to initiate schooling at age four rather than age six would take advantage of the child's lively capacity for instruction in these years. This is confirmed by everything we have recently discovered from researches in early learning. Two years that might otherwise be wasted would be put to good use; and, in addition, starting at age four rather than age six would bring basic schooling to an end at age sixteen rather than age eighteen. If it were at all possible, it might even be better, for the cure of adolescence and the achievement of earlier maturity, to terminate basic schooling at age fourteen or fifteen.

My second comment concerns the ideal of the educated man under the circumstances of contemporary life—in our kind of society and our kind of culture. As an idealistic democrat, I have tried to reconceive that ideal in a way which makes it attainable in some degree by all human beings, not just the exceptional few for whom the ideal, as traditionally formulated, was exclusively realizable. If our kind of society and culture is dedicated to the education of a whole people, not just the development of a small class of educated persons, then the notion of *the educated person* must hold out a goal toward which every human being can strive and which, given facilitating circumstances, he can achieve in some measure. This makes sense if we define *being educated* not in terms of the traditional intellectual virtues or in terms of certain high attainments with respect to the arts and sciences, but rather in terms of having competence as a learner and using that competence to continue learning throughout a lifetime and to engage in other of the creative pursuits of leisure. Every human being, from those with the humblest endowments up to the most gifted among us, can become an educated person in this sense.

Since the purpose of schooling is not to produce educated men and women but rather to facilitate their becoming educated in the course of a lifetime, it serves that purpose well only if basic schooling for all tries to make the young learners rather than learned and tries to make them avid for learning rather than turn them away from it; only if advanced schooling for some initiates them in the process of becoming learned, both in general and in specialized fields; and only if other facilities for becoming learned, whether in educational institutions or by other means, are provided by society for all, those who have had advanced schooling as well as those who have had only basic schooling. A choice in favor of undifferentiated basic schooling and in favor of the proposed reorganization of our educational institutions would, I submit, help us to school a whole people in a manner that would facilitate their becoming an educated people as a whole.

10

Liberal Schooling
in the Twentieth Century

(1962)

In "Liberal Schooling in the Twentieth Century," Adler deals with
the substance of a liberal education. Having demonstrated the necessity
of making general, liberal education available to all and of making it
have the same quality for all, he turns his attention here to the content
of a liberal education. Here, however, he comes directly into conflict with
prevailing opinion. He argues that the liberal arts are the skills of learning
and as such their acquisition is a necessity and not a luxury. They are
the preparation for all further learning. Without them education cannot
prosper, and neither can a free and responsible people. They are in fact
indispensable. There is no room for compromise in his argument for a
liberal arts curriculum. Never published before, this article is taken from
a lecture that was part of a series on Modern Education and Human
Values sponsored by the Pitcairn-Crabbe Foundation in November 1962.

G . V . D .

THE PROBLEMS of education are many and various. They include such things as the proper organization of a university, the
nature and aims of professional or vocational training, the preschool training of the child, the continued learning of adults after they
have completed school, the preparation of teachers, not to mention all
the political and economic problems which have to do with the support
and regulation of educational institutions by public or private agencies.

I shall not deal with any of these but shall limit myself to the consideration of liberal schooling, especially at the college level. What, ideally, should a liberal arts college try to do? What should be its educational objectives, and the means or methods of achieving them? Or, to put the same questions in a slightly different form, what should the bachelor of arts degree signify—what sort of intellectual competence, what kind of learning, should it certify?

Putting the question in this last way enables me to say immediately that the worst mistake we can possibly make—yet one that is nevertheless generally made—is to suppose that the bachelor of arts degree, honestly earned, signifies that its possessor is an educated man or woman. Nothing could be further from the truth, even if we allow ourselves to imagine the best possible student who has spent four years most conscientiously and industriously at a college which was as perfect in faculty and curriculum as any college could be. The reason is simply that youth itself—immaturity of mind, character, and experience—is the insuperable obstacle to becoming educated. We cannot educate the young; the best we can do for them is to school them in such a way that they have a good chance to become educated in the course of their adult life.

The discussion is, therefore, not about liberal education as a whole, which involves much more than can ever be accomplished in school. It is narrowly concerned with liberal schooling—with what can be done in high school and college to help a person become liberally educated later on. And it is concerned with that problem under the conditions of life and learning in the twentieth century. Perhaps I should be even more specific and say: conditions of life and learning today in a technologically advanced industrial democracy such as the United States.

An industrial democracy, of the kind we now have in America, is a brand new kind of society. It is, perhaps, the first affluent society which has ever existed on earth. From the point of view of the circumstances and opportunities of terrestrial existence, it represents far and away the most radical transformation of human life that has happened in the West. Hence it would not be unreasonable to expect that our educational institutions should also undergo a transformation to meet these altered conditions. Nevertheless, it is my judgment, which I shall try to defend, that in essence the objectives of liberal schooling must remain precisely what they were in earlier ages under quite different conditions. Whatever was the best schooling for the few should now become the schooling for all.

It may be objected, however, that I have not considered the radically altered conditions of learning which now prevail. Industrial democracy may not necessitate an essential change in the objectives of liberal schooling, but only require us to make it as universal as democratic suffrage and the opportunities for leisure. But other changes in our culture, which directly affect the content and processes of learning, may call for a change in the very substance of what should be accomplished in the course of liberal schooling.

What do those who might raise this objection have in mind? They would call our attention, I think, to the fact that we live in the age of science fully matured, an age of specialized research, dominated by the centrality of the scientific method, and by the fruits and promises of technology. They would also call our attention to the fact that the number of learned professions, or of technically specialized vocations requiring specialized schooling, has multiplied many times over and is still on the increase. They would most of all stress the occurrence of what is sometimes called the "knowledge explosion," and which, if it is not really that, certainly deserves to be called the "research explosion," or at least the "publication explosion."

Whatever it should be called, it must be admitted that, in all specialized fields of inquiry, in all those areas where knowledge can be advanced or applied, rapidity of change is positively accelerated to a degree that has become alarming to both teacher and student—or anyone who is concerned with acquiring a reasonable measure of proficiency and competence in some chosen sphere of learning. Does this fact affect the objectives of liberal schooling—its content and methods? Must we not adjust or adapt the process of learning in school to the radically altered way in which learning is itself advanced through ever-increasing specialization and at an ever-increasing rate?

My answer to these questions is negative. The two theses I will try to defend are: first, that all students should be given a general liberal schooling, devoid of any specialized study, before they engage, at the university level, in the pursuit of professional or technical competence in some special field; and second, that this general liberal schooling should be the same for all, without regard to their individual differences, their future interests, or their professional inclinations.

While the altered conditions of learning in the twentieth century do not call for any change in the objectives of such general liberal schooling, they do most emphatically intensify and extend the need for it. As specialized learning becomes more and more fragmented, as the demands for greater and greater technical competence in more and more limited areas of knowledge increase, the greater is everyone's need for the skills of learning itself, which are acquired through a mastery of the liberal arts, and the greater is everyone's need for some elementary appreciation of the common humanities, the things that are not only common to all fields of learning, but also remain relatively constant across the centuries, because man himself—our common human nature—remains the same. Everything else in our cultural environment can change, and at any rate; but so long as human nature remains unchanged, the task of liberal schooling is the same in the twentieth century as it always was.

These propositions are, in our day, not popular with educators, parents, or the general public. The general practice of our educational institutions runs counter to them. They are regarded as opposed to the general trend of the times. If earning a living and getting ahead in the world are the ends of life, why waste too much time, or any at all, in the liberal arts or the humanities?

I must, therefore, make some effort to explain and defend these unpopular propositions. I must begin by reiterating the two, quite limited objectives of liberal schooling. They are, first, to give the young a measure of competence in the liberal arts, which are nothing but the skills of learning itself—the skills of reading, writing, speaking, listening, observing, calculating, and measuring. I do not mention thinking, because the ability to think, clearly and well, is implicit in all the other more specific skills of learning. In addition to competence in the skills of learning, a liberal school should give the young a preliminary and necessarily superficial acquaintance with certain general and common features of the world of learning itself. Instead of giving them a false sense of being learned, this should give them a deep awareness of how much remains for them to learn during the remainder of their lives. If a liberal college succeeds in doing these two things well—if it provides the young with both the means and the incentives to go on learning —it will have accomplished all that it should or can do for the young in order to prepare them for the life of learning in which they must engage after they leave school if they are ever to become educated men and women.

Training in the liberal arts is indispensable to making free men out of children. It prepares them for the uses of freedom—the proper employment of free time and the exercise of political power. It prepares them for leisure and for citizenship. And acquaintance with the traditions of our culture prepares them for citizenship in the republic of learning as well as for participation in the affairs of the state.

These are the only two parts of basic education which are indispensable for men as men. They are not only a necessary preparation for all further specialized schooling, but also for the pursuit of truth and the performance of one's social and political duties.

The reason for this is simply that to be human is to have the power and the need to exercise the liberal arts. There is no other part of intellectual learning that is necessarily common to all men. All men do not need to be engineers, lawyers, physicians, priests, businessmen, or scientists. But all men are obliged to conduct their affairs by rational communication with their fellowmen. All are obliged to think. These things can be done well or poorly. The only choice for a man, then, is not whether he will or will not be a liberal artist. He cannot be human without being one. His only choice is being a good or bad liberal artist, and the purpose of liberal schooling is to make him a good one.

Even at the risk of some repetition, let me quote here a statement on this point by Robert Maynard Hutchins, in a recently published book:

The liberal artist learns to read, write, speak, listen, understand, and think. He learns to reckon, measure, and manipulate matter, quantity, and motion in order to predict, produce, and exchange. As we live in the tradition, whether we know it or not, so we are all liberal artists, whether we know it or not. We all practice the liberal arts, well or badly, all the time every day. As we should understand the tradition as well as we can in order to understand ourselves, so we should be as good liberal artists as we can in order to become as fully human as we can.

The liberal arts are not merely indispensable; they are unavoidable. Nobody can decide for himself whether he is going to be a human being. The only question open to him is whether he will be an ignorant, undeveloped one, or one who has sought to reach the highest point he is capable of attaining. The question, in short, is whether he will be a poor liberal artist or a good one.

The single most impressive fact about this proposition concerning the primacy and indispensability of training in the liberal arts is the fact that it has been affirmed throughout the whole tradition of Western education. The neglect of this truth or its denial did not appear until the last century. It is only during the last hundred years that parents, teachers, and students themselves are content with shoddy substitutes for the liberal arts or are willing to dispense with training in them entirely. As Hutchins says: "The tradition of the West in education is the tradition of the liberal arts. Until very recently nobody took seriously the suggestion that there could be any other ideal."

If we contemplate this fact, or the larger fact that all of the traditional principles of education, including this one about the primacy of training in the liberal arts, have been seriously controverted only in the last hundred years, we may be able to gain some insight into the educational controversies of our own day; and with it, some understanding of the prevalent tendency to substitute vocational training or specialized learning for general liberal training at the level of basic schooling, which should come to its completion with the awarding of the bachelor's degree.

Let us suppose that a college were to be guided solely by traditional principles in its effort to provide basic liberal schooling for the young. What steps would it have to take to achieve the appointed goals? How should it be organized? What should its program of studies be like? What should be the character and competence of its teachers? There is probably no single set of positive answers to these questions which would elicit the agreement of all educators. There are undoubtedly many different and equally effective ways of providing the young with training in the liberal arts and acquainting them with the traditions of our culture and the broad outlines of the world of learning. I am reluctant, therefore, to propose, in positive terms, anything that would pretend to be the one right or ideal curriculum for a liberal arts college. But I do have the temerity to lay down a series of negative injunctions, proscribing the things which a college must not do if it is sincerely devoted to the ends which basic liberal schooling should achieve. Let me state them for you.

First, a liberal arts college should not allow any form of special training for specific jobs, vocations, or even learned professions to intrude itself into the curriculum. This is not to say that liberal schooling has no relation to earning a living. The point is rather that the method and content of liberal schooling should be the same without regard to how the young to whom it is given have to earn a living after graduation. Liberal schooling will, in fact, prepare them to earn a living in the one way that it should. A person well trained in the liberal arts is able to learn anything more readily than a person not so trained. Hence he is better prepared for whatever specialized learning may be a necessary condition of earning a living, whether that further learning takes place on the job or in the course of further schooling.

Second, a liberal arts college should not provide any elective courses in its curriculum, nor should it afford any opportunities for specialization in particular subject matters. Whatever subject matters are chosen for study, they should be chosen because they are the materials best suited for disciplining the young in the liberal skills, and not because it is supposed that the young should master these subject matters and become learned in them. The liberal arts are the same for all men, and so is the need of all men to be trained in these arts. All the facts about individual differences in talent, interest, inclination, or future occupation are irrelevant to the purposes of liberal schooling. Just as at the earliest stage of education, there is no question that every infant should be taught to walk and talk, so at the college stage of education, there is no question that every boy and girl should be taught to talk well, read well, write well, listen well, and, of course, think well.

Third, the faculty of a liberal arts college should not be divided into departmental groups, each representing special competence in some particular subject matter, and narrow interest in some limited field of learning. This does not mean that the members of a college faculty must eschew all special scholarly interests, or that they should be chosen for their general incompetence and lack of all scholarly attainments. It means only that as college teachers, engaged in administering a program of liberal schooling, they should be willing to submit themselves to the whole course of study which the college is prescribing for its students. Only in this way can they themselves develop the general competence which they should possess as teachers of the liberal arts. Furthermore, as college teachers they should not be expected to carry on specialized research. They should win the honors and emoluments appropriate to their careers by their excellence as teachers, not by their contributions to the advancement of knowledge. Their achievement of a high degree of excellence as teachers will, of course, depend on their deepening and broadening their own general and liberal education, which the college should encourage by forming study groups for its teachers and by allowing them sufficient periods of time free from the burdens of teaching, just as a university allows its professors free time for research.

Fourth, no textbooks should be used in a liberal arts college; there should be no lectures in courses; and formal lectures should be kept to the minimum and should, wherever possible, be of such generality that they can be given to the whole student body. Each of these related negatives rests on the same fundamental reason. Since liberal schooling is concerned with the discipline of the intellect, not the short-term cultivation of the verbal memory, the materials and methods of teaching should avoid anything that permits students to memorize formulary answers just long enough to hand them back on examination papers. Textbooks are largely devices for enabling students to memorize answers without learning to read or think in the process. Lectures in course are often, too often, nothing more than oral recitations of, or commentaries on, textbook materials. Neither textbooks nor lectures in courses require much activity on the part of the student's mind as opposed to his memory. To elicit intellectual activity on the part of the student, whatever the student is asked to read should be sufficiently over his head to require a genuine effort at understanding; and instead of lecturing hour after hour, the liberal arts teacher should teach mainly by asking, not by telling, and in classes that are small enough for the purposes of effective discussion. An occasional formal lecture out of course may supplement the Socratic method of teaching, which should be the model emulated by all teachers in a liberal arts college.

Fifth, written examinations, especially of the objective or true-false type, should be eliminated in favor of oral examinations. The reason for this is closely related to what has just been said about memory and mind. Only an oral examination can succeed in separating the facile verbalizers and memorizers from those in whom genuine intellectual skills are beginning to develop and whose minds have become hospitable to ideas. Written examinations, even term papers or senior essays, are inadequate for this purpose. Where serious written work is undertaken by the students, it should not only be examined for its excellence in writing, but it should also be made the basis for examining the student orally to see if he can defend his thesis with some depth of understanding that goes below the surface of his written document.

These five negative recommendations, if adopted, would still allow for a variety of different positive programs, differently organized and differently administered. The negatives, if enforced, merely create the right sort of vacuum, so that whatever positive content then rushes in to fill the void has some chance of being right. If all these negative injunctions were to be accepted by a faculty which understood that the basic objectives of liberal schooling were the liberal skills and a broad acquaintance with the humanities, I would be confident that any curriculum which they devised would make bachelors, that is, initiates in the liberal arts of those upon whom the college conferred that ancient and honorable degree.

Perhaps I ought to add a word of explanation about my use of that much abused term "humanities." When I say that the course of study in a liberal arts college should be exclusively humanistic, I do not mean to exclude the study of mathematics or of the natural sciences. When these subjects are approached in a certain way, they are as much a part of the humanities as are philosophy, history, and the social sciences, or the fine arts of poetry, music, painting, and sculpture.

The mark or measure of the humanistic approach to any subject matter or field of learning is the awareness that there is a permanent aspect to any subject matter, even those in which the most rapid cumulative advances take place. What is permanent in any field of study are those constant features of it which derive from the constancy of human nature itself. Another way of saying this, perhaps, is to say that the humanistic approach to any subject matter is philosophical, in the sense that it looks for the universal and abiding principles, the fundamental ideas and insights, the controlling canons of procedure or method, all of which are determined by the faculties of man as inquirer or learner.

In addition, I would like to say that when the approach to any subject matter is humanistic in the sense just indicated, the study of it will serve to cultivate the liberal skills rather than lead to a learned mastery of the subject itself. This holds true even of the great books, which certainly cannot be mastered by college students. With the exception of a few great books in mathematics, astronomy, and physics, the great books do not yield their secrets to the young. Why, then, give them to the young to read and discuss? The answer which Stringfellow Barr once gave to this question goes right to the heart of the matter. He said that the great books in the hands of a college student were like a large bone being gnawed at vigorously by a very young puppy. The puppy might not succeed in getting very much nourishment from the bone, but it certainly gives him plenty of exercise.

That is precisely the point—about the great books or any other subject matter, humanistically treated, in a liberal arts college. The materials being studied are not there for the nourishment which they provide, but for the exercise which they afford—exercise in the liberal arts in order to develop the skills of learning. If, as a by-product, any nourishment is derived, it will tend to be of the sort that is proper at this stage of education; namely, a general and superficial acquaintance with the permanent features of the world of learning itself.

There is one more question to which I would like to address myself in closing. Since I have so severely limited the objectives of basic liberal schooling to the acquirement of proficiency in the liberal arts and to some appreciation of what I have called the humanities, it may be asked whether college is the appropriate institution for a course of study thus delimited. Is not high school the proper place for training the young in the arts of reading and writing, speaking and listening, and for giving them an initial appreciation of the humanities? Or if high school will not suffice, should we not at least try to limit basic liberal schooling to the first two years of college, leaving the upper years for specialized programs of study, elected according to the differing interests of particular students?

These are reasonable questions, and they deserve reasonable answers. Before I try to answer them, let me remind you of two facts.

On the one hand, we must face the fact that the graduates of our high schools, as they are currently operated, do not enter college with sufficient training in the liberal arts or a sufficient appreciation of the humanities. They are neither well-read nor are they able to read well. Their proficiency in writing, speaking, and listening is as poor, if not poorer. Their general intellectual orientation, if they have any at all, is likely to be fuzzy and foggy. They are hardly disciplined initiates into the world of learning, equipped with the skills of learning to a degree which warrants their pursuing specialized studies at the college level. And if a college does nothing at all to remedy their obvious deficiencies in the liberal arts, it makes a travesty out of the Bachelor of Arts degree which it will confer on some of them four years later.

On the other hand, we must also face the fact that the leading professional schools—in law, medicine, and engineering—have long complained that they must take the graduates of our colleges and teach them how to read and write before they can teach them law, medicine, or engineering. Some years ago when I was on the faculty of the Law School of the University of Chicago, a substantial portion of the law student's first year had to be devoted to tutoring in the basic skills of reading and writing. I suspect that the situation has not changed for the better. The Bachelor of Arts degree, which should certify that a young man or woman has the liberal skills prerequisite to specialized study, no longer certifies anything of the sort; and the professional schools have come to realize with dismay that they cannot rely on it. If what should be done in high schools is not done there, and if what should be done in college is not done there, then finally it must be done where, certainly, it is most inappropriate—at the level of professional or graduate study. This means that it will be done only for a few.

If I had any hope that, in the foreseeable future, the educational system of this country could be so radically transformed that basic liberal training would be adequately accomplished in the secondary schools and that the Bachelor of Arts degree would then be awarded at the termination of such schooling, I would gladly recommend that the college be relieved of any further responsibility for training in the liberal arts. It could become, what it has of late been so desperately trying to be, the antechamber of the graduate schools—the beginning of specialized study.

I am at present without such hope. I also think that the graduate and professional schools should be relieved of a responsibility that is certainly not theirs, except by the default of all prior schooling. The colleges of the country must, therefore, provide the remedy for the deficiency of our high schools. If they are reluctant to devote all four years to training in the liberal arts, then at least the first two years of college should be given over to what Hutchins has recently called the six Rs—remedial reading, remedial writing, and remedial 'rithmetic.

This may appear to be a desperate measure, but that is what the present deplorable situation seems to require. The college represents the last chance to do what should be done for our future citizens and our future men of leisure, as well as for our future specialists, technicians, and scholars. The college is, in a sense, the point of no return. The deficiencies of schooling which are not remedied there may become, for many students, permanently irremediable. And that would be a disaster—a measureless personal as well as social disaster—which we should do everything in our power to avoid.

11

What Is Basic
About English?

(1941)

In this essay Adler uncovers a fact that at first may seem surprising. No longer reigning supreme, an outcast of American schooling, liberal education has put itself into the protective custody of teachers of English and taken shelter in the English departments. There it cowers, a shade of its former self, threatened by advancing scientific scholarship and declining public interest.

Adler explains why liberal education has declined and how English departments have aided its demise. Adler recommends what he calls "academic suicide"—that the teaching of English should be "abolished in favor of the restoration of a truly liberal curriculum." "What Is Basic About English?" was read at a general session of the National Council of Teachers of English, November 1940, and was first published in College English *(April 1941).*

G.V.D.

I HOPE all teachers of English know, as well as I do, how complete and dismal is the failure of liberal education in this country—at both high school and college level. I am sure that all weep, as much as I do, about the fact that few, if any, of their students can read better than sixth-grade children, or write well, or speak well, or listen well. They certainly do not know how to read a book, either for comprehension or for appreciation, either to receive instruction or to delight in beauty.

Instead of dwelling on these well-known and lamentable facts, instead of repeating the therapy I have prescribed in *How to Read a Book*, I am going to try to explain why liberal education has fallen to such low estate, how it has happened, and what can be done about it. And central to my explanation is the peculiar status of the teacher of English. The history of the teaching of English reveals, I think, the gradual decay of the liberal arts and the progressive degradation of the curriculum to its present state.

On the other hand, the teacher of English is the most indispensable man on any faculty, for he is the only one left who is at all concerned with the liberal arts as the disciplines which train a mind for the most characteristic function of human life—communication. With the progressive decomposition of the curriculum under the shattering impact of the elective system and the insidious encroachment of the sciences, especially the social sciences, upon the field of humane letters, the English teacher has become the last defender of the faith that something can be learned from books. I mean books—not textbooks; I mean great literature—not current journalism about current events.

On the other hand, and paradoxical though it seems, the very reasons which make the English teacher the indispensable man are the reasons why English departments and English courses should be completely abolished as such. It is precisely because the English teacher is the last—and often a very frail—vestige of the liberal tradition in our education, it is precisely because he still cherishes literature and the liberal arts—though his devotion (under dire threats) is often secret and unconfessed—that the English teacher should commit academic suicide.

I am not recommending suicide as an empty gesture or as an expression of despair. I am thinking of a militant martyrdom. My simple thesis is that English—its courses, teachers, and departments—should be abolished in favor of the restoration of a truly liberal curriculum in secondary and collegiate education. The English teacher should cease to be a separate academic entity, only on the condition, of course, that every other teacher would become a teacher of English, or, to say more precisely what I mean, a teacher of liberal arts; for my main point is that what the English teacher is now trying to do, often half-heartedly, often unwittingly, and almost always inadequately, should be done by the whole faculty in a curriculum which is not atomized into courses or made chaotic by departmental prerogatives. Only if it is thus done can what the English teacher is trying to do be well done.

Perhaps I have now explained my title, the question, *What Is Basic About English?* In asking this question I am not thinking about the tragic possibility that English may be the only language left in which civilized men can think and talk freely, even though that fact by itself would make it terribly basic. Nor am I thinking of the semantic invention known as basic English.

What I have in mind is simply this: that if one asks what functions the teaching of English performs in contemporary education the answer will show that these functions are so basic educationally that they cannot be performed well in a single course or series of courses which the natural and social sciences still permit to exist in an innocuous corner of the curriculum.

I shall, in short, try to argue that what is basic about English is not the English language, but language and all its arts; not English literature, but literature in all its forms and all its books. I shall try to persuade you that every English teacher who is not a traitor to the tradition he has inherited should become a fighting exponent of the curriculum which is now widely known as the St. John's curriculum—the curriculum which devotes all its teachers' and students' energies to the liberal arts and the great books. And, let me add at once, there are no teachers of English at St. John's, as there are no teachers of philosophy, or science, or history, because every teacher at St. John's is doing what the best teachers of English try to do and fail in doing simply because it cannot be done as an isolated and restricted part of a curriculum. It can be done only when the whole curriculum is devoted to liberal pursuits and humane letters and every teacher is a master of the arts, toward bachelorhood in which he is trying to help his students.

To say what is basic about English and to support my appeal that teachers of English abolish themselves and become undepartmentalized liberal artists, I shall now proceed to show, if I can: first, how the liberal arts have suffered from having ceased to be the whole of liberal education and having become mainly the preoccupation of English teachers, their concern and almost no one else's; second, how the study of literature —and here I mean the reading of great books—has become a special privilege instead of a general vocation, as the result of its being left almost entirely to English teachers, for in their hands literature has been reduced to belles lettres, or, worse, to lyric poetry, or to poetry written in English.

Throughout all this please remember that though I come to bury Caesar, I have also come to praise him. Although I ask teachers of English to immolate themselves for their faults and their inadequacies, I also speak a panegyric for the valiant effort they have made to keep the light of genuinely liberal learning shining, however dimly, somewhere behind the bushel basket of the elective system.

First: the liberal arts are three and one—an educational trinity which must function as a unity and should not be dismembered. By the three liberal arts I mean the arts of grammar, logic, and rhetoric. (For the sake of brevity, I am omitting the consideration of that specialized version of these arts which belongs to the quadrivium—the liberal arts of mathematics—the grammar, logic, and rhetoric of mathematics, as a special universe of discourse.)

When the arts are thus named, the English teacher may suppose they do not all belong to him; for does not logic belong to philosophy, and is not rhetoric the province of that specialized fellow, the teacher of elocution or public speaking? But suppose I were to name the arts, not in terms of their analytical principles or in terms of their fundamental rules of operation, but rather in terms of the operations they regulate according to sound principle. What would these operations be? They would be writing and speaking—the initiation of communication; and reading and listening—the reception of communication. And, of course, I do not mean the arts of writing or reading poetry, or the arts of speaking or listening to political propaganda. I mean the arts of writing and reading anything, the arts of speaking about or listening to discourse on any subject matter.

Thus named, all these operations fall within the province of the teachers of English who, as they usually deal with them, unfortunately restrict them to certain very limited subject matters. To the extent that teachers of English are concerned with these four operations, they are concerned with the three arts; and in so far as they are properly concerned with these operations, and with their arts, they should transcend every limitation of subject matter, for they should be concerned with every type and every phase of communication.

But you may object that I have omitted the most important operation and the most essential of the liberal arts, namely, the art of thinking.

Let me reply at once that all human thinking is of two sorts: the sort which is involved in discovery—learning without the aid of teachers; and the sort which is involved in instruction—learning with the aid of teachers, who already know what the student must learn.

Although in the history of the race and its cultural growth learning by discovery must take precedence over learning by instruction, in the biography of any individual, learning by instruction is foremost. There is no point in any individual starting out to discover anything until he is well versed in what other men have already discovered and are prepared to teach.

The book which more than any other has misled millions of American teachers and distorted American education is Dewey's *How We Think*, for it is concerned only with learning by discovery and the sort of thinking that there goes on. But below the level of the university, apart from men competent in scholarship or research, the major learning is by instruction, and the kind of thinking therein involved is inseparable from processes of communication. In so far, therefore, as I restrict myself to the basic education of youth—youth incompetent to discover anything by itself—I can say that there is no significant operation of thinking apart from such operations as reading and listening, writing and speaking, and there is no art of thinking other than the three liberal arts as arts of language or communication.

Now let me explain why the three arts are co-implicated—always interdependent—in all the operations of communication. There are three things involved in all communication, whether in initiating it or receiving it. They are language, thought, and the persons who think and discourse. (By "language" I mean any language, not just English; by "thought" I mean, broadly, every state of mind or soul, feelings, intentions, perceptive experiences, as well as ideas and intellectual judgments. And, let me add, there is a fourth thing which I did not mention because it is simultaneous with thought and speech—namely, the object referred to by both thought and speech.)

The three arts get their distinction from the three aspects of every communication, just mentioned. Thus: (1) Grammar is the art of ordering language to express or to receive thought. (2) Logic is the art of ordering what is to be expressed in language or of judging what has been expressed, and here there is a limitation; for logic is restricted to the communication of thought in the narrower, or more intellectual, sense; and it must be completed by poetics as the art of ordering feelings and imaginations to be expressed, or of judging such expressions. (3) Rhetoric is the art of ordering both language and thought in order to reach another mind or person effectively; or, if you are the mind or person being reached for, rhetoric is the art which guides you in yielding or resisting.

The three arts cannot be separated, for no one of them is sufficient to regulate good writing or reading. Each requires the supplementation of the other two; the three must interpenetrate one another; they are mutually supporting disciplines for the simple reason that language without thought is nonsense; thought without language is ineffable; and both without consideration of the human context in communication are lacking in direction. (Discourse is not simply rational, but social, for man is not just rational, but socially so.)

Not only are the three arts (of grammar, logic, and rhetoric) mutually interdependent, but they are also in a certain order. Considering the ends and nature of communication, rhetoric is the dominant art: it is the art of writing, not a phrase or sentence, but a whole composition, a whole poem, a whole speech, a whole book; it is the art of reading, not just a part, but a whole communication. The use of grammatical and logical techniques must be guided by ultimate rhetorical consider-ations—the intention of writer and reader. Of the two remaining arts, grammar and logic, grammar is ordered to logic when the intention is to explain or to instruct.

In order to explain the ordering of the arts in their tri-unity, let me expand a little on the multiple dimensions of rhetoric and show you how these dimensions involve a diversity of logics and grammars.

The most fundamental division which rhetoric considers is the di-vision made by the difference between two intentions men have in writing: instruction and delight—to convey the truth or to create beauty. This is the familiar distinction between science and poetry, between intellectual and imaginative literature, between the use of language to express knowledge of reality and the use of language to create imitations of reality.

There are, of course, subordinate distinctions. Thus:

1. In the intellectual dimension there is the fundamental division between the theoretic and the practical, the former aiming to convince
   about the truth, the latter directed to persuade in matters of action
   or feeling. There is, in short, a theoretical rhetoric as well as a

practical rhetoric in the sphere of intellectual communication. Unhappily, many regard rhetoric as restricted to the practical, to problems of oratory and propaganda.

2. In the imaginative dimension there are all the distinctions of poetry into epic, dramatic, and lyric, whether in prose or verse, and whether we call them epics or novels, dramas or plays.

But, for our purposes, it is sufficient to point out that these distinctions require us to cultivate two different sorts of grammar—a logical and a poetic grammar; they also require us to cultivate many different sorts of logic, each with an appropriate grammar, a theoretic and a practical logic, and within the domain of theoretic logic and grammar we must be sensitive to such varieties of logic as the historical, the scientific, and the philosophic.

All this, I say, follows from a proper consideration of the liberal arts as united in a triplicate unity and under the aegis of rhetoric as concerned with the most fundamental canons of style, or, shall I say, the styles appropriate for every sort of writing, the styles to be detected by every sort of reading.

I have said all this—much of which must be familiar to many of you—because of the educational significance it has. If what I have said is true, what follows for liberal education? What must be done to make youth competent as liberal artists and worthy of the B.A. degree in terms of the only relevant criterion, namely, that they know how to read and write? I enumerate only some of the more obvious consequences:

1. None of the arts can be well taught merely as a science, having principles, or as a discipline, having rules, in separation from exercises in all the artistic operations, namely, in reading and writing, listening and speaking. (Thus, grammar cannot be well taught as a set of rules in isolation from the operations to be regulated, namely, writing and reading; this is even more true of logic. Yet much of our teaching is done contrariwise: students who have memorized grammatical rules cannot put them into practice, cannot detect simple and complex sentences, dependent or independent clauses, in difficult discourse; students who can recite all the rules of the syllogism cannot discover arguments and their relation in the reasoning of great minds, whose books they may be trying to read. Of course, much worse than this is the situation in our progressive schools where writing and reading are

done in complete isolation from any acquaintanceship with the rules of grammar and logic.)

2. None of the arts can be well taught in isolation from the other two; for all three must be practiced simultaneously in reading and writing, speaking and listening.

3. None of the arts can be well taught if restricted to some limited subject matter, such as the poetic dimensions of literature or the practical dimension of rhetoric.

4. Since the rules which govern any form of writing are the same rules which govern the reading of that form of literature, no student can learn to write well what he has not been taught to read well, and conversely; and here reading is certainly prior, in the order of learning, to writing, for reading is easier than writing, as listening is easier than speaking.

5. The practice of the arts requires worthy materials to operate on, for rules of art will not work on matter itself inartistically contrived. What I mean is that the greatest books in every dimension of literature must be the materials read if reading is to be well taught, for how shall anyone be able to practice reading, according to good rules, what was not written according to such rules; and, similarly, great literature of all forms must provide the models to guide the novice in practicing writing according to the rules of these arts.

In the light of these five points—and there are many others—you can see how defective and even defunct the teaching of the liberal arts has become in our education because it has been relegated to English courses, almost exclusively, or because the arts have been separated by departmental divisions or divided according to mistaken notions about what is proper at different levels of education.

1. Thus grammar belongs to the English teacher, whereas logic belongs—if it exists at all—to the philosophy department. As a result of this departmental separation both grammar and logic lose their artistic usefulness; grammar becomes nothing but a set of conventional rules of English usage; and logic becomes an abstract science which has nothing to do with the business of reading and writing.

2. Furthermore, as falling to the English teacher, grammar is considered only, or primarily, in the dimension of poetic rhetoric, and all the grammatical problems related to logical rhetoric are ignored or inadequately treated.

3. Furthermore, grammar is primarily treated in relation to writing, if

it is given any application at all; and it is seldom invoked in the reading of difficult texts as part of the business of interpretation and criticism.

4. Furthermore, logic, in separation from grammar, and as the special province of the philosopher, degenerates into a discussion of scientific method and ceases to be the basic discipline of writing and reading, not even of writing and reading philosophy itself, as the writings of most contemporary philosophers so painfully reveal.

5. Furthermore, rhetoric, in separation from both grammar and logic, and relegated to courses in public speaking, ceases to be the dominant art, regulative of all forms of intelligent communication, and becomes a minor appendix of the curriculum. It is rhetoric in its most degraded state—little better than elocution. And without rhetoric, the other two suffer! We deal with short passages, not wholes!

Let me picture in another way the disastrous educational consequences which flow from the dismemberment of the trinity of liberal arts.

First, the results of separating grammar and logic. (Equally bad results flow from the separation of grammar and poetics, but I shall confine my discussion to the first of these two separations, because the second is less drastic in English teaching.)

1. Grammar becomes purely conventional instead of formal. It is English grammar instead of universal grammar—the grammar of any language. As a result, both teacher and student wonder why they are bothering about grammar except for the purposes of polite speech and superficial correctness by conformity to "good usage." But usage is arbitrary in large part; and the rules of a purely conventional grammar lack the intelligibility which belongs only to a universal grammar integrated with logic and poetics and subservient to rhetoric.

2. Logic becomes a purely formal science instead of a useful liberal art. It degenerates, as we have seen, into symbolic logic or logistics, which has absolutely no relation to anything. Even though logic be mastered as it is taught in philosophy courses, such mastery means nothing in the way of liberal discipline, any more than the mastery of the rules of a game would be significant if the game itself were never played. The student does not become a better reader or writer, a better interpreter or critic, a better thinker, a more orderly mind.

3. The quickest way to establish both of these foregoing points is to indicate the parallelism between the basic grammatical units (units of discourse) and the basic logical units (units of thought).

a. The parallelism is: words and phrases—terms or concepts; sentences—propositions or judgments; paragraphs—syllogisms or arguments.

b. The fundamental fact here is that there is no one-one correlation between the two sets of units. Thus, one and the same term can be expressed in various words or phrases, and one and the same word or phrase can express various terms; similarly, a single English sentence, especially if complex or compound, or both, does not express a single proposition but a whole series of them, and so forth.

c. Now the separation of grammar and logic prevents the student from being able, in reading, to come to terms with an author by penetrating beneath his language; he may know all about propositions and arguments, but he won't be able to find any when he is reading a book; and if you ask such a student to write a series of propositions he will give you some half-formed or overcomplicated sentences in an undisciplined effort to express his thoughts.

d. When I say that college graduates cannot read or write I am simply pointing to the fact that they have no effective discipline in either grammar or logic, either none at all or, what is almost as bad, the inadequate sort which comes from the departmentalized functions of English and philosophy professors. This is easily tested: ask a college graduate as I have done when he gets to law school, to find the separate propositions in a single sentence or their connection in a paragraph; ask him to translate what a sentence says into another sentence saying the same thing but in different words; ask him to explain what an argument means by pointing to the objects or experiences which the words refer to.

4. What I have here said mainly concerns the writing and reading of intellectual literature, theoretic or practical; but the same holds for the reading and writing of imaginative literature in any of the forms of poetry; for even though grammar and poetics both belong to the English teacher, he deals with them separately—so pervasive is the atomization of everything into separate courses, given by specializing professors.

Second, the results of separating rhetoric from grammar and from logic. Here I do not speak of the separation of rhetoric from poetics, for the opposite has taken place: in so far as rhetoric is not just public speaking, it is reduced to a concern about poetic style.

1. Let me begin, therefore, by commenting briefly on the notion of style. Style is the most general rhetorical fact. But as treated by teachers of English, style is restricted to the consideration of poetic excellence: to effectiveness in the field of imaginative literature.

2. As a result, our students, if they are taught to be sensitive to, and critical of, whole literary works at all, have such sensitivity developed only with respect to belles lettres, and sometimes they are so specialized as to be trained in the appreciation of lyric style and not even dramatic or epic composition. Certainly they have no training in the analysis of expository works as wholes, no sensitivity to excellence in logical, as opposed to poetic, rhetoric. They would not be able to tell you the difference between the style of Plato and the style of Euclid, or why the Platonic style is more suitable to the matter which St. Augustine expounds than to the matter of Galileo, who tries to use that style; or why the Euclidean style is more suitable to the matter of Newton than to the matter of Spinoza, even though the latter also tries to use Euclidean style.

3. Furthermore, if rhetoric is treated in the logical dimension at all, it is concerned with oratory, or practical discourse, and even here the effectiveness of oratory is not made intelligible in terms of its grammatical and logical aspects, for rhetoric as customarily taught by English teachers is taught apart from logic and as a course which comes much later than grammar.

I conclude, therefore, that the liberal arts have fallen on evil days as the result of curricular arrangements that separate them into departments which prevent them from being taught properly and which give to the English teacher an impossible task—impossible even when the English teacher somehow realizes what it is, and even less possible when the English teacher does not know the burden which has been unintentionally imposed on him.

Anyone will see this at once by considering the educational work done by the Greek sophists and philosophers, the Roman grammarians and rhetoricians, the medieval masters of the liberal arts, the Renaissance humanists—in each case dominating the whole of basic education —and then comparing the work now being done by English teachers in their little corner. And if such intuitive perceptions have no authority in this day of educational tests and measurements, I suggest a test which will show the enormity of the failure in its full extent. Students have been tested on their ability to read sentences and paragraphs, and on such tests we all know that the average high school graduate is not much better than a sixth-grader, that the best high school seniors are less than reasonably competent. But all such tests, even though they reveal educational failure, are much too easy. Test the best high school graduate or, for that matter, the best college graduate, or even the candidate for the Ph.D. on his ability to read a whole book intelligently —and let the book be a great book worthy of the effort—and you will be able to measure in no uncertain terms how complete today is the failure of liberal education.

Second, discourse is heterogeneous, but the liberal arts are unified, and therefore all kinds of reading and writing must be done together and not under existing departmental separations. This second point follows from what has already been said. If the aim, in teaching reading and writing, is not simply the ability to write or read a sentence or at most a paragraph, but rather a whole work, then the teaching of writing and reading must be undertaken by a comparative study of all the different types of works, for otherwise the student will lack the rhetorical distinctions and principles necessary for guiding him in the use of grammatical and logical or poetic techniques.

For the same reason that many English teachers now realize that it is necessary to acquaint the student with every poetic form—with regard to his skill in writing as well as his skill in reading—they should also see the general principle which is here involved. If it is true that the student has not learned to write well or read well, from the point of view of imaginative compositions, if he can read only lyrics or only plays, then it is more generally true that to possess the liberal arts of reading and writing, without qualification, he must be able to do every sort of writing and every sort of reading—at least every sort of reading.

Now this cannot be accomplished if English teachers restrict "literature" to belles lettres; or, if when they extend their assignments to include other materials, such as philosophical essays or scientific works, they treat them all as if they were belles lettres. Though a naturally great teacher in his day, John Erskine used to commit this fallacy in reading books with his students: he had only one set of criteria for interpreting them or judging them, exclusively "literary" or aesthetic criteria. For him to say that every great book should be read as literature meant that only poetic excellence was worth discussing. . . . The opposite error is, of course, equally regrettable, namely, the historical, sociological, or scientific reading of great works of poetry.

The truth, it seems to me, is that every great work has a primary rhetorical dimension, poetic or expository, and exists in one of the subordinate forms of these. According to that dimension and form it must meet certain criteria of stylistic excellence; it must be submitted to proper principles of interpretation and criticism, involving distinctions in grammar and logic. (This does not exclude secondary interpretations, for every great work has more than one rhetorical dimension.) If this be right, then the liberal arts cannot be well taught unless in the teaching of them every different sort of book is read in the context of books of every other sort; and unless every different type of writing is undertaken in imitation of the great models of every rhetorical type.

I need not take your time to tell you that, under present educational conditions, the great books are not read together and in intimate juxtaposition any more than the arts are taught together or in relation to all the books. Certain books belong to the English department; others are specialized in by the philosophers; the great works of mathematics, science, and history are not read at all, because these departments use textbooks for the sake of getting subject matter memorized by students who cannot read the great books in these fields and through them come to understand, not memorize, the principles of these subject matters.

I know, of course, that a large number of the great books on the St. John's list are scattered throughout the variety of elective courses in an ordinary college curriculum. Many of them are, however, treated as supplementary rather than required reading, despite the violence done a great book by making it supplementary to something which is its inferior—an ordinary teacher's lectures or the textbooks written by his colleagues.

But even if all were required, I would not be satisfied as long as they were split up into a hundred courses, separated one from another, and separated from instruction in the liberal disciplines of reading and writing. Shakespeare, Montaigne, Machiavelli, Descartes, Leonardo, Galileo, Bacon, Rabelais, Harvey, Newton, Milton, Locke—here, for example, is a heterogeneous collection, all of which should be read together by the same students *with the same teacher.*

It is, for the most part, only in the English department that books are read, not for their subject matter alone, but as occasions for developing skill in reading and writing; and even that is rapidly becoming less so as English teachers spend most of their time on the history and sociology of whatever it is they read.

From all of this I conclude that as books are now read in most high schools and colleges—even if they were the great books, as unfortunately in many cases they are not—the reading of them is not done in a way that facilitates the major aim of liberal education, the development of liberal artists, the production of disciplined, as well as cultivated, minds.

I return, therefore, at the end, to the point with which I began: what is basic about the teaching of English is the vestige of the traditional liberal education it still exhibits, however poorly and inadequately. Hence, if teachers of English recognize themselves as the only surviving academic representatives of this tradition, they should find it in their hearts to work for the abolition of the sort of educational system which now prevents them, or anyone else, from doing the main job effectively.

If you, then, ask me what I am proposing to substitute, I can answer you in two ways: (1) I can refer you to the St. John's curriculum as the only curriculum which is genuinely devoted to liberal education; or (2) I can answer you by stating three negations which, if established, would create an educational vacuum into which genuinely liberal education would have to rush, if teachers and students still got together. The three negations are: abolish all departments, abolish all electives, abolish all textbooks.

Furthermore, let me point out that what I am saying applies equally to high school or college, for we waste four years in American education, or certainly at least two. The kind of liberal education I am talking about should follow elementary schooling and precede the specialized education of the university. It should be the secondary level of education, and whether you call it secondary or collegiate, whether you call the four-year course in which it is given a high school or a college course, makes no difference, for this is the education which should terminate in a B.A. degree restored to its proper meaning.

Finally, let me say that although the great books introduce every subject matter into this scheme of education, its aim is not a mastery of subject matter but the acquisition of discipline. The great books, and all the subject matters, are involved, because without them it is impossible to acquire discipline, to train minds in all the skills of reading and writing, speaking and listening, and, perforce, the skills of thinking. But the point always to be remembered is that the sort of education which consists in the mastery of a subject matter can never be acquired in high school or college, for the students are much too young, and much too immature and inexperienced, to get such an education in the full sense. All that they can get is the sort of education which consists in acquiring the disciplines of learning itself, so that, whether they go on to the university or not, they will be prepared to take care of their own education from that point on. This is the whole meaning of a liberal education as signified by bachelorhood in the liberal arts, for that degree should not be taken as marking the accomplishment of learning but only as indicating a man who, because liberally disciplined, is now able to pursue learning by himself.

PART THREE

Teaching and

Learning

12

Teaching, Learning,
and Their Counterfeits

(1976; 1987)

*In "Teaching, Learning, and Their Counterfeits" we learn that gen-
uine teaching, as opposed to indoctrination, is a cooperative art, an
activity that helps but cannot by itself bring about genuine learning.
Part of this essay "Teaching and Learning" was written for* From Par-
nassus, *a collection of essays in honor of Jacques Barzun, edited by
William R. Keylor and Dora B. Weiner (New York: Harper & Row,
1976); part of it was unpublished. The conception of teaching and
learning it presents is the basis of the Paideia program.*

G.V.D.

EVERYONE KNOWS, or certainly should know, that indoctrination is not genuine teaching and that the results of indoctrination are the very opposite of genuine learning. Yet, as a matter
of fact, much that goes on in the classrooms of our schools is nothing
but indoctrination. The results that are measured by our standardized
tests are not products of genuine learning.

All learning is either by instruction or by discovery—that is, with
or without the aid of teachers. The teachers who serve as instructors
may be alive and in direct contact with those whom they instruct, as
is always the case in classrooms or tutorials, or they may be present to
the learner only in the form of books. The teacher who instructs by his
writings cannot engage in discussion with those who are reading his
works in order to learn; he can ask them initial questions, but he cannot

ask any second questions—questions about answers they give to his initial questions. He is, therefore, seriously limited in his performance of the art of teaching, though he may have done what he could to apply the rules of that art in his effort to communicate what he knows.

That the effort to communicate what a man knows is not, *in itself,* effective teaching follows from the fact that such efforts are seldom if ever successful and, at best, they succeed only in part. Successful teaching occurs only when the mind of the learner passes from a state of ignorance or error to a state of knowledge. The knowledge acquired may be either something already known by the teacher, or something about which he himself is inquiring. In either case, the transformation effected in the mind of the learner is learning by instruction only if another human being has taken certain deliberate steps to bring about that transformation. What the teacher does must be deliberately calculated to change the mind of the learner. Merely motivating someone to learn is not enough; stimulation is not teaching.

Since whatever can be learned by instruction must necessarily have been learned first by discovery without the aid of teachers, it follows that teachers are, absolutely speaking, dispensable. Nevertheless, they are useful because most human beings need instruction to learn what they could have learned by discovering it for themselves. If we recognize, as we should, that genuine learning cannot occur without activity on the part of the learner (passive absorption or rote memorization does not deserve to be called learning), then we must also recognize that all learning is a process of discovery on the part of the learner.

This alters our understanding of the distinction between learning by discovery and learning by instruction. If the latter is not to be identified with passive absorption or rote memorization, then the distinction divides all active learning into two kinds—unaided discovery, discovery without the aid of teachers, on the one hand; and aided discovery, or discovery deliberately assisted by teachers, on the other. In both cases, the principal cause of learning is activity on the part of the learner engaged in the process of discovery; when instruction occurs, the teacher is at best only an instrumental cause operating to guide or facilitate the process of discovery on the part of the learner. To suppose that the teacher is ever more than an instrumental cause is to suppose that the activity of a teacher can by itself suffice to cause learning to occur in another person even though the latter remains entirely passive. This would view the learner as a patient being acted upon rather than as an agent whose activity is both primary and indispensable. In contrast, the instrumental activity of the teacher is always secondary and dispensable.

These basic insights are epitomized by Socrates when, in the *Theaetetus*, he describes his role as a teacher by analogy with the service performed by a midwife who does nothing more than assist the pregnant mother to give birth with less pain and more assurance. So, according to Socrates, the teacher assists the inquiring mind of the learner to give birth to knowledge, facilitating the process of discovery on the learner's part.

Teaching, like farming and healing, is a cooperative art. Understanding this, Comenius in *The Great Didactic* again and again compares the cultivation of the mind with the cultivation of the field; so, too, Plato compares the teacher's art with the physician's.

In arts such as shoemaking and shipbuilding, painting and sculpture (arts which I call "operative" to distinguish them from the three cooperative arts), the artist is the principal cause of the product produced. Nature may supply the materials to be fashioned or transformed, and may even supply models to imitate, but without the intervention of the artist's skill and causal efficacy, nature would not produce shoes, ships, paintings, or statues.

Unlike the operative artist, who aims either at beauty or utility, the cooperative artist merely helps nature to produce results that it is able to produce by its own powers, without the assistance of the artist—without the intervention of the artist's accessory causality. Fruits and grains grow naturally; the farmer intervenes merely to assure that these natural products grow with regularity and, perhaps, to increase their quantity. The body has the power to heal itself—to maintain health and regain health; the physician who adopts the Hippocratic conception of the healing art attempts to support and reinforce the natural processes of the body. The mind, like the body, has the power to achieve what is good for itself—knowledge and understanding. Learning would go on if there were no teachers, just as healing and growing would go on if there were no physicians and farmers.

Like the farmer and the physician, the teacher must be sensitive to the natural process that his art should help bring to its fullest fruition —the natural process of learning. It is the nature of human learning that determines the strategy and tactics of teaching. Since learning which results in expanded knowledge and improved understanding (rather than memorized facts) is essentially a process of discovery, the teacher's art consists largely in devices whereby one individual can help another to lift himself up from a state of knowing and understanding less to knowing and understanding more. Left to his own devices, the learner would not get very far unless he asked himself questions, perceived problems to be solved, suffered puzzlement over dilemmas, put himself under the necessity of following out the implications of this hypothesis or that, made observations and weighed the evidence for alternative hypotheses, and so on. The teacher, aware of these indispensable steps in the process by which he himself has moved his own mind up the ladder of learning, devises ways to help another individual engage in a similar process; and he applies them with sensitivity to the state of that other person's mind and with awareness of whatever special difficulties the other must overcome in order to make headway.

Discipline in the traditional liberal arts imparts the skills by which an individual becomes adept at learning. They are the arts of reading and writing, of speaking and listening, of observing, measuring, and calculating—the arts of grammar, rhetoric, and logic, the mathematical arts, and the arts of investigation. Without some proficiency in these arts, no one can learn very much, whether assisted or not by the use of books and the tutelage of teachers. Unless the teacher is himself a skilled learner, a master of the liberal arts which are the arts of learning, he cannot help those he attempts to teach acquire the skills of learning; nor can his superior skill in learning provide the learner with the help he needs in the process of discovery. The teacher must put himself sympathetically in the position of a learner who is less advanced than himself, less advanced both in skill and in knowledge or understanding. From that vantage point, he must somehow reenact—or simulate— for the learner the activities he himself engaged in to achieve his present state of mind.

The Hippocratic understanding of healing as a cooperative art provides us with analogical insights into the cooperative art of teaching. Hippocrates, whom we in the West regard as the father of medicine, wrote treatises setting forth the rules of healing as a cooperative art. They were rules for controlling the regimen of the patient—the food he ate, the air he breathed, his hours of waking and sleeping, the water he drank, the exercise he engaged in, and so forth. By controlling the patient's regimen—his diet, his hours, his activities, his environment —the physician helps the body to heal itself by its natural processes.

Administering drugs, introducing foreign substances into the body, Hippocrates regarded as the least cooperative of all medical treatments. Surgery he regarded as a drastic measure to be resorted to only when all cooperative methods failed; it was, strictly speaking, an *operative* rather than a *cooperative* procedure.

In the sphere of teaching, the analogue of surgery is indoctrination, the result of which is rote memorization, or some passive absorption of information without any understanding of it. Indoctrination does violence to the mind, as surgery does violence to the body, the only difference being that there is never any excuse for indoctrination, while there can be justification for surgery.

Teachers who regard themselves as the principal, even the sole, cause of the learning that occurs in their students simply do not understand teaching as a cooperative art. They think of themselves as producing knowledge or understanding in the minds of their students in the same way that shoemakers produce shoes out of pliable or plastic materials.

Only when teachers realize that the principal cause of the learning that occurs in a student is the activity of the student's own mind do they assume the role of cooperative artists. While the activity of the learner's mind is the principal cause of all learning, it is not the sole cause. Here the teacher steps in as a secondary and cooperative cause.

Just as, in the view of Hippocrates, surgery is a departure from healing as a cooperative art, so, in the view of Socrates, didactic teaching, or teaching by lecturing or telling rather than teaching by questioning and discussion, is a departure from teaching as a cooperative art.

Lecturing is that form of teaching which is analogous to the use of drugs and medication in the practice of medicine. No violence may be done to the mind if the lecturer eschews any attempt at indoctrination; but the lecture, even when it is attended to with maximum effort on the part of the auditor, is something that the mind must first absorb before it can begin to digest and assimilate what is thus taken in. If passively attended to and passively absorbed by the memory, the lecture has the same effect as indoctrination, even if the lecturer scrupulously intended to avoid that result. At its best, the lecture cannot be more than an occasion for learning, as challenge to the mind of the auditor, an invitation to inquiry. The lecture, in short, is no better than the book as a teacher—an oral rather than a written communication of knowledge.

If, however, the lecture is always accompanied by some discussion of whatever matters are didactically presented, if there is an active interchange between teacher and students through questioning, didactic teaching can, to some slight degree, become genuine teaching of knowledge understood instead of being an indoctrination of opinions to be committed to memory, retained, regurgitated on examinations, and then largely forgotten when the tests have been passed.

Analogous to the fully cooperative therapeutic technique of controlling the patient's regimen is the fully cooperative pedagogical technique of engaging the learner in discussion—teaching by asking instead of teaching by telling, asking questions not merely to elicit answers for the sake of grading them (as in a quiz session, which is not teaching at all), but asking questions that open up new avenues of inquiry.

When instruction is not accompanied by discovery, when instruction makes impressions on the memory with no act of understanding by the mind, then it is not genuine teaching, but mere indoctrination. Genuine teaching, in sharp distinction from indoctrination, always consists in activities on the part of teachers that cooperate with activities performed by the minds of students engaged in discovery.

The Greek word for mind, *nous*, identifies it with understanding. What we do not understand at all we retain solely through memory. Memory is a by-product of sense-perception; understanding, an act of the intellect. Statements that are verbally remembered and recalled should never be confused with facts understood.

Correlated with this distinction between mind and memory is the distinction between knowledge and opinion. To know something as opposed to holding a mere opinion about it is to understand it in the light of relevant reasons and supporting evidence.

Students acquire knowledge by the activity of their own minds, with or without the aid of teachers. How do they come by the opinions they hold, especially those acquired in the course of schooling?

They have adopted them on the naked authority of teachers who acted as if they were productive, not cooperative, artists—teachers who indoctrinated them by didactic instruction that was not accompanied by any acts of thinking or discovery on their part.

I have used the phrase "naked authority" to signify the authority teachers arrogate to themselves when they expect students to accept what they tell them simply because they are teachers. The only authority to which genuine teachers, as opposed to indoctrinators, should appeal is the authority of the relevant reasons or the evidence supporting whatever is to be learned. In the absence of such authority, teachers cannot help students acquire knowledge that is understood. They can only indoctrinate them with opinions they may or may not retain for long in their memories. Opinions adopted on the naked authority of teachers have little durability. Opinions remembered, with that memory reinforced temporarily by "boning up for tests," are opinions for the most part soon forgotten.

Much more durable are the habits of skill that are formed by the kind of teaching that is coaching, which is more cooperative than didactic teaching even when what is thus taught is illuminated by understanding through discussion. Habits are not memories. They can only be formed by coaching, never by lectures and the reading of textbooks.

Most students passing, at the end of one academic year, the standardized tests currently used, which are largely tests of memory, would probably not be able to pass them if they were given the same tests without warning at the beginning of the next academic year. But if the habitually possessed skills of students in reading and writing were measured by the level of their performance at the end of one academic year and then measured in the same way at a later time, little would be lost.

The understanding of ideas and knowledge understood, once acquired, has maximum durability. What is understood cannot be forgotten because it is a habit of the intellect, not something remembered. Anyone who comes to understand that a truth is self-evident only if it is undeniable because its opposite is unthinkable will understand it forever. To test or measure the understanding of students, the only effective instrument is an oral examination, a probing of the mind by persistent questioning that penetrates its depths as far as possible.

The misunderstanding of teaching and learning that prevails today has resulted in the deplorable fact, amply attested by Professor John Goodlad in *A Place Called School*, that 85 percent of all classroom time is consumed by unrelieved didactic teaching that is not genuine teaching at all, but sheer indoctrination. It results in the short-lived, mainly verbal, memory of mere opinions adopted on the naked authority assumed by indoctrinating teachers.

The conception of the teacher as one who has knowledge or information that he or she transmits to students as passive recipients violates the nature of teaching as a cooperative art. It assumes that genuine learning can occur simply by instruction, without acts of thinking and understanding that involve discovery by the minds of students.

The way in which we test or examine students and the way in which we grade them determines what teachers teach and how they teach, and what students learn and how they learn. Our present methods call for indoctrination rather than genuine teaching, and for memorizing rather than genuine learning.

Unless we radically change our present methods of testing and grading students, we cannot expect our teachers to become cooperative artists instead of mere indoctrinators, and we cannot expect our students to become genuine learners instead of mere memorizers.

All our written tests should be open-book examinations so that students prepare for them not by boning up on what they have not adequately remembered, but by trying to deepen their understanding of what they were taught, or sharpening their thinking about it. If habitual skills are to be evaluated, they should be tested by performances judged adequate or inadequate. And to measure levels of understanding, the only effective instrument is an oral examination.

Four things are needed in the training of teachers to make them cooperative artists:

1. They themselves should possess whatever knowledge students are expected to acquire through their didactic efforts, but this by itself is never enough. They must also have an understanding of everything they know in order for them to be able to supplement their didactic performance by questioning, by answering questions, by leading discussions that will help their students acquire genuine knowledge, knowledge accompanied by understanding.

2. Teachers should have the intellectual skills they are expected to coach and they should know how to form the habits of those skills in the students they coach.

3. They should have an understanding of the ideas and issues that they wish to help students to comprehend through discussions in Socratically conducted seminars. For this purpose they should be trained in the art of conducting seminars by observing others conducting them, by participating themselves as students in seminars conducted by others, and by conducting seminars under the critical scrutiny of masters of this art.

4. Most important of all, they should be so prepared for the profession of teaching that they understand their own primary role as that of learners. A school should be a place where teachers learn, not just a place where students learn. A learner-teacher is one whose teaching involves genuine intellectual activity on the teacher's part as well as on the student's part, not just recitation by the teacher and memorization by the students.

13

The Order of Learning

(1941)

This complex and profound discussion is essentially a practical guide to the art of teaching. It deals with the means of education—in this case, the activity of the teacher. Adler's question is: Given ideally perfect ends of education, how shall the basic means be ordered? The answer here is that the order of teaching must follow the order of learning and not the order of knowledge. In other words, instruction follows or imitates discovery. What follows from this thesis is the understanding that the liberal arts, as skills, are the arts of teaching and learning and as such must precede the mastery of the fundamental subject matters.

Taken from an address given for the western division of the American Catholic Philosophical Association in April 1941, the article was published in The Moraga Quarterly *(Autumn 1941). It is included here with only a few changes. The occasion explains the context of the discussion with reference to Catholic education, but the question concerns all.*

G.V.D.

I AM deeply appreciative of the honor conferred upon me by your invitation to address you this evening. It is a great privilege to be able to attend two meetings of the Catholic Philosophical Association in the same year. I have been attending the Christmas meetings of the eastern division for the last seven years, and I think you will realize with what background and what sincerity I can pay you this compliment: I have never before seen so perfectly constructed a program—so unified, so comprehensive, so balanced. The officers and members of this division are to be congratulated. I wish they would come East some time and arrange our meetings for us.

I have a private reason for pleasure in the perfection of the program you have just completed. When I first read the announcement of the papers to be given during these two days, I was embarrassed by the fact that there seemed to be nothing left to talk about on the subject of education. It looked as if the only appropriate thing to do at this dinner was to get up and say Amen. But then I found another angle from which to view the proceedings and my place in them. Just because the program was so beautifully rounded and balanced, I could feel relaxed about my own final part in it. The program was so balanced, no harm would be done if I was unbalanced. All the major points having been made, all the important themes being covered, I could feel free to do a minor and unimportant job. I could indulge myself in a little tirade, expressing one of my pet prejudices about contemporary education.

1. The Means of Intellectual Virtue

The theme I have chosen to discuss is the order of learning. *I am going to deal with the means of education, not with the ends.* Nor am I going to consider the means in every way—but only with respect to their ordination to one another. I am concerned with the order of studies, on the one hand, and with the order of a teacher's activities relative to those of his students, on the other. The question I propose to answer is: Given ideally perfect ends, how shall the basic means be ordered? But even this question is too large for treatment after dinner, so I must restrict the matters to be considered somewhat further.

I shall limit myself to purely natural education—that is, education defined in terms of natural and temporal happiness, as its ultimate end, and the natural virtues, as its proximate ends. I shall neglect religious education entirely, not because it is negligible—far from it, it is the least negligible part of education—but for two reasons which I wish to state: first, because it is beyond my competence to treat of such matters; and second, because it is beyond the province of strictly philosophical discussion to consider such matters, regardless of the personal competence of an individual who may combine in his person the gifts of both the philosopher and the theologian. One may combine the gifts, but the gifts are never the same, and should never be confused.

There is one further restriction on my discussion this evening which

I should like to announce. I shall neglect moral education entirely—a much more difficult, and also a more important, topic than intellectual education, to which I shall confine myself. I note that one of your papers was on whether virtue (moral, I assume, must have been meant) can be taught. I hope the answer was clearly negative. As I understand the essence of teaching, it simply cannot be the adequate or effective instrument for forming moral virtue. Plato and Aristotle were clear about this, and clearly in agreement. The intellectual virtues are preeminently teachable, as the moral virtues are not. With respect to them, we should be able to solve the problem of means, as no one yet has with respect to the development of moral virtues, if ever a solution will be reached. And so I address myself to the problem—interesting because narrow and solvable—of the means to intellectual virtue: the order of studies which aim to cause the perfection of the mind.

The intellectual virtues are the proximate ends of all truly *liberal* or *intellectual* education. (I shall use these two words interchangeably.) Even here there is one last restriction. Prudence belongs with the moral virtues. It is formed as they are, not by teaching or by schoolwork, but somehow mysteriously by practice, under guidance, in many ways. Hence, I am left with four virtues, divided into the arts, on the one hand, and the three speculative virtues (understanding, science, and wisdom) on the other. And here certainly wisdom is the highest end and the controlling principle in any consideration of the means.

I think this problem is something Catholic educators should consider. I say "Catholic educators" because they alone today rightly understand the ends of liberal or intellectual education to be the four intellectual virtues: understanding, science, art, and wisdom. They alone know this, and know what the virtues are. In this, they stand in sharp contrast to their secular colleagues who in the last hundred years have so misconceived the aims and ends of liberal education that it has almost vanished from the scene. But though our secular colleagues are wrong about the ends of liberal education, they are often quite sound about the means—especially about the order of teaching as an art of using the means—and this is most true, you will be surprised to hear me say, in the case of the extreme progressive educators who have unwittingly returned to some ancient truths about educational method. They do not use the means for good educational results, because they misdirect them through ignorance or misconception of the ends. But Catholic educators can, I think, be charged with an opposite fault: knowing the right ends, they frequently fail to achieve them because they misuse the means, because they violate the nature of the learning process itself.

I warned you this might become a tirade, expressing a pet peeve of mine. You may remember an article I published in *The Commonweal* several years ago, asking "Can Catholic Education be Criticized?" My answer was Yes—not about the ends, but about the means. Let me repeat here the conclusion I then formulated:

> I can understand why a Catholic educator might be impervious to any critic who attacked the ends of Catholic education, because somehow these ends are implicated in the central truths of the Christian religion, and thus there is a dogmatic confirmation for the conviction of reason about them. *But certainly this is not the case with the means!* The truth of Catholicism in religion and philosophy, for example, is no warrant for the efficacy or intrinsic excellence of the way religion and philosophy are taught in Catholic schools. Only the liberal arts can provide the standard for judging excellence in teaching, for measuring the efficiency of educational means, or for inventing others; and the liberal arts are neither pagan nor Christian, but human.

I am deeply concerned about this point, deeply disturbed by seeing the miscarriage of education in Catholic institutions, precisely because I know their ends are right. Furthermore, is not their fault a worse one than the fault of the secular educators? Is there not more excuse for the secular educators being mistaken about the ends, than for Catholic educators being mistaken about the means? Let me explain why I think so.

I said before that secular educators, especially the radical progressive group, were singularly right and eminently sound on many points concerning the means. I had in mind the fundamental soundness of the project method (though I abhor the name), the method which stresses activity on the part of the learner as indispensable, which emphasizes the great importance of understanding the problem before knowing the answers, which places the acquirement of skills before the mastery of subject matters in the domain of basic general education.

Now I say that all of these right procedures appear to be radical innovations only because they were forgotten or corrupted by the decadent classical education of the last century, against which progressive education arose in justifiable rebellion. Truly, all these procedures are founded on ancient insights about the order of teaching and learning, insights which every Catholic educator must possess if he understands the nature of man and of human teaching, according to the principles of the philosophy he generally affirms. Let me briefly enumerate some of these points. *The Catholic educator knows:*

1. *The difference between intellectual habit and sensitive memory.* Hence he knows that verbal proficiency, which is a work of sensitive memory, must not be confused with the habit of understanding.

2. *That habits of understanding can be formed only by intellectual acts—acts on the part of the student, not simply acts by the teacher.* Hence he knows that the teacher is always a secondary cause of learning, never a primary cause, for the primary cause must always be an act on the part of the learner's own intellect.

3. *That the intellect depends on sense and imagination, and also that it can be swayed and colored by the motion of the passions.* Hence he knows that the discipline of the liberal arts must precede the process of acquiring the speculative virtues, for it is the liberal arts which rectify the intellect in its pursuit of truth—the arts of grammar and logic which protect the intellect against the deceptions of verbal and other symbolizations, and all the wayward imagery of sense; the arts of logic and rhetoric, which guard against the incursions of passion, and the coloring of thought by irrelevant emotion.

4. *That the intellectual virtues are always a mean state between vicious extremes of saying too much or saying too little—dogmatic affirmations in excess, or skeptical denials in defect.* Hence he knows that truth is always an eminent synthesis of false extremes, a sober resolution of false issues made by extreme positions; he knows that the truth can be genuinely possessed only by a mind which sees the truth always as a correction of manifold and divers errors, and never by the mind which tries to be alone with the truth in an artificially antiseptic environment.

The Catholic educator knows all these things, because they are fundamental truths in his philosophy of man. But, unlike his secular colleague, who may not acknowledge these truths at all, or certainly not know them so deeply, but who nevertheless seems to practice according to their meaning, *the Catholic educator, who knows them, often violates them in practice by educational methods which (1) put a premium on verbal memory instead of intellectual habit; (2) proceed as if the teacher were the only active cause of learning, and as if the learner could be entirely passive; (3) neglect or wrongly subordinate the liberal arts to a supposed mastery of subject matter; (4) try to do the impossible —namely, to give the students genuine possession of the truth without ever really perplexing them first by the problems or issues which the truth*

resolves—and this requires a vital experience of error, for genuine per-
plexity is usually killed along with the dummy opponents who have been
made into straw men for quick demolition.

Before I proceed now to a brief statement of the order of learning,
based upon these truths, let me anticipate one objection I have received
from Catholic educators *as to means.* I am told that Catholic education
must give its college graduates a fundamental body of truths for the
guidance of their lives. I am told that this necessitates the covering of
much ground. You can guess my response. I simply ask what is the
point of covering ground, if the students' feet never touch it, if they
never learn through independent exercise to walk by themselves, with
head erect and unafraid of all intellectual opposition and difficulty.
What is the point of memorizing truths, if they can really guide us only
when they are genuinely possessed, if they can protect us from falsehood
only to the extent that we understand them as fully refuting errors—
real, live errors, not dummy ones concocted for the purposes of an easy
victory. I would feel happier about the graduates of Catholic colleges
if they were really to understand a few truths well—understand them
as solving problems which vigorously challenge the mind and perplex
it—rather than be able to recite, from merely verbal memory, a whole
catechism of philosophical answers to problems they did not really
understand or take seriously. I would be happier if they were merely
disciplined in the pursuit of truth and in the rejection of error, rather
than be, as they now are in so many cases, unable to give an account
of what they know because it is known by memory rather than possessed
by intellectual habit.

I shall proceed now to a brief discussion of the order of learning in
the field of the intellectual virtues. I shall, first, consider the ordination
of the liberal arts to the speculative subject matters. I shall, then,
consider the methods of teaching the speculative subject matters. And,
finally, I shall draw some conclusions and summarize my insights in
terms of the state of philosophy in contemporary culture—for the present condition of philosophy is not unrelated to the way it is taught and
learned.

2. Art and Subject Matter

My thesis here is simply that mastery of the liberal arts must precede
the mastery of the fundamental subject matters, which constitute the

matter of the speculative virtues. Though wisdom comes first in the natural order of the virtues—graded according to their intrinsic excellence—the arts, least of the intellectual virtues, come first in the temporal order, the order of human development.

You may tell me that this order is now generally observed: that logic is a basic course in all Catholic colleges, and that it is a discipline preparatory for the study of the basic subject matters. May I disagree, not with the facts, but with such interpretation of them? Logic can be taken, or given, in one of two ways: *either* as a speculative science itself, albeit a science in the second intention, in contrast to metaphysics and physics as sciences of the real (and hence in the first intention); *or* as one of the liberal arts, an organon, a body of rules for the regulation and rectification of the mind, not in itself, for in itself the human intellect is absolutely infallible, and needs no art at all, but rather in its dependence upon sense and imagination, and in its subjection to passion. (I am saying that logic, as a science, may deal with pure thought; but logic, as an art, is not an art of thinking, of pure intellectual activity, for such does not exist; it is always an art, necessarily conjoined with grammar and rhetoric, which regulates the operations of the intellectual imagination, thinking with symbols and against the impulse of passion.)

When logic is considered as an art, it cannot be divorced, you see, from the other two liberal arts of grammar and rhetoric. The three arts form a trinity, and each of the arts becomes corrupted and ineffective —an empty and meaningless routine—when separated from the others. This, by the way, is precisely what has happened to the liberal arts during the last four centuries. And scholasticism, with its arid logic, divorced from grammar and rhetoric, is as much to blame for this sad state of affairs as the most anti-intellectual movements in education.

The teaching of logic in Catholic colleges—*as a science*—is not a liberal discipline. The textbook logic which is taught, as a set of formulas without practice in the intellectual operations to which they are relevant, does not discipline the mind in writing, speaking, and listening. What good is it to know all the kinds of propositions, if a student cannot discover how many propositions are being expressed in a complicated sentence, and how they are related? What good to know all the principles of the syllogism if the student cannot recognize the congeries of syllogisms, or reasonings, that occur in a paragraph expressing a complicated argument? The proof of my point here is very simple. Though they are given a course in the science of logic, as their secular fellows are not, the graduates of Catholic colleges cannot read or write any better than their secular fellows. If they had been liberally disciplined, if the liberal arts had been acquired by them through years of exercise in their practices, then they would be vastly superior in the performance of all these liberal operations.

Furthermore, logic as a science is completely out of order when it is put first in the course of philosophical studies. Logic the organon, which really means the three arts of the trivium in complex conjunction, does come first; but logic the science comes last—even after metaphysics, after all the sciences of the real—precisely because second intentions follow first intentions, are derived from them, and depend upon them.

Let me explain, therefore, that by a proper teaching of the liberal arts, I mean only a teaching of the fundamental practices which these arts regulate: the performance of reading, writing, speaking, listening, measuring, and observing. Arts are habits. Hence they are not possessed at all by students who can verbally recite their rules. The rules are important only as regulating the performance of acts, which acts in turn, often repeated, then form the habits, which are the arts as vital transformations of the soul's operative powers. This can be done only in a scheme of education which orders learning in the following manner: (1) *on the elementary level,* gives the predispositions for intellectual discipline, by the study of multiple languages, especially the highly inflected ancient ones; by the routines of mathematics; and by the cultivation of the senses and imagination as the intellect's most important adjuncts; and (2) *on the secondary or collegiate level,* spends all of the four years primarily on the liberal arts, and not on the mastery of subject matters.

In short, a liberal education, crowned by the bachelor of arts degree, should consist in an ability to read and write, speak and listen, observe and think. A college graduate should be a liberal artist, and nothing more—as if this were not enough to hope for, and strive for, with all one's might and main.

Let me explain this last point, for it is likely to be misunderstood. First, let me say that I make no distinction between secondary and collegiate education. The B.A. degree should be given at what is now the end of high school, or at least at what is now the end of the sophomore year of our so-called colleges. After that comes the university. The three levels of education—and there is no place for a fourth—are rightly ordered when the first, or elementary, is seen as entirely preparatory and preintellectual, predispositive toward liberal training; when the second, or general, is seen as entirely liberal, partly terminal and partly preparatory for the study of subject matter; when the third, or specialized, is seen as devoted to the mastery of special subject matters, to the acquirement of the speculative virtues. (I shall return to this point later.)

I do not mean that the liberal arts are ever ultimate ends, ends in themselves. On the contrary, they are only intermediate ends, and as such, means to further and higher ends. They are specifically the indispensable means to the speculative virtues as ends. The acquisition of the arts is for the sake of mastering subject matters. But I wish to repeat one point: *they are not only means, they are indispensable as means.* Lacking real skill in the liberal arts, no one can become a master of an intellectual subject matter.

In order to acquire the arts, the subject matters must be used. This preliminary use of subject matter must not be confused with the ultimate approach to it after the arts have been acquired. When the basic subject matters are used at the collegiate or secondary level, they must be subordinated to the acquirement of the arts: they are then merely the matter on which the mind is being exercised to learn how to think—not, *then*, to learn what to think. That comes later. This is not a misuse of subject matter, as, of course, it would be, if it were the only use.

May I conclude this section of my remarks by the summary statement *that unless and until students become reasonably competent liberal artists, they are incompetent to approach or learn—really learn—any of the fundamental truths in the basic subject matters, for the means of forming the speculative virtues are lacking.* Teachers can indoctrinate students. Teachers can stuff their memories with pat verbal formulas —in Latin or in English—but they cannot teach them as if they were rational animals, instead of parrots, simply because their rational powers have not been sufficiently disciplined in the difficult arts of learning itself. The liberal arts, in my conception of them, are nothing but the arts of teaching and being taught. They are the basic skills of learning, and must, therefore, precede the effort of the mind to learn. Just as I would make mastery of the liberal arts—the old, but not meaningless, degree—the only requirement for one who wishes to teach the young in school or college (how many teachers would there be, if this standard were imposed?), so I would make bachelorhood, or a novitiate in the arts, the one test for admission to the university as the place where subject matters are studied. This would close our universities down quicker than any military draft is likely to do.

To all of this, let me add a few brief comments. First, this is not a defense or apologia for the St. John's plan. What I am proposing is the fundamental order of the best ancient and medieval educational systems. It was the order, the very wise order, proposed by Plato in *The Republic*. It was the medieval order, which really put Platonic policy into actual practice; the work of the liberal arts faculty served to prepare boys for the universities, where under the auspices of the three basic faculties (law, medicine, and theology) they studied the subject matters. Having become skilled in learning, which meant they could read and write with reasonable competence, they were now admitted to the status of competent learners. It was the original intention of the Jesuit *Ratio Studiorum*, which has not—may I be forgiven for saying—been sufficiently retained in spirit, as well as in letter, by post-Renaissance Jesuit institutions. And although it is this order which St. John's is trying to reestablish, that should certainly not stand in the way of Catholic colleges adopting it, for the idea is fundamentally a Greek and medieval idea. It was not invented by the proponents of the St. John's scheme. It is an idea that belongs to all the great traditions of Catholic education, and yet Catholic institutions today do not exemplify it in practice.

Second, this basic educational idea, about the priority of the liberal arts to the study of subject matter, also has significance for the relation of all schooling to adult education. Real learning must be the work of more mature persons than boys and girls in school and college. Children are too young, too inexperienced, too unstable, to acquire wisdom. Hence, they should be given what they, at their age, are able to receive: the formation of the artistic, not the speculative, virtues. If they graduate from college liberal artists, then, whether they go on to the university or not, they will be able to continue the pursuit of truth throughout a life of adult learning, when maturity makes the formation of speculative habits possible.

Finally, there is the question, Where, *institutionally*, should the subject matters be taught and studied? I have already indicated the answer: in the university. The answer is, of course, practical, only if the B.A. is given earlier than it is at present. If Catholic educators say this is not possible, because of the opposition of the various accrediting agencies, I can only answer that until Catholic institutions throw off the yoke of the accrediting boards, and exercise a free judgment on basic educational questions, they will never be able to realize in practice any of the principles which belong to Catholic education.

We are now prepared to consider my second and last major point: the order of learning in the field of the speculative virtues, the order of studies at the university level. And here, to limit my discussion, I shall consider the teaching of philosophy as a case in point.

3. The Order of Teaching and Learning Philosophy— the Order of the Means to the Virtue of Wisdom

Here I have two fundamental points to make, which I shall try to make briefly. The first concerns the *objective order* of the subject matters themselves; the second concerns the *methods of teaching* the subject matters, with reference to the distinction between the order of knowledge and the order of learning.

By the objective order of the subject matters I mean, of course, the order of the objects of knowledge *secundum se*—the order of things known according to their intrinsic knowability, rather than their relative knowability, that is, their knowability to us.

In the first place, it is necessary briefly to condemn all the Wolffian errors—all the false divisions of subject matter, the wrong ordering of the parts of philosophy, invented by Christian Wolff, most unfortunately adopted by later scholasticism, and now dominating the philosophy curriculum of so many Catholic institutions. The correction of the Wolffian errors—the wrong divisions, the wrong orderings—can be made simply by anyone who understands the Thomistic theory of abstraction, which Wolff violates at every point. (I shall not concern myself further with Wolff but rather go at once to the right objective ordering of subject matters.)

Theology is certainly first if the objective ordering be in terms of the object which is most knowable in itself, though not to us. This indicates at once that the objective ordering of subject matters cannot be the same as the subjective ordering, for the latter must be in terms of what is most knowable to us as coming first, and, in these terms, theology would come last.

If we apply these principles to all the fundamental theoretic subject matters, we will find that, just as in the objective order, theology precedes metaphysics, and metaphysics, the philosophy of nature, and the philosophy of man, which is one of its parts, and the whole of philosophy, as dealing with essences, the whole of science, as dealing with phenomenal accidents; so in the subjective order, the members of this series are perfectly reversed: science should be studied before philosophy, and the philosophy of man before the philosophy of nature, and these before metaphysics and theology.

There are two other points of order, which I must mention in passing: (1) the priority of the theoretic to the practical (which, curiously enough, is both an objective and a subjective priority, for the theoretic is both more knowable in itself and to us); and (2) the priority of objectively constituted subject matters such as metaphysics and the philosophy of nature, to such problematically constituted subject matters as the philosophy of law, or of art, or of education, or of knowledge itself.

Now within each sphere of subject matter, there is supposed to be an order of principles and conclusions. There is some truth in this, of course, but I think it has been excessively oversimplified by the scholastic acceptance of Aristotelian logic, as giving a true and adequate account of the intrinsic structure of bodies of knowledge. In this connection, let me make the following observations:

a. Aristotelian logic is primarily the logic of philosophy, and not at all the logic of science; and in so far as Aristotle did not clearly distinguish philosophy and science, his logic is both confused and inadequate.

b. Even as the logic of philosophical knowledge, it is restricted to the philosophy of nature, to what Aristotle calls physics. The *Organon* is totally inadequate as an account of metaphysical knowledge: its concepts, judgments, or purely analytical reasonings. The supposition that Aristotelian logic is applicable to metaphysics results in the false notion that metaphysics is exclusively, or even primarily, a deductive science, demonstrating conclusions from first principles.

c. In general, the influence of the *Posterior Analytics*, as giving the picture of the structure of scientia—any scientia—is disastrous; for, in fact, the only science there pictured is mathematics, and primarily geometry. As Gilson has pointed out, Aristotle's logic, and especially the *Posterior Analytics*, cannot be applied to any of Aristotle's own philosophical works. His own *Physics* and *Metaphysics* violate the account of scientia given in the *Posterior Analytics*.

d. The major errors which have arisen in the scholastic tradition, as
a result of following Aristotle's *Organon* as if it were a good, a true,
and an adequate logic, are these: an attempt to expound both physics
and metaphysics in a too-simple deductive order, whereas in truth,
these basic philosophical subject matters are circular rather than
linear in the connection of their propositions; a misconception of
first principles, especially the law of contradiction, as if they were
sources of deductive demonstration, as if other truths could be drawn
from them deductively, whereas they are merely regulative principles of other inferences; the failure to see that most of the basic
truths of philosophy, being existential judgments, are the result of
a posteriori inferences from fact, not deductive inferences from prior
analytical principles.

All of these points, though they are primarily concerned with the
intrinsic and objective order of knowledge itself, have some significance
for the order of learning, and of teaching in relation to learning. But,
certainly, one thing is already clear: the objective order of subject
matters—of objects as knowable in themselves and apart from us—does
not and cannot determine the right subjective order of teaching and
learning. We must find other principles, peculiarly relevant to the
subjective order, in order to make these determinations. Let us proceed
to them at once.

There are two basic principles which, it seems to me, help us
determine the order of learning, and to adjust that subjective order to
the objective order of subject matters.

The first of these is the very nature of teaching itself. Teaching,
like agriculture and like medicine, is a *cooperative art*, not a simply
productive art, transforming the obediential potentialities of inert matter. Teaching, as a cooperative art, must work with the determinate
potentialities of living matter—and the rules of teaching must be adapted
to the very nature of learning.

The second principle is the basic distinction between discovery and
instruction as types of learning. Discovery is learning without a teacher;
instruction is learning with a teacher's aid. But both are, *as learning*,
essentially the same, and the order of learning must be essentially the
same, therefore, whether the learner proceeds by discovery or by instruction. Furthermore, what is most important of all, since the teacher

is always only a cooperative cause, and never a primary or sole cause, of learning, the intellectual activities which occur without aid in the case of discovery must be going on also in the case of instruction.

From these two principles, we can conclude that the order of teaching must follow the order of learning, and that this order is primarily the order of discovery, for, as we have seen, even in learning by instruction, the primary causes of learning are the same sort of acts which cause discovery, when the learning goes on without a teacher's aid. The significance of this point—which I think is of the greatest importance—may not be grasped unless it is put into contrast with the now prevalent error. Today, in most cases, teaching proceeds as if the order of teaching should follow the order of knowledge, the objective order of knowledge itself, even though we know that this objective order cannot be followed in the process of discovery. In fact, it is completely reversed. Instruction which departs from the order of discovery also departs from the order of learning, for the way of discovery is the primary way of the mind to truth, and instruction merely imitates nature in imitating discovery. The objective structure of knowledge in no way indicates the processes of the mind in growth.

Now the order of discovery is primarily inductive and dialectical, not deductive and scientific. Let me explain. The usual distinction between induction and deduction—going from particulars to universal or universals to particulars—has always seemed to be somewhat superficial, if, in fact, it is correct at all. Rather, it seems to me, the deductive order is going from what is more knowable in itself to what is less knowable in itself; and thus there is an objective foundation for less intelligible truths in more intelligible ones—the intelligibility being intrinsic to the object known, being *secundum se,* not *quoad nos.* In contrast, the inductive order is going from what is more knowable to us to what is less knowable to us. Thus, the deductive order is the demonstration of conclusions from prior principles, or, where demonstration does not take place, the analytical expansion of prior truths in terms of their consequences; whereas the inductive order is the discovery of self-evident principles, on the one hand, and, on the other, it is the inferential procedure whereby every basic existential proposition is known—*for no existential proposition (concerning God, or substance, or the diversity of essences) can be demonstrated deductively.* All *a posteriori* inferences are inductive, not deductive, and these are among the most fundamental inferences of the mind in the discovery of truth about things. The other fundamental step is the intuitive induction of first principles.

Therefore, the methods of teaching any subject matter should be primarily inductive and dialectical, rather than deductive and simply expository, for the former method is a conformity of teaching to the order of learning, as that is naturally exhibited in the order of discovery, which teaching must imitate as a cooperative art; whereas the latter method is a conformity of teaching to the order of knowledge itself, and this is an order which should not determine teaching, for it does not determine learning. The practical implications of this conclusion can be quickly drawn:

First, for any subject matter, and for philosophy preeminently (precisely because it is wisdom and the most difficult sort of knowledge to possess by way of speculative habit), teaching must be by the Socratic method.

Second, the Socratic, or dialectical, method is the only way to avoid the substitution of verbal memory for intellectual habit. It always puts questions before answers. It does not rest when a student gives a verbally right answer, but always tries to undermine the right answer to test it, for if it is just parrotlike speech, the answer will not stand the dialectical attack. It places the highest value on questions, rather than upon answers; for a question in search of answers is an educational dynamo, whereas an answer in search of the question it answers is an educational dud.

Third, it follows, of course, that lectures and textbooks are taboo, for the most part, because lectures usually are deductive or analytical expositions following the order of knowledge, rather than dialectical inquiries adapted to the order of discovery; and textbooks are even worse than lectures as manuals for the memory, rather than challenges to the mind.

Fourth, right teaching must be done either without any books, *if the teacher is a Socrates,* or, if the teacher is not a Socrates the only books he can use to good effect are the very greatest books, on a given subject that have ever been written, for only such books will be above both himself and his students; only such books will stimulate him to inquire and thus to lead his students in inquiry; only such books will pose both teacher and students problems, rather than give them simply codified, and readily memorizable, answers.

Fifth, the simplest test for right teaching—teaching well-ordered as an aid to learning—is this: that the teacher should find himself actively engaged in discovery of the truth, at the same time that he is helping his students (though they be moving at a lower level) to make discoveries also, proportionate to their age and condition. When the teacher proceeds by the wrong method—by lecture-expositions and quizzes on textbooks or manuals—it seldom, if ever, happens that the teacher himself learns anything new. His state of mind is not an inquiring one. That shows he is not really doing the work of a teacher, for the work of a teacher must conform to the work of learning, and this can only take place if the teacher is really learning at the same time that he teaches.

Finally, it is only by such dialectical and inductive procedure that the truth is learned, not in complete abstraction from the problems it solves or the errors it corrects, but in the context of complicated alternatives. This again is the trouble with textbooks. They seldom make the problems live, or state the errors vigorously enough to make them real dangers and real obstacles to the mind.

14

Two Essays on Docility

(1940)

"Two Essays on Docility" considers the relation between students and their teachers. Adler tells us that docility is necessary for learning, but that it is not easy to achieve. Avoiding subservience on the one hand and indocility on the other, docility entails having an open mind, suspending judgment, and being disposed to seek the help of teachers and books in gaining knowledge. These essays first appeared in The Commonweal *(April 1940).*

G. V. D.

1. Docility and Authority

IN HIS *Treatise on Temperance*, Saint Thomas discusses the virtue of studiousness and the vice of curiosity. The virtuous pursuit of learning must not only be moderate, but rightly motivated. *Studiositas* inclines a man to be serious and steadfast in the application of his mind to things worth learning. In contrast, the zest with which many men devote themselves to scholarship and research seems to express curiosity rather than a virtuous exercise of the desire to know.

Now there is another virtue—not explicitly discussed by Saint Thomas—which disciplines us in the life of learning.[1] Docility is the virtue which regulates a man's will with respect to learning from a teacher. Studiousness concerns a right attitude toward subject matters. If men learned only by discovery—each seeking out the truth entirely by himself—studiousness would be sufficient. But men also learn by instruction; in fact, that is the way most men learn for the most part. Therefore, they must adopt a right attitude toward their teachers, to the instruments as well as to the matter of instruction. It is through docility that we recognize the teacher as a doctor, and respect his authority as we respect that of a physician working for our health.

I place docility in the group of virtues annexed to justice, for it consists in rendering to teachers what is their due. As we owe piety to God as the source of our being, and to our parents as the source of our becoming, so docility is a kind of piety toward teachers as among the sources of our learning. There is also an element of gratitude in docility, responsive to the charity of teaching; and an element of humility, because through docility we are rightly ordered to our superiors. We cannot be instructed by our peers, or at least not in the respects in which there is peerage or equality in knowledge. Unless the teacher has an authority which comes from greater knowledge or skill, he cannot justly be our master, nor need we be docile as his students.

In order to define the vices of excess and defect—which I shall call *subservience* and *indocility*—it is necessary to discuss the nature of the doctoral authority. When Saint Thomas says that "the argument from authority based on human reason is the weakest" (*Summa Theologia*, I, 8, Reply to Objection 2), he is obviously not recommending indocility, for that would belie the practice of his whole life as a respectful and grateful student of Aristotle and Saint Augustine. What he is saying is simply that the weakest ground for affirming a conclusion is the fact that it has been affirmed by another, even if that other be the master of those who know or a father of doctrine. If we affirm a principle that is supposed to be self-evident, without its being evident to us, or a conclusion that is supposed to be demonstrated, without being able to demonstrate it, merely because another man has said it, we are being subservient, not docile. We have acquired an opinion, not knowledge; and if we persist in it through a sort of verbal memory, rather than a truly intellectual penetration of the truth, we have been indoctrinated, not instructed.

But, then, wherein lies the authority of teachers? We must distinguish between the intrinsic possession of such authority and its extrinsic signs. With respect to all teachable matters, a man has as much authority intrinsically as he is able to speak the truth. Strictly, it is the truth alone which has the authority over our minds in the realm of knowledge as opposed to the realm of opinion. Whereas opinion is an affirmation by the intellect as moved by the will or the passions, knowledge is a motion independent of the will. To know is to judge entirely in the light of reason. The truth as we see it in such light compels our judgment. If the authority of a teacher consisted in nothing but the truth he spoke, then we could justly recognize his authority only to the extent that, by the natural light of our own reason, we could independently discriminate between truth and falsity on the point of doctrine. There would be no need for docility toward him as a man.

The need for docility arises from the supposition that a student lacks knowledge or the skill to get it and that a teacher, having what the student lacks, can help him. Although the student must never accept what the teacher says *simply because he says it*, neither can he reject it on that ground. In the field of natural knowledge, the student must ultimately make up his own mind in the light of natural reason, but until he is able to do that finally he should try to get all the help he can from those who offer to teach him. Docility is needed, therefore, to dispose him to seek and to use such help wisely and well. If a teacher claims to demonstrate something which the student cannot see at once to be the case, docility requires that the student suspend judgment— neither accept nor reject—and apply his mind studiously to the teacher's words and intentions. He must, with patience and perseverance, continue to submit his mind to instruction, which means nothing more than that he suffer the teacher to continue cooperating with his own active intellect.

Unless there were extrinsic signs of authority, which marked the proper objects of docility, the student would be unable to direct himself properly with respect to available instruction. Such signs are not wanting. Assuming that an educational system is wisely administered, those who hold the office of teacher are signified as having sufficient authority for the grade of student allotted to them. Unlike the political office, which has a certain authority in itself even when held by a bad man, the doctoral office is truly emptied whenever students who have exercised docility discover its occupant to be unworthy. If the *de facto* rule of a usurping despot is tyranny, the *de facto* pressure of an inadequate teacher can only be effective as indoctrination, and that, as we have seen, is a kind of violence. Docility requires the student, nevertheless, to respect the office of the teacher until his incompetence is unmistakably revealed.

There are other extrinsic signs. Quite apart from his office, a teacher may command respect because of his past performances. A teacher who has succeeded in bringing us to the light many times in the past despite our intransigence, is one who deserves our patience in the present instance where we are still in the dark. This is the mark which honors the great teachers of all times. In the tradition of European learning, some men have been the teachers of many generations, of many epochs. The fact that these men are so generally honored by the tradition as great teachers—men who both know and can communicate—is the most compelling extrinsic sign of an authority to which we must respond with docility.

I have elsewhere developed the distinction between dead and living teachers. The living teachers—the local embodiments of learning—are seldom the great teachers. The great teachers are usually dead, though, in another sense, they are eminently alive for us as teachers through their books. Books are instruments of instruction, and obviously call for docility in those who would learn from them, as much as living teachers do. The virtue is essentially the same, whether exercised toward the book of an absent teacher or toward the ministrations of one who is present. When I speak of a "great teacher" or a "great book" I mean one who merits the extrinsic marks of teaching authority because possessing that authority intrinsically, by virtue of a great store of knowledge and great power to disseminate it.

It would be a mistake for those of us who are teachers to suppose that the problem of achieving docility is a problem only for our students. To the extent that we, too, are students, the moral problem exists for us as well. It exists for anyone and everyone who is actively engaged in the life of learning. Those who understand the obligations of that life do not give up learning when they begin to teach. On the contrary, a good teacher is usually one who is himself an active student of the subject matter in which he gives instruction. Authority and docility will be combined in him, for he is both a teacher of those who know less than himself and a student of the masters of his subject matter. One might even guess that there will be a certain proportion between his attainment of authority and his exercise of docility.

I want to consider the problem of docility as it exists for all of us, whether we be merely students in the early stages of our education, or teachers who have realized the need to continue study. The problem, it seems to me, has significant implications for education under modern cultural conditions, precisely because modern culture is so ambivalent about tradition. In its horror of subservience, the modern mind tends to the opposite vice of brash indocility. On the other hand, those who deplore modernism and try to combat it too often return to the first extreme, mistaking subservience for docility.

The opposition of these extremes is the prevailing tension between the mood of secular and Catholic education. These two systems of education have contrary vices, each a reaction to the other—too little or too much respect for traditional authorities. I might add that the attitude which is characteristic of secular or Catholic faculties toward the great teachers of the past is reflected in the attitude of secular or Catholic students toward their living teachers. The one is usually indocile, the other subservient. (The subservience may be merely outward. I speak only of appearances.)

The temper of a culture with respect to its intellectual tradition underlies its educational efforts. If docility is indispensable to sound educational policy and practice, we must rectify the culture itself in terms of this virtue. How shall this be done? We are frequently told that historical scholarship is the way. We are told that the proper study of philosophy, and even science, is impossible without thorough historical orientation. Both modernism and its equally bad opposite, "modern scholasticism," spring from corrupt history, or the lack of historical insight. In their enthusiasm, the exponents of history as the magic open sesame tend to identify the historical attitude with docility. They soon become infected with historicism, which is simply the error of making historical scholarship, truly enough a necessary condition of rectitude in learning from the past, into a sufficient condition.

I propose, therefore, to examine the service of history in the life of learning, by considering its relation to the achievement of docility. But before I can discuss these larger implications of the problem, it is necessary first to consider docility from the point of view of the individual person who is trying to be virtuous in his attitude toward teachers and books.

For most of the moral virtues, the mean between the extremes of excess and defect is a subjective mean. The mean in the case of courage, lying somewhere between foolhardiness and cowardice, is not objectively ascertainable, and as such the same for all men. It is rather a mean that is relative to the individual temperament of each man who tries to be courageous, a mean which a man's own prudence must appoint after due consideration of the conditions of his life, the complexion of all his natural tendencies, and the circumstances of particular acts.

The mean of docility is subjective in this sense. The definition of docility as the right amount of respect for the authority of teachers (or books) is by itself insufficient to determine action. It is a truth too remote from the exigencies of practice to direct us in the particular decisions we have to make. In this particular case—with this teacher or book, in view of my temperamental weaknesses, my tendencies to be indolent or impatient, and in connection with this point of doctrine about which I have strong feelings—what is the *right amount* of respect due those who are trying to instruct me? There is the practical question. And I cannot cultivate the habit of docility unless I can decide such questions prudently time after time as they arise.

Aristotle gives us two practical rules to guide us in the casuistry of applying moral principles to particular cases of action.

As it is difficult to hit the mean exactly, we must take the second best course, and choose the lesser of two evils, and this we shall do best in the way we have described, i.e., by steering clear of the evil which is further from the mean. We must also observe the things to which we are ourselves particularly prone, as different natures have different inclinations, and we may ascertain what these are by a consideration of our feelings of pleasure and pain. And then we must drag ourselves in the direction opposite to them; for it is by removing ourselves as far as possible from what is wrong that we shall arrive at the mean, as we do when we pull a crooked stick straight (*Nicomachean Ethics*, II, 9).

Let us consider the second suggestion first. If by temperament we tend to be impatient of authority, we should pull ourselves in the direction of subservience, for by so doing we shall be going toward the mean. If our temperament is of the opposite sort, we should struggle against our reluctance to exercise an independent judgment. Such counteraction of our natural weaknesses assists us to make a prudent determination of the mean relative to ourselves.

But if the mean of docility is hard to hit exactly, which is the better error to make, the worse vice to avoid, subservience or indocility? I, for one, cannot answer this question *absolutely*, that is, without any reference to circumstances. But it can be answered *relatively* by considering the generality of cases of different type. Thus, I would say that for modern culture generally the aim should be to avoid indocility; for Catholic students, in contrast to those in our secular colleges, the motion should be away from subservience; and, in general, it is worse for those who are in the early stages of study to be indocile than subservient, whereas, on the contrary, for those who are mature and who should assume a responsibility of independent judgment proportionate to their competence, it is worse to be subservient.

The casuistical questions which a man faces in trying to be docile are more difficult than those which arise in the field of other moral virtues; but these are always the most difficult questions, not only for each of us to decide for ourselves, but for anyone to prescribe ways of answering for others. Perhaps, therefore, the best thing I can do is to put down some of the considerations which weigh heavily with me when I am trying to read a book with docility.

In the first place, I try never to forget that the only ultimate factor which can decide my judgment—whether I shall agree or disagree with the author who is my teacher—is the natural light of my own reason. Remembering this, I will not assent to anything I do not see, be it principle or conclusion or the reasoning from the one to the other. I know, of course, how often I have failed to abide by this precept, how often I have adopted, for example, statements by Aristotle or Saint Thomas, because of emotional predispositions rather than intellectual light. I respect them so much as teachers that I have often permitted them to indoctrinate me—the fault being mine, not theirs, the respect being excessive, rather than right. For many years, I affirmed, and repeated to my students as if I knew it to be true, the Aristotelian error about natural slavery. If it is the error I now see it to be, it could not have been a truth I saw. As I review my own life on this point, I realize that I never did *see* the point. I merely accepted it because Aristotle had spoken.

In matters of natural knowledge, no human authority should prevail against the light of your own reason. But we know that our thinking is fallible. We know how often we suffer the illusion that we see the truth, only to discover later that we have judged too soon. Hence the second maxim I try to follow is this: one should suspend judgment long enough to be sure that one really understands what the teacher is trying to say before agreeing or disagreeing with him. Life being short, and the responsibility for making up one's mind on important questions being urgent, how long is long enough? This is a matter which everyone must determine for himself in conscience. If to disagree rashly leads to indocility, to agree without reservation, without making the effort to be sure one really knows what is being agreed to, is subservience. Docility demands sufficient *suspension* of judgment so that when I judge I shall be acting in the light of reason, and not in terms of passionate devotion or equally passionate opposition to the author I am reading.

There are a number of factors I consider in estimating the delay of judgment proper in a given case, the amount of effort to understand which should precede making up my mind. One is the degree of extrinsic authority that tradition has accorded the teacher. I should be less impetuous in judging Aristotle and Saint Thomas than in the case of some nineteenth, or even sixteenth, century scholastic textbook. If there is a probable correlation between the extrinsic signs of authority and its intrinsic possession, then certainly it is sound to say that the more authority a teacher *seems* to have, the more pause he should give you. This maxim should operate in the case in which you are, for whatever reason, inclined to disagree, as well as when you are favorably predisposed. Here, too, my biography is full of faults. So much of what David Hume says was repugnant to my reason fairly early in my study of philosophy, that I tended to reject him in entirety without due consideration of the extrinsic authority he certainly has in a large area of the modern tradition. I now know that I went astray here, failing through indocility to see the contribution of Hume's positivism for the understanding of empirical science, as through subservience I have parroted errors from Aristotle and Saint Thomas.

The rule of practice must, therefore, be sharpened on both its edges, for it must cut two ways. Wherever I am emotionally, or even intellectually, inclined to agree, I should suspend judgment before concurring, lest I merely indoctrinate myself. Wherever my disposition is of the contrary sort, I should hesitate to disagree, lest I reject without understanding what greater patience would have made intelligible and acceptable to my mind. And, in both cases, my conscience must determine the degree of patience due the author by reference to the marks of extrinsic authority he bears. I must add here that, in addition to the reputation which tradition has conferred, the degree to which I have come to feel his authority because of his previous successes as a teacher in my own life ought also to be considered.

This first factor is qualified by two others. On the one hand, I must take into account my own position in the scale of learning. Thus, in a given subject matter I may have achieved competence to a greater or less degree. In proportion as I have competence—which means, in proportion as I approach peerage with the great teachers in that field —I am entitled to make up my mind more quickly. What would be indecent impetuosity in the beginner may be protracted deliberateness in the learned. On the other hand, I must know myself as a creature of passions and prejudices in order to make due allowance for every sort of waywardness that could interfere with a prudent determination of the mean of docility in this case, as conditioned not only by the author's authority in relation to my knowledge, but also by my idiosyncrasies in relation to the author.

In this process of casuistry, it makes a difference whether I am a student being instructed by living teachers, or at once a teacher of students as well as a student of the dead masters. If I am in that middle position—which should be the position of every good teacher, modest enough to recognize his limitations—the duty of docility is more heavily incumbent upon me, for I have the obligation to exhibit it in my teaching, as well as practice it in my studying. I shall return to this point in a later discussion of the bearing of docility on the role of the teacher.

One other thing makes a difference. When I am dealing with the great teachers of the past, I must bridge the gap of time. The continuity of tradition is not perfect. I must be deeply conscious of my own place in cultural time, in order to realize that the author I am reading lived and thought in a different climate of opinion. If my cultural location confers certain advantages on me, I am not indocile if I take advantage of the superiority which modern birth gives me over the greatest teachers of the ancient and medieval past. If I exaggerate that advantage, I am, of course, lacking in true docility; but a vicious subservience results equally from minimizing it.

This last point raises the whole question about the dependence of docility, in an individual teacher, in an educational system, or in a whole culture, upon the cultivation of a historical sense—a sense of the present as moving into the future, as well as a sense of the present growing out of the past. This point, too, I shall discuss in a subsequent essay.

2. Docility and History

The attainment of docility is, as we have seen, a personal problem which each of us must solve in his private life of learning. But there is also an institutional problem of docility, involving the curriculum and administration of studies in an educational system. I am thinking of the two points which in my prior article were left for further consideration. The first has to do with the relation between living teachers and dead ones (books) as instruments of instruction. The second concerns the precise place of scholarship, and historical orientation generally, in learning from the past.

The curriculum of St. John's College, Annapolis, has generated controversy bearing on both these points. Some critics have questioned the advisability of placing the great books in the hands of the young, without definite instruction by living teachers that explicitly discriminates between true doctrines and false. When such critics follow out the implication of the amendment to the St. John's plan, they usually end up by suggesting lecture courses, textbooks, and manuals, devised for putting blinders on the students and leading them along the straight and narrow path to the truth. This is not an amendment of the St. John's plan, but an abolition of it. It substitutes the way of indoctrination for the discipline of docility.

Other critics have wondered whether the paraphernalia of historical scholarship can be so cavalierly dispensed with. The program of getting the tradition to reveal its secrets by going directly to the books seems to underestimate the importance of the philological approach to past cultures. Even though the books are read in chronological order, little effort seems to be made to place each book precisely in its cultural setting, to read the mind of each author as a product of complex historical determinations. Paradoxically, an educational program which exudes so profound a respect for the past seems to have little or no respect for the historical methods by which men try to relive the intellectual life of prior epochs.

I would like to consider these two points, not only as they bear on the St. John's curriculum, but in their educational implications generally.

The critics who fear a shallow eclecticism, or, what is worse, sophistry and skepticism, as the inevitable result of making the great books the students' *only* teachers, cannot be lightly dismissed. Their error lies not in their insistence that sound educational policy requires living leadership, but rather in their misconception of the role the living teacher should play. The tradition of great books contains both truth and error, mixed in varying proportions in different cases. This holds for ancient and medieval authors, as well as moderns. The student who reads both Plato and Aristotle and does not recognize the obligation to decide between them on crucial points is not learning *from* the past, but merely *about* it. The same can be said for issues which put Saint Augustine and Saint Thomas on opposite sides. The objective is to know the truth about God, man, and nature, and the ends of human life, not what anyone, however great his authority, thought about these matters. The deviation from a right aim is even greater if it be supposed that students should become acquainted with the sheer diversity of opinions on major questions in order to become, through the conflict of authorities, emancipated from authority itself.

There are two extremes here. One position, which may be taken by some of the exponents of the St. John's plan, is to make the living teacher *merely* a liberal artist, *merely* a dialectician, whose only office is to sharpen the student's wits as a reader of the books. While I would certainly insist that it is the teacher's business to cultivate in every way the student's skill in reading—analytically, interpretively, critically—I would also insist that that is not enough. For, as Plato teaches us, dialectic cannot be distinguished from sophistry *as an intellectual method*. It differs only on a moral count—in virtue of its use as means toward the truth. If the reading of the great books is merely for the sake of making liberal artists of the students, they will end by being sophisticated, but not learned or wise.

At the opposite extreme is the position, embodied in much of Catholic education, that the shortest way to the truth is the best. Why take the long and devious path that leads through the great books, with all their difficulties and conflicts, if a living teacher can present the right doctrine in lectures supported by textbooks written by himself or his colleagues; or if he can assign a textbook and get the students to repeat what it says instead of doing that himself in lectures? If the great books should be read, let the teacher do that in the course of his own education or in the privacy of his study. Let him cull the truth from the errors, and feed the young the unblemished fruits.

Here the opposite error is made. Students who are not trained in the liberal arts—and apart from the discipline of reading great books they cannot be—are incapable of the *activity* of being taught. They are entirely given to the *passivity* of being indoctrinated. They are not trained to be docile, for docility is required only in the active exercise of one's intellectual powers. Only when independence of judgment is encouraged (more, demanded), must docility be cultivated. Textbooks and lectures elicit memorization and, with it, instill subservience. Furthermore, the supposition that the living teachers are the refinery through which the riches of the past are purified before they reach the student in the form of lectures and textbooks is open to question. Teachers are usually the product of the educational system in which they serve in their turn. If the system is one in which they do not read great books with *their* students, it is unlikely that *their* teachers read great books with them. Hence it is likely to be the case that their lectures or textbooks are condensations or repetitions of other textbooks and lectures, rather than magnificent renditions of the tradition.

The solution, as always, is a union of the half-truths drawn from the extremes. The living teacher must not only be a disciplinarian of the liberal arts; he must also argue for the truths and against the errors that he himself has found, or finds, in the books he reads with his students. He must be both *doctor* and *docile*. The assumption is that the person who conducts a reading seminar is more mature than his students—more skilled in reading, and hence able to initiate them into its intricacies, as well as more learned in doctrine, and hence competent to discover the truth to those who seek it in the books. The living teacher is truly a mediator between the novices in learning and the masters of knowledge, through being himself in a mean state between them. On the one hand, he participates in the role of *teacher* through possessing more of the knowledge the great books contain, than do his students. To this extent, he has some authority in his own right, is entitled to instruct and deserves docility from them. On the other hand, he participates in the role of *student* through being still engaged in the search for knowledge at its fountainheads. To this extent, he must exhibit docility to his students, for only by manifesting it in his own practice of the liberal arts, can he genuinely persuade his students to follow in his footsteps.

The solution thus avoids two errors: the fallacy of supposing that a curriculum which makes the great books the major teachers must completely exclude doctrinal judgments on the part of the minor teacher; and the mistake of making the minor teacher the chief source of doctrine, permitting him to masquerade as a major teacher, usurping an authority not rightly his. The latter error is made by any educational program which substitutes manuals and lecture courses for the great books. It forces a teaching personnel, that might be able to function

well as mediators, to exceed their powers, to offer themselves as reposi-
tories of learning. It cannot breed docility, failing so signally to exhibit
it, for the pretense by which the minor teacher becomes an oracle
instead of a medium is a counterfeit made possible only by subservience
or indocility.

What I have said of this second error applies equally, though perhaps
differently, to Catholic and secular institutions. If the first error is made
at St. John's, then the program is subject to one of the charges brought
against it. I wish to argue only that that error is entirely accidental to
the program. That being so, there is no excuse for Catholic educators
in not separating essence from accidents, and not adopting what is
fundamentally sound in the St. John's plan.

With respect to the role of historical scholarship, there are also two
false extremes. For the sake of sharpening the point within the brief
scope of this article, let me consider the relation of history to the study
of philosophy. For one thing, the problem of docility is much more
acute in seeking philosophical wisdom than in acquiring scientific
knowledge; and this is related to the fact that textbooks are much less
pernicious in science than philosophy. For another thing, the history
of philosophy—in fact, the history of culture, and of science also—
appears to have a certain philosophical significance which the student
of philosophy cannot well ignore. The student of science suffers less
from ignorance of general cultural history. Hence, education in philosophy is a good field for the examination of the relation between
docility and history.

At one extreme are those who claim that history is irrelevant to the
study of philosophy. Curiously enough, these are usually the same
people who try to teach philosophy *systematically*, out of textbooks or
manuals. Philosophical knowledge consists of a set of doctrines which
are timelessly true and which, therefore, can be expounded without
any regard for the historical accidents of cultural time and place. If I
understand them correctly, the students of M. Gilson have attacked the
simplemindedness of this position as a root cause of error and super-
ficiality in modern scholasticism. But, it seems to me, they go to the
opposite extreme, and in doing so go further than their leader himself.
They commit the error of historicism. Though all they affirm is that
history is an indispensable instrument in the discovery of philosophical

truth, they become so enamored of the instrument that in practice, if not in theory, they subvert the end to the means. The philological study of texts, the delineation of affinities between minds separated by centuries, the tracing of streams of influence and divergence—all these things become more important than bare philosophical argument.

I am extremely sensitive to the difference between scholarly competence and expertness in philosophy, to the difference between seeking to penetrate the truth by thinking, and seeking to get inside the minds of other men, to think their thoughts by acts of historical imagination. Partly this may be due to my own acknowledged incompetence in historical scholarship. Life being short, I have made what seemed to me an inevitable choice between scholarship and philosophy. I doubt if anyone's energies are ample enough to permit an adequate devotion to both. To take eminent examples, Gilson and Maritain, it seems to me, have made opposite choices, though each, of course, enjoys some competence in the other's field.

But my sensitiveness here is due even more to the fact that I have seen so many young men start out to become philosophers and end up as historians or philologians. I would say that they gave up the harder task for an easier one. Truly it is easier to "speculate" about what Aristotle thought, even if such speculation must be supported by the most careful adduction of evidences, than it is to speculate, as Aristotle did, about the nature of things. (Perhaps this is why many philosophy departments in both secular and Catholic universities direct their doctoral candidates into fields of historical research rather than encourage "young men" to undertake genuine philosophical work.) Not only is it easier, but one's fundamental intellectual integrity is less affected. To have one's scholarship corrected does not get into one's soul as much as to have one's philosophical judgments refuted. Those who substitute scholarship for philosophy avoid sticking their necks out in a way that invites serious intellectual challenge. The scholar may have his own philosophical opinions, but he usually manages to bury them in his interpretation of other men's thought. He has effaced himself behind what other men stood for and thus avoids standing too openly for anything himself.

Observe that I marked the word "speculate" when I spoke about historical research. For this, it seems to me, is speculation in the sense of conjecture, not speculation in the sense in which philosophy is speculative knowledge. In fact, history at its best stands to philosophy, as opinion does to knowledge. No matter how perfectly all the historical techniques are employed, it is impossible to *know with certitude* what Aristotle or Plotinus thought about anything. In contrast, the philosophical thought of Aristotle and Plotinus is either certainly true or false. It is either knowledge or not knowledge, but never probable opinion. The reason why cultural history is opinion should be obvious. It is an effort to reach a decision about the singular mind of a particular man in terms of such contingent and inadequate data as written documents. To indulge in scholarly disputes about what a dead philosopher meant by his words seems to me a poor substitute for philosophical controversy about a truth in issue. For if agreement is reached in the one case, the disputants rest only in opinion; whereas in the other they share a common knowledge.

But scholarship and history need not be substituted *for philosophy.* Therein lies the reconciliation of the two false extremes. So long as the means are properly subordinated to their end, no disorder results from the use of historical scholarship as an aid in the reading of great philosophical books. Just as we correct an error which may occur accidentally in the execution of the St. John's program, by insisting that the reading of books be ordained to the end of acquiring doctrine as well as skill, so we correct the excess of historicism by placing scholarship in the service of an intelligent reading of books. When this ordering of means to ends is clear, historicism is as effectively avoided as eclecticism.

It may be said, however, that it is not historicism, but its opposite, which a program like St. John's must avoid. The problem here concerns the relation between the liberal arts and historical techniques as components in the complex skill of reading books. May I suggest a solution briefly? There are two major steps in reading: interpretation and criticism. One must do one's best to understand an author before agreeing or disagreeing with him. Historical scholarship bears exclusively on interpretive reading; when it is properly subordinated as a means, its end is exegesis; all of its techniques are of service to the grammatical art. But exegesis is not *the* end; nor is grammar the highest art. Exegesis is for the sake of a fair critical judgment, grammar for the sake of logic and rhetoric. A liberal education must, in short, include historical scholarship as a supplement to grammatical art in reading, and just as surely must it subordinate these techniques to the ultimate purpose for which logical and rhetorical skill is exercised—the independent judgment of a mind about the living truth. When history and grammar dominate the process, docility is confused with the effort to achieve a "sympathetic understanding" of dead men's minds.

There is another aspect of the relation between history and docility. To the extent that we engage in learning from great teachers of the past, a well developed "historical sense"—a sense of the motion of history—gives us the perspective and orientation needed for docility. We in the modern world have this historical sense much more highly developed than any earlier epoch of European culture. We owe it to the technical achievement of modern historical scholarship.

The truth is timeless, but human thought, intricately conditioned by its concrete cultural situation, is dated. Historical relativity cannot be avoided, but through acknowledging the limitations imposed upon any thinker by his time and place, we can disengage the truth from its historical accidents. The imagery which embodies thought, and the language in which it is expressed, are always local. By discerning these externals as belonging to a cultural moment, we can transcend them a little, and find the timeless in the heart of time. The truth itself, *whenever* it is achieved or *however* it is embodied and expressed, is not explained by history. But history does explain the errors men have made in the search for truth. The truth our ancestors won belongs to us as much as to them. History helps us to possess it by enabling us to transcend the cultural accidents which separate us from them. The errors our ancestors made are theirs alone. We shall make others, perhaps, but we should not repeat theirs. History helps us to reject such mistakes by showing us their causes in the cultural limitations of past epochs. Aware that we are subject to similar limitations, we should be able to look down at the past without pride.

Historical relativity is greater in some fields of thought than in others, in politics, for instance, more than in ethics, in the philosophy of nature more than in metaphysics. To disengage the political truths of Aristotle and Saint Thomas from the accidents of local imagery and language, as well as from the fallacies that surround them, requires much more historical insight than a similar effort in ethics. Unless we have such insights, we are likely to be subservient, accepting errors because they accompany truth, or we may be indocile, rejecting the truth because of the errors, or because the truth is strangely garbed in foreign dress.

The modern student should be able to attain a greater docility precisely because he has better historical perspective and orientation. The ancient and medieval worlds lacked the historical sense. To the extent that their works reveal them as students of their predecessors, we can see how Aristotle and Saint Thomas suffered from this privation, characteristic of their times. With greater historical knowledge, Aristotle might have been less indocile toward the pre-Socratics, and Saint Thomas might have been less subservient toward Aristotle.

The historical sense is not simply a sense of the past. It is even more a sense of the future, and an awareness of the present as a point in motion between past and future. Through realizing the slow, and often imperceptible, progress of history, we can take advantage of the respects in which our present cultural location elevates us above the past, and at the same time we can appreciate the limitations of the present as we look forward to the future. Thus we can combine gratitude toward the past on whose shoulders we stand, with humility toward the future. Neither fawning nor unduly self-reliant, we recognize ourselves as creatures of time. Through a docility thus fortified by a historical sense, we are emancipated both from the dead hand of tradition and from the provincialism of the present moment. Only the docility of the living present can make the tradition live and perpetuate itself through myriad transformations.

If I were asked to name the virtue which most singularly distinguishes Jacques Maritain as a philosopher, I would say his docility. All of its manifestations will be detected by those who see how deeply his Thomism is motivated by a sense of the future. Philosophy is perennial for him, not as a monument which endures the ravages of time, but as a living thing which enjoys time as its dimension of change and growth. The dead bones of philosophy are not building materials. Not a reverence for relics, but for the spirit they have disembodied, is the docility which encourages Maritain to regard Saint Thomas as a cooperator in the work of preparing for a philosopher greater than Saint Thomas, as he was greater than Aristotle.

We have considered all the impediments to docility, the difficulties to be overcome in ourselves, in our educational systems and in our culture. It would be wise, in conclusion, to remember a point that is central in the whole theory of virtue, namely, the integration of the virtues. No one of the cardinal virtues, nor any of their parts, can be possessed in isolation from all the rest. Whether it be considered as a part of prudence, in relation to practical matters, or as a part of justice, in relation to the theoretic life in which there are doctors and students, docility is impossible apart from fortitude and temperance. One may be docile by natural temperament, but that is not the true virtue which belongs only to those whose will is rectified by the simultaneous possession of all the principal virtues.

It has become sufficiently clear how courage is indispensable to docility. Perhaps a word more is needed to indicate the need for temperance also. It may suffice to recall that a part of temperance is the virtue most closely related to docility, *studiositas*. No one can be docile who is not rightly directed in the matter of pursuing knowledge. Studiosity opposes the vice of curiosity. It appoints the right end of all our intellectual labors. The means of learning will be well used only if they are used for the right end. As Saint Thomas tells us (*Summa Theologica*, II-II, 167, 1), we must avoid studying for the sake of taking pride in our knowledge; we must not seek to know the truth "above the capacity of our intelligence, for by so doing we fall easily into error"; we must make a proper estimate of the worth of various subject matters as these are disposed in a true hierarchy of studies; and the due end, to which all our efforts in research must be referred, is the knowledge of God.

15

Education Beyond Schooling—
The Task of a Lifetime

(1942; 1952)

The proposition that education is primarily a matter for adults and therefore for all adults is essential to Adler's view of education. Youth, he maintains, like Aristotle before him, is an obstacle to education. Two corollaries of this proposition are (1) that liberal education for all must be begun in school so that all may go on with their education after schooling, and (2) that, although all of us must earn a living, nobody needs to go to school in order to learn how to earn a living. Suggestions for education beyond schooling, as the task of a lifetime, follow.

This essay includes small sections of an unpublished essay called "Have You Changed Your Mind?" and of the article, "What Every Schoolboy Doesn't Know," which was published in Pulse *(March 1942). Most of the essay was published under the title "Adult Education" in the* Journal of Higher Education *(February 1952).*

G.V.D.

THOSE OF US who are engaged in adult education have been thinking for some time of how to avoid using that term, because in the minds of the general public it has such an unfortunate connotation. If, by issuing an edict, I could get everybody to use words the way I would like them to, I would try to set up the following usage: use *schooling* to signify the development and training of the young, and *education* to signify the learning done by mature men and women.

Then we could say that after schooling, education, not adult education, begins.

Most of us, and most professional educators, hold a false view of schooling. It consists in the notion that it is the purpose of the schools—and I use the word *schools* to include all levels of institutional education from the kindergarten to the college and university—to turn out educated men and women, their education completed when they are awarded a degree or diploma. Nothing could be more absurd or preposterous. This means that young people—children of twenty or twenty-two—are to be regarded as educated men and women. We all know, and no one can deny, that no child—in school or at the moment of graduation—is an educated person. Yet this is the apparent aim of the whole school system—to give a complete education. At least this is the conception that governs the construction of the curriculum and the conduct or administration of the school system, and it is the conception of most parents who send their children to schools and colleges.

That this misconception is widespread is shown by the fact that most of us also hold a false view of adult education. We think of it as something for the underprivileged. Some unfortunate people, deprived of schooling in youth by economic circumstances or hardships, in later life, while they are working all day to support a family, go to night school to make up for their lack of schooling in youth. Night schooling or remedial schooling—to compensate for lack of sufficient schooling in youth—is, for a great many people, the essence of adult education. When the majority who are more fortunate think of it in this way, they conclude that adult education is not for them, but only for the unfortunate few who lacked sufficient schooling in youth.

Another false and very misleading notion is that adult education is an avocation, a hobby that occupies a little of your spare time, something a little better than canasta or television, but not much. On this level, adult education consists of classes in basket weaving, folk dancing, clay modeling, or, what is not much better, lectures on current events.

These are all wrong notions—wrong notions of the meaning of what schooling is or should be, and wrong notions of what fundamental education for adults should be. Perhaps the easiest way to correct these errors, and state the contrary truth, is to point out what every school child does not know. Every school child, particularly at the moment of graduation from school, does not know how much he does not know—and how much he has to learn. This is perfectly natural, and children are not to be blamed for it. It is one of the blindnesses of youth. But there is hardly an intelligent adult—a college graduate two or three years out of college—who will not readily and happily confess that he is not an educated person, and that there is much more for him to learn.

When the graduate, two, three, or five years out of college, recognizes the fact that he is not educated, or that his education or training was far from completed in all the years of schooling, he usually has one or another incorrect explanation of the fact. If he is a gentle and generous person, he is likely to say: "The fault was mine. I went to a good school. The curriculum was good. I had a fine set of teachers. The library facilities and all the other conditions in my formal schooling were excellent; but I wasted my time. I played cards or took the girls out, or went in for extracurricular activities, or something else interfered with study. If only I had studied, I would now be an educated person." This, I assure you, is quite wrong. At the opposite extreme, there is the person who is less generous. He puts the blame on somebody else. He says: "It was the school's fault. The teachers were no good; the curriculum and the facilities were poor. If all these had been better, I would now be educated." This opposite extreme is equally wrong.

Consider the brightest student at the best imaginable college—much better than any which now exists—with the most competent faculty and with a perfect course of study. Imagine this brightest student in the best of all possible colleges, spending four years industriously, faithfully, and efficiently applying his mind to study. I say to you that, at the end of four years, this student, awarded a degree with the highest honors, is not an educated man. He cannot be, for the simple reason that the obstacle to becoming educated in school is an inherent and insurmountable one, namely, youth.

The young cannot be educated. Youth is the obstacle. Why is this so? We know the answer almost as soon as we ask the question.

What do we mean by young people? What are children? In asking this question, I use the word *children* for all human beings still under institutional care. I do not care what their chronological age is, whether it is fifteen or twenty-two. If they are still within the walls of a school, college, or university, they are children. They are living a protected, and in many ways an artificial, life.

What is our conception of being a child? It is obviously a conception of human life at a stage when it is right to be irresponsible to a certain degree. Childhood is a period of irresponsibility. In addition to being irresponsible, the child or young person, precisely because he is protected or safeguarded, is greatly deficient in experience. Most or all of the things that make us adults or mature occur after we leave school. The business of getting married, of having children, of having our parents become ill, or dependent on us, or die, the death of our friends, our business and social responsibilities—these are the experiences that age us. And aging is part of what makes us mature. We cannot be mature without being aged, and aged through pain and suffering and grief. This kind of suffering children are spared, but they pay a price for being spared it. They remain immature, irresponsible, and unserious, in the basic sense of that word.

Let me indicate this in still another way. In recent years, teachers in colleges and universities have had the experience of having, in the same classroom, the returned G.I., continuing his education on the G.I. Bill of Rights, and ordinary boys and girls right out of high school. The difference between those two groups of students in the same classroom is like the difference between black and white. The actual ages are not too far apart—sometimes the G.I. is hardly more than a year or two older than the boy sitting next to him. But the one is a man and the other is a child. And the difference between a man and a child is a difference wrought by experience, pain, and suffering, by hard knocks. It cannot be produced by schooling.

It follows, then, that, precisely because they are immature, properly irresponsible, not serious, and lacking a great deal of experience, children in school are not educable. I do not mean they are not trainable. In fact, they are much more trainable than we are. As we get older, our nervous system becomes much less plastic. It is much harder for us to learn languages, shorthand, or ice skating. The child, in all matters of simple habit formation, is much more trainable than the adult; but the adult is much more educable, because education is not primarily a matter of training or habit formation. Though these are preparations for it, education in its essence is the cultivation of the human mind. Education consists in the growth of understanding, insight, and ultimately some wisdom. These growths require mature soil. Only in mature soil, soil rich with experience, can ideas really take root.

When I say adults are more educable than children, I am really saying that adults can think better than children. If this were not so, adults ought to stay away from the polls and send their children there instead. But if an adult can think better than a child, then he must be more educable than a child. Basic learning—the acquisition of ideas, insight, understanding—depends on being able to think. If adults can think better than children, they can also learn better—learn better in the fundamental sense of cultivating their minds. This is not a novel educational insight, this insistence that education belongs to the mature, and schooling, at the level of training and habit formation, to the young. In our own century, with scientific evidence on adults' ability to learn, Thorndike of Columbia has come to the conclusion, after painstaking research, that while the ability to learn seems to reach its height at twenty-five and drops until at forty-five it corresponds to what it was at eighteen, "the change from 18 to 45 is so slight that there is no reason for diffidence, on the part of those in the prime of life, about undertaking new branches of learning." He estimates the decrease after twenty-five at no more than 1 percent a year. Professors Sorenson and Price of Minnesota, conducting further investigations of the problem, found that "the decline in the mental abilities of adults is functional; it results from disuse and not from organic degeneration."

In fact, all the great periods of Western culture have recognized and acted on the simple basic truth I have stated as my central thesis. If we go back to the Greeks, for example, we find in the works of the two greatest thinkers of antiquity, Plato and Aristotle, the presence of this fundamental insight.

The *Republic* of Plato outlines the ideal education of the best men to govern the ideal state. The course of study is as follows. Notice its time schedule. From the beginning until the student reaches the age of twenty, the curriculum is confined to music and gymnastics, to the cultivation of the sensibilities and imagination and to the acquisition of all the basic bodily coordinations. Between the ages of twenty and thirty there occurs training in the liberal arts, particularly the arts of mathematics (arithmetic, geometry, astronomy, and music), and the basic arts of grammar and logic. Then, at the age of thirty, the young person begins the study of philosophy for five years. At the age of thirty-five he goes out into the world. He leaves the academy and undertakes civic duties or public responsibilities, thus becoming a little more mature. He returns to the academy at fifty to resume the study of philosophy and begin the contemplation of ideas. Here is a time schedule which recognizes how slowly the processes of education take place and how much maturity is required before the understanding of ideas can occur.

In the opening chapters of Aristotle's *Ethics*, he points out that you can train the characters of young men, you can form the moral virtues in them by reward and punishment; but, he says, you cannot teach them ethical principles because they are immature. Lacking moral and political experience, being more or less under the influence of wayward passions, they cannot possibly understand moral and political principles, nor are they in a position to make sound judgments on moral questions. Think of how we violate this insight in our schools today. One of the major subjects for the young, soon after kindergarten, is social studies. Aristotle would not have thought it possible to teach these to young children, because to understand the theory of society requires mature experience and judgment.

If it is true that education is primarily a matter for adults, then it is necessary for all adults, not just for those who suffered deprivation in youth through lack of this or that part of formal schooling. It is no longer just necessary for the other fellow; it becomes a matter which each of us must face for himself.

Let us turn, first, to the consequences of this proposition for the school system. I assume, without any argument at all, that we are committed to a democratic society, a democratic government, and democratic institutions. And I assume that this means the acceptance of the basic truth of human equality, which expresses itself in the political principle of universal suffrage. What distinguishes democracy from all other forms of government is the extension of the franchise to all citizens, men and women, without regard to race, creed, or color. The only just limitations on suffrage involve the exclusion of infants and children, the mentally incompetent, and criminals who have forfeited their political rights by acts of moral turpitude. No one else is justly excluded according to a democratic conception of government. The educational consequence of this political principle is the precept of equal educational opportunity for all. Schooling must be universal and compulsory because, in a democracy, all children must be trained for citizenship. This means building enough schools and finding enough teachers to take care of the whole population of future citizens in our democratic society.

It may be claimed that we have almost succeeded in doing this in this country. It is true that we have, in the course of the last fifty years, recognized the educational obligations of a democratic society. We have built a tremendous number of schools and trained a vast horde of teachers. We have poured great funds of taxpayers' money into school budgets. This is satisfactory as far as it goes, but it does not go nearly far enough. Anyone who has children in school, or knows anything about what is going on in most of the schools today, public or private, knows that most of the children are not being democratically educated. Most of the children—I think I can even safely say more than 75 percent—are, in fact, being given almost no education at all. They are being given vocational training. Vocational training is training for work or for the life of a slave. It is not the education of the future citizen, of the free man who has leisure to use. Liberal education, as distinguished from vocational training, is education for freedom, and this means that it is education for the responsibilities of citizenship and for the good use of leisure.

No one has to go to school in order to earn a living. Our grandfathers did not. Perhaps we need schools to train men for the learned professions, but not for the ordinary jobs of an industrial society. The basic tasks of an industrial society can be learned on the job. We need to go to school, not in order to learn how to earn a living, but in order to learn how to use the life for which we are going to earn a living—to learn how to occupy ourselves humanly, to live our leisure hours well and not play them all away. We need to learn how to do well what we are called upon to do as moral and political agents, and to do well what we must do for the cultivation of our own minds.

These are the aims of liberal education. Liberal education must be begun in school. If we understand what democracy is and what leisure is, and that to be a free man is to be a man of leisure as well as a citizen, then it follows that all children not only should go to school but should also be given a liberal education there. I would go so far as to say that all vocational training should be removed from the schools. I would go even further and say that by liberal education for all children I mean the same kind of education for all, up to what is now regarded as the bachelor of arts degree.

It was all right, objectors say, to try to give all who went to school the same kind of liberal education a hundred years ago when we had a much smaller and a much more select school population. But now that we have democratically taken all the children into school, it is no longer possible to give the same kind of education to all. I reply that we must undertake to give the kind of education that was given in the eighteenth century to the small governing class (the Thomas Jeffersons, the Alexander Hamiltons, the John Adamses, the men who wrote the Constitution and the Declaration) to the large governing class now— all the citizens of the United States today. Nothing else will do. Nothing else is democratic.

I admit that children are containers of different sizes. They do not all have the same capacity. But the question is not one of the amount of education to be given each child, for no child can receive more than his capacity permits. The question is the kind of education to be given each child, according to his capacity.

Let me illustrate this with a simple metaphor. Let the child of low intelligence and weak natural endowments be represented by a pint container, and the child of extremely high endowments and intelligence, by a gallon container. According to the democratic concept of education, you must put into the pint container whatever kind of liquid you put into the gallon container, even though only one pint can go here and a gallon there. It will not do to put cream into the gallon container and, say, water—dirty water, at that—into the pint container. Vocational education is the dirty water we are now pouring into our pint containers. Liberal education is the cream we are giving the few.

I think that schoolteachers, parents, and the country in general, have been misled on this point because the problem is so difficult to solve. The teachers took the wrong turn, though the easier one, when they were first faced with the problem at the beginning of the century. They discovered that they did not know how to put cream into the pint container. Instead of doing what was required of them—taking the time to face and solve this very difficult problem of finding pedagogical techniques, methods, or means for putting cream into every container, large or small—they backed away, and accepted vocational training for the great majority of children as much the easier thing to do. This profound mistake we must now correct. We must give liberal training, training in the liberal arts, to all the children who are going to inherit the rights of citizenship and the leisure time of free men in their adult years.

What do I mean when I speak of liberal training for children? I do not mean a great deal of learning, because I do not think that liberal education can be accomplished in school. I do not contemplate the production of educated men and women at the age of sixteen. I recommend only these two things: first, our children should be disciplined in the liberal arts, which means the ability to read and write and speak and think as well as they can. Second, our children should experience some intellectual stimulation and be enticed by learning itself. I would hope that somehow the feast of knowledge and the excitement of ideas would be made attractive to them, so that when they left school, they would want to go on learning. In school they must be given, not learning, for that cannot be done, but the skills of learning and the wish to learn, so that in adult life they will want to go on learning and will have the skills to use in the process.

Let us turn now to the consequences of this basic educational proposition for adults. Here, too, the consequences are serious. If my understanding of the relation of schooling to education is right, then education is necessary for all adults—just as much for those who have gone through colleges and universities as for those who have not gone beyond elementary school. The person who has had more schooling has some advantage in the long process of learning, but actually all adults, as they begin their adult life, are on much the same footing so far as the goals of education are concerned. To understand this, the difference between education—that is, adult education—and schooling must be made clear.

There are three remarkable differences between the education that takes place in adult life and the kind of thing that goes on in the schools at any level. In the first place, adult education must be voluntary. You cannot compel adults to undergo a course of study or a process of learning because, if you have to compel them, that means they are not adults. It is proper to compel children to go to school or to compel their parents to send them. The common good of the republic and the individual good of the human beings who are its citizens require it. Adults are responsible for their own welfare and they participate in their own government. Therefore, they must engage in education voluntarily, not under compulsion.

The second characteristic of education in adult life is equality among all those involved. Let me explain. In the schools there are teachers and pupils, and the relation between teacher and pupil is one of inequality—not simply because the teacher knows more than the pupil but because the teacher is mature, whereas the pupil is a child. A widespread American illusion is that the best thing in the world to be is a child. Nothing could be further from the truth. A child is the most imperfect of all human beings. Our job is to make him an adult. Except for those progressive schools where teachers mistakenly try to become equal with their pupils by getting on the floor with them, and by asking their opinions about everything, the classroom situation is one in which the teacher is superior.

Now in adult-learning situations, we do not have teachers in this sense. The leader may know a little more than the other persons participating in the class, but that is not the point. The point is that he is one mature human being talking with others, and the conversation is taking place between equals. Adult learning is quite different from what goes on in the schools. Most Americans think of adult education as schooling, and therefore misunderstand it. They think it consists in going to school, listening to lectures, taking notes, passing examinations. That is not adult education; that is a perversion of it. That is putting schooling into adult life where it does not belong. Adult education, or basic education for adults, involves a relation of equality among all the persons participating.

The third characteristic of education for adults is the most important. Basic education in adult life, which succeeds all the years of schooling, is and must be interminable—without end, without limit. In this country we have eight years of elementary school, four years of high school or secondary school, four years of college, three years of medical or law or engineering school. This is quite proper, for these spans of time, these terms of years, are intended to provide time for a course of study embodying a subject matter or discipline to be acquired by the student. It is proper that he be certified when and if, upon examination, he shows himself competent. It is proper for a person to say, "I completed my legal education in three years," or "I completed my four-year college program." But think of an adult saying, "I have been going on with my learning for the last five years, from thirty to thirty-five, and now I have completed my adult education." No more preposterous words could be uttered. For if anyone were to say, at the age of thirty-five, "I have completed my adult education," all one could respond is, "Are you ready to die? What are you going to do with the rest of your life?"

Adult education does not consist of a course of study or a subject matter to be mastered in a fixed number of years, something to take an examination on and pass, and then be finished with forever. That is not the point. Adult education, once begun, is interminable. Nothing but serious illness relieves any adult of his responsibility to continue learning year after year, every part of every year, until the end of his life.

There are two reasons for the interminability of adult education: one in the nature of the human mind itself, and one that derives from the goal of learning. Let us consider the second first.

What is the ultimate goal toward which every part of schooling, or education, is directed? It is wisdom. We would all like to be a little wiser than we are—to have a little more understanding, a little more insight, a little more comprehension of the human situation, of the conditions of our lives, of the world in which we live; to know better the difference between good and evil. But how long does it take to become wise? The answer is: a lifetime. Hence if wisdom is the ultimate goal of the whole process of learning, then that process must go on for a lifetime.

The other reason for the interminability of adult education lies in the nature of the mind itself. The human mind is not a muscle. It is not an organic thing, in the sense of an ordinary bodily organ. But it is a living thing. And like any other living thing, there are certain indispensable conditions of its vitality. If the body is to be kept healthy, alive, and in repair, it must have food and exercise regularly. What is true of the body is true of the mind. The mind unfed weakens just as the body does. The mind not sustained by the continual intake of something that is capable of filling it well or nourishing it, shrinks and shrivels. And the mind unexercised, like a muscle unused, atrophies, grows weak, becomes almost paralyzed. Hence, just as we know that we cannot support the life of the body this week on the basis of last week's feeding, so we ought to realize that we cannot support the life of the mind this week on last week's reading, much less last year's reading, or the reading done in college.

The process of keeping the mind alive and growing is as perpetual and continual a process as that of keeping the human body alive. But whereas there are limits to the body's growth, the mind, unlike the body, can grow every year of our lives. Until there is a real physical breakdown, real decrepitude, the human mind can grow. The only condition of its growth is that it be fed and exercised. Yet these are the very conditions most of us do not provide for our minds.

Anyone who supposes that he has a set of ideas left over from college days which he can carry around with him the rest of his life, to pull out of a drawer when he wants to use them, is supposing something that simply is not the case. Any ideas we want to think with, we must rethink. We must give life to them by the use we make of them.

What follows from all this for the education of adults? Every adult who has had the best liberal training we can give in school years needs continuing liberal education throughout all the years of adult life. This is a large order. If we really mean every adult citizen, that is a large number; and if we really mean all the years of adult life, that is many years. The whole school system, from kindergarten through college, only occupies sixteen years; and yet, if the education of adults began at twenty-two, that would involve thirty or forty years more of learning.

How can we solve a problem of such magnitude? We cannot solve it unless we have some conception of what adults must do in order to sustain their minds, keep them alive, keep them growing. Most adults do not do their part, because they wrongly suppose that an education is something one should have got somehow in school and college. If, for whatever reason, they did not get it there, it is now too late to get it. But as we have seen, the fallacy here consists in failing to see the one reason why education could not be gotten in school. When we see through that error, we also see why adult life is the time to get the education no young person can ever obtain. Any adult who achieves this vision is at last on the highroad of learning. It is not a royal road. It is steep and rocky, but it is the highroad—in fact, the only road. It is open to anyone who has some skill in learning, and must be taken by anyone who has the goal of learning in view—understanding the nature of things and man's place in the total scheme.

The program of adult learning must be something that will sustain learning through many years; something that treats adults as adults, not as children in school; something they can do voluntarily; something that is in every way proper for the mind. With all these requirements in view, I can think of only one program that fully and properly fits all the circumstances of the case. That program is simple as to plan. The plan involves two parts. First, the adult who, because of bad or insufficient schooling, lacks the disciplines of learning, must acquire these for himself. He acquires them the way every schoolboy acquires them—by habituating himself to the formal process of asking and answering the question "Why" with respect to every phenomenon he confronts. Take questions like the following, remembering that the important thing in answering each question is the *why*.

Is freedom good? Is it good in itself or only as a condition for getting other good things? Is it the greatest good?

Does God exist? Did God create the world?

How does man differ from other animals? Does man have an immortal destiny?

What is truth, and how do we know it when we see it? Is anything either right or wrong for *all* people at *all* times, and, if there is, how does one discover it?

Are pleasure and pain standards for judging whether a line of conduct should be pursued or avoided? Are there other standards? Are they better than the standard of pleasure and pain?

Is that government best which governs least? Is all good government self-government?

Is war always wrong, and, if it isn't, under what conditions is it right?

Should all men work together on the same basis, or should they work, some as masters and some as servants? Would you rather be a well-fed slave or a starving freeman? Should there be any limit to the acquisition, possession, or transmission of private property, and, if there should be, what limits should be set, and by whom?

In what does human happiness consist, and how does it differ, if at all, from the happiness of other kinds of creatures?

These are some of the hardest questions men can ask themselves, and all men ask them at one time or another, though they may use other words to do so. If the education we received in school was any good at all, we probably learned some answers to questions of this sort. However superficially we held these answers, the teachers we had and the books we read did something to form our minds. Now the question is whether we have done anything for ourselves since then, whether through experience, through facing practical problems, through further reading, we have deepened the formation of our minds by the continued exercise of our mental faculties.

Second, having the requisite skills, the adult must pursue for the rest of his life the same curriculum of studies which, for centuries, have been regarded as the content of liberal education. By the content of liberal education I mean the basic subject matters of history, philosophy, science, and humane letters—and all the great books which constitute the tradition of our common culture in these fields. For even if these subject matters were studied in college, even if all the great books had been "read," they remain the materials of adult education because college boys and girls are too young to master them.

First, the great books are great because they are inexhaustible. Unlike most of the things we read, the great books are indefinitely rereadable.

Second, the great books were written for adults, not for children. The great books are for adults in the sense that theirs is the level at which adults operate and think. I do not mean that we should not— in fact, I firmly believe that, for the liberal training of children in school, we should—start young people reading the great books in school and in college. They cannot understand them at that age; but in addition to the obvious fact that students must be taught to read and these are good books for the purpose, the great books must be read several times to be read well, and it is a good idea to get the first reading done as early as possible.

Third, the great books deal with the basic problems, both theoretical and practical, of yesterday and today and tomorrow, the basic issues that always confront mankind. The ideas they contain are the ideas all of us have to think about and think with. The great books represent the fund of human wisdom, at least so far as our culture is concerned, and it is this reservoir that we must draw upon to sustain our learning for a lifetime.

If the great books are worth studying in school and college, as a condition of gaining skill in intellectual pursuits, they are certainly worth studying for the rest of one's life, not only to increase that skill, or, perhaps, to gain it where the schools have failed, but for the sake of transforming one's self, slowly, painfully, but rewardingly, into an educated person. An educated person is, after all, one who, through the travail of his own life, has assimilated the ideas which make him representative of his culture, which make him a bearer of its traditions, and which enable him to contribute to the improvement of that culture. Clearly no school boy or girl can be educated in this sense, any more than he can be a man or woman before the hour of maturity has struck.

The plan, I say, is simple. Its successful execution is something else. But it is ostrichlike to pretend there is an easier way to become educated.

What Is an Idea?

(1958)

*An idea, Adler tells us, is not a word. It is not a fact. It is not a
feeling. The great ones grow and change. They have a long past, a living
present in which they are imperfectly understood, and a future in which
they may be explored. "What Is an Idea?" was written for the November
22, 1958, issue of the* Saturday Review of Literature. *Since then, under
Mortimer Adler's direction, members of the Institute for Philosophical
Research have inquired into a number of the great ideas and published
their results as follows:* The Idea of Freedom, *by Mortimer J. Adler,
published by Doubleday & Co., Vol. 1 in 1958 and Vol. 2 in 1961;*
The Idea of Happiness, *by V. J. McGill;* The Idea of Justice, *by Otto
A. Bird;* The Idea of Love, *by Robert Hazo; and* The Idea of Progress,
by Charles Van Doren—all published by Frederick A. Praeger, 1967.

G.V.D.

WHAT is an idea?
Ideas are my business. I've been at it forty years now,
and I have not yet found a new idea. But the old ones—and
I am just getting started on some of them—have kept me going. And
in all this time I have come to some conclusions and, I believe, a clearer
notion not only of what an idea is but of what it is not.

It is not just a word, nor is it a string of words. Words are performing
their highest function when they express ideas, but they do not constitute
the ideas they express. This is clearly shown by the fact that different
persons all using the same word may not have the same comprehension
of the idea which that word expresses.

Consider the word "love." It has many meanings which we recognize as soon as we consider the difference between romantic love and conjugal love, the difference between love of country and love of God, or the difference between the love that parents readily bestow upon their children and the love that children slowly develop for their parents. All these meanings of the word—all these kinds of love—have something in common. All are related aspects of a single, very large idea—the idea of love. But as most people employ the word in ordinary speech, they have only a small part of this idea in mind; and when young people use it they seldom have in mind the same part that older people have. Few who use the word ever have the whole idea in mind, for it takes a lifetime of experience and thought to comprehend it fully.

An idea is not a fact of any kind, nor a collection of facts, no matter how massive or recondite. The telephone book is full of facts, but it doesn't contain a single idea. A history book is full of facts, none of which is an idea, though if the writer is given to philosophizing about history he may illuminate the facts with some basic idea, such as the idea of progress, the idea of chance, or the idea of fate. Suppose we are dealing with the idea of "progress," in itself abstract and general. To grasp it, we consider one example after another, each a concrete or particular instance of the essential idea. We look at the changes that have been made in transportation to increase comfort and speed. We call attention to the advances that have been made in the conquest of disease. We may even point to improvements in certain social or political institutions, such as the treatment of criminals or the protection of human rights. But none of these things is the idea of progress, though each may exemplify it. Moreover, if we did not have some idea of progress in the first place, we would not have chosen these examples to illustrate what we have in mind and to hold that idea before us.

Ideas influence our actions no less than feelings, desires, emotions, and purposes do, but not in the same way. Our particular passions or desires determine the attitudes we take and move us to the things we do. But if we ever recognize the discrepancy between what we do and what we ought to do, we are moved by ideas, not passions. Particular loves and hates may lead us to befriend certain minority groups and persecute others. But if we ever question such discrimination—our own or someone else's—we do so in virtue of ideas about love and man (especially insights about the fraternity and equality of men) that move us to judge our attitudes, and even perhaps to overcome our prejudices.

Some of the positive attributes of an idea have already been indicated by the difference between ideas and words, facts, examples, and emotions or desires. An idea alters and grows. Having a life, it can have a history—a past, present, and future. Each of the great ideas is a complex and organic whole, a dissectible structure of related parts. It has an interior, and in this sense it is like a domain which can be probed, pried into, explored, approached from many angles, taken apart in many ways.

Ideas may look alike from the outside, but the more we look into them the more we find that each is a world of its own, with its own special history and its own special structure. Yet each also belongs to a vaster world or universe of thought in which ideas group themselves as so many constellations or galaxies. In themselves and in relation to one another they comprise the configurations of the human mind, as intricate and varied in their crisscrossing patterns as the starry heavens. And like each individual star, every idea is a source of life and light which animates and illuminates the words, facts, examples, and emotions that are dead—or deadly—and dark without them. The idea of Government, for example, moves in the orbit of such other ideas as State, Law, Constitution, Citizen, Democracy, Revolution. The idea of Virtue not only has such ideas as Wisdom, Temperance, Justice, Prudence, and Courage as its satellites, but it also is one of the focal points in a group of ideas that includes Desire, Duty, Sin, Happiness, and Pleasure and Pain. The more fully one investigates any great idea the more one has to delve into others. The pursuit is endless—and fascinating.

None of these things would be true if ideas were words, or facts, or examples, or feelings. Nor would words, facts, examples, or feelings play the roles that they do in human life if ideas did not intervene to give them meaning and direction. Apart from ideas, great or small, they would not be discussable, interpretable, or even relatable. But while all ideas have the properties mentioned, the nature of ideas is most clearly seen in the case of the relatively small number of great ideas that are the main points of reference in the universe of human thought.

What are these "great ideas"? Working with a large research staff, I spent eight years directing the construction of a reference work entitled *The Great Ideas* or *Syntopicon*, which aimed at a systematic and comprehensive inventory of the fundamental ideas to be found in the great

The 102 Ideas

Angel
Animal
Aristocracy
Art
Astronomy
Beauty
Being
Cause
Chance
Change
Citizen
Constitution
Courage
Custom and
   Convention
Definition
Democracy
Desire
Dialectic
Duty
Education
Element
Emotion
Eternity
Evolution
Experience
Family
Fate
Form
God
Good and Evil
Government
Habit
Happiness
History
Honor

Hypothesis
Idea
Immortality
Induction
Infinity
Judgment
Justice
Knowledge
Labor
Language
Law
Liberty
Life and Death
Logic
Love
Man
Mathematics
Matter
Mechanics
Medicine
Memory and
   Imagination
Metaphysics
Mind
Monarchy
Nature
Necessity and
   Contingency
Oligarchy
One and Many
Opinion
Opposition
Philosophy
Physics
Pleasure and Pain
Poetry

Principle
Progress
Prophecy
Prudence
Punishment
Quality
Quantity
Reasoning
Relation
Religion
Revolution
Rhetoric
Same and Other
Science
Sense
Sign and Symbol
Sin
Slavery
Soul
Space
State
Temperance
Theology
Time
Truth
Tyranny
Universal and
   Particular
Virtue and Vice
War and Peace
Wealth
Will
Wisdom
World

books of the Western world. In the beginning, we drew up a list of some seven hundred possible candidates for inclusion in our encyclopedic catalogue of great ideas. Then we started to examine them. After two years we found that most of these notions were parts or bits of more inclusive ideas. When we came to count up the really big and independent ideas that could stand by themselves, we determined that the irreducible minimum numbered 102.

The *Syntopicon* was published in 1952 as an adjunct to the fifty-two volume *Great Books of the Western World*. Since then I have been continuously at work on ideas with my colleagues at the Institute for Philosophical Research, and so far we have not found any ideas of a magnitude comparable to the 102. Nor has dropping any from the list been suggested.

None of the 102 great ideas is a recent discovery in the sense in which there are really new inventions in every age. The ancient Greeks had a name for every one of them. All have been objects of speculation and inquiry since the beginning of thought. They have always been the common stock of the human mind. Innumerable men have engaged in the discussion of each one of them. The vast literature which exists on every great idea reflects not only the continuity of human thought about them, but also the wide diversity of opinions to which such thought inevitably gives rise. In the sphere of the great ideas we can find all the fundamental disagreements—and agreements—of mankind.

When I say that there are no new ideas—or no great ones that are new—I do not mean that there is nothing new in the world of ideas. On the contrary, most of the great ideas have kept on changing and growing in substance and scope, to whatever extent thinking men have been at work on them century after century. Unlike facts, which remain fixed for all time once they are established, the great ideas, once discovered in the dim past, remain the same in the way in which living organisms remain the same while developing.

In every epoch, intellectual geniuses have added not new ideas but new facets to the same enduring ones. Some of the great ideas have been more energetically or creatively pursued at certain periods or places than at others. Ideas like Prophecy or Angel have had a livelier history in antiquity or the Middle Ages than in modern times. The opposite is true of such ideas as Progress and Evolution. But the lineage of these goes back to antiquity. As Mark Twain wryly observed, "The ancients stole all our ideas from us."

Even more important than the living presence of a great idea is its future. Each is still unfinished business, each is still imperfectly understood. For six years the staff of the Institute for Philosophical Research has worked on a single idea—Freedom. We studied its past by trying, so far as possible, to read through all the major writings on the subject. We explored the whole range of differing conceptions and theories which eminent thinkers have advanced or held about freedom, assessing this idea's present significance by taking stock of all that has been thought about it in the past and is being thought about it now. This stocktaking, we hope, will reveal the fundamental agreements and disagreements which unite and divide men, together with the arguments by which they have carried on the debate of the issues.

Later we plan to undertake similar inquiry and investigation of such fundamental ideas as Justice, Law, Love, Wealth, Knowledge, and Government. The venture is a formidable one. Taking four or five years for the exploration of an idea, it will require much more than several lifetimes to examine human thought on all 102 of the great ideas, each of which has a future larger and more interesting than its past.

One thing we know from the experience we have had in constructing the *Syntopicon* and in examining the idea of freedom. Every one of the great ideas is a unique adventure. Each has an interior structure and life of its own, not to mention its difference from others in size and complexity. Some great ideas—God, State, Man, Knowledge, and Wealth—involve as many as forty or fifty different topics. Some, like Fate, Element, and Honor, require only ten or fifteen. Some have a relatively simple order of parts. Some have a complex and intricate structure. But all have enough scope and variety to deserve a fuller treatment than can be given in a short essay. In the *Syntopicon*, the treatment of liberty took about twenty-one pages. When *The Idea of Freedom*, the first volume of which has recently been published, is completed, it will run to about 1,500 pages.

Whether we know it or not, we are all philosophers. We all think —well or sloppily, enthusiastically or inattentively. The slightest sense perception—a falling leaf, a twinkling star, a smiling child—awakens our minds as well as arouses our feelings and forces us to ask: Why? What? Whence? Whither?

Not to engage in this pursuit of ideas is to live like ants instead of like men. The ant can live without ideas because the whole course of its life is fixed. But man has the freedom—and, therefore, the necessity—to choose and to choose in terms of ideas.

We often think of ourselves as living in a world which no longer has any unexplored frontiers. We speak of pioneering as a thing of the past. But in doing so we forget that the greatest adventure of all still challenges us—what Mr. Justice Holmes called "the adventure of the human mind." Men may be hemmed in geographically, but every generation stands on the frontiers of the mind. In the world of ideas, there is always pioneering to be done, and it can be done by anyone who will use the equipment with which he is endowed. The great ideas belong to everyone.

17

Invitation to
the Pain of Learning

(1941)

In Adler's view of education, learning is not something one acquires externally like a new suit. It is, in his own words, "an interior transformation of a person's mind and character, a transformation which can be effected only through his own activity." It is as painful, but also as exhilarating, as any effort human beings make to make themselves better human beings, physically or mentally. The practices of educators, even if they are well-intentioned, who try to make learning less painful than it is, not only make it less exhilarating, but also weaken the will and minds of those on whom this fraud is perpetrated. The selling and buying of education all wrapped up in pretty packages is what is going on, but, Adler tells us, it is not the real thing. This essay was published in The Journal of Educational Sociology *(February 1941.)*

G.V.D.

O NE of the reasons why the education given by our schools is so frothy and vapid is that the American people generally—the parent even more than the teacher—wish childhood to be unspoiled by pain. Childhood must be a period of delight, of gay indulgence in impulses. It must be given every avenue for unimpeded expression, which of course is pleasant; and it must not be made to suffer the impositions of discipline or the exactions of duty, which of course are painful. Childhood must be filled with as much play and as little work as possible. What cannot be accomplished educationally through elaborate schemes devised to make learning an exciting game must, of necessity, be forgone. Heaven forbid that learning should ever take on the character of a serious occupation—just as serious as earning money, and perhaps, much more laborious and painful.

The kindergarten spirit of playing at education pervades our colleges. Most college students get their first taste of studying as really hard work, requiring mental strain and continual labor, only when they enter law school or medical school. Those who do not enter the professions find out what working at anything really means only when they start to earn a living—that is, if four years of college has not softened them to the point which makes them unemployable. But even those who somehow recover from a college loaf and accept the responsibilities and obligations involved in earning a living—even those who may gradually come to realize the connection between work, pain, and earning—seldom if ever make a similar connection of pain and work with learning. "Learning" is what they did in college, and they know that that had very little to do with pain and work.

Now the attitude of the various agencies of adult education is even more softminded—not just softhearted—about the large public they face, a public which has had all sorts and amounts of schooling. The trouble is not simply that this large public has been spoiled by whatever schooling it has had—spoiled in the double sense that it is unprepared to carry on its own self-education in adult life and that it is disinclined to suffer pains for the sake of learning. The trouble also lies in the fact that agencies of adult education baby the public even more than the schools coddle the children. They have turned the whole nation—so far as education is concerned—into a kindergarten. It must all be fun. It must all be entertaining. Adult learning must be made as effortless as possible—painless, devoid of oppressive burdens and of irksome tasks. Adult men and women, because they are adult, can be expected to suffer pains of all sorts in the course of their daily occupations, whether domestic or commercial. We do not try to deny the fact that taking care of a household or holding down a job is necessarily burdensome, but we somehow still believe that the goods to be obtained, the worldly goods of wealth and comfort, are worth the effort. In any case, we know they cannot be obtained without effort. But we try to shut our eyes to the fact that improving one's mind or enlarging one's spirit is, if anything, more difficult than solving the problems of subsistence; or, maybe, we just do not believe that knowledge and wisdom are worth the effort.

We try to make adult education as exciting as a football game, as relaxing as a motion picture, and as easy on the mind as a quiz program. Otherwise, we will not be able to draw the big crowds, and the important thing is to draw large numbers of people into this educational game, even if after we get them there we leave them untransformed.

What lies behind my remark is a distinction between two views of education. In one view, education is something externally added to a person, as his clothing and other accoutrements. We cajole him into standing there willingly while we fit him; and in doing this we must be guided by his likes and dislikes, by his own notion of what enhances his appearance. In the other view, education is an interior transformation of a person's mind and character. He is plastic material to be improved not according to his inclinations, but according to what is good for him. But because he is a living thing, and not dead clay, the transformation can be effected only through his own activity. Teachers of every sort can help, but they can only help in the process of learning that must be dominated at every moment by the activity of the learner. And the fundamental activity that is involved in every kind of genuine learning is intellectual activity, the activity generally known as thinking. Any learning which takes place without thinking is necessarily of the sort I have called external and additive—learning passively acquired, for which the common name is "information." Without thinking, the kind of learning which transforms a mind, gives it new insights, enlightens it, deepens understanding, elevates the spirit simply cannot occur.

Anyone who has done any thinking, even a little bit, knows that it is painful. It is hard work—in fact the very hardest that human beings are ever called upon to do. It is fatiguing, not refreshing. If allowed to follow the path of least resistance, no one would ever think. To make boys and girls, or men and women, think—and through thinking really undergo the transformation of learning—educational agencies of every sort must work against the grain, not with it. Far from trying to make the whole process painless from beginning to end, we must promise them the pleasure of achievement as a reward to be reached only through travail. I am not here concerned with the oratory that may have to be employed to persuade Americans that wisdom is a greater good than wealth, and hence worthy of greater effort. I am only insisting that there is no royal road, and that our present educational policies, in adult education especially, are fraudulent. We are pretending to give them something which is described in the advertising as very valuable, but which we promise they can get at almost no expense to them.

Not only must we honestly announce that pain and work are the irremovable and irreducible accompaniments of genuine learning, not only must we leave entertainment to the entertainers and make education a task and not a game, but we must have no fears about what is "over the public's head." Whoever passes by what is over his head condemns his head to its present low altitude; for nothing can elevate a mind except what is over its head; and that elevation is not accomplished by capillary attraction, but only by the hard work of climbing up the ropes, with sore hands and aching muscles. The school system which caters to the median child, or worse, to the lower half of the class; the lecturer before adults—and they are legion—who talks down to his audience; the radio or television program which tries to hit the lowest common denominator of popular receptivity—all these defeat the prime purpose of education by taking people as they are and leaving them just there.

The best adult education program that has ever existed in this country was one which endured for a short time under the auspices of the People's Institute in New York, when Everett Dean Martin was its director, and Scott Buchanan his assistant. It had two parts: one consisted of lectures which, so far as possible, were always aimed over the heads of the audience; the other consisted of seminars in which adults were helped in the reading of great books—the books that are over everyone's head. The latter part of the program is still being carried on by the staff of St. John's College in the cities near Annapolis; and we are conducting four such groups in the downtown college of the University of Chicago. I say that this is the only adult education that is genuinely educative simply because it is the only kind that requires activity, makes no pretense about avoiding pain and work, and is always working with materials well over everybody's head.

I do not know whether radio or television will ever be able to do anything genuinely educative. I am sure it serves the public in two ways: by giving them amusement and by giving them information. It may even, as in the case of its very best "educational" programs, stimulate some persons to do something about their minds by pursuing knowledge and wisdom in the only way possible—the hard way. But what I do not know is whether it can ever do what the best teachers have always done and must now be doing; namely, to present programs which are genuinely educative, as opposed to merely stimulating, in the sense that following them requires the listener to be active not passive, to think rather than remember, and to suffer all the pains of lifting himself up by his own bootstraps. Certainly so long as the so-called educational directors of our leading networks continue to operate on their present false principles, we can expect nothing. So long as they confuse education and entertainment, so long as they suppose that learning can be accomplished without pain, so long as they persist in bringing everything and everybody down to the lowest level on which the largest audience can be reached, the educational programs offered on the air will remain what they are today—shams and delusions.

It may be, of course, that the radio and television, for economic reasons must, like the motion picture, reach with certainty so large an audience that the networks cannot afford even to experiment with programs which make no pretense to be more palatable and pleasurable than real education can be. It may be that the radio and television cannot be expected to take a sounder view of education and to undertake more substantial programs than now prevail among the country's official leaders in education—the heads of our school system, of our colleges, of our adult education associations. But, in either case, let us not fool ourselves about what we are doing. "Education" all wrapped up in attractive tissue is the gold brick that is being sold in America today on every street corner. Everyone is selling it, everyone is buying it, but no one is giving or getting the real thing because the real thing is always hard to give or get. Yet the real thing can be made generally available if the obstacles to its distribution are honestly recognized. Unless we acknowledge that every invitation to learning can promise pleasure only as the result of pain, can offer achievement only at the expense of work, all of our invitations to learning, in school and out, whether by books, lectures, or radio and television programs will be as much buncombe as the worst patent medicine advertising, or the campaign pledge to put two chickens in every pot.

Part Four

Thinking About
Moral Values

18

Virtue and Happiness

(1979)

In "Virtue and Happiness" Adler defines both of those terms and joins them together in a conception of human happiness that is very old, although it will be new for some readers. Like "This Prewar Generation" (q.v.), this essay deals with a recurring theme in Adler's writings. It is that moral relativism and moral subjectivism, so common among the best educated in this century, are the result of poor thinking about what is really good for us. This is the cause of much distress and a threat to our political life as well.

In this essay Adler shows us how to think more cogently about moral values. As happens so often in these essays, he acts here as teacher as well as critic, not merely commenting on American education, but explaining how to improve it.

"Virtue and Happiness" is a transcript taken from the tapes of four weekend seminars led by Adler, which were arranged by and held at Spring Hill Center in Wayzata, Minnesota. It was subsequently published in the center's Dialogue series (June 1979). Those discussions focused on current issues in democracy that are relevant to the four fundamental ideas of equality, liberty, justice, and property. The conclusion that moral virtue is necessary for individual happiness as well as for a just society is not the whole story. That virtue alone is not sufficient for happiness is also, Adler tells us, important to know. In his book The Time of Our Lives Adler gives us his fullest treatment of the subject of moral philosophy and of the distinction he makes in this essay between the psychological conception of happiness and happiness as an ethical ideal.

G.V.D.

I N T H E T W E N T I E T H C E N T U R Y there is prevalent in our universities and among the leaders of intellectual life what I would call moral relativism and moral subjectivism. This position, technically called the theory of noncognitive ethics, states that only questions of fact can be answered by statements that are true or false. Questions of value about what is good and bad, or right and wrong, or statements about what ought to be done or ought not to be done, are not in the sphere of knowledge. Statements answering such questions are neither true nor false. The leading proponents of this view in Oxford, Cambridge, and American universities would say that when a person makes a moral judgment, he is either merely expressing his emotions or formulating prescriptions that are only his own personal prejudices and preferences. Bertrand Russell summarized this position by saying, "Ethics is the art of recommending to others the things they should do in order to get along with one's self." In other words, science belongs in the area of our knowledge of nature, our knowledge of man even, but when one gets into the field of morals, we cannot have objectively valid philosophical knowledge.

This is a very serious matter. It is as deep a question as the question about whether there are natural rights or only legal rights. In fact, the view that there are only legal rights and no natural rights, that things are right and wrong only because the power behind law makes it so, is very similar to the position that moral judgments are subjective matters of opinion and not objectively valid knowledge of right and wrong.

What lies behind noncognitive ethics is a definition of truth that goes back as far as Plato and Aristotle. Aristotle very clearly defined truth in the fourth book of the *Metaphysics*. A man thinks truly, said Aristotle, when he thinks that that which is, is, and that that which is not, is not. A man thinks falsely if he thinks that that which is, is not, and that that which is not, is. In other words, truth simply consists in putting *is* and *is not* in the right place in one's thinking.

One can recognize this definition to be correct at once because we all know what a lie is. A lie consists in saying the opposite of what you think or believe. For example, if you are a stockbroker, and you honestly think the market is going up tomorrow and you tell somebody the market is going down, you are lying. Particularly if you are not merely misstating what you think but are intending to deceive him.

A great professor at Harvard at the beginning of the century, Josiah Royce, said that a liar is the man who willfully misplaces his ontological predicates, putting *is* where he should say *is not*, or *is not* where he should say *is*. If that is what truth is, then the contemporary philosophers who say that ethics is noncognitive have a certain basis for saying so because a statement that contains the word *ought* cannot agree with the way things *are* or *are not*. Only descriptive propositions, or propositions that say *is* or *is not*, can be true if truth consists of agreement between thinking *is* or *is not* with the way things *are* or *are not*. In this view, then, what can *ought* or *ought not* (or *good* and *bad*, or *right* and *wrong*) possibly agree with? If truth consists in the agreement of what the mind thinks or says to itself and the way things are, how can such statements as "You ought to seek knowledge," "You ought not to steal" or "You ought not to commit murder" be true?

However, Aristotle tells us that the truth of descriptive statements is only one kind of truth. The other kind of truth belongs to normative statements or, as he would say, practical statements. (A statement that says *ought* or *ought not* is practical, i.e. normative, whereas a statement that says *is* or *is not* is theoretical, i.e. descriptive.) The criterion of the truth of a normative statement, says Aristotle, is that it agrees with "right desire." What does he mean when he says a statement which contains *ought* or *ought not* is true or false according to whether or not it agrees with right desire? Right desire, as opposed to wrong desire, consists in desiring what you ought to desire. This almost looks circular, but pushing that idea a little further, what ought you to desire? The answer to that question must be that one ought to desire that which is good. The meaning of the word *good* is identical with the meaning of the word *desirable*. The desirable is the good and the good is the desirable. Whenever we desire anything we desire it under the aspect of its being good. We never desire anything that we deem to be bad. (I am not saying whether, in fact, it is or is not really good, but only that we deem it to be good.)

In the fourth chapter of the third book of his *Ethics*, Aristotle makes a distinction between two kinds of desire: natural desires and acquired desires. That underlies his distinction between real and apparent goods. He says that those things which we by nature tend to seek in perfecting ourselves or fulfilling our capacities are really good. For example, he says that man by nature desires to know. If by nature man desires to know, then knowledge is really good. There are many other desires that are not "by nature"; we acquire them out of our experience and we acquire them from contact with our fellowmen. Those desires also are desires for the good; we deem them to be good *because* we desire them. In sharp contrast, we desire real goods *because* they are good. In the case of apparent goods, we deem them to be good because we desire them.

If that is so, then what we ought to desire is inexorable. Out of that comes one true, self-evident proposition: real goods ought to be desired. To test whether this proposition is self-evident, try to assert its opposite: you ought to desire that which is really bad for you or you ought not to desire that which is really good for you. If you understand the meaning of *ought to* and you understand the meaning of *really good*, then *really good* and *ought to* go together and *not really good* and *ought not to* go together.

So we have one normative proposition that is self-evidently true: real goods ought to be desired. All other normative truths are derived from it. Let me take the simplest case of a practical syllogism. Knowledge is really good for me. That is a statement of fact. How do I know this? Because I know that I need knowledge, my nature craves knowledge. I have an intellect that needs knowledge as I have a stomach that needs food. Food is really good for me. Knowledge is really good for me. Therefore, I ought to desire knowledge. That conclusion follows at once.

The truth of these *ought* propositions comes from the truth of that first proposition. I ought to desire whatever is really good for me. Knowledge is a real good, wealth is a real good, health is a real good, friendship is a real good, love is a real good, pleasure is a real good. These are real goods in terms of what I understand my nature to need. Ultimately, the factual basis of my conclusions under that general premise rests in my understanding of what appetites or tendencies are inherent in my nature.

Curiously enough, it is that single sentence of Aristotle's about normative truth consisting in conformity with right desire that leads us to understand the truth of that first normative proposition (I ought to desire whatever is really good for me) and the truth of all the conclusions that I can draw from that proposition.

This takes us back to the first book of the *Ethics* in which Aristotle enumerates a series of goods and talks about happiness. The English word *happiness* is used by us in two quite different senses: the psychological meaning and the moral, or ethical, meaning. The psychological meaning of the term is the most prevalent today. In its modern, psychological use, happiness is something you feel. What kind of summer did you have last summer? A happy summer. You are describing a summer in which your pleasures and joys and satisfactions outweighed your pains and discontents and frustrations. It could even be a summer in which you had nothing but pleasures and joys and satisfactions.

Psychological happiness is something you enjoy from moment to moment. Happiness, in the ethical sense, is not something you experience, it is not something you ever enjoy, and you never have it at any moment in your life. To be sure, a happy life should have a great many happy moments in it. The second use of the word *happy* in the foregoing sentence is psychological, the first use of the word is ethical. An ethically happy life should have a lot of psychologically happy moments.

Psychological happiness is a state of mind. What it really means is that you are happy when you get what you want. Your happiness can be measured from moment to moment in terms of the current state of your wants and their satisfaction. That is purely psychological and has nothing to do with morality or ethics. Most people use the word *happiness* that way, in terms of apparent goods, or the things that they deem to be good.

Let us take the classic case of the pathological miser. All he wants, he says, is gold. Not to spend, though; he wants to see it piled on the table, and in the flickering candlelight of his dark, dank cellar he looks at the gold and touches it. That is all he wants. In order to get what he wants, he sacrifices health, he has no friends, he does not participate in the life of the community, he has allowed himself to become ignorant, and his mind has been stultified. But he has what he wants. Is he happy or not? Psychologically, he is perfectly happy. Morally, he is the most miserable creature alive. He is stunted. He is dwarfed. He has corrupted his human nature. Ethically, he is as far removed from happiness as anyone in the world can be. But he says that he is the happiest man alive. Here is the chasm between the psychological meaning of happiness and the ethical meaning of happiness.

What is the ethical meaning of happiness? Aristotle says that happiness is an end which is not a means to anything else. No one, he says, can complete the sentence "I want to be happy because. . . ." You want to be happy because you want to be happy. Any of the goods I mentioned—health, wealth, knowledge, friends—are a means to my happiness, but happiness is not a means to anything else. Even the miser, the man who has misconceived his happiness, is using the word *happiness* to name the last end, the end for which everything else is a means. If that is the case, says Aristotle, then happiness must be completely self-sufficing: it must leave nothing to be desired. For example, if the miser wanted both gold and friends and had only gold, he would not call himself happy because he lacked something he wanted. In the psychological and the moral sense, the man who calls himself happy has nothing more to desire. All his desires are satisfied.

If happiness is the ultimate end that we seek and is not a means to anything else, and happiness leaves nothing more to be desired, says Aristotle, then happiness cannot be counted as one good among many. For if happiness were one good among many, then you could have happiness but not some other goods that you desired. If one understands what Aristotle means by happiness, one can never call it, as it has been miscalled throughout the history of Western thought, the *sumum bonum*, the highest good. Happiness is not the highest good; rather, it is the *totum bonum*, the whole of goods. The happy man is the man who has acquired, in the course of a complete lifetime, all the things that are really good for him. He has nothing left to desire.

Among all of the goods there is an order, and some are means to others. For example, wealth is really good: one needs a certain amount of external goods for subsistence. One needs health. One needs friends. One needs a good society in which to live. One needs to be a citizen and to participate in political life. One needs to be self-governing. One needs knowledge. Among these goods that constitute the parts of happiness, some are limited goods and some are unlimited goods. Wealth is not an unlimited good; you can have too much wealth. Knowledge is unlimited; you cannot have too much knowledge. Pleasure is a real good, but you can have too much pleasure. In order to pursue happiness one must moderate achieving certain goods to allow for possession of other goods. The happy man is the man who achieves in a lifetime the *totum bonum* in which all real goods are present.

Happiness is the end of life, the goal we all seek. Think of that curious meaning of the word *end*. When you and I say we are going to Venice and think of Venice as the termination of our journey, we get there and come to rest. In Christian terms, the ultimate goal is eternal salvation; when you die and go to heaven and achieve the state of the blessed in the presence of God, you have it, you enjoy it. But happiness in this life is a very peculiar thing. It is an end you never reach because it is a temporal whole. It is, therefore, not like a terminal end, which is something you arrive at, enjoy, and possess at a moment in time (or forever in the case of eternal happiness).

Happiness in this life is like a performing art. When a conductor conducts a symphony, the symphony does not exist at any moment. The first movement is over, the second movement is over, the third movement is over, the fourth movement is over, and when it is all over, you do not have the symphony. You have heard it and it is now done. It was a good symphony if it was played well, but at no one moment is it a good symphony. The conductor has an ideal of the total performance which he is trying to produce at successive moments and this ideal guides him in what he does. A life is exactly like a symphony. It is a temporal whole, it has parts, it is ordered. And just as the conductor must at every moment be thinking of producing that whole in time, so you and I are obligated to try to live decent lives and are, at every moment, making choices to produce a whole life.

An architect can go through the long process of building a building. When he is finished, he has the building. It is there, in space. It can be lived in and enjoyed. That goal is quite different from the goal of the conductor who conducts a symphony and never has it at any moment. The difference between the two kinds of works, spatial wholes and temporal wholes, is very important to understand. You can produce a temporal whole, but you cannot have it or enjoy it. That is why you cannot, in this life, obtain happiness at any moment. You are conducting your life to make it a good life the way the conductor of the symphony is conducting the music to make it a good performance. But when can you say it is a good performance? Only when it is finished!

You cannot call a football game *good* at the half, because it is only a half-played game. If you go out in the middle of a football game and your friend says to you, "It's a good game, isn't it?" you should say, "No, it is not a good game, but it is becoming one. If the third quarter is as good as the first two, and the fourth quarter also, it will have been a good game when it is finished."

A final illustration. The first book of Herodotus tells the story of an early Greek wise man named Solon who was visiting the great Lydian king, Croesus, a man of untold wealth. Croesus said, "Tell me, wise man, of all the men you know, who is the happiest?" And Solon replied, "Harmodius and Aristogiton." Croesus said, "Tell me about them." And he told him about them. Croesus then said, "Tell me about some other people who are, in your judgment, happy." Solon named some others. Finally, Croesus got very impatient and said, "But why don't you think of *me* as happy? Look at the power I have. I am king of Lydia and the wealthiest man in the world. Why don't you call me happy?" And Solon said, "You are not dead yet." In fact, within the next year the Persians invaded Lydia and Croesus was killed in battle. His life ended abruptly. Aristotle uses the story to make his point. One cannot ever reach the *totum bonum* in this life, one can only pursue it.

You cannot teach ethics to the young, you cannot teach them moral philosophy. When you are young, you cannot understand this. You have to be older to understand the notion of making a whole life for yourself. Children and young people up to the age of twenty or twenty-five are thinking of today, tomorrow, and the next day. It is very hard for them to think of their actions today as somehow directed toward the construction of a whole life. It is beyond their imaginations. And yet to lead the moral life, you must have that curious kind of goal in mind as you make choices from moment to moment throughout a lifetime.

Now, says Aristotle, there are three principal means to happiness: acquiring the real goods that constitute happiness; being virtuous, or cultivating the habit of making good choices; and being blessed by good fortune. An essential element in acquiring those real goods is the habit of making choices among the things that are presented to you in order to create that temporal whole. That is what Aristotle means by the word *virtue*, the good habit of freely choosing the right means to that end.

The other factor in happiness is good fortune, and here is what is so extraordinary about Aristotle. Almost every other moralist would say that it is quite enough to be virtuous. Aristotle says no, that virtue makes a *man* good but not a *life* good. Take the case of Priam, the king of Troy: a virtuous man, a virtuous father, a virtuous husband, and a virtuous king; but he died with his city destroyed, his wife taken into slavery, and his sons killed. Was this his fault? No, ill fortune. He was a virtuous man, but, not through any fault of his own, he did not have a good life because it did not end well. Some of the goods that belong to happiness are not within our power. One can recognize when fortune is smiling and take advantage of it. Some people are slow to take advantage of the good twists of fortune and miss those opportunities. We can make good choices and yet all kinds of accidents can happen to us, no matter how virtuous we are.

Each of these two factors, virtue and fortune (good habits and good luck), are necessary for happiness, but neither one by itself is sufficient. A man with good fortune but bad habits of choice will not achieve a happy life. A man with virtue, or good habits of choice, but beset by bad fortune will not lead a happy life. This is not only good common sense but it has a bearing on the tragic aspects of any life, even for the virtuous man, who is beset by misfortune.

Only Aristotle says that virtue is not enough. For example, other theories of happiness take the view that the purpose of organized society is to ensure the happiness of its citizens. But if virtue were enough, the state could not contribute to it. The state cannot make you virtuous. In the historic view that virtue is enough, Epictetus, the virtuous slave, is regarded as happy as Marcus Aurelius, the virtuous emperor. But Aristotle says that a man must have other goods that organized society can help in providing, even for the virtuous man. Take the simple case of health. You can be virtuous about watching your diet, exercising, and keeping your body clean, but if the organized society in which you live is not concerned about giving you health care and does not provide a healthy environment, your health can be ruined.

There are many other things that no individual can provide for himself that the state must provide in order to promote human happiness. But the state cannot make human beings virtuous, since virtue is a habit of good choice and the habit is formed by free choices. The state certainly can support the development of such choices, but it is never, by itself, sufficient. Only in Aristotle's theory of happiness is there any point to the state serving human welfare and promoting happiness. If virtue were enough, the state would have no function so far as happiness is concerned.

What is virtue? It is a habit of choice, says Aristotle. We are choosing all the time and we do it by habit most of the time. The number of times we are conscious of making choices is very small, but because we have habits of choice, the choices we make become habituated. Every moment of our lives we are choosing to do this or that. The choice is virtuous, says Aristotle, if the choice is for an important real good in terms of our life's development. The virtuous man is one whose choices are always directed to that end.

The three aspects of virtue are justice, temperance, and courage. One must desire the right end and one must make judgments, or be prudent, about the right means to it. Sometimes there are wrong means,

means that are ill-adapted to the end. Prudence is an intellectual virtue judging about means. Prudence is involved in all the other virtues because the means that one chooses are the end in the process of becoming.

In the last chapter of the sixth book of the *Ethics*, Aristotle says you cannot be good without being practically wise, and you cannot be practically wise without being good. He means by *wise* not philosophical wisdom but prudence—practical wisdom. For example, there are good thieves and bad thieves, clever thieves and bunglers. The question is, Is the very clever thief, the thief who knows how to steal and get away with it, a prudent thief? No, says Aristotle, he is not a prudent thief because he cannot be prudent if he is a thief. He can be a clever thief but not a prudent thief because prudence means choosing the right means to the right end, not the right means to a wrong end. Just as you cannot be a prudent thief, you cannot be a prudent coward or a prudently unjust man, or a prudently intemperate man.

If you are prudent, you must have the other virtues, and similarly, in order to be just, temperate, or courageous, you must make a prudent judgment about means. In the case of temperance and courage, says Aristotle, you must choose between indulging in certain immediate pleasures or postponing them for the sake of a long-term good. In the case of courage, you must at times be willing to undergo certain pains for a long-term good.

If I have virtue, I must be making prudent choices in terms of what is really good for my whole life and to do that I must not only have temperance and courage, I also must have justice. If I am unjust, I am not really thinking about what is good for me. When I act unjustly, it indicates that the direction of my whole life is not toward the *totum bonum*, but toward something else—toward the accumulation of wealth, as if wealth were an end, not a means, or toward the accumulation of power, as if power were a real good. If that is the case, I cannot be temperate or courageous in the full meaning of those terms. Although I appear to be injuring only others, in fact I am injuring myself as well.

Why should I be just? I should be just because being just is part of pursuing my own happiness. The pursuit of happiness is cooperative, not competitive. Happiness is the only thing that you can pursue without doing other people in by virtue of pursuing it. If you pursue power as an end, for example, you may step on other people in the course of pursuing it. If you pursue unlimited wealth as an end, you may be tempted to step on other people in the process of doing that. But if you pursue happiness, you cannot possibly step on anybody else. In fact, you will help those within the range of your conduct to pursue happiness also. Happiness is the only completely cooperative pursuit.

Those two points—that the pursuit of happiness is cooperative and that virtue is not enough—are not only good answers to the moral question, but also provide a very important understanding of an extraordinary line in the Declaration of Independence. "We are endowed with certain inalienable rights," Jefferson wrote. "Among these are life, liberty and the pursuit of happiness." Locke enumerated the basic rights as life, liberty, and estates. Jefferson dropped the word *estates*. George Mason, in drafting Virginia's constitution, said that among the rights are the rights to pursue and *attain* happiness. Jefferson dropped the word *attain*. We have a right to pursue happiness, Jefferson said, but not a right to attain it because obviously it is not within our power to attain it. He must have understood Aristotle's meaning of happiness. In other words, Jefferson is saying in that extraordinary line that we are endowed with certain inalienable rights and, among these, are life, liberty and the right to anything else we naturally need in order to pursue happiness.

Among those things are certain goods that society can help us achieve. Jefferson says that, to secure these rights, governments are instituted among men. For example, I have a natural need for knowledge. Do I have a right to knowledge? No, because no state can give me knowledge. What I do have a right to is help from the state in gaining knowledge. I have a right to schooling. I am deprived if I am deprived of schooling. Schooling is an instrumental but not indispensable means to knowledge. I could, in fact, gain knowledge without schooling, but I am helped in my pursuit of knowledge by the advantages of schooling. The state at that point is an accessory to my pursuit of happiness.

Is power over other men a real good? If we really did need power in order to pursue happiness, we would then have a natural right to it. Jefferson tells us that the state should try to secure our natural rights. But how can it secure the right of all its citizens to have power over others? That is not cooperative, but conflictful and competitive. If I have power over you, you do not have power over me. One of us has to be dissatisfied. The goods that are really good for us are the ones that all of us can possess without excluding anyone else from possessing them. They are *common*, not *individual*, goods.

An understanding of that fundamental proposition in the Declaration of Independence is closely connected with Aristotle's conception of happiness and of natural rights. Natural desires indicate what is really good for us as opposed to what is apparently good for us merely because we desire it. We have a natural right to those goods that by nature we need in order to lead a good life.

Are the only things that we should desire those which we need by nature? Is every man's happiness identical with everyone else's? The answer is no, because in the complex lives we lead, we are different individuals with different temperaments and different wants. We have the same needs but different wants. Among our wants are many innocuous things. They are innocuous because we can want and get them without interfering with the pursuit of happiness by others. The individual pursuit of happiness is the same for all in that it involves striving for the same real goods. It is different in that we have different acquired desires which are not inimical to our pursuit of happiness or injurious to others. We are proscribed from wanting that which can be achieved only by injuring others or that which prevents us from achieving the *totum bonum*.

Another way of saying this is in terms of what I call the main activities of life: sleep, work, play, leisure, idling, and rest. Sleep consists of all biologically necessary activities: eating, slumbering, cleansing one's self, exercising. Those activities occupy a certain amount of time and involve some of the real goods—the health and vigor of one's body. Whereas sleep is biologically necessary, work is only economically necessary. I use the word *work* in a limited sense: that which is necessary to gain the means of subsistence. In this sense, work is purely a means to an end. Subsistence-work has no justification except that it is exchanged either for money or for the commodities which are the means of subsistence. If you are not equipped with inherited wealth, then you must spend at least six or eight hours a day in sleep and six to eight hours a day in work. That leaves another eight or ten hours of free time.

The next two basic activities are playing and leisuring, or more correctly, playing and leisure-work. Playing is good because it is an activity in which we engage simply for the pleasure of doing it. It is the only activity that has no extrinsic end. When play is relaxing or when play removes the strains of tension, it is therapeutic play, it is not real play. Real play is done for its own sake.

Most people think that the only way they can fill time is sleeping,

working, and playing. That is wrong. A life built upon only those three
things is really an aborted life. Imagine that you had to sleep six hours
a day and you did not have to work for a living. What would you do
with the rest of your time? Play?

So we come to the fourth kind of activity, leisure-work. Most people
do not have wealth without toil, though some are very fortunate to earn
their subsistence by doing what they want to do. They are fortunate
because although they may think they are working for a living, they
are really not. They are engaged in leisure-work and getting paid for
it. They would continue to do exactly what they are doing if wealth
were secured for them. If that is not the case, they are working, not
leisuring. I earn my living by editing, writing, lecturing, and teaching.
If I did not have to earn a living I would do exactly the same things. I
would not change my life at all. (If people didn't pay me to lecture,
I'd pay them to listen.) A good life need involve no subsistence-work.
A good life must have three things: sleep, in its broadest sense; play;
and leisure-work.

What is the essential character of leisure-work? Subsistence-work is
for an extrinsic compensation. But leisure-work is intrinsically rewarding. It does not have to be extrinsically compensated. It is the kind of
activity that produces the things which make a life good. As Aristotle
says, one plays for the sake of work and works for the sake of leisure.

The two other activities of life are idling and rest. Idling is a very
important element. When the motor of an automobile is turning over
but the gear is not engaged, the car is going nowhere; it is idling. When
I come into a room and sit down with an empty stare on my face, I
am idling. I do that a certain amount of time every day because all
kinds of things occur to me. I sit there and do nothing; I don't try to
think but I let the motor run without going anywhere. Many creative
things happen in idling.

To understand the meaning of the last activity, rest, one must refer
to Genesis. On the seventh day, Genesis says, God rested. You know
that God did not sleep, work, play, leisure, or idle on the seventh day.
What did God do? When He rested He looked at the world and said
it was good, very good. He admired it. Rest, to put it another way, is
contemplation. The third commandment is to keep the Sabbath day
holy as a day of rest. In orthodox Judaism, not an ounce of work is
done on the Sabbath. You can't even light the stove. You can't cut a
piece of bread. You must do nothing. If these things have to be done,

they have to be done by a Gentile, not by a Jew. The only thing you can do on the Sabbath is pray. The day is spent in prayer, which is rest. Most of us have very little of it in our lives.

The greatest of the goods of happiness are the things we create in our leisure pursuits. All leisure activities are creative. The leisure worker learns, grows morally, intellectually, and spiritually. For example, friendship is a creative activity. Do you think friendship is easy? No, friendship is a hard job. You cannot have a large number of good friends because you have to devote time to them, you have to devote thought to them, and you have to devote activity to them. It is a creative activity that is spiritually enriching, but it is work, leisure-work.

Sex can be sleep, play, work, or leisure. When it is performed as a biological necessity, it is sleep; when it is performed just for sexual, sensual pleasure, it is play; when, as in prostitution, it is performed to earn a living, it is work; and when it is performed as an aspect of love, it is leisure. So you cannot look at the activity and say what it is. You have to ask how it is being done and for what reason it is being done.

Augustine, in a single sentence, sums it all up by saying, "Happy is the man who has all that he desires provided that he desires nothing amiss." In other words, he has desired what he ought to desire and not desired what he ought not to desire. The Aristotelian way of saying this is: "Happy is the man who has all that he desires virtuously." Moral virtue is the habit of desiring nothing amiss.

The Christian view, of course, is that this life is a vale of tears and suffering, and at its best, happiness in this life is a very poor thing indeed, mixed with tragedy and grief. As creatures of God with immortal souls, our end is not in this life, but hereafter. Our end is the vision of God, if we achieve what Christians call *salvation*. For this end, ordinary moral virtue is not enough. You must have the theological virtues of faith, hope, and charity. How do you acquire these theological virtues? By what you do? Not at all. They are gifts of God's grace. The doctrine of grace and salvation is very strict. You cannot earn salvation, but you can predispose yourself by what you do to be receptive to divine grace.

The pursuit of eternal happiness is quite different from the pursuit of temporal happiness. Can one and the same man aim at these two ends, one in this life and one in the next life? Is it possible to live so that one can achieve a good earthly life and also achieve eternal salvation? I do not see any conflict between those two, particularly if you have God's grace. If you do not have God's grace, you may achieve one but not the other.

If you think of happiness as a whole life—twenty-four hours a day, so many days a week, so many weeks a month, so many months a year, and so many years to a life—it is a temporal whole, and virtue consists in making those choices from moment to moment that will produce a whole good life, if it is attended, of course, by the accidents of good fortune.

19

A Sound Moral Philosophy

(1982)

In the prologue to this book (q.v.) Adler says that in the two essays that follow he once again comes "to the defense of objective and absolute truth in moral philosophy." In this essay, "A Sound Moral Philosophy," which is a review of After Virtue *(1981) by Alasdair MacIntyre, Adler credits Professor MacIntyre with recognizing the failure of modern thought to achieve a sound moral philosophy. He also credits MacIntyre with acknowledging the achievement in moral philosophy to be found in Aristotle's* Ethics.

While he applauds MacIntyre's assertion that the concept of moral virtue is necessary to a sound moral philosophy, Adler protests that that concept by itself is not sufficient. This review appeared in The Great Ideas Today, *1982, a publication of Encyclopaedia Britannica, Inc.*

G.V.D.

IN MY JUDGMENT, Aristotle's *Nicomachean Ethics* is the only sound, practical, and undogmatic moral philosophy in the whole Western tradition. That judgment is shared to some extent but not wholly by Professor Alasdair MacIntyre in his book *After Virtue*.

After Virtue is a fine piece of historical scholarship in the field of moral philosophy. It ranges over the whole tradition of Western thought in the field of morals from the early Greeks to the present day. It is well worth reading for the comprehensiveness and clarity of the intellectual narrative it presents, if for no other reason. But there is another reason for reading it, and that is its central message, to which a reader should pay close attention. It is this on which I wish to concentrate within the brief compass of this review. Other reviews of this book have paid too much attention to the historical scholarship, too little to the book's philosophical message, and none to the relation of the one to the other.

The briefest way to summarize the philosophical thesis of *After Virtue* is to explain the title. Professor MacIntyre maintains, and I think quite rightly, that without the Greek, and especially the Aristotelian, conception of moral virtue as an habitual disposition of man's appetites or desires that put him on the pathway toward leading a good human life, moral philosophy is simply bankrupt.

When Rome replaces Greece, and Roman Stoicism (with its insistence that nothing more than a will in conformity with the laws of nature and of reason is needed for a sound morality) ignores the sound common sense in Aristotle's insight that good fortune as well good habits are needed for a good life, Western moral philosophy turns in the wrong direction.

A brief respite from this misdirection occurs in the late Middle Ages, when the moral theology of Thomas Aquinas reinstates Aristotle's conception of the role of moral virtue and of good fortune in the pursuit of temporal (and, therefore, imperfect) happiness. But after that, and especially from the eighteenth century down to our own day, Western moral philosophy goes the whole way toward its present bankrupt condition. As MacIntyre clearly and cogently points out, all attempts to lay the foundation of a sound morality *after* the concept of virtue is abandoned are necessarily doomed to failure.

To touch only the high spots, among the points to which MacIntyre calls our attention are (1) Hume's failure to find a basis for moral sentiments in the passions; (2) Kant's unsuccessful version of ancient Stoicism's appeal solely to the laws of reason; (3) the fumbling efforts of J. S. Mill's utilitarianism to restore happiness as the ultimate end to be sought, rendered self-defeating by Mill's hedonistic error of identifying happiness with the maximization of pleasures or satisfactions without any basis for differentiating between good pleasures or satisfactions and bad pleasures, and also by his substitution of the general happiness (or the greatest good for the greatest number) for individual happiness as the ultimate end; and, finally, (4) the complete denial of objective truth to any moral judgments (judgments that categorically prescribe what ought to be sought and ought to be done), which leads to the emotivism and the so-called noncognitive ethics prevalent in our own day.

In surveying this demise of sound moral philosophy, MacIntyre heaps excessive and unwarranted praise on the part that Nietzsche played, attributing to him penetrating critical insights that justified the wholesale dismissal of all the modern views with which he was acquainted, and substituting for them nothing but his own brand of nihilistic skepticism. That, in my judgment, makes Nietzsche the villain rather than the hero of the story.

In the first place, we did not need Nietzsche to justify our dismissal of the errors made by moral philosophers since the eighteenth century. An understanding of all the fundamental insights that make Aristotle's *Ethics* the only sound, practical, and undogmatic moral philosophy would have sufficed for that. In the second place, Nietzsche's contribution, if it has any merit at all, is nullified by the nihilistic skepticism which he thought was the only alternative to the doctrines he rejected. His ignorance, misunderstanding, or neglect of Aristotle's *Ethics* is unacceptable. MacIntyre's juxtaposition, in several chapters, of Nietzsche vs. Aristotle, as if this presented us with a genuine choice, is also unacceptable.

That, however, is not the only serious fault with the philosophical message that is interlaced with the historical narrative in MacIntyre's book. The bankruptcy of moral philosophy in modern times does not stem solely from the loss of the concept of moral virtue and the attempt to substitute for it moral laws or rules of conduct, the validity and utility of which have been so successfully challenged. It stems also from the loss of the other elements that, in Aristotle's *Ethics*, are inextricably connected with the concept of virtue.

These elements are as follows:

1. A nonhedonistic and totally nonpsychological conception of happiness as identical with a whole life well lived, because virtuously conducted and accompanied by the blessings of good fortune;

2. An understanding that happiness, so conceived, is not experienceable or enjoyable at any moment in the individual's life, that it functions as the ultimate end for which everything else is a constitutive or an operative means in the same way that an architect's vision of a building to be erected functions as the end to be aimed at, with the one difference that the building, when erected, exists and endures, whereas a good life when completed is over and done with;

3. The crucial insight that moral or prescriptive judgments have a

different kind of truth from that of factual or descriptive judgments, by conformity with right desire instead of by conformity with reality;

4. The distinction between natural and acquired desires, together with the distinction between real and merely apparent goods—real goods being the objects of natural desires (or inherent human needs), and merely apparent goods seeming to be good only because individuals have acquired desires for them and so happen to want them;

5. The understanding that though everyone uses the word *happiness* as the name for an end that is never a means—that is, something to be sought entirely for its own sake—not all human beings have the same ultimate good in mind when they pursue happiness;

6. The rejection of individualistic relativism on the grounds that the happiness everyone ought to seek is the same for all because the real goods we naturally desire are the same for all; which leads to

7. The conception of happiness not as the *summum bonum* but rather as the *totum bonum*, a whole life made good by the cumulative attainment of *all* the real goods that are the objects of the natural desires common to all human beings because they share the same specific nature; and to

8. The distinction between these real goods as the constitutive elements of happiness (or a whole life made good) and the moral virtues as the operative or functional means whereby happiness is achieved, but

9. Only, of course, if their presence is accompanied by the blessings of good fortune.

All of the foregoing nine points are summarized in the single sentence in which Aristotle defines happiness as a whole life that is lived in accordance with complete virtue and is accompanied by a moderate amount of the external goods that are the goods of fortune. The role that virtue plays cannot be understood without an understanding of all the other elements in the picture. Virtue, as Aristotle says, may make a man morally good, but by itself it does not produce the happiness of a morally good life.

Though MacIntyre insists that without the concept of moral virtue a sound moral philosophy cannot be developed, his account of the role that moral virtue plays in a sound moral philosophy is deficient because he either neglects entirely or does not pay sufficient attention to all the other elements in the picture, with which moral virtue is inextricably connected. This has serious consequences for his discussion of virtue and for his effort to replace Aristotle's ethics with a doctrine that he thinks will be more acceptable, more congenial or palatable, to contemporary tastes.

For one thing, he fails to distinguish between two radically different senses of the word *good*—the adjectival use of *good* (along with *better* and *best*) to grade objects of any sort (e.g., a good knife, and good coffee), for which such other words as *fine, finer,* and *finest* can always be substituted; and the substantive use of the word in the plural to name goods that are objects of desire. With the exception of the adjective *good* in the phrase "a good man," only the latter use of *good* has moral significance.

This failure on MacIntyre's part underlies his erroneous dismissal of Hume's correct insight that valid prescriptive judgments, which declare what we ought to seek or do, cannot be derived from true descriptive statements about what does or does not exist in reality. There is no way of validating prescriptive judgments except in terms of Aristotle's distinction between prescriptive and descriptive truth, one by conformity to right desire, the other by conformity to reality. In the light of this distinction, it is then possible to formulate one self-evident prescriptive principle: we ought to desire everything that is really good for us; all real goods ought to be desired.

Nothing more than this one self-evident first principle is needed to arrive at other prescriptive truths based on true descriptive statements about the natural desires or needs of all human beings, the objects of which are all real goods that are rightly desired and, therefore, ought to be desired.

MacIntyre's deficient understanding of Aristotle's ethics may also account for his failure to see that another basic difference of the greatest importance between Aristotle's moral philosophy and modern ethical doctrines is the primacy of the good over the right in the one, and the reverse of that in the other.

For Aristotle, the ultimate end to be sought by the individual is his own happiness, the totality of all real goods attainable by virtue and good fortune in a whole life. It is not the general welfare of the political community, nor the general happiness—the happiness of others. One aspect of moral virtue, justice, is concerned with the welfare of the community and the happiness of others; but, unless each individual knows what is really and ultimately good for himself or herself and aims at it, the individual cannot know what is really good for others, to which they have a right because they need every real good for their happiness. Nor will the individual be inclined to avoid injuring others by depriving them of real goods or interfering with their attainment of them, unless he understands that he cannot aim at, or attain, what is really good for himself without also acting justly toward others; that is, without injuring them.

The moral laws or rules of conduct that modern ethical doctrines substitute for the concept of moral virtue are exclusively concerned with right and wrong conduct toward others rather than with the good that the individual ought to seek for himself or herself.

Last, but not least, of the consequences of MacIntyre's argument to be pointed out is his rejection of Aristotle's teaching concerning the unity of virtue. The reason why this point is important is that to omit or reject it prevents us from understanding what Aristotle meant by "complete" or "perfect" in that crucial sentence in which he defined happiness as a life lived in accordance with complete or perfect virtue, not just in accordance with some virtues in the absence of others or together with the vices that replace them. It also prevents us from understanding why an individual is obliged to act rightly or justly toward others in order to pursue happiness for himself or herself.

This can be made intelligible only if it is impossible to be courageous, temperate, and prudent without also being just, precisely because the four virtues named are not virtues capable of existing separately. They are only four aspects of virtue, the existence of any one of which is impossible without the coexistence of the other three.

Not to understand the unity of virtue and the inseparability of its four cardinal aspects is not to understand moral virtue itself. Moral virtue is the habit of right desire. Desire can be right in two ways, not one—right in aiming at the end which ought to be sought because it consists in the totality of all real goods, and right in the choice of the means to be employed in acting for the rightly desired end. Prudence is that aspect of virtue which is involved in the right choice of means; temperance and courage in private life, and with them justice in relation to others, are the aspects of virtue which are involved in rightly desiring or aiming at the one ultimate good—the happiness we are all morally obliged to seek.

The intemperate individual, the glutton, drunkard, or sluggard, cannot be prudent, because any means chosen will be chosen for the wrong end. Similarly, the unjust individual, the thief, cannot be prudent; he can only be cunning and clever, Aristotle tells us, because his conduct is not directed to the right end.

For the same reason, an individual cannot be temperate *and* cowardly, or courageous *and* intemperate; that is, an individual cannot have an habitual right desire for the end he ought to seek (as indicated by his being temperate or courageous) and at the same time also have an habitual wrong desire for things he ought not to seek, because the latter are incompatible with the end he ought to seek (as indicated by his being cowardly or intemperate).

This brings me finally to MacIntyre's own project of trying to retain something akin to the notion of virtue (but certainly not identical with the Aristotelian conception of it as summarized above) and to develop a moral philosophy for our day that will be more congenial than Aristotle's doctrine to current prejudices—for that is all they are.

One of these prejudices, MacIntyre tells us, is the scientific prejudice against Aristotle's "metaphysical biology," which, in his view, provides the indispensable underpinnings for Aristotle's moral philosophy. This scientific prejudice, it should be pointed out, is to be found mainly if not exclusively among social scientists, not biological scientists. It is a prejudice against the notion that all human beings, as members of the species *Homo sapiens*, share a common, specific nature and all the species-specific properties that genetically belong to that specific nature.

If the affirmation of a specific nature and species-specific properties is metaphysical biology, then twentieth-century biological science is metaphysical when it looks upon the genetic code as having programmed, in the same way, the development of individual members of a species, all drawn from the same gene pool. The same picture, but not the same words, is to be found in Aristotle's doctrine that individuals of the same species have the same potentialities for development and their normal development consists in the actualization of such potentialities.

This basic biological insight, which is not metaphysical at all in any correct sense of that term, does, of course, underlie Aristotle's moral philosophy. The crucial notion of the natural desires that are inherent in all members of the human species because of their common human nature (together with the notion of the real goods they aim at) rests on the biological fact that all human beings have the same specific potentialities (i.e., the same genetic program) for development and that these potencies are appetitive tendencies to be fulfilled by their actualization.

To say, as Aristotle does, that all men by nature desire to know is to say that all, having minds, have a potentiality for knowing, and that this potentiality is a natural desire or tendency—a need to be fulfilled by the acquisition of knowledge, which is something really good for every human being to possess.

The other contemporary prejudice that Professor MacIntyre wishes to placate by his deflated version of Aristotle's moral philosophy is one that he calls "individualistic liberalism." Briefly stated, it consists in the opinion that everyone should be free to conceive happiness in his own way and to seek it accordingly. Those espousing such individualism are necessarily affronted by a doctrine which proclaims that happiness can be rightly and wrongly conceived, that rightly conceived it is the same for every human being, and that, with minor differences in accidental respects, it must be pursued in the same way by all—that is, by virtuous conduct accompanied by the blessings of good fortune.

Any attempt to avoid these two contemporary prejudices, neither of which is defensible, must result in a moral philosophy that is as defective as Mill's utilitarianism. MacIntyre makes no reference to an excellent contemporary work in moral philosophy (G. H. von Wright's *The Varieties of Goodness*) which, like his own, expresses great admiration for Aristotle's *Ethics* while, at the same time, giving reasons for substituting something else for it that is not as good.

Professor von Wright tells us his reason for turning away from Aristotle's teleological ethics in the direction of Mill's utilitarianism. Referring to Aristotle and Mill as representative of the two main variants of teleological ethics, he writes:

> The one makes the notion of the good of man relative to the notion of the *nature* of man. The other makes it relative to the needs and wants of individual men. We would call the two variants the "objectivist" and the "subjectivist" variant respectively. I think it is right to say that Aristotle favoured the first. Here my position differs from his and is, I think, more akin to that of some writers of the utilitarian tradition.

The same prejudices are here apparent—*against* the affirmation of man's specific nature and *for* individualistic liberalism. Neither prejudice, in my judgment, can be regarded as a good reason for replacing

Aristotle's *Ethics* with a moral philosophy that is less sound, and that is especially deficient because it cannot combine a principle of moral obligation with the teleological consideration of means and ends.

It must be said in Professor MacIntyre's favor that he acknowledges the deficiencies in what he has been able to come up with so far as a substitute for Aristotle's *Ethics*. He promises further developments in a forthcoming book, but I do not think he can succeed in the project he has set for himself if he persists in the positions he has taken so far.

20

Ethics:
Fourth Century B.C. and
Twentieth Century A.D.

(1988)

In "Ethics: Fourth Century B.C. and Twentieth Century A.D." Adler
demonstrates the extremes to which a denial of objective validity to moral
judgments can lead. He also questions the proposition advanced by
Bernard Williams in his book Ethics and the Limits of Philosophy
(1985); namely that while moral philosophy may be bankrupt in modern
times, Aristotle's Ethics, though sound in ancient Greece, is no longer
tenable for us. What, Adler asks, has changed in the world to make
Williams think this? Human nature? Our moral problems? This review
first appeared in The Great Ideas Today 1988, a publication of Encyclopaedia Britannica, Inc.

G. V. D.

IN 1986, on the one hundredth anniversary of Yeshiva College in
New York City, the president of the college, Norman Lamm, gave
a convocation address that was later published in the New York
Times. He said that "until about fifty years ago, it was commonly
accepted that the university was responsible for offering its students
moral guidance." Since then moral skepticism, the view that value
judgments, judgments about what is good and evil, right and wrong,
cannot have objective validity, has been regnant in our colleges. It did
not begin in the 1960s, as one might suppose by reading Allan Bloom's

book *The Closing of the American Mind.* In 1940 I wrote an article for *Harper's Magazine,* entitled "This Prewar Generation," which described the inroads then of moral skepticism at the University of Chicago, Bloom's university.

"Such value-agnosticism in the academic enterprise," President Lamm went on to say, "is self-destructive. . . . An educational system that is amoral in the name of 'scientific objectivity,' thus devours its own young. . . . Permitting a generation of students to grow up as ethical illiterates and moral idiots, unprepared to cope with ordinary life experiences, is a declaration of educational bankruptcy."

"Moral idiots" is strong talk, but it does express the repugnance that is evoked by those who deny objective validity to all moral judgments. In doing so they take the view expressed by the sophist Thrasymachus in Plato's *Republic* that might is right—that those who have the power to tyrannize over others, whether that be an absolute despot or a democratic majority, cannot be rationally condemned as unjust or as violating human rights. Those who are oppressed by such tyranny may not like it, but they cannot, in the court of reason, contend that it is wrong.

Lest readers suppose that I am conjuring up an amoral monster, let me quote some statements by Judge Robert Bork, who when I wrote this was President Reagan's nominee for a seat on the Supreme Court. Bork has been quoted as saying that no "system of ethical or moral values" has "objective or intrinsic validity of its own." He has written that "every clash between a majority and a minority claiming power to regulate involves a choice between gratifications"; and that "there is no principled way to decide that one man's gratifications are more deserving of respect than another's." The majority's gratifications should prevail because might is right.

Where did Judge Bork learn to think and talk this way? At the University of Chicago in the 1940s. From whom did he learn it? From his professors in the social sciences who think and talk that way, and also from Professor Carnap and other logical positivists in the philosophy department who regard ethics as a noncognitive discipline, concerned only with what feelings, desires, or impulses are expressed in talk about good and evil, right and wrong. All judgments about such matters are entirely subjective, relative to the individual and the circumstances of the time and place.

I have been aware of this academic rejection of moral philosophy as genuine knowledge—as a body of valid truths—since the 1930s. In various ways, in articles and lectures, I have attempted to combat it. Finally, in 1970, I published *The Time of Our Lives: The Ethics of Common Sense*, in which I reformulated the fundamental truths of Aristotle's *Nicomachean Ethics* in twentieth-century terms, exposed the modern errors in ethics perpetuated by Hume, Kant, Nietzsche, John Stuart Mill and other utilitarians, and in a lengthy postscript demonstrated why it can be said that Aristotle's *Ethics* contains the only sound, totally undogmatic, and thoroughly pragmatic moral philosophy that we have in the whole twenty-five centuries of Western thought.

Its soundness rests on the fact that only one self-evident prescriptive truth is required as a basis for all its prescriptive conclusions; its undogmatic character stems from the fact that it sets forth no *ad hoc* rules of conduct but instead attributes leading a good life to the effects of moral virtue and the benefits of good fortune: its pragmatic appeal is that it offers us an attainable goal in response to the question everyone must ask, "How should I live?" or "What is the right conduct of life?"

Since 1970 I have written other books in which in different contexts I have carried forward the main message of *The Time of Our Lives*: in 1978, the chapters in Part III of a book entitled *Aristotle for Everybody*; in 1981, chapters 10–13 in *Six Great Ideas*; and in 1985, chapters 5, 6, and 8 in *Ten Philosophical Mistakes*.

It is against this background that I would now comment on two recently published books by professors of philosophy—*After Virtue*, by Alasdair MacIntyre (1981), and *Ethics and the Limits of Philosophy*, by Bernard Williams (1985), especially the latter.

I was delighted by the critique of all post-seventeenth-century attempts to provide a sound moral philosophy that I found in the books by MacIntyre and Williams, which more than amply confirmed the criticism I myself had leveled at Hume, Kant, and J. S. Mill and other utilitarians in *The Time of Our Lives*. I was further delighted by the praise that both authors lavished on Aristotle's *Ethics* as a great contribution to moral philosophy that we have inherited from antiquity.

At the same time, I was sorely puzzled and disturbed by the fact that both authors, each in his own way, found Aristotle's contribution flawed by its antiquity, so that it no longer remained as sound for us today as it once was for Greeks in the fourth century B.C.

Here I part company from them. In my view, Aristotle's moral philosophy is just as objectively true, just as pragmatically sound, just as practically wise today as it was then. In my view, human nature is exactly the same today as it was in Greek antiquity. In my view, all the manifold changes in our social, political, and economic institutions that have occurred since then, combined with all the extraordinary technological innovations that condition our lives today, are totally irrelevant to the problem we all face when we ask ourselves the primary ethical question: *"How should I conduct my life?"*

I reviewed Professor MacIntyre's book in *The Great Ideas Today*, 1982, summarizing it by saying that, according to Professor MacIntyre, modern thought (lacking as it does the Aristotelian conception of moral virtue as a well-established habit of the will that directs it to the right final end and confers on it an habitual right choice of means to that end) is bankrupt when it tries to answer the question: *How should I conduct my life?*

I went on to say that the bankruptcy of moral philosophy in modern times does not stem solely from the loss of the concept of moral virtue, but also from other elements in Aristotle's *Ethics* that are inextricably connected with its concept of moral virtue. Central to this is a non-hedonistic and nonpsychological conception of happiness as a normative, not a terminal, final end, requiring nothing less for its realization than a whole life well lived in accordance with virtue, and accompanied by a moderate possession of those external goods that are not entirely within the power of the individual to obtain, but which become ingredients in his or her life partly through the blessings of good fortune.

Apart from certain other defects in MacIntyre's understanding of Aristotle's *Ethics*, which I pointed out in my 1982 review of his book, my main objection to it was the fact that Professor MacIntyre tried to salvage the truth in Aristotle's ethical doctrine by abandoning Aristotle's conception of human nature, which is the rock on which his whole ethical edifice is built, while defending the un-Aristotelian view that everyone should be free to conceive happiness in his or her own way.

Professor MacIntyre's abandonment of Aristotle's conception of human nature came about, he tells us, in obedience to the scientific prejudice against Aristotle's "metaphysical biology" as well as to the existentialist dogma that there is no such thing as a common and constant human nature. MacIntyre's rejection of the view that the lineaments of a morally good life as a whole are the same for all human beings was his attempt, he tells us, to placate a twentieth-century "individualistic liberalism" that insists upon allowing each individual to decide for himself how to live well.

After Virtue was Professor MacIntyre's faulty attempt to retain some currency for such truth as there is in Aristotle's *Ethics* by deflating it to accommodate these two contemporary prejudices, neither of which is defensible. I concluded my review of MacIntyre's book by saying that neither prejudice can be regarded as a good reason for replacing Aristotle's *Ethics* with a moral philosophy that is less sound, and that is especially deficient because it cannot combine a principle of unconditional moral obligation with a teleological consideration of means and ends.

Bernard Williams, the author of *Ethics and the Limits of Philosophy*, also reviewed MacIntyre's earlier book, and he gave it unstinting praise. However, in his own book, he did not follow MacIntyre by trying to resurrect Aristotle's *Ethics* in contemporary, if also somewhat deflated, terms. Professor Williams does believe that modern thought is completely bankrupt in moral philosophy, especially the dogmatic rationalism of Kant, and the hedonistic utilitarianism of J. S. Mill; he also thinks that in Greek antiquity Aristotle's *Ethics* was a remarkably sound solution of the problem of how to live well. But unlike Professor MacIntyre, Williams does not think that what was sound about Aristotle's ethical doctrine can be resuscitated in the contemporary world.

If that is really the case, then philosophy, so far as ethics is concerned, is today completely bankrupt. It may have achieved certain successes in other fields in the twentieth century, but it is now barred from attaining any truth with regard to morals. For us and our descendants, there is no valid philosophical solution to such questions as: How should I conduct my life? What should I do to live well? How can I succeed in the lifelong pursuit of happiness?

But are we in fact at this pass? I do not believe it. To someone like myself, who thinks that Aristotle's *Ethics* is just as true objectively and just as sound practically in the twentieth century as it was in the fourth century B.C., the question that must be asked of Professor Williams is: What has changed in the world to cause him to change his view of Aristotle's *Ethics*—in his view, philosophically tenable and relevant for ancient Greeks, but, in his view, philosophically untenable and irrelevant for us today?

Before I try to answer this question, let me say at once that if Professor

Williams were correct in his two main contentious—(1) that modern thought is bankrupt with regard to moral philosophy and (2) that Aristotle's moral philosophy, while practically sound and objectively true in Greek antiquity, is no longer tenable in the twentieth century or relevant to the conditions of life today—then we might have to concede that moral skepticism or Nietzschean nihilism cannot be condemned; that there are no objectively valid moral judgments about what is good or evil, right or wrong; and that Thrasymachus was correct in arguing against the Socratic view of justice and in asserting that might makes right.

But I do not think *both* of these contentions are right. Rather, as readers of books I have published since 1970 (cited earlier in this essay) already know, I heartily subscribe to the first of them and just as wholeheartedly reject the second. Hence I have never felt obliged to concede that moral skepticism is the only position we can adopt. On the contrary, at least fifteen years before Professor Williams stated his objections to accepting any longer the moral wisdom contained in Aristotle's *Ethics* as a guide to living well, I wrote *The Time of Our Lives*, in which many of his objections were anticipated and, in my judgment, satisfactorily answered. Those that were not then anticipated can be answered now, I believe, as well.

Professor Williams attributes to Socrates in Plato's *Republic* the question that is the right starting point for moral inquiry and reflection. The question is, How should one live? "It is no ordinary matter that we are discussing," says Socrates, "but the right conduct of life" (*Republic*, 352D). Professor Williams comments on this by adding that the Greeks were impressed by the idea that "such a question must, consequently, be about a whole life and that a good way of living had to issue in what, at its end, would be seen to have been a good life. Impressed by the power of fortune to wreck what looked like the best-shaped life, some of them, Socrates, one of the first, sought a rational design of life which . . . would be to the greatest possible extent luck-free."

With such help as he obtained from Plato, sifting the truths that he found in his teachings from the errors he also detected there, Aristotle formulated the rational design for living well that, according to Professor Williams, Socrates originally sought. This rational design belonged to practical philosophy in that it guided or directed us in our freely chosen actions, but it had its theoretical foundation in Aristotle's philosophical psychology—his conception of human nature and its species-specific potentialities.

If Aristotle's theory of human nature has been shown by modern science to be incorrect, it was incorrect in the fourth century B.C. as well as today; and it follows that Aristotle's moral philosophy, which had its basis in his view of human nature, was without foundation in antiquity as well as today.

If Professor Williams is right in claiming that Aristotle's moral philosophy is no longer valid for us because we can no longer accept his philosophical psychology as true, then Professor Williams must be wrong in thinking, as he appears to think, that it was a sound moral philosophy in antiquity.

Against Professor Williams, I contend that since the beginning of human life on earth some forty-five million years ago with the appearance of the species *Homo sapiens sapiens*, specific human nature has not changed in any essential respect. The potentialities that constitute specific human nature are constant from generation to generation, and they will remain constant as long as the human species endures on earth.

Aristotle's philosophical psychology is an analysis of those potentialities, from which is derived his account of man's inherent, natural needs for their fulfillment or actualization. This in turn leads to his insight about the distinction between real and apparent goods in relation to the distinction between natural and acquired desires—needs and wants.

It is a short step from this to the one underlying self-evident principle of moral philosophy—that we ought to want what we need, which is to say that we ought to desire everything that is really good for us, and that a good human life as a whole consists in the cumulative attainment of all the things that are really good for every human being, through moral virtue and good luck, together with getting such innocuous apparent goods as one or another individual may want for himself or herself.

The pursuit of happiness is the same for all, so far as the attainment of real goods is concerned, but different for different individuals according to differences in the apparent goods that we want, resulting from individual differences in temperament, nurture, and the differing circumstances of time and place.

Nothing that we have discovered by experimental or empirical investigation in modern scientific psychology alters in one jot or tittle the main truths in Aristotle's philosophical psychology, as I think I have conclusively shown in a book entitled *The Difference of Man and the Difference It Makes* (1967). Hence the reason for rejecting Aristotle's *Ethics* as no longer tenable in the twentieth century cannot be that we now know that his account of human nature is false and so his moral philosophy is without foundation. It may not be generally acceptable in the academic world today, but that is quite different from asserting that it is false.

Another way of saying the same thing is to call attention to the accounts given in antiquity of human life, of human problems, and of the ways human beings succeed or fail in solving them. When we read the two great epics of Homer, the tragedies of Aeschylus, Sophocles, and Euripides, the histories of Herodotus, Thucydides, and Tacitus, and the biographies written by Plutarch (which President Truman read regularly to understand what was going on in Washington), we cannot fail to acknowledge that human beings were the same in Greek and Roman antiquity as they are today.

They are, humanly speaking, our contemporaries, even though our institutions differ from theirs and the external conditions of our lives differ even more remarkably from theirs. But our moral problems do not differ from theirs. Success and failure in solving these problems depend on the same two indispensable factors—moral virtue and the blessings of good fortune—both necessary, neither by itself sufficient. That, in brief, is the central teaching of Aristotle's *Ethics*.

Another charge that Professor Williams levels against the acceptability of Aristotle's *Ethics* is that ancient moral thought was egotistic —too self-centered, too much emphasis on the individual's own personal happiness and not enough concern with the individual's obligation to the well-being of others (pp. 8, 14, 35, 49). But on all of these points, Professor Williams's understanding of Aristotle's *Ethics* is, I believe, deficient.

In the first place, he has overlooked the fact that, for Aristotle, happiness (or a morally good human life as a whole) is a *common* good, the same for all men. When the individual directs his life toward happiness as the final end of all his actions, he is aiming not only at his own ultimate goal but at the ultimate goal he shares with all other individuals.

Second, justice is one of the four aspects of moral virtue by which the individual chooses means to this ultimate goal, and justice is concerned with the happiness of others. The morally virtuous man in seeking his own happiness through temperate, courageous, and prudent choices (the three other aspects of his moral virtue) also seeks it through just choices.

What are such choices? *Negatively,* not to do anything that injures others and either frustrates or prevents them from succeeding in their pursuit of happiness. *Positively,* to act for the good of the organized community, the public common good, in which all individuals participate and which contributes to their individual happiness by providing them with real goods they need to lead good lives, goods they cannot obtain for themselves entirely by their own efforts. The best state, says Aristotle in the *Politics,* is one that aims at the happiness of all its citizens.

Still another objection that Professor Williams makes to the contemporary acceptability of Aristotle's *Ethics* is that his conception of virtue "no longer has any, or enough, sense for us"; that the virtues today are "unpopular as an ethical conception"; and that any list of virtues we today would draw up would differ markedly from Aristotle's catalog of them, thus showing "how pictures of an appropriate human life may differ in spirit and in the actions and institutions they call for."

Once again, Professor Williams has failed to observe the crucial passages at the end of Book VI where Aristotle argues soundly for the unity of moral virtue and for the existential inseparability of all the various aspects of moral virtue he inventories at length in Books III and IV. Aristotle alone maintains that there is only moral virtue in its singleness, one habit of right direction to the end of life and of the right choice of means, not a plurality of numerous, existentially distinct, virtues.

Not even his most docile disciple, Thomas Aquinas, agrees with him on this central point, while agreeing with him that the four cardinal aspects of moral virtue are temperance, courage, justice, and prudence. All other aspects of moral virtue are affiliated with and subordinate to these four cardinal aspects of moral virtue as a single, integral habit of right choice of means to a rightly appointed end—a good life as a whole.

Nor does it follow, as Professor Williams thinks it does, that because our social and cultural life differs markedly from that of the ancients, so too must our ethical thought differ from theirs. Granted that our social and cultural life differs from theirs, our fundamental moral problems remain the same.

Professor Williams also neglects two essential and quite original contributions that Aristotle makes to moral philosophy. One is his distinction between theoretic or descriptive truth, as defined in *Metaphysics*, Book IV, 4–5, and practical, normative or prescriptive truth, as defined in *Ethics*, Book VI, 2. Here, Aristotle tells us that such truth is not the conformity of the mind's descriptive judgments (is and is not) to what in reality is or is not, but rather the conformity of the mind's prescriptive judgments (ought and ought not) to right desire.

The other is the distinction made (in *Ethics*, Book III, 4–5) between (1) natural desires that, rooted in man's natural potentialities, are our basic needs, the same for all human beings, and (2) acquired desires —the wants that result from nurture, training, and experience and therefore differ as individuals differ from one another in their temperaments and biographies.

These two distinctions taken together constitute the core of Aristotle's *Ethics*. All our natural desires or needs are right desires, so we ought to want what we need, for those are the things that are really good for us. The one self-evident principle of moral philosophy is that we *ought* to seek everything that is really good for us and nothing else. The principle is undeniable because the opposite is unthinkable.

The objects we want in addition are only apparently good, deemed good because we want them, but only so regarded *when* we want them, not *later* when we may regret having obtained them. They may turn out to be really bad for us. Those that do not turn out to be really bad are *innocuous* apparent goods; and we are permitted to include the satisfaction of such innocuous wants in our pursuit of happiness. It is only in this respect that one individual's happiness or morally good life differs from another individual's.

Professor Williams is quite right in calling attention to the grievous errors Aristotle made about natural slaves and the inferiority of women to men (p. 35). But when we expunge those errors of fact, the essential moral truth of Aristotle's *Ethics* remains intact and undisturbed.

Saint Augustine incompletely summed up that moral truth by saying, in his little treatise on *The Happy Life*, that happy is the man who, in a complete life, obtains everything he desires, *provided he desires nothing amiss.* This statement stresses the role moral virtue, or right desire, plays in the pursuit of happiness and implies the distinction between real and apparent goods. But it omits the role that the blessings of good fortune play.

Aristotle takes account of that in his own summary statement when he says in *Ethics*, 1, 10, that happiness consists in a complete life well lived in accordance with moral virtue (a rightly habituated will), and accompanied by a moderate possession of health and wealth along with other external goods that are, to some degree, beyond the power of the individual to obtain by his or her own efforts, and that are, therefore, the blessings of good fortune.

Moral virtue and good fortune are both necessary; but neither by itself is sufficient. The morally virtuous individual may be a morally good human being, but he or she may be prevented from completing a good life by accidents beyond the individual's control.

Finally, Professor Williams holds a view of the advances made by philosophy in the twentieth century that is both wrong, in my judgment, and also detrimental to his own thesis that Aristotle's *Ethics* was a good philosophical book in antiquity but one that does not measure up to contemporary standards of good philosophical writing.

He says that philosophy today is more rigorous and stringently an-alytical than it was in Greek antiquity; and in consequence, that we are rightfully more skeptical than Aristotle about reason's reflective powers to achieve philosophical truth (p. 3).

That statement undermines the praise that Williams later in his book showers on Aristotle as a relatively sound moral philosopher in antiquity. But it is also questionable whether all the gimmicks of an-alytical and linguistic philosophy in the twentieth century, trying to solve pseudo-problems inherited from the preceding three centuries of philosophical thought, constitute a real advance in philosophical thought.

The fundamental mistakes of modern philosophy, none of which were made by Aristotle, remain uncorrected today by contemporary thinkers whom Professor Williams regards as philosophically superior to Aristotle. That they are more skeptical than Aristotle in dealing with metaphysical and moral problems is certainly true, but that they are *rightfully* so is highly questionable.

Above all I would contend that the basic premises of Aristotle's philosophical psychology (his conception of human nature) are true, whereas the psychological presuppositions of contemporary positivism and of modern analytical and linguistic philosophy are false. That is what makes Aristotle's *Ethics* sound and also accounts for the bankruptcy of moral philosophy since the seventeenth century.

Part FIVE

Paideia:

Its Inception and

Development

21

Reconstituting the Schools

(1983)

The Paideia project for the reform of basic schooling (K–12) is in some sense this book's reason for being. Launched in 1982, Paideia is a product of these essays—a program to carry out the principles they espouse, a solution to problems they pose. With the advent of Paideia, a liberal education of the highest quality can be made available to all American children, and not just to the college bound.

The essays that follow provide an introduction to the program and some insights into its operation. A fuller explication can be found in three small books: The Paideia Proposal *(1982),* Paideia Problems and Possibilities *(1983), and* The Paideia Program *(1984), all published by Macmillan.*

How the democratic goals of education are met in the Paideia proposal, what the proposal is and what it is not, and how three kinds of teaching and learning are related to the goals they serve and the materials they employ are explained in "Reconstituting the Schools." How the changes called for in basic schooling relate to the improvement of our colleges and universities is also considered. This essay is from a discussion about The Paideia Proposal *that took place at the Center for the Study of Democratic Institutions in Santa Barbara. It appeared in* The Center Magazine *(September/October 1983).*

G.V.D.

THERE ARE five related and widely prevalent errors in American education that *The Paideia Proposal* attempts to correct. The first error is to think that only some children are educable, even though all have a right to aspire to become truly educated human beings.

The second error is to suppose that the process of education is completed in our educational institutions during the years of basic schooling or even during the years of advanced schooling after that. Nothing could be further from the truth. Education never is completed in the school. Youth and immaturity are insuperable obstacles to becoming educated.

The third error is to suppose that teachers are the sole, primary, or principal causes of the learning that occurs in students. That is not the case. The primary cause of all learning—unless it be rote memory, which is not learning at all—is the activity of the student's mind. The best that the best teacher can do is to assist that activity.

The fourth error is probably at the heart of the matter, and the correction of this error is at the heart of *The Paideia Proposal*. The error is to suppose that there is only one kind of teaching and one kind of learning, the kind that consists in the teacher lecturing, or telling, and the students learning what they hear said or what they find in textbooks. That's the least important kind of learning and teaching. There are two much more important kinds of learning and teaching, and all three must be in basic schooling, from kindergarten through the twelfth grade.

Finally, there is the error of supposing that schooling—basic or advanced—is primarily a preparation for earning a living, and that it will not hold the attention of students unless that is manifestly so. Obviously one of the objectives of schooling is to prepare the young to earn a living, but that is the least important objective. One of the great troubles with our schools is that both teachers and parents make the mistake of thinking that job preparation is the primary objective.

My book, *The Paideia Proposal*, is dedicated to Horace Mann, John Dewey, and Robert Hutchins. To Horace Mann because in the middle of the last century he struggled valiantly to see that on the eastern seaboard the children had at least six years of free compulsory schooling. It turned out that six years became the rule well into this century. It is only in the last forty or fifty years that compulsory schooling has been extended to twelve years, but that in part is a debt we owe to Horace Mann.

To John Dewey because, in 1916, in his book *Democracy and Education*, Dewey put those two words together for the first time in history. By doing so, he showed that in our kind of society, all the children who go to school are destined to have the same kind of future;

therefore, the objectives of schooling should be the same for all. They should all have exactly the same quality of schooling.

And to Robert Hutchins for a single sentence that sums it all up: "The best education for the best is the best education for all." An extraordinary passage that Bob Hutchins was fond of quoting came from John Amos Comenius in the year 1657:

> The education that I propose includes all that is proper for a man, and it is one in which all men who are born into this world should share. Our first wish is that all men be educated fully to full humanity. Not any one individual, not a few, or even many, but all men, together and singly, young and old, rich and poor, of high and lowly birth, men and women; in a word, all whose fate it is to be born human beings, so that at last the whole of the human race become educated, men of all ages, all conditions, both sexes, and all nations.

In the title of my book, *paideia* is the Greek word for general human learning; the Latin of *paideia* is *humanitas*. I mention that because one of the terrible errors in the world today, and particularly in America, is a misunderstanding of the meaning of humanities. People think that it denotes what is left over when you finish with the sciences. Humanities, *humanitas*, is strictly the equivalent of *paideia*, which means general, unspecialized, untechnical human learning.

The subtitle of the book describes it as "an educational manifesto." We used the word "manifesto" to echo the *Communist Manifesto*, because we are intending a revolution, and a revolution is nothing but a reversal in direction in any social institution. The quality of schooling has been declining for the last sixty years. We must start climbing back. The ideal is a goal to be aimed at and achieved by a series of cumulative steps in the right direction. It will not be reached quickly. It may take twenty-five, thirty, even fifty years to produce the changes we have in mind.

Now it is much easier, of course, to state principles and policies than to implement them. Therefore, the Paideia group has written a second book, *Paideia Problems and Possibilities*. It will be published in the fall of 1983. In the course of the last year, we have met with members of sixty or seventy educational organizations across the country. We have picked up more than fifty questions and problems which we state carefully and answer.

We are planning a third book, *The Paideia Program*, scheduled for publication in 1984. It will be a group of essays written by the members of the Paideia group. The first two have already been written: one on mathematics and the mechanical arts; the other on language and the language arts. Everything in the Paideia program, diagrammed on page 23 of *The Paideia Proposal*, will be commented on in detail in our third book. (See page 285 below.)

All these will be short books like our eighty-four-page first book. We decided that if the *Communist Manifesto* had been written in three hundred pages, there never would have been a revolution. Anyone who needs more than an hour to read it can't read. There is no jargon in it, no educationese, no pedagese. If I could have raised the money to do it, I would have liked to have dropped *The Paideia Proposal* from airplanes on the roof of every home in the United States.

Several things our proposal is not. It is not a return to basics. Of course, we are concerned with skills, including the skills of reading, writing, and arithmetic. But we are concerned with much more than skills.

Our program is not a return to the classics, as that word is so often taken to mean, simply going back to Greek and Roman antiquities. We are concerned with classics where the classics mean anything of enduring value.

Our program is also not just an appeal for an improvement in the quality of education for some students. It is an appeal for the improvement in quality for all, without any exception whatsoever. And, since it is for all, it is not elitist. People who call it elitist because it is dedicated to a high quality of education misuse the word elitist.

The first and most important distinguishing characteristic of *The Paideia Proposal* is that it takes democracy seriously. It takes seriously the commitment of the democratic society to the objective of a high quality of basic schooling for all children.

Most Americans do not know that democracy is not fifty years old. Democracy, properly defined in the modern sense as constitutional government with truely universal suffrage, and the securing of all natural or human rights, was not in existence at the beginning of this century. At that time women were still disfranchised, human rights were not secured, and economic rights were not even dreamed of.

It is therefore not surprising that we do not have a democratic system of education. We have instead an antidemocratic, or undemocratic, system of education, a holdover from the nineteenth century and the first years of this century. We have a two-track educational system. We separate the children into the sheep and the goats, and we do not give them the same quality of schooling. It is about time—now that democracy is just beginning to come into existence—that we try to create, over the next hundred years, a system of schooling that fits a democratic society.

Our proposal is also concerned not just with secondary schooling, but with all twelve years of compulsory schooling as an integrated unit. And in terms of all the developmental psychology we know, the best way to divide those twelve years is in two parts of six years each.

Another characteristic of our proposal is that, given the same objectives for all students, we must use the same means, which is a required curriculum, for all. The required curriculum calls for the elimination of all electives in the upper six years of schooling, with the exception of a choice of a second language to be mastered, and the elimination of all specialized job training throughout. The kind of vocational training that now goes on in schools is worse than useless; it is undemocratic in the extreme. As John Dewey observed in 1916— and the situation is ten times worse today—vocational training is the training of slaves, not free men.

Our proposal does not prescribe the particulars of a curriculum for the whole country. It says there should be a required curriculum everywhere, but we have not defined that curriculum. It would be presumptuous to do that in a country as pluralistic as ours, with more than fifteen thousand separate autonomous school boards and/or school districts, each with the authority to determine what is to be studied in its own area. If we had a Ministry of Education in the United States as they have in France, you could do that. What we did instead is present a curricular framework, within which any sound curriculum must be constructed in different ways, in different school districts, to meet different populations under different circumstances.

Finally, our proposal regards basic schooling as preparation for continued learning, either in higher institutions or in adult life. To become an educated person is an accomplishment of one's mature years, after all schooling, basic or advanced, has been completed.

In sum, *The Paideia Proposal* calls for:

1. The same quality, not just the same quantity, of schooling for all the children, so that all will have an equal educational opportunity.

2. The schooling must be general, not specialized; liberal, not vocational; humanistic, not technical; thus fulfilling the meaning of the words *paideia* and *humanitas*—the general learning that should be in the possession of every human being.

3. The objectives of basic schooling should be the same for all, because all have the same three elements in their future, as John Dewey pointed out: the demands of work; the duties of citizenship; and the obligation of each individual to make as much of himself or herself as possible.

These three common objectives can be achieved only by a completely required course of study, whose only elective is a second language. Incidentally, we are the only country in the world that does not require a second language in its basic schooling.

4. The curriculum or course of study must include three kinds of learning: acquisition of organized knowledge; development of the intellectual skills of learning; and an enlarged understanding of ideas and values. These three kinds of learning and the corresponding three kinds of teaching must be integrally related to one another.

5. Individual differences, especially inequalities in natural endowment and in nurtural environments from which the children come, call for compensatory efforts in the form of preschool tutoring for those who need it, and remedial or supplementary instruction for those who need that.

6. Every school must have a principal who is truly the principal teacher in that school, its educational leader, not merely its administrative or clerical head. We tend to forget that the word "principal" is an adjective. An adjective needs a noun. And the noun that goes with principal is teacher. It's the only thing that could possibly go with it. It's our American equivalent for the British term headmaster. In Britain the teachers are masters, and the headmaster is the head teacher. A school without a principal is no school at all. I know that in every school there are clerical and administrative chores to be done; but let them be done by clerks working for the principal. The principal should be the educational leader of the school. Unless that is the case, I do not think you can have a real learning community.

Two important comments on the foregoing are in order. The first concerns the often misused words "liberal" and "humanistic." Liberal has had two uses traditionally. As an adjective for education, it meant nonvocational, that is, learning for the sake of learning itself. Vocational meant learning for the sake of earning. But that does not address the fact that carpentry, for example, may be a component of liberal schooling and liberal learning, if it is carpentry for the sake of acquiring the skill of thinking with one's hands and tools. If it is carpentry to earn a living, it is not liberal. Chemistry is liberal only if it is chemistry for the sake of learning that particular branch of the physical sciences. If it is chemistry to become a chemical engineer, it is not liberal.

The second meaning of the word liberal is as an adjective modifying arts. Liberal arts are not fine arts. The fine arts are totally useless; that is their glory. The liberal arts are useful. It is important that we not include under the liberal arts all the things they are not. When we refer to "liberal arts high schools" or "liberal arts colleges," we do not mean liberal arts as such. Any course, and any combination of elective courses of study, can be part of a liberal arts college curriculum. But the liberal arts themselves are the arts of the trivium and the quadrivium, which, in modern form, include reading, writing, speaking, listening, and all the mathematical disciplines and scientific skills. Those are the liberal arts. They are skills. Arts are skills. The Greek word *techné* is the word that names them all. Nevertheless, in America today there is a gross misuse of these terms. We speak of a "liberal arts curriculum" in which no liberal arts are taught at all, and in which most of the elective components in that curriculum are either not arts or skills, or if they are arts, they are literary and other fine arts, not liberal arts.

The same kind of misuse applies to the word "humanities." Humanistic learning is simply general, not specialized, learning. In the Greek lexicon, the distinction is between *paideia*, or general learning, and *episteme*, which is the knowledge of the scientist, the expert. In Latin, the distinction is between *humanitas* and *scientia*. *Paideia* is the root word in "encyclopaedia"; the meaning of encyclopaedia is the great circle of general learning. *Paideia*, or *humanitas*, in this traditional sense, includes mathematics, all the sciences—natural and social— just as much as it includes history, philosophy, and the fine arts. Everything that belongs to general human learning is humanities.

When Robert Hutchins came to the University of Chicago, he did something that perpetuated this mistake. He's been forgiven for it, because it was in the air. He divided the university into four divisions. Three of these were the physical sciences, biological sciences, social sciences. What was left over he called the humanities. And it really was what was left over. But what was left over is no different from the other three subjects. The humanities at the University of Chicago, under Mr. Hutchins, included philology, history, philosophy. But these subjects were just as specialized and narrow in their scholarship as were the sciences in their specialized research. The humanities at Chicago was no more *humanitas*, in the sense of general learning, than physics and mathematics were. Humanities, as general learning, must include all the subject matters, not just some.

The curricular framework as diagrammed (see figure on page 285) is clear. Each of the three columns designates a kind of learning that must continue, in ascending difficulty, for the full thirteen years, that is, from kindergarten through grade twelve. The first column is the acquisition of organized knowledge in the basic fields of subject matter, which are language, literature and the fine arts, mathematics and the natural sciences, history, geography, and the study of social institutions. The kind of teaching that assists, but only assists, this kind of learning is didactic teaching. It is teaching by telling, teaching by lecturing, teaching by textbook assignments and by examinations on those textbook assignments, teaching by class exercises and blackboard work. Unfortunately this least important kind of teaching is the only kind that most teachers do. It is the only kind that schools of education pay any attention to. They do not do this very well, but they do pay attention to it. They pay little or no attention to the other two kinds of teaching and learning.

The second kind of learning and teaching (column 2) is the development of the intellectual skills. Now a skill, a *techné*, or an art—the three words mean the same thing—is a habit. You do not have an art except by having it through habit formation. This is true of all the bodily skills. Forget about the intellectual skills for the moment. Think of the skills that are taught in a gymnasium or on the playing field. What kind of teaching helps the formation of the habits which are these skills? It is coaching. You would not think of someone trying to teach another how to play basketball or how to swim by lecturing that person. You need a coach, a fellow who says, don't do it this way, do it that way; stop putting your right foot forward when you should put your left foot forward; keep your eye on the ball; throw your shoulder back. Whatever it is you are doing, you must do it over and over and over again under a coach's eye until you form the correct habit. Coaching is the only way that skills—intellectual or physical—can be formed. And it only can be done by a coach with four or five trainees, not thirty or forty, at one time. You could not do coaching in a million years with thirty students.

Now, since schools of education do not prepare our teachers to coach, and since they have classrooms and curricular arrangements in which coaching cannot be done, our children do not learn how to read, write, speak, listen, or how to do the mathematical or scientific oper-

THE PAIDEIA CURRICULAR FRAMEWORK

	Column 1	Column 2	Column 3
Goals	Acquisition of organized knowledge	Development of intellectual skills— skills of learning	Enlarged understanding of ideas and values
Means	*by means of* Didactic instruction, lectures and responses, textbooks and other aids	*by means of* Coaching, exercises, and supervised practice	*by means of* Maieutic or Socratic questioning and active participation
Areas, Operations, and Activities	*in three areas of subject matter* Language, Literature, and the Fine Arts Mathematics and Natural Science History, Geography, and Social Studies	*in the operations of* Reading, writing, speaking, listening Calculating, problem-solving, observing, measuring, estimating Exercising critical judgment	*in the* Discussion of books (not textbooks) and other works of art and involvement in artistic activities, e.g., music, drama, visual arts

The three columns do not correspond to separate courses, nor is one kind of teaching and learning necessarily confined to any one class.

ations well. They never will be able to do these things if they are not coached. These skills can be developed in no other way. We have to get coaching of the skills back into the schools. Coaching is ten times more important than the acquisition of organized knowledge (column 1) which most people forget anyway. I regard myself as an educated human being, and I have forgotten almost everything I learned in school as described in column 1 of the table. But I have not forgotten the skills I formed. They have remained with me all my life, and I have improved them. The first kind of learning is evanescent; the other two kinds are permanent.

The third column is even more important than the second. The first column is knowing *that*; the second is knowing *how*; the third is knowing *why*. The enlargement of the understanding of basic ideas and values cannot be done by didactic teaching, and it cannot be done by coaching. It must be done by discussion, by the Socratic method of asking questions in seminars that run for two hours, in which the things discussed are books, not textbooks. No one can discuss a textbook. You have to have books that are readable and discussable, that deal with ideas and values. And you have to have other works of art that enhance those values. These are almost absent from the schools today.

The great joke is that the only place in the school system where this kind of teaching and learning goes on today is kindergarten. The kindergarten teacher does sit on the floor with her students. They sit in a circle, and she tells them a story or a fable. They ask questions, and they enjoy it. That kind of teaching persists a short while in the first grade. But by the time the children get to the second grade, it stops. What should persist through the whole twelve years is almost entirely absent in our schools.

There is an organic or biological analogue of this. For our life, for our body's health and vitality, we need three nutriments: fats, carbohydrates, and proteins; and we need them in a certain balance or proportion. One can imagine what our body would be like if we had a diet solely of fats. Well, our schooling is that kind of diet. It consists almost solely of column 1 teaching, and unassimilated at that. It is teaching and learning that is unalloyed by the "carbohydrates" and "proteins" found in the second and third columns.

The three columns are diagrammed in two dimensions as if they were separate; but all the work we have done indicates that in a properly constructed curriculum, these three kinds of learning and teaching are organically related to each other. Our teachers are totally untrained for the third kind of teaching. They may have a bit of training for the column 2 kind of teaching, coaching. They have none for the third kind, which enlarges understanding. It is only the rare, gifted teacher who does it at all, and then not because of anything that he or she learned in a school or department of education.

In addition to the threefold course of study which runs through twelve years, there are three auxiliaries: twelve years of physical education; six years of manual training, including cooking, sewing, typing, machine repair—all the manual skills—not for any vocational purpose, but because learning how to do things with one's hands is just as much a matter of mental agility as learning how to do things with words; and, in the last two years, a general—I emphasize the word general—introduction to the world of work.

A comment on this last point is in order. Vocational training, as it is now conducted, is worse than useless, but it will also become totally outmoded because ten years from now computers and robots will be doing most of the unskilled and semiskilled work. Computers will direct robots and will program other computers.

The only kind of preparation for work that makes any sense is schooling in the liberal arts, the intellectual skills, the skills of judgment, the skills that help a child to learn how to learn whatever he or she needs to learn in life. That is the only proper preparation for the world of work. It is not preparation for a particular job; that kind of training goes back to the guild system when the children of glassblowers became glassblowers, the children of metalworkers became metalworkers, and so on. It is not only undemocratic to narrow a child's future to any particular slot, it is also foolish, since most of those slots will disappear anyway.

We haven't begun to think of what is involved in preparation for work over the next ten, fifteen, or twenty years. Our country, as everyone is beginning to realize, needs radical reorganization of our industrial life. We can no longer compete in the world economy with a nineteenth-century model of industry. Those jobs are gone forever.

That is the Paideia proposal for the kindergarten and the next twelve years of schooling. Obviously some children will go on to advanced schooling, some to college, some to universities. But all children must be prepared to continue learning throughout their adult life, whether they go on to college or university or not.

There are implications in the proposal for our colleges and universities, which are in a bad state on both the undergraduate and graduate levels. The members of the Paideia group, many of whom are college presidents or deans, have given up on the colleges, as did Robert Hutchins fifty years ago. It took Mr. Hutchins from 1930 to 1943 to create what I would say is a general college at the University of Chicago, a college devoted entirely to general liberal learning. In 1943, we had a completely required college curriculum at the University of Chicago. That was so radical that it almost brought on a faculty revolt. Indeed, it was so radical that within twelve months of Mr. Hutchins's leaving the university to join the Ford Foundation, members of the graduate school undid the whole thing. Our colleges and universities are under the control of the graduate schools which are specialists' schools. They are not interested in general education at all. They are interested in research in their specialties.

To create a good college, Robert Hutchins made the college faculty an autonomous ruling body of the University of Chicago. This faculty was in no way responsible to the graduate school. There were appointments to the college faculty, promotions within the college faculty, salaries determined by the college faculty, curriculum developed by the college faculty, all this independent of the graduate school. In short, the college became autonomous, because that was the only way you could make a good college at the University of Chicago. But, as I say, within twelve months of Robert Hutchins's leaving, that program and setup were dismantled, and the college of the University of Chicago became like any other college elsewhere. The only college in the country that Hutchins and I had anything to do with that still persists as a college in which general, liberal, humanistic learning is required for four years is St. John's College at Annapolis, Maryland, and Santa Fe, New Mexico.

There are no departments at St. John's College. There are no professors. Every member of the faculty must teach the whole curriculum. That is the only way you can make it work. That is the ideal.

St. John's College has been in existence since 1937. It has never enrolled much more than 380 or 390 students. Why? Why has general education at Chicago been thrust aside; why has it been thrust aside at Harvard? Why was Hutchins's general education at Chicago undone? The answer to that is also one of the reasons for the Paideia proposal. Today, college comes too late in a young person's life. The years of the young in college are eighteen to twenty-two. That is too close to the time when one leaves home, gets married, earns a living. Asking the young or their parents, under those circumstances, to subscribe to four years of general, unspecialized, unvocational education, an education that does not directly prepare for any profession, will, of course, be resisted and rejected. And it probably should be that way.

So we decided that if we are going to have general human schooling in this country, it has to be accomplished in the first twelve years of compulsory schooling.

That program is right for another reason; namely, that that is the only schooling that is common to all children. General learning should be common to all, and it should occur in schooling that is common to all—grades kindergarten through twelve—not in college, which is for less than half the population.

Now, agreed that colleges will continue to be specialized and departmentalized, that their catalogues will continue to be crammed with elective courses—Harvard alone has four thousand courses in its catalogue!—let all that stand. The Paideia group says, if we have the *paideia* precollege schools underneath, let's at least have some continuation of general, liberal, humanistic learning at the college level. The proposal—it is only a proposal—that I have made, at the invitation of a number of college presidents, to their faculties, is, keep your catalogue and all your elective majors, but have just one minor for all four years, something which all students will be required to take. That minor, in the form of a seminar, will consist of the reading and discussion of books and the discussion of works of art. When I propose that to college faculties, they smile indulgently, until I make the next statement, which is that this will work only if all members of the faculty lead these seminars. At that point they throw their hands up. "You cannot expect us to do that. What books would you have us read?" I name some books. "Oh, we cannot do that. Most of those books are not in our field." That is the statement that ruins everything. The students can read them, but the faculty cannot because they are specialists. It is very difficult to get a college faculty in this country to undertake great books seminars with students.

*   *   *

Another demon we must exorcise is the Ph.D. degree. The Ph.D. degree has no ancient lineage. There were no Ph.D.s in the medieval universities. They had only four degrees. One was the teaching degree, the master of arts. The master was strictly a teacher, and he taught the same arts that the students were to learn, the liberal arts. The other three degrees were professional in nature: doctor of law, doctor of medicine, and doctor of theology.

Eventually there grew up in the nineteenth-century German universities research in the fields of science, the humanities, philology, and history. The German universities wanted to recognize these new specializations just as law, medicine, and theology had been recognized. Again, humanities was the name for whatever was left over after you accounted for the natural and social sciences, and in Germany the humanities teachers were called the faculty of philosophy. So the degree was called "doctor of philosophy," but it had nothing at all to do with philosophy.

Today there isn't an actual doctor of *philosophy* in our country. There may be a few in the departments of philosophy, but for the most part they, too, are not philosophers. We don't refer to someone as a "doctor of philosophy"; we say "doctor of philosophy in education," or "doctor of philosophy in physics," or "doctor of philosophy in engineering," or accounting. Today you can be a doctor of philosophy in anything.

The meaning of the Ph.D. degree in the German universities was, in the beginning, acceptable, because it meant a degree that signified the accomplishment of specialized research in a given field like philology or history or mathematics. It did not mean a degree that prepared anyone to teach. It had nothing to do with teaching. The great teachers in Germany were the teachers in the humanistic gymnasium, and those were not Ph.D.s. They should not have been Ph.D.s. At Oxford and Cambridge universities, well into this century, the highest degree, other than the professional degrees, was the master of arts, as it should be. Finally Oxford and Cambridge yielded. And, of course, the American universities slavishly imitated the Germans, but with a difference. The American universities came to regard the Ph.D. degree as a certificate for a teacher. That is why our college faculties are staffed today with

Ph.D.s. One of the great letters in all of American literature is William James's letter to the president of Bryn Mawr College, who had refused to hire James's best student to teach philosophy because the student did not have a Ph.D. James's letter became the classic little essay entitled "The Ph.D. Octopus."

We ought to restructure the whole thing. We ought to have a "Sc.D." which would stand for doctor of science of scholarship, and use that in place of the Ph.D., for all graduate degrees other than law, medicine, and theology. The Sc.D. would not signify a teacher at all. If we want to signify someone who is prepared to teach, and since the master of arts degree no longer means that, let us resuscitate the old degree (now an honorary degree) of L.H.D., doctor of humane letters. That would be for the teacher of general, liberal, humanistic studies.

Then let us require—for the sake of our culture, if nothing else—that all Sc.D.s and all L.H.D.s should also be Ph.D.s in the proper meaning of Ph.D., that is, doctors of philosophy, meaning that they must have some acquaintance with the fundamental ideas and values of our civilization. Let them be philosophical experts and philosophical teachers in the sense in which both John Stuart Mill in his famous address as rector of St. Andrew's and Cardinal Newman in his *Idea of a University* meant philosophy, not in its narrow sense as used in our philosophy departments today, but in its general sense.

What we are saying is that everyone should be a generalist first and a specialist second.

Robert Hutchins never tired of saying that the university should be a community of learning, a community of scholars. But how can we say a university is a community when students and teachers have nothing in common? You can go to every college in the country at graduation time and ask this question of the seniors: What one book have all of you read in the last four years and discussed with one another? To which there would be no answer at all. No answer, not even in the Catholic colleges. All may have read certain textbooks, but not one book in common. So it is ridiculous to think of the university as an intellectual community today.

This is a serious matter that goes beyond the education of the young, if it continues. The man who called the shots on that is José Ortega y Gasset. I recommend to you, as *the* most important educational document in the twentieth century, his *Revolt of the Masses*, particularly chapter 12, "The Barbarism of Specialization." That was written in 1930. What Ortega describes there is true to a much more intense degree today.

The ideal of a truly educated human being, something to which every child has a natural right to aspire, is in some degree attainable only at the end of life, in the ripeness of maturity, certainly not much before one reaches the age of fifty or sixty. There is such a thing as terminal schooling. But education is for a lifetime. We can give certificates, diplomas, and degrees to signify the completion of schooling. The only thing that signifies the completion of education is a death certificate.

22

The Three Columns Revisited

(1987)

In 1987, after five years of observing and promoting the implementation of the Paideia program in schools, beginning in Chicago and Atlanta, Adler in this essay enlarged on the activities, outcomes, and the means of better evaluating the outcomes, of the three kinds of teaching and learning. The Wednesday Revolution mentioned here is the establishment of a series of weekly seminars, in all grades from kindergarten through grade twelve. It is essential to the Paideia program as a whole, but useful by itself as a way of introducing the program into a school. The Wednesday Revolution is discussed in chapter 24. "The Three Columns Revisited" first appeared in a special edition of The Paideia Bulletin *(May 1987).*

G.V.D.

Introduction

IT HAS BEEN five years since the three-column table that depicted three types of teaching and learning was first published in *The Paideia Proposal*. It was repeated in the later Paideia books: *Paideia Problems and Possibilities* and *The Paideia Program*.

Since then, I have had a great deal of experience in discussing the three kinds of teaching and learning with principals and teachers all over the country, especially in the many schools that have already introduced elements of the Paideia program or have indicated a serious interest in initiating it.

As a result, I think that I can now explain the differences of the three types of teaching and learning more clearly, and that I can also clarify what is involved in the conduct of seminars in a way that will answer many questions that teachers have asked about it, and will give them greater guidance in their efforts to engage in this kind of teaching.

With respect to each of the three kinds of teaching and learning, I propose to proceed as follows: first, to define the outcome to be achieved; second, to indicate the several modes in which that kind of teaching can be done; third, to discuss the relative effectiveness and durability of the learning that results; fourth, to comment on the method of teaching involved in each of the three kinds; and, finally, to consider the means of evaluating the outcomes.

I will begin with the first column, didactic teaching—the kind that is now done by most teachers. Here I will only suggest how this kind of teaching can be improved in relation to the kinds of teaching to be done in the second and third column.

The second column—coaching—is a more important element in the Paideia program. Coaching is also the element that should be associated with the conduct of seminars in the three-hour period called for by the Wednesday Revolution. I will, therefore, treat coaching second.

From the point of view of the Wednesday Revolution, and of the Paideia program as a whole, seminars are the most important element and the one for which teachers are least prepared by the training they have received. It is on this subject, which will come third, that I have the most to say.

Column 1: Didactic Instruction

OUTCOME. Information or knowledge of the facts in a field of subject matter.

EFFECTIVENESS AND DURABILITY. The poorest, least effective didactic teaching involves merely the imparting of information about matters of fact, information that is memorized by students mainly for the purpose of passing the tests that measure their possession of such information.

More effective didactic teaching would involve the acquisition of knowledge by the student rather than mere information. Knowledge consists of information about the facts accompanied by some understanding of them. This cannot be achieved by didactic teaching that is not augmented by discussion of the information imparted by the teacher or by textbook readings assigned.

To make didactic teaching more effective, a fifty-minute period should be divided into two phases; the first phase, running for thirty minutes, in which the teacher lectures; the second phase, running for twenty minutes, in which the teacher engages in discussion with the students, getting them to ask questions or asking them questions about the meaning of the facts covered in the first phase.

Mere information imparted by teachers and memorized by students is the least desirable of all the products of teaching and learning. Nor is there any reason why it should long endure after standardized tests have been passed. Most information can easily be looked up in reference books. Genuine knowledge of matters of fact is more durable than mere information about them, but it is less durable than habitual skills firmly established and continually used, and much less durable than the understanding of ideas achieved in seminars.

EVALUATION. Short-answer tests can measure the amount of information retained, but they cannot measure as well or at all the understanding of that information which turns it into genuine knowledge of matters of fact. Open-book examinations requiring the understanding of facts to be found in those books is recommended for a better evaluation.

Column 2: Coaching

OUTCOME. Some improvement in a skilled performance, the skills in question being language, mathematical, or scientific skills, in all of which thinking is involved, so that there is no need for any special or separate coaching of thinking skills.

METHOD. Critical observation by the coach of the performance of those being coached, with the on-the-spot correction of mistakes in performance and the recommendation of ways to correct these mistakes, together with repeated exercise of the right ways to improve the performance.

MODALITIES. Here there is only one mode of coaching, but that one mode is more or less effective according to the number of students being coached at the same time and the amount of time that is devoted to the coaching of each student.

Most effective, of course, is the coaching of a single individual for a sufficient period of time to observe improvement in the performance of the skill. Least effective is coaching a group of twenty or twenty-five students in a period of time that does not allow for attention to individual students. In between these extremes is a spectrum of more and less effective conditions for coaching.

The importance of coaching is so great that it should be attempted even when the conditions for undertaking it render it less effective than ideal conditions provide.

DURABILITY. Skills are habits, not memories. Habits are much more durable than memories, especially than the memory of information acquired without much understanding of the facts remembered. But the durability of habits depends upon their being continually exercised; if they are not, they weaken from disuse. Hence the skills perfected by coaching can turn out to be less durable than the understanding achieved by seminars, but they tend to be more durable than the mere information imparted by didactic teaching unaccompanied by any discussion of what is thus taught.

Column 3: Seminars

OUTCOME. The educational result to be aimed at here is the understanding of ideas and issues, never information or even knowledge about a body of subject matter. It should always involve consideration of the significance of what has been read (in the case of books) or what has been experienced (in the case of works of fine art). That, in turn, should lead to the agreement or disagreement of the participants concerning the main points that have come out in their attempt to understand what has been read or experienced, accompanied by their reasons for holding opposing views or their reasons for judging certain statements to be either true or false.

MODALITIES. In its simplest mode, the conduct of a seminar does not call upon the teacher to give any background information, nor need there be any coaching by the teacher of the intellectual skills of reading, writing, speaking, and listening. The rudimentary seminar here involves mainly questions and answers about what has been read.

In more complex seminars, the teacher may have to provide some background information during the course of the discussion. The teacher may also have to engage in the coaching of reading, especially when it is necessary to help the students obtain a full understanding of the text read in order to get the ideas and issues in it clear enough to be discussed. Nevertheless, the seminar should always begin with questions that open up what is involved in trying to understand the text and conclude with questions that call for agreement and disagreement about what has been understood, or judgments about the truth or falsity of the propositions that have been understood. Since the seminar leader is a participant in the seminar as well as its leader, he or she can engage in this part of the discussion by expressing his or her own views and defending them if they are challenged by the other members of the seminar.

EVALUATION. The outcome of this kind of teaching cannot be measured by any short-answer tests, but only by oral examinations. However, increased skill in reading and writing resulting from seminars can be measured by traditional tests.

EFFECTIVENESS. The increased understanding that is the ultimate result of the seminar is the most durable of the three kinds of learning. Whatever is understood is rarely if ever forgotten.

THE MATERIALS TO BE READ FOR SEMINAR DISCUSSIONS. These materials are divided into two types. They are either narratives (stories, plays, histories, biographies) or they are expository works (science, philosophy, essays, documents, etc.).

The simple mode of the seminar is possible only in the case of narratives. With such materials, the seminar should always begin with having the participants tell the story, with the correction of mistakes or omissions as the story is successively told by different participants. The telling of the story provides the basis for a discussion of the significant points raised in the narrative.

For expository texts as opposed to narrative ones, the simple mode of seminar conducting is seldom, if ever, effective. Here the complex mode must be resorted to, with varying degrees of admixture of declarative and interrogative speech on the part of the teacher, as well as coaching by the teacher of reading and speaking, together with probing questions by the leader to get at the truth or falsity of what comes to be understood.

Here, instead of opening by having the story told, the leader must employ questions that direct attention to passages in the text that require careful interpretation to get at what they mean. What the author is trying to say must be sufficiently clear to everyone around the table before questions can be asked that aim to get at the truth or falsity of what is being said.

To make this happen, the author should be regarded as a participant in the seminar, which cannot be the case unless what the author is trying to say has been sufficiently understood before questions about what he has said can be asked.

THE CHOICE OF THINGS TO BE READ. First and most important of all, the materials chosen for seminar discussions should always be sufficiently over the heads of the students at any grade level that they have to reach up to understand what they have read. If what is assigned is completely intelligible to them at a glance, it is not material suitable for seminar discussion, because a seminar should always result in the students understanding more after they have discussed what they read than before the discussion started.

Second, and almost equally important, the reading assigned should be short enough for adequate discussion during the short period of a single seminar. In the case of very long narratives—a modern novel, for example—only parts can be read for a single seminar, and it may take a number of seminars to discuss the whole. In the case of expository works, it is seldom the case that a whole book can be discussed in a single seminar. Parts, chapters, or sections should be assigned rather than the whole. The whole work may require an extended series of seminars, which amounts to a tutorial on that book.

Third, teachers should never assign things to be read that do not interest them or catch their minds in a way that involves them in asking questions about its meaning as they make an effort to understand it.

Finally, in choosing a set of readings for a sequence of seminars, no attention at all should be paid to the field of subject matter in which the materials fall. A haphazard chronological ordering of them is much better than any attempt to order the materials so that they cover themes or topics in a particular subject matter.

THE DIMENSIONS OF THE SEMINAR. Every seminar has two dimensions: a vertical dimension from top to bottom (from beginning to end) and a lateral or horizontal dimension (from side to side).

The movement of the seminar in its vertical dimension should be directed and controlled by the seminar teacher through the ordering of the main questions that the teacher plans to ask, bearing in mind that the purpose of the seminar is increased understanding of ideas, *not* covering predetermined ground.

The movement of the seminar in its lateral or horizontal dimension should be open to all the possible answers that the teacher's questions elicit from the participants in the seminar. It should be open to all the possible thoughts that the participants can express.

Seminars vary in the degree to which they are controlled and open according to the demands for understanding the text read before the participants discuss its significance and the truth and falsity of what is being said.

A discussion of the Declaration of Independence is likely to be most controlled. Only somewhat less controlled is a discussion of two books, such as Aristotle's *Politics*, Book I, and Rousseau's *Social Contract*, Book I. In contrast, the discussions of Plato's *Apology*, Machiavelli's *Prince*, and of *Antigone* by Sophocles are much more open.

When a seminar is open in both of its dimensions, it is not truly a seminar. It is a poor counterfeit of a seminar—a bull session or a rap session.

When a seminar is directed or controlled in both directions, it is not truly a seminar either; it is didactic and dogmatic. It also is a poor counterfeit of the seminar—a quiz session in disguise.

THE IMMENSE VARIETY OF SEMINARS. There is no one right way of conducting seminars. Every book or piece of reading assigned calls for a unique approach appropriate to that particular reading and accommodated to the students participating in the seminar at a particular grade level.

Even for a given book or reading assignment at a particular grade, two seminar teachers may conduct good seminars in quite different ways. What is common to all these different ways of conducting seminars is the result they achieve: some increase on the part of the participants in the understanding of what has been read and some exercise of thought on their part in dealing with differing interpretations of what has been read and differing judgments about its truth or falsity.

I have been conducting seminars for sixty-five years, since 1923. In that time, I have conducted many thousands of seminars with many hundreds of readings, often conducting seminars dealing with the same reading materials many, many times. My files contain innumerable notes that I have made for the conduct of all these seminars. An examination of my files would discover the extraordinary variety that occurred in the conduct of all these seminars, varying with different books, varying with different groups of participants, and varying even with the same reading material at different times in my life, with different participants, and under different conditions.

In the course of sixty-five years, I have improved in my ability to conduct seminars, but even at the beginning, when I was quite young, I did well enough simply because I was a little older than the students and worked a little harder than they did in my effort to understand the book being read and to think of the questions it raised for them to consider.

Any teacher who understands this and regards himself or herself as a superior learner with regard to any book that is the subject for seminar discussion cannot fail to help the students in the seminar to become learners also.

MISUNDERSTANDINGS TO BE AVOIDED. In the last five years, I have, at the invitation of elementary and high schools across the country, done a great many demonstrations of seminar performance with students at the elementary and secondary level and also with their teachers. I have also shown one or another of the five videotapes of seminars I conducted with seniors at the Millbrook High School in North Carolina (now available from Encyclopaedia Britannica Educational Corporation in Chicago).

The readings have included narratives, such as *Hamlet* and *Antigone*, documents, such as the Declaration of Independence and the Preamble to the Constitution, and philosophical writings, such as Plato's *Apology*, the first book of Aristotle's *Politics* together with the first book of Rousseau's *Social Contract*, and Machiavelli's *Prince*.

In the case of the videotapes made in North Carolina, teachers were present who asked me questions about the conduct of the seminars; my discussion with them is recorded on these videotapes. In other cases, I have garnered questions and comments from teachers who observed the performance of the seminars.

From all this experience, I have slowly, much too slowly, become aware of grave misunderstandings of what is involved in the conduct of seminars. The misunderstandings are partly my fault, for in my first efforts to contrast didactic with Socratic teaching, I oversimplified the contrast between them and used words loosely in a manner that made my oversimplification easily remembered. I now must correct that oversimplification. The widespread misunderstanding of the difference between didactic and Socratic teaching must be corrected once and for all.

The misunderstanding that I am referring to is manifested in the questions I have been asked by teachers who have observed demonstration seminars. They ask: Weren't you a bit too didactic? Didn't you talk too much instead of just asking questions? Weren't you making them too aware of their lack of understanding of the meaning of certain words and passages, or their misunderstanding of the text on one point or another? Didn't you intimidate them by exposing the inconsistencies or contradictions into which they had fallen? Or by telling them that what they said was incorrect—plainly false? Or by leaving them up in the air when they could not answer your repeated query, "What reasons do you have for saying that?" By pointing out that the arguments they advanced were unsatisfactory, by telling them they had not listened carefully to the question they were undertaking to answer and so the answer they gave was not relevant, and even by going so far as to tell them that their use of language was so confused that what they said made very little sense?

I hope that questions of this sort do not indicate that the teachers who asked them cannot recognize or acknowledge that students may fail to understand what they read, misunderstand it, or understand it inadequately; that students may be irrelevant as well as relevant in their answers to questions, either because they do not listen well enough or because they do not have a sharp enough sense of what is and is not relevant; that the opinions that students express may be wrong or right, false or true, incorrect or correct; that the arguments they try to advance in support of their opinions may be cogent or not, adequate or inadequate; that they may or may not understand what certain crucial words in a text mean; that their use of words may be so garbled that what they say makes very little sense.

If teachers do recognize all these alternative possibilities, why then are they made so uncomfortable by the fact that I do not hesitate to call a student's attention to his or her mistakes or deficiencies when they become apparent in the course of a seminar? Why, in addition, does my doing that and being so strict with students about what they have to say and how they say it cause teachers to make the comment that my demonstration seminar was really not a good seminar, *as they understand what a good seminar should be,* because it was too didactic and not Socratic enough, because I talked too much and even was too dogmatic, instead of just asking questions and allowing anything that anyone said to get by without comment or correction?

There are three answers to the questions I have just asked.

First, the teachers who ask such questions or make such comments have misunderstood what a good seminar should be. They have misunderstood that because of my own initial oversimplification of the distinction between didactic and Socratic teaching.

That oversimplification consisted in drawing the line between the two kinds of teaching in terms of teachers *uninterruptedly talking at students,* on the one hand, and teachers *persistently questioning* students, on the other hand. A didactic teacher is a telling teacher; a Socratic teacher is a questioning teacher; and that's all there is to it.

To correct this misunderstanding of the difference between didactic and Socratic teaching, let me draw another line, this time between two kinds of teacher-talk, between didactic teacher-talk and Socratic teacher-talk. Didactic teacher-talk is controlled by the purpose of imparting information—*telling* students what they should take note of and try to remember for the purpose of passing tests they will take later. Socratic teacher-talk is utterly different. Sometimes it is for the purpose of presenting factual information that provides a background for understanding the text being discussed. Most of the time it is for the purpose of enabling the teacher to ask a question that will then be sufficiently clear to the participants in a seminar so that they can try to answer the question intelligently and relevantly. Socratic teacher-talk is always aimed at getting the students to understand and think about something, never at getting them to take note of it and remember it for the sake of passing a test, never imparting information for its own sake.

Another way of pointing out the root of the widely prevalent misunderstanding of the difference between didactic and Socratic teaching is to note that the difference does not consist simply in the distinction between declarative and interrogative speech on the part of the teacher, as if all declarative speech by a teacher is didactic, and only interrogative speech is Socratic.

The difference, as I have tried to point out, lies in the purpose of speech on the part of the teacher, whether it be declarative or interrogative. The fact that a teacher conducting a seminar engages in declarative speech for more minutes than he or she engages in interrogative speech does not make that teacher any less Socratic in purpose than a teacher who reverses that ratio and engages in more interrogative than declarative speech.

One might say that the ideal Socratic seminar occurs when the teacher is able to resort only to interrogative speech—that there is no declarative, but only interrogative teacher-talk, only the asking of questions.

That may occur with very simple texts of the narrative variety and with the very best students in terms of their capacity for understanding the text being discussed and their capacity for thinking about it. But when the text is a difficult expository text and when, in relation to that text, the students the teacher confronts are obviously having serious difficulty in understanding it and thinking about it, then for the teacher to proceed in a purely interrogative manner would be ineffective.

If the aim of the seminar is to help students understand and think about what they have read, merely questioning them will not succeed at all. A great deal of teacher-talk that is declarative, not interrogative, may be required, but *always for the purpose of leading up to the critical questions that the students must try to answer.*

The amount of such teacher-talk is not the measure of a good seminar or the indication of a bad one. The only proper criterion for a judgment of whether the seminar was good or bad is whether the seminar raised good questions and raised them clearly enough for the students to have their minds actively engaged in trying to understand and think about what they read, regardless of the amount of time spent in teacher-talk that is interrogative.

The amount of declarative as opposed to interrogative teacher-talk that occurs in a good seminar depends on the amount of help the students at a certain level of capacity need in order to be able to understand and think about questions concerning a text at a certain level of difficulty.

The five demonstration seminars that were videotaped in North Carolina all involved different amounts of teacher-talk on my part (the Declaration of Independence the largest amount because the students needed the most help in understanding it and thinking about it). Nevertheless, they were all equally Socratic seminars and not in any way didactic, if the right criterion for judging them is appealed to, namely, the *purpose* of the teacher-talk that is declarative rather than interrogative.

The second of the three explanations of the prevalent misunderstanding of what a Socratic seminar should be attributes the cause of this misunderstanding to the little rule book distributed by the Great Books Foundation for the guidance of novices in conducting seminars, either for adults or for children in schools.

At the time of the establishment of the Great Books Foundation, in the creation of which in the 1940s I was instrumental, I wrote the first manual for leaders, none of whom were expected to be teachers. Since then other manuals have been produced, but all of them including the current one are addressed to persons who may or may not have the responsibility that a teacher must discharge.

The Great Books Foundation manuals for moderators are, in other words, intended for moderators who are *not* necessarily teachers, but only persons who are willing to assume the responsibility of chairing a discussion in which all the participants are on *an equal footing* with regard to the text read and discussed. Such moderators are not teachers in relation to students. Both teachers and students should be learners in a seminar, but teachers must be superior to the students in that process, for if they are not superior, they are not teachers.

Socrates was a teacher. He was certainly superior as a learner to the persons he interrogated for the purpose of helping them learn to understand and to think. If teachers wish to imitate Socrates, they must be teacher-moderators, not the ordinary moderators given guidance by the Great Books Foundation.

Teachers always regard themselves as superior to their students when they engage in didactic teaching, because they have the information or even sometimes the knowledge that their students do not have and should acquire. They should also regard themselves as superior learners when they engage in Socratic teaching—in the conduct of seminars. If they cannot do this, then in their conduct of seminars they are not teachers, for they are no better than their students in understanding and thinking about the text read and discussed.

Their being Socratic moderators, or teacher-moderators, means that they can tell the difference between a correct and an incorrect, a relevant and an irrelevant, a more or less true, a more or less adequate, answer to whatever questions they ask. It also means that they are able to engage in good declarative teacher-talk as well as to ask good questions. Declarative teacher-talk is good if it helps the students understand and think about the questions posed, just as interrogative teacher-talk is good if it poses the best, the most critical and penetrating questions, about the text read.

Finally, I come to the third explanation of the widely prevalent misunderstanding of what a good Socratic seminar should be. More than an explanation of that misunderstanding, it points to the reason why many teachers will recoil from the correct understanding that I am here offering, to replace the misunderstanding that now prevails.

The reason that many teachers will resist or even resent being told that in conducting seminars as Socratic moderators of them they should regard themselves as superior to their students (as they do regard themselves as superior when they are engaged in didactic teaching) lies in a malaise that pervades the whole academic world.

In our schools and colleges, both students and teachers suppose that, outside the sphere of mathematics, the exact sciences, history, and even sometimes social studies, there are no right and wrong answers to questions, no true and false propositions, no adequate and inadequate arguments or explanations.

That being the case, how dare teachers correct students in seminars when the questions raised are not about matters of fact or answerable in terms of well-established knowledge in a given field of subject matter? And if they dared to do so, wouldn't they be faced by students who challenged their right to do so?

The cultural or intellectual malaise of which I speak can be described as phony tolerance. It denounces as dogmatic and authoritarian anyone who regards one person's opinion as better than another's. It translates everyone's right to hold whatever opinions can be espoused into an acquiescence in the view that all opinions are equally tenable, no one better, sounder, truer than another.

Freedom of thought and expression includes the freedom to be wrong as well as to be right; it does not abolish the distinction between right and wrong. It also involves the freedom to change your mind when contrary evidence advanced and reasons given should cause you to change your mind when you are wrong. Your right to hold whatever opinion you happen to espouse in no way guarantees that the opinion you happen to hold is right, nor does it mean that you should not yield to correction and not change your mind if it can be shown that you are wrong.

Teachers who, in conducting seminars, fail to correct students when they are wrong, because they misunderstand the meaning of freedom of thought and discussion, do not discharge their obligation as teachers. Students who resist being corrected or cry out that they are being intimidated by their teachers who correct them do not discharge their obligation as students. They lack the essential virtue of students— docility, which is a mean between subservience and contentiousness. The use of the word "intimidation" indicates that both the teachers and the students misunderstand their relationship and their mutual obligation to one another.

I recommend to all who aspire to become truly Socratic or teacher-moderators of seminars that they read the best statement ever made about freedom of thought and expression. It is to be found in the second chapter of J. S. Mill's great essay *On Liberty*. I also recommend reading the chapters on truth in a book of mine, *Six Great Ideas*, especially chapters 6–8.

This is the medicine that may help cure the malaise I have called phony twentieth-century tolerance. Without that cure being effected for students and teachers, there is little hope that they will ever enjoy the profit, and the pain as well as the pleasure, of good Socratic seminars.

SOME FINAL OBSERVATIONS. On rereading what has been set forth above, I would like to add a number of qualifications and comments.

I have said that I think that the teacher-moderator should not hesitate to exercise a corrective influence upon the speech and thought of students in a seminar. But while doing so is not only desirable but also necessary if teachers are to discharge their responsibilities, this should be done with clear awareness of the fact that the correction of errors is not the sole or main purpose of the seminar, as it is in the process of coaching. It is more important to keep the seminar moving and to allow a good discussion, aimed at clarifying ideas, to exercise its own corrective influence.

Not all questions have right and wrong answers; in fact, the most difficult and penetrating questions usually do not. They should elicit a variety of competing answers, all of which should be considered and weighed against one another, in the light of whatever evidence may be offered and whatever reasons may be advanced in favor of one or another.

One of the most important results of a good seminar is to leave the students with difficult issues unresolved, matters to be pondered. On such matters, unanimity of opinion is not to be sought, but rather a shared understanding of the alternatives to be considered.

There are three kinds of declarative teacher-talk, not two. The two that have been mentioned are (a) didactic telling, which consists in the imparting of information to be memorized (i.e., the indoctrination that is a counterfeit of genuine teaching); and (b) declarative speech on the part of a seminar leader solely for the purpose of preparing the participants in a seminar to understand the questions that the moderator wishes them to consider and answer.

Here the declarative mode of speech is always followed by the interrogative. In didactic telling by teachers that normally consumes the whole of a fifty-minute period, the declarative mode of speech is uninterrupted; it is not accompanied or followed by questions; nor is its main purpose preparation for the asking of questions.

To call such didactic telling by teachers "lecturing" is a misuse of that word. While a formal lecture may consist in uninterrupted declarative speech for an hour or more, it is something quite different in character and purpose from ordinary classroom declarative teacher-talk. Using the term "formal lecture" for (c) the third kind of declarative teacher-talk, let me indicate what differentiates it from the kind of didactic telling that aims at imparting information to be memorized.

The formal lecture may stand by itself or it may be one in a series of formal lectures. Its controlling aim is to present the lecturer's analytic understanding of an idea, a problem, an issue, or some complex area of knowledge or inquiry. Its controlling aim is to provide the audience with an occasion for thinking and for increased understanding.

If the formal lecture is followed by a question and answer forum in which points raised in the lecture are discussed, it may go beyond providing an occasion for thinking. It may, like the seminar, actually help the students engage in thinking about the matters being considered. If the formal lecture is not followed by a sustained discussion, it falls short of what seminars can do to provoke, encourage, and help the thinking of students. But, with or without such sustained discussion, the formal lecture is a kind of teaching that, in purpose, is much more like the conduct of seminars than it is like the didactic telling of ordinary classroom talk for the sole purpose of imparting information to be memorized.

In its vertical dimension, the sequence of questions that constitute the teacher's plan for conducting the discussion controls its movement from its opening to its closing considerations. But in its horizontal dimension, the responses of students determine the latitude of the discussion—the extent to which it expands at each stage of its development. In this dimension, students may—in fact, it is to be hoped they will—engage in cross-table talk, questioning one another, expressing opposite views, arguing with one another, and agreeing or disagreeing about where the truth lies. The more the seminar is an experience of active learning for the students, the sooner they will become active learners in their reading of texts for future seminars and the sooner they will be able to engage in learning by themselves without the help of teachers, which is the ultimate desideratum of all teaching.

Since questions, asked by either teachers or students, lie at the heart of seminars, a word more should be said about the variety of questions that can be asked. Each type of question—questions of fact, of interpretation, of judgment—performs a different function. Some questions call for Yes or No answers; some elicit a wide range of alternative responses, which may or may not be compatible with one another; and some generate strictly contradictory, or at least contrary, answers that challenge students to put themselves on one side or the other of a clearly defined issue that seeks resolution. Confronting contradictions and attempting to resolve them is probably the most illuminating experience in the pursuit of truth. Hypothetical questions are also very useful because they call attention to assumptions and consequences.

23

A Declaration of Principles
by the Paideia Associates

(1988)

In 1988, after six years of presenting and assisting in the imple-
mentation of Paideia, the Institute for Philosophical Research was joined
in that effort by the University of North Carolina at Chapel Hill. By
then Paideia reforms were in effect in a hundred school districts in fifteen
states. A National Center for the Paideia Program was established to
preserve and perpetuate the Paideia program, and to help train teachers
to carry out its essential tenets: that the three kinds of teaching and
learning occur throughout the years of schooling, that the minds of
students are actively engaged in learning, and that ways are found to
promote equal educational opportunity for all. The "Declaration of Prin-
ciples" that follows was drawn up by the Paideia Associates to help guide
the future efforts of the National Center located at Chapel Hill. The
declaration could also serve as an Educational Bill of Rights for all
American children.

G.V.D.

Wᴇ, the members of the Paideia Associates, hold these truths to be the principles of the Paideia program:

1. That all children are educable;

2. That, therefore, they all deserve the same quality of schooling, not just the same quantity;

3. That the quality of schooling to which they are entitled is what the wisest parents would wish for their own children, the best education for the best being the best education for all;

4. That schooling at its best is preparation for becoming generally educated in the course of a whole lifetime, and that schools should be judged on how well they provide such preparation;

5. That the three callings for which schooling should prepare all Americans are (a) to earn a decent livelihood, (b) to be a good citizen of the republic, and (c) to make a good life for one's self;

6. That the primary cause of genuine learning is the activity of the learner's own mind, sometimes with the help of a teacher functioning as a secondary and cooperative cause;

7. That the three kinds of teaching that should occur in our schools are didactic teaching of subject matter, coaching that produces the skills of learning, and Socratic questioning in seminar discussions;

8. That the results of these three kinds of teaching should be (a) the acquisition of organized knowledge, (b) the formation of habits of skill in the use of language and mathematics, and (c) the growth of the mind's understanding of basic ideas and issues;

9. That each student's achievement of results should be measured against that student's capacity to learn, and should not be related to the achievement of other students;

10. That the principal of a school should be the principal teacher and educational leader of the school community;

11. That the principal and faculty of a school should themselves be actively engaged in learning; and

12. That the desire to continue their own learning should be the prime motivation of those who dedicate their lives to the profession of teaching.

24

Reforming Education—
No Quick Fix

(1988)

One of the difficulties in implementing the Paideia reform is the amount of time it takes to effect. The changes required in the practices of teaching and the structure of schooling cannot happen quickly. There is no quick fix, says Adler.

Far from being disheartened by that realization, Adler proposes a first step toward reforming any school if it wants to experience any of the effects of Paideia. He calls that first step the Wednesday Revolution.

Although changes in schooling in the United States tend to become mired in politics, Adler has high hopes for Paideia, if it is given the time and effort it requires. In 1939, in the essay in this book called "Tradition and Progress in Education," feeling far less hopeful than in 1988, Adler wrote: ". . . pessimism must not lead to despair, for much is at stake that makes it imperative to keep working for reform so long as a chance remains." The essay that follows was taken from Mortimer Adler's inaugural lecture as university professor at the University of North Carolina at Chapel Hill on September 21, 1988.

G.V.D.

REFORMING EDUCATION in the way that the Paideia proposal recommends cannot be accomplished in a short time. An adequate reform of basic schooling in this country cannot be a quick fix—in a future as short as the next few years, or even as extensive as the remaining years of this century. I hope I am not unduly optimistic if I say that it probably can become a recognizable reality in this country sometime before the next century reaches its midpoint.

When I state all the obstacles that must be surmounted and the radical changes in our educational establishment that must take place before the Paideia reform can be substantially accomplished, the reader may not feel as optimistic as I do. In any event I trust he will agree that a quick fix is out of the question.

The two major obstacles to reform have been mentioned elsewhere. One is the persistent failure of educators to recognize that a proportionate equality of results can be achieved when children who differ markedly in the degree of their educability are given the same quality or kind of schooling. The other is the persistent refusal of the educational establishment to replace the scheme of grading that puts a student in his or her niche on the bell-shaped curve by an assessment of the student's achievement wholly in terms of that student's capacity without reference to any other individual's achievement.

When comparative and competitive grading is replaced by individual and proportionate grading, it will no longer seem unreasonable and impractical to have the less able and more able students engage in exactly the same course of study. Even the preposterous charge that the Paideia program is elitist will disappear, because that charge stems from the disbelief that the objectives the Paideia proposal sets can be fulfilled by the less able students. Once it is understood that the fulfillment will be proportionate, such disbelief will be overcome.

The obduracy of these two obstacles is reinforced by the educational mandates enacted by state legislatures that specify the amount of ground to be covered in various subject matters and by their uncritical, almost superstitious, reliance on the scores students achieve in standardized tests, mainly tests of memorized information. For the educational establishment as well as for the state guardians of schools, test scores are treated as indications of the extent to which the required ground covering has been done. But they are also usually regarded as educationally significant. However, while they may be prognostic of a child's ability to get through school, passing from one grade to another, or from one level of schooling to another, they do not provide us with an appraisal of the child's progress in the long process of becoming a generally educated human being—the advance made toward a more skillful, thoughtful, and cultivated mind.

These same obstacles are also reinforced at the high school level by college entrance requirements that put undue reliance on standardized test scores as measures of adequate ground covering in specified subject matters. If the twelve years of basic schooling were, with the Paideia reform, to become a first step in the general, liberal, and humanistic education of the growing individual, many high school graduates, thus trained and cultivated, would have no need to go to college for the kind of specialized technical, preprofessional or preoccupational training that most of our colleges now provide. Since only some students go on from high school to college, college entrance requirements should not be allowed to stand in the way of Paideia's plan to give all students in high school the same quality of general schooling.

Still other obstacles exist. Many parents have the wrong expectation of the profit to be derived from schooling. They think that the only purpose of schools is to prepare their children to earn a living. While that certainly is an objective to be served, it is, in terms of human values, less important than preparation for citizenship and for leading a richly rewarding, good human life. Even with regard to earning a living, most parents do not understand that in our high-tech economy, preparation for earning a good living is more readily secured by those who can read, write, speak, and figure well and who have learned how to think critically and reflectively, rather than by those given specialized job training in vocational training courses.

If all these obstacles were somehow to be removed, we would still be left with the inadequate preparation of teachers to perform the tasks set by the Paideia reform. They come from schools or departments of education with the minimum education and training they need to be certified by the states, but that bare minimum is definitely not enough for most of them to be effective coaches of the basic intellectual skills. They may be totally in the dark when it comes to the kind of teaching that is involved in Socratically conducted seminars about great or good and always difficult books dealing with basic ideas and issues.

A recent report of the Carnegie Foundation recommended the abolition of the undergraduate bachelor of science degree in education leading to the state certification of teachers. Schools of education should become research institutions at the graduate level of the university and not places for the training of schoolteachers. Those planning to enter the profession of teaching should have four years of general, liberal education at the college level, and then three years of practice teaching under supervision. They, too, need coaching if they are to develop the intellectual skills involved in teaching and also learning, for the best teacher is one who learns in the process of teaching.

To become an effective Socratic conductor of seminars, to become an effective coach of the intellectual skills, and to become a didactic teacher who not only lectures effectively but is also able to engage students in discussion, takes a long time even for those who have had a better education and training than most of our teachers have experienced. In schools that have opened their doors to Paideia, where we have attempted to do something about the enlightenment and training of the teachers, progress is slow. We are compelled to counsel patience and persistence. Teachers must be prepared to accept the amount of time it will take for them to feel comfortable in their new roles.

Finally, the reigning values of our society are hardly congenial to the objectives of the Paideia reform. The pay of teachers must become competitive with that of other equally demanding occupations. The professional status of the schoolteacher must be given the respect of the community in the same measure as that given other professions. Above all, money-making and other external indices of social success must become subordinate to the inner attainments of moral and intellectual virtue. The educational revolution that Paideia is trying to promote must be accompanied and supported by revolutions in other institutional aspects of society. For that to occur, ample time must be allowed.

We are thus led to the conclusion that an adequate reform of public education in our school system cannot be accomplished by anything like a quick fix. We suspect that anyone who thinks otherwise cannot fully understand the shape of an adequate reform or all the obstacles to be overcome in achieving it.

A recent U.S. secretary of education is just one among many who suffer the illusion that a desirable reform of our schools can be accomplished in a few years—if only principals and teachers would enthusiastically accept their recommendations and follow them to the letter. That illusion is evidence of the deep chasm that exists between what they think of as desirable reforms and what the Paideia program outlines as a radical reform of basic schooling from kindergarten through grade twelve and a reconstitution of the whole process of teaching and learning

If an adequate educational reform cannot be a quick fix, and if it takes the better part of two generations to achieve it, we cannot avoid the practical questions: that being the case, what should we do? Give up in despair because our hopes cannot be quickly and easily realized?

Or do something even if it consists only in the first steps that must be taken in a long march toward that goal?

Well, suppose we wished to travel to a place that was a hundred miles away. Suppose that terminus was so highly desirable for us that we were unwilling to give it up. And suppose there was no way of getting there except by walking. What should we do? On those assumptions, the only answer is: start walking tomorrow in the right direction, and keep on walking day after day.

What would be the analogy in an educational reform—a first step toward the distant realization of the Paideia ideal? It is something I have called the Wednesday Revolution. It consists in taking three hours from the thirty classroom hours a week at all levels of schooling from the third grade to the twelfth, and in those three hours each week having all or most of the teachers in the school engage in two activities: (1) Socratically conducted seminars, and (2) coaching of reading, writing, and speaking.

An hour and a half approximately should be devoted to each. Whatever else the school is engaged in should be relegated to the other twenty-seven hours. The three-hour Wednesday Revolution may actually occur on Wednesday, but it may take place on any other day of the week.

Where this has been done in schools that have welcomed Paideia, the results have been heartening. The combination of seminars and coaching does more than increase an understanding of basic ideas and issues. It has demonstrable effects on the ability of students to read difficult books; in fact, it is only by struggling with difficult books, books over one's head, that anyone learns to read.

The effects on other intellectual skills—writing, speaking, thinking —are also manifest. Most important of all is the effect on teachers. They find reading the books assigned and conducting the seminar discussions intellectually refreshing and exciting, as compared with the boredom they usually experience with the repetition of the lesson plans that guide their didactic teaching of subject matters.

The Wednesday Revolution is easier to install in the elementary grades from three to eight than it is in the four years of secondary school. That is because of the departmentalization, the specialization, and the electives that dominate the high school scene. Secondary school principals think it impossible to satisfy all their constituents with anything less than a full schedule of thirty hours a week. They do not know how to free up three hours for seminars and coaching—activities that have nothing whatsoever to do with subject-matter instruction.

One suggestion that some of my Paideia associates have made to high school principals was anticipated many years ago in an address I delivered to the National Council of Teachers of English entitled "What Is Basic About English?" It is reprinted in this volume, on pages 151–64. In that address I recommended that teachers in the English departments of our secondary schools should restore the liberal arts of grammar, rhetoric, and logic (which the teaching of English replaced in the secondary curriculum) by devoting half of their teaching time to coaching students in the skills of reading, writing, speaking, and listening. The other half of their teaching time should be devoted to conducting seminars, for these great or important books should be read and discussed in a two-hour session around a seminar table, not in an ordinary classroom.

The books to be read should not be limited to those written in English. This should not become a course in English literature—its novels, plays, lyrics, and essays. Instead it should be devoted to the great works of history, biography, philosophy, theology, natural science, social science, and mathematics, as well as the great works of fiction in the whole tradition of Western literature—in English translation, of course. Its aim should not be a survey of Western civilization, but an effort to understand the basic ideas and issues in Western thought.

Every seminar should involve at its conclusion the assignment of a short composition in which students would attempt to state how their understanding of the book discussed in the seminar was increased by their participation in the discussion. That composition should be corrected and rewritten until it is well done.

This is the primary job that should be done by English teachers in our high schools. If it were done and if high school principals could also persuade some of their history and their social science teachers to join in this effort with their English teachers, at least in the seminar part of it, that would be the way to initiate the most important part of the Paideia reform in our secondary schools, as the Wednesday Revolution is the way to do the same thing in our elementary schools, from the third to the eighth grade.

The Wednesday Revolution is only a first step in the right direction. But if taken, and if, as the wedge of the Paideia reform, it has the effect of making the principal and teachers of a school, and also its students, parents, and school board, more receptive to other aspects of the complete Paideia program, then the ultimate consummation, though it may still be far off, will tend to become a more and more practicable ideal rather than what it is for most people now—a utopian dream.

It is not only a practicable ideal, it is a practical necessity. In the middle of the last century, when a constitutional democracy in this country was still a hundred years away, Horace Mann wrote:

The establishment of a republican government without well-appointed and efficient means for the universal education of the people is the most rash and foolhardy experiment ever tried by man.

How much truer that statement is today when we now have universal suffrage! Not only the prosperity of our high-tech economy but, even more so, the well-being of our political democracy depends upon the reconstitution of our schools.

Our schools are not turning out young people prepared for the high office and the duties of citizenship in a democratic republic. Our political institutions cannot thrive, they may not even survive, if we do not produce a greater number of thinking citizens, from whom some statesmen of the type we had in the eighteenth century might eventually emerge. We are, indeed, a nation at risk, and nothing but radical reform of our schools can save us from impending disaster.

Whatever the price we must pay in money and effort to do this, the price we will pay for not doing it will be much greater.

Great Books, Past and Present

1. A Liberal Education for Adults

The great books movement aims in the direction of universalizing liberal education for adults—making it as commonplace as schooling for children and youth, and extending it, as far as the franchise goes, to all citizens. The success achieved so far may be a source of satisfaction, but more than that it gives confidence to the hope that in the years to come those reading and discussing great books in community groups will be numbered in the hundred thousands and even millions.

The great books, however, have been the subject of much educational controversy in recent years; and almost in proportion as they have increasingly taken hold, both in our colleges and in adult education, they have also been attacked or at least disapproved. It is to be expected that such rejections should occur along with their widespread acceptance.

To review the basic idea behind the great books movement, I turn to our critics for help, ignoring that part of the educational controversy which concerns the place of the great books in a college curriculum. Much discussion, however, is relevant to the great books as a means of liberal education for adult men and women.

Friendly criticism can be and has been helpful, but unfortunately most of the published attacks have not been of that sort. They give us little or no help. This does not mean that the great books program cannot be amended or improved. It means only that our most vocal critics have not understood well enough what we are doing to have found the real difficulties or flaws. I think we can do a better job of criticizing ourselves. We can make a better estimate of the difficulties to be overcome. We can qualify our aims so that they have a better chance of fulfillment.

Most of the criticisms which have been expressed represent misunderstandings. They do not create genuine issues between us and our would-be opponents. They accuse us for the most part of making claims for the great books that we do not make; they impute to us theories we do not hold; they attribute to us aims we do not have or goals we do not seek.

The fault may be ours for not having made ourselves clear; but quite apart from whose fault it is that so much of the criticism of the great books is based on misinformation and misunderstanding, the fact remains that almost all the attacks knock down straw men. We stand by untouched, ready to admit that our critics are quite right in attacking the picture of the great books movement that they have in their heads. But it is in their heads, not in reality. If anyone in reality misused or abused the great books in the ways mentioned by our critics, I think most of us would join them in a vigorous attack on such educational tomfoolery.

Let me illustrate the lack of real issues between our opponents and us by stating what would be very real issues, indeed, if anyone—they or we—were to make certain extreme statements.

For example, if we were to say that the great books are the *only* books worth reading by adults, or if they were to say that the great books are not worth reading *at all*, then there would be a genuine opposition of minds. But no one, at least no one to my knowledge, has ever said anything so preposterous.

Or if they were to say that the great books can make no contribution at all to the continuing development of the adult mind, or if we were to say that nothing but the reading and discussion of the great books is required to give the adult a complete and rounded education, then again a real issue would be joined. But again no one seems to hold such extreme views.

Or if we were to say that engaging in the great books program by itself makes good men and good citizens, or if they were to say that the great books program has no bearing at all on the development of good men and good citizens, then once more we and our opponents would confront one another in flat contradiction. But neither we nor they say any such thing.

Finally, to take one more example, if they were to say that it is enough for a man to know the facts of life and current events or, if ideas and theories are important, the ones currently discussed will suffice; or if we were to say that no knowledge of current events or information about matters of fact is necessary and that the only ideas or theories worth paying attention to are those considered in the past, then another clear conflict would exist. But neither they nor we have ever talked such nonsense.

Since none of these issues exists—because no one has ever asserted any of these quite false notions which, if ever uttered, it would be necessary for all men of sound sense to join in denying—what is all the shouting about? What are the actual complaints or criticisms, and what is our answer to them?

I do not pretend to give an exhaustive enumeration of them, but what I shall offer seems to me truly representative of the adverse opinions which have been publicly expressed. Most of these are easy to answer, because for the most part we need do little more than agree with our opponents, while at the same time calling their attention to the fact that it is not us they are attacking but a bogey man of their own creation. In only a few cases, as we shall see, is there a genuinely relevant point to consider and something positive to say in reply.

Objection: It has been said that the books to be read are chosen in an authoritarian manner and that it is undemocratic for people to have to submit to book lists made for them by their betters.

Reply: If this were true, it would be a telling point. But of all the book lists ever made, the list of the great books results from the most democratic or popular method of selection. Neither we nor anybody else can make a book great by calling it one. We did not choose them. The great books were chosen by the largest reading audience of all times, as well as by a consensus of expert opinion.

A best-seller is a best-seller, not by authoritarian judgment, but by popular consent. So the fact that certain books have interested a vast multitude of men through the centuries is one of the signs that they are great books. It is not the only sign, but it is that mark of a great book which shows it to be not the choice of a special elite, but the choice of mankind generally.

Those of us who have compiled great books lists have simply recorded the prevailing judgment of the many and the wise. Ten percent of any great books list may involve questionable choices, in the sense that in this area there may be a reasonable difference of opinion concerning whether a certain book should or should not be included. But this margin of error is hardly damning nor does it defeat the purpose of the program.

Objection: It is said that the list of great books from which our reading courses are constructed is defective in two particular respects; first, in the omission of the best contemporary books; and second, in the omission of the great works of oriental thought and culture.

Reply: As a matter of fact, both charges are absolutely correct; but as a matter of principle, we think that good reasons can be given for these two omissions.

We omit contemporary books from our reading lists because it is almost impossible to judge whether a contemporary book is a great book. The tests of time cannot be applied, nor do we have sufficient perspective. This does not mean that some contemporary books will not some day become great books; not does it mean that the best of contemporary books are not eminently worth reading. The persons who engage in the reading and discussion of the great books are not precluded thereby from doing other reading. In fact, many of them do. They naturally tend to combine their reading of the great books with the reading of good current books. But since we are concerned with the contribution which the great books can make to our lives, we think it wise to restrict our list to those books that are unquestionably great.

As for the omission of oriental literature, the answer is simply that it is a difficult enough task for us to understand the roots and sources of our own civilization. Only after we are very well grounded in the basic elements of our own culture can we safely embark on the effort to understand cultures and traditions that must necessarily be quite foreign to us.

Objection: It has been said that the great books program deals only with "old books," that it encourages going back to the past, that it cultivates an interest in the dead and done with rather than in the living present.

Reply: While it is true that, with few exceptions, no books by contemporary or living authors are included, it is definitely not true that the great books program deals only with "old books." The fact is that more than half of all the authors read lived and wrote in the last three hundred years—the period we call "modern times"—and that all the reading courses come down to authors who have only recently died, and to books which are exercising an immediate influence on contemporary thought. Furthermore, the reason why we have steadfastly avoided the use of the word "classics" and have insisted instead upon "great books" is that the word "classics" usually connotes a reverence for antiquity for its own sake. But we are not interested in any of these books as antiquarians.

Like our opponents, we disapprove of those who seek to dwell in the past in order to escape from the pressing realities of the present. Our interest in the great books goes no further than the contribution they can make to understanding and meeting present problems. That they can make a great contribution, even though most of them were written from two to twenty centuries ago, simply means that many, if not all, of our fundamental problems today have always been the problems confronting men in the realms of thought or action.

Objection: It has been said that no one is competent to deal with the crucial problems of our own times until he has familiarized himself with the best current thinking on current problems. In the same general vein, it has been said that it is necessary to come to grips with the challenge of real life; that it is necessary to be well informed about current events, and to become intimately and directly acquainted with the present-day scene.

Reply: With all of this we agree. No one of sound mind could say anything to the contrary.

You cannot have ham and eggs unless you have some ham and unless you have some eggs. You cannot think as well as possible about the problems of the present unless you have *both of two things:* on the one hand, whatever the past can contribute by the best thinking it has been able to do about its problems, which are either identical with our problems or very closely similar; on the other hand, as great a familiarity with the present scene as can be obtained from direct experience and from the reading of other materials than the great books.

Objection: It has been said that the great books represent a single philosophy which is dogmatically imposed upon the students in great books groups, to the exclusion of alternative views and without facing the issues between opposing views.

Reply: Anyone who has read the great books knows that there is no philosophical position, religious doctrine, moral belief, or social theory stated in them which is not also contradicted in them. For every view that the mind of man has taken on any fundamental problem, the great books contain, not one, but many opposite views. It would be strange, therefore, for anyone who wished to impose a single philosophy or point of view upon the human mind to recommend the reading of the great books.

It may be said that dogmatism or the imposition of a single line of opinion is achieved by the way the great books discussions are conducted. But again it is strange that the great books classes should be conducted by the method of discussion, consisting largely in the exchange of opinions and in the criticism of any opinion that is proposed, whether by the leaders or the members of the class. It would be so much easier to impose a dogmatically held doctrine by the lecture method. In fact that is the way it is usually done, not by the Socratic method of teaching. So much so is this the case that another group of our opponents think that the method of the great books discussion group is *too dialectical*—too open-minded to a variety of opposite opinions —and they favor lectures rather than discussions.

Those who have one particular doctrine which they would like to see propagated fear that the great books discussion groups tend toward a kind of shallow eclecticism—the mere play of opinion rather than the pursuit of the truth. Those who espouse no doctrine at all, except perhaps the doctrine that no doctrine should be espoused, fear that great books discussion groups may try to discover the truth by a dialectical process of dealing with and clarifying opinions.

Both fears are justified; but the fact that the great books program is criticized from these opposite extremes is some evidence of the fact that it tries to hold the middle ground between dogmatism and sophistry.

Objection: It has been said that in the tradition of the great books, there is not only much truth but much error, and that the present generation must be safeguarded against adopting false values or attitudes from the past.

Reply: We agree completely. Since almost every position taken in the great books is also contradicted in the great books, the great books necessarily contain as much falsity as they contain truth. Our task in reading and discussing them must, therefore, be to judge for ourselves where the truth lies and by the development of our critical faculties to make up our own minds on most basic questions. That is the aim of the great books discussion groups. That is the principal point which dictates the method by which they are conducted. We also think that if the reading and discussion of the great books develops a critical faculty, it should be exercised not only on the great books themselves, but on other things, especially contemporary books, political speeches, newspapers, and magazines. It is just as important for us to be critical of all the errors and false values in contemporary thought as of the mistakes and illusions of the past. The reading and discussion of the great books is intended to serve both these purposes at once.

Objection: It has been said that the great books courses at their best constitute only a minimum program of liberal education for adults, and that much more than this should be done to give adults a rounded education in the years after school.

Reply: We agree with this. At University College of the University of Chicago we offer courses of study which involve much more, and therefore take much more time, than the great books reading groups do.

There can be no issue here about minimum and maximum for we have never claimed that the great books program was a complete curriculum of liberal education. Many of the things our opponents would like to see added to round it out, we would like to see added for any adult who had enough time to give to his continuing education.

But most adults have very little time to give, over and above the demands which work, family, and civic responsibilities make upon them. Hence it is reasonable to propose an essential or indispensable minimum of liberal education which they should undertake in the course of every passing year. We do claim that the reading and discussion of the great books constitutes that minimum; and we claim that this minimum is indispensable, though not sufficient, for any adult whose mind is to grow and develop with the years. We are even tempted to claim—and here some of our opponents may wish to disagree—that no alternative program of adult education can succeed as well in providing the indispensable minimum.

Objection: It has been said that, for whatever values there may be in the study of great books, there are other and better ways of studying them than in the manner proposed by the Great Books Foundation or the University of Chicago. For example, in distinction from the Chicago Plan, it has been proposed that only twenty or twenty-five great books be read in a four-year course of study beginning with the ancients and coming down to the moderns, that these books be read as complete wholes, and that they be very carefully examined by all the techniques of textual commentary and criticism.

Reply: This plan of study should certainly be tried once more, and perhaps those who try it may succeed better than we did when we first organized the study of the great books precisely in that way. We gave it up because we found by experiment that it did not work. We found, again by experiment, that adults need to be introduced to the whole tradition of Western culture before they can profit from a more extensive study of any of its parts. That is why we try in the first six or seven years of the great books program to cover a great many books and authors, even though we do not read all the books through as wholes, and even though we know that our reading and discussion even of the parts is quite superficial. Moving over the surface should precede plumbing the depths at any point.

The selection we have chosen for the first six years of great books readings, the way the readings are organized in each year, and the way the successive years are related to one another, all these things are calculated gradually to open up the whole field of human learning for the beginning reader.

On one point, however, we differ sharply from the critics who propose a four-year course of study of the great books. Our first six years of readings is only a beginning; and there is no end. We propose that adults shall continue to read the great books throughout their lives. After they have covered the surface in the first six to ten years, they will be able in the next ten or twenty to profit from reading a smaller and smaller number of books and reading them much more intensively —not only as wholes, but with concentration on the interpretation and criticism of the text.

Objection: It is said that the proponents of the great books program claim for their program that it is either the best or the only way to educate adults liberally. This claim is denied, and it is held, on the contrary, that other programs and methods are either better or just as good.

Reply: Here we strike what, among all the claims and counterclaims so far considered, may be the first real issue; for we *do* claim that the great books program is the ideal minimum for adult liberal education, aimed not at one year, or at four, but at a lifetime of study.

Our contention that the great books program is the ideal minimum—the best or the only one—may seem to be so extreme as to deserve vigorous contradiction. Nevertheless, as I shall try to show, we are here making a very moderate claim and one which, it seems to me, can be reasonably defended.

To answer this last objection I shall, therefore, try to state as briefly as possible the claims we make for the great books program. I cannot believe that there will be much disagreement with this statement from anyone who has the decency to pay attention to it before trying to dispute or refute it. But if there is, then we may find some real issues instead of the false ones based on misinformation about, or misunderstanding of, the great books program.

For a program of adult education which consists in the reading and discussion of the great books, we claim simply that it is good for the mind.

It is good for the mind in a number of ways. It requires the individual to develop certain basic intellectual skills. Since we are interested not merely in reading the great books but in reading them well, we are concerned with the art of reading. Since we are interested not merely in discussing the great books, but in talking to one another intelligently and intelligibly about the great ideas, problems, and subject matters they consider, we are concerned with skill in communication.

Over and above the development of these arts or skills, the great books program is good for the mind by increasing the individual's opportunity for gaining insight, understanding, and perhaps ultimately a little wisdom. *We cannot promise any of these things.* We do not claim to be able *to give* individuals such extraordinary gifts as insight, understanding, and wisdom. The most we can say—and this is a great deal—is that the reading and discussion of the great books provides conditions favorable for the acquisition of these mental qualities.

The great books contain the best materials on which the human mind can work in order to gain insight, understanding, and wisdom. But they are not a pumping station. The individual mind must work, must be active, if it is to keep awake and grow. Insight, understanding, and certainly wisdom are not easily come by. They cannot be achieved in a year or two. One cannot have too much of them.

Hence it is obvious that anyone who is interested in the pursuit of these good things of the mind must be prepared for a lifetime's undertaking; and certainly anyone who wishes to keep his mind awake and growing as long as he is alive must also be willing to keep it active throughout life. Such a long-term undertaking as the pursuit of understanding and wisdom and the continual growth of the mind throughout life requires not only the best materials to stimulate the mind's activity and for the mind to work upon, but also a set of materials which shall be inexhaustible year after year.

Our basic claim is that the great books constitute precisely that set of materials. By everyone's admission they are the repository of whatever insight, understanding, and wisdom Western man has so far accumulated. By everyone's admission they set forth the ideas, the problems, the principles, and subject matters of the arts and sciences, which make our culture what it is. By everyone's admission, they are books which cannot be mastered on the first reading; and anyone who will make the experiment for himself will find that he can return to them again and again with profit—in fact he must do so if he is to learn what they have to teach.

There may be materials to read and discuss, other than the great books and the great ideas, which can provide the individual with an opportunity for gaining insight, understanding, and wisdom, and which can stimulate and profit the mind for a lifetime. But I do not know what they are. Certainly there can be no better books. Apart from books of any sort, experience, acquaintance with the facts of life and active participation in its tasks, are necessary conditions for the vitality and growth of the mind. But except for the rare individual, almost the genius, they are not by themselves sufficient, even as the best reading of the great books is not by itself sufficient.

Our claim, then, for the great books program, conceived as a lifetime undertaking, is that it is the only or certainly the best way for the individual to acquire understanding and wisdom. If there are other ways of doing this, they have yet to be proposed. If when proposed they turn out to be better, then by all means they should be preferred.

Let me try to protect this moderate claim from being misunderstood by mentioning the things we do not claim for the great books program.

We do not claim that the great books provide *all the knowledge that is worth having*. Far from it. I have very carefully avoided the use of the word "knowledge" in referring to the goods of the mind at which the great books program aims. I do not mean that some knowledge, and perhaps very fundamental knowledge, may not be obtained from the great books; but I wish to emphasize the fact that for many special areas of knowledge other books or sources of information may be much more useful, and in many cases indispensable.

We do not claim that the great books will develop all the virtues or excellences of which men are capable, certainly not the moral virtues. A good mind is one thing. A good man and a good citizen is another. But unless having a good mind, having some understanding and wisdom, is a disadvantage to an individual in his efforts to lead a good life, the great books program does not lessen his chances. And if, on the contrary, there is some advantage to a man, both as a citizen and in his private life, to have the best mind of which he is capable, then whatever the great books program can do to improve the mind will certainly help a man in the pursuit of happiness and in the performance of his civic duties.

But we do not claim that the reading and discussion of the great books will necessarily make men better men or better citizens, for we do not claim that they necessarily produce better minds. We have merely said that they provide the best opportunity for the improvement of the mind; and if that opportunity is taken, *and many other factors cooperate*, the result may be a better man and a better citizen.

We do not claim that the great books will save the world, prevent the next war, or avoid atomic suicide. We do not claim that the great books will safeguard democracy from its enemies or guarantee the attainment of social and economic justice. But if democracy requires citizens who are not only free men politically and economically but also citizens who have free minds, then the great books program helps democracy to flourish to whatever extent it is able to cultivate the critical faculties—the ability of the individual to judge all questions on their merit and to exercise an independent judgment. And if our culture or civilization is worth saving from atomic destruction, then it is also worth saving from dissipation and neglect.

A culture can endure and thrive only to the extent that it is possessed by individuals, some of whom may add to it, but all of whom should be the vehicles of passing it on to the next generation. To the extent that the great books constitute the monuments of our culture, the substance of our intellectual tradition, the more individuals who in any degree actually possess some of that culture through the reading and discussion of the great books, the more favorable are the conditions for its transmission and progress.

We have often described the great books as enacting a great conversation through the ages—a conversation about the basic ideas, the fundamental problems, the major subject matters which concern the mind and heart of man. They are the ideas with which any individual must think about his own life and the world in which he lives. They are the problems which any society must face. They are the subject matters which represent the things worth inquiring into and learning about, certainly for anyone who wishes to understand a little about the nature of the world, of society, and of himself.

The reading and discussion of the great books draws the individual into that conversation, and because the other participants in it are the greatest minds of all time, there is a good chance for most of us that we can profit by association with our betters. But in addition to that profit, there is also the pleasure or delight of being able to talk to one another about the great themes which have always occupied and frequently perplexed the mind of man.

Good conversation is intrinsically enjoyable, and it is an enjoyment which many of us too seldom experience. The pleasure of being understood by others; and of understanding others; the solace which each of us in his loneliness can get from a meeting of minds on common ground; the enrichment of human association by making companionship intellectual as well as emotional—these are some of the promises which I do not think it is too much to make for the great books program.

I would like to add just one more. Adults are related to one another in families as well as in the state and in other organizations or societies. To the extent that the great books program helps to increase the ability of men and women to communicate intelligently and intelligibly with one another, it enriches all forms of association. In the case of the family it may perform a very special service. Here adults are related to children, and as parents have responsibility for their training and development.

The circumstances of modern life have greatly weakened the vitality of the home, and particularly the position of parents in relation to their children. For the most part, they are no longer the symbols of knowledge and wisdom, the sources of guidance and counsel. With the increase of schooling up to the collegiate level, with the intervention of other social agencies in the life of the child, with the general breakdown of discipline and even of good manners, the parent exercises less and less authority over his children and gets less and less respect from them.

The only authority the parent should have is, of course, an authority based upon his greater experience and wisdom. Only such things deserve respect—not sheer age or physical power. I do not claim for the great books program that it can reverse the general tendency of our times toward the dissolution of the family and toward the loss of a proper relationship between parents and children; but I do say that parents who have greater understanding and more wisdom stand a better chance of gaining the respect of their children, as well as of serving them better, than those whose minds actually lag behind their superficially better-educated children.

The boy or girl who has gone through school or even graduated from college has very little understanding and almost no wisdom. At that age, such qualities of mind are not to be expected. They cannot be achieved even by the best schooling in the world. Greater maturity is required for the possession of these things, a maturity involving experience, the shouldering of responsibilities, participation in the tasks of life. Having these advantages of maturity, the parent can profit much more from putting his mind to good use than can his children in school or college. Even if children were to read the great books, that would not enable them to gain the understanding and wisdom which is open to their parents. Hence the great books program may offer an opportunity for parents to improve their own minds in a way which will not only benefit them as adults in an adult world, but as parents in relation to their children.

I have stated as moderately as possible the things we claim for the great books program as a program of adult liberal education to occupy each individual for a lifetime. I have stated as carefully as I know how the things we do not claim, so that there may be an end to criticisms or objections based on misconceptions of what we are seeking to do.

I said at the beginning that we who are involved in this program should be able to state its difficulties or shortcomings better than those who criticize it from the outside, and who unfortunately often do not take the time and trouble to examine the facts. I should like now, in conclusion, briefly to indicate some of these difficulties.

First, the success of the great books program depends upon the voluntary cooperation of the individuals who engage in it. The great books cannot make them think. Thinking is hard. It is probably one of the most painful things that human beings are ever called upon to do. Since what an individual gets out of reading and discussing the great books necessarily depends on what he puts into it in time and effort, we cannot hope to succeed with all individuals, or to the same degree with all.

Second, the leaders of the great books discussion groups are not, like the authors of the great books, the greatest minds of all times. For the most part, they are ordinary men and women who have volunteered to take the responsibility of helping their fellow men do what they themselves regard as worth doing.

They serve the program well to the extent that they themselves teach through learning. Their function as teachers, or as we call them "leaders," is not to lecture, not to indoctrinate, not to declare what is right and true, not to impose their own opinions or their own interpretations of the book, not to hand out what they may think is their own superior understanding of an idea or their own superior wisdom about a problem. Rather by asking questions, by examining the answers, by directing the discussion and by keeping the conversation both on the point and moving along, they increase the chances of anyone in the group, including themselves, to improve in the skills of reading and talking and to gain the understanding and wisdom which are the sole aims of the program.

Things being as they are, the leaders may often fail, and they may never succeed to any great extent. Despite all these reservations, I think it remains true that an individual will not only be more likely to read the great books but will also be more likely to read them well, if he undertakes to read them socially, that is, in the company of other individuals with whom he regularly meets for discussion.

Finally, the great books are difficult, not easy, to read. In fact, they are perhaps the most difficult books, in the sense that they are the richest, the most profound. They are not the most difficult in the sense of being the most technical. In that sense textbooks and specialized treatises by professors or scholars are much more difficult.

No one should expect to understand the great books very well on the first reading, nor even, perhaps, fully to master them after many readings. Their difficulty requires them to be read and reread. It requires patience and perseverance. It demands mental effort and may, therefore, cause considerable pain. Like all the other good things of life, what the great books have to offer is hard to get. But the great books are also rewarding, even on the first reading; and they are increasingly profitable as one returns to them again and again.

It is precisely the difficulty of the great books which makes them more readable than other books and more worth reading. It is precisely because they raise problems which they do not finally answer that they can provoke us to think and inquire and discuss. It is precisely because their difficulty challenges our skill in reading that they can help us to improve that skill. It is precisely because they often challenge our accepted prejudices and our established opinions, that they can help us develop our critical faculties.

The difficulty of the great books comes not from the fact that they are poorly written or badly conceived but rather from the fact that they are the clearest and simplest writing about the most difficult themes which confront the human mind. It is precisely because they are difficult in this way that they offer us the opportunity to gain understanding and wisdom.

Understanding and wisdom are not reserved for a chosen few. They can be had in some degree by all men—according to the degree of native talent and in proportion to the effort made by each individual. The difficulty of the great books, therefore, does not limit the program to an intellectual elite, but it does limit it to those men and women who care enough about improving their minds—who want understanding and wisdom badly enough—to be willing to put their minds to work, and who have sense enough to see that mental activity must be sustained through all the years of their life, not just the years spent in school or college, if they are going to keep their minds awake and growing.

2. What Books in Western Civilization Are Great Books, 800 B.C. to A.D. 1900

There have been many definitions offered of the great books, or statements about what constitutes the greatness of a great book. Mark Twain's definition was certainly the wittiest. He said that the great books are the books that everyone wishes he had read but that no one wants to read.

More seriously and recently, Carl Van Doren said the great books are the books that never have to be written again. They did the job they set out to do so perfectly that they cannot be improved upon.

For John Erskine, the relevance of the great books is not limited to the century in which they were written. They are always relevant to whatever century happens to be the present era. Though their relevance today may be different from what it was in earlier centuries, it is as great today. We do not read great books as cultural antiquities or as enduring monuments of the past. We read them for the light they throw on the fundamental ideas that no century has outlived and the perennial issues that no century can avoid.

In 1937, Scott Buchanan defined a great book as one meeting a number of prerequisites, which he enumerated. Probably no book ever written has fully met all these criteria, but the great books come nearer to doing so than any others.

His five criteria were:

1. It is a book that has been read by the largest number of persons . . . that have, over the centuries, had more readers than other books, and that have "stood the test of time."
2. It is a book that has the greatest number of alternative, independent, and consistent interpretations. . . .
3. It raises the persistent unanswerable questions. . . .
4. It must be a work of fine art. . . .
5. It must be a masterpiece of the liberal arts.

To these demanding criteria for selecting great books I would like to add my own.

First of all, they must be eminently discussable books by virtue of the fact that they deal in a variety of ways with basic ideas and issues. This excludes all textbooks, which are totally undiscussable; and all books that convey information but little knowledge; and even those books that contain a body of organized knowledge but do not challenge our minds to engage in reflective thought and the search for understanding. This means that a great book must have many passages in it that are substantially relevant to the great ideas and issues in the tradition of Western thought.

Second, unlike most of the books that are published each year, even those worth reading once (which is usually less than 2 percent of the total number published), the great books are not only worth reading more than once, but must be read many times to be fully understood, if fullness of understanding can ever be achieved in the case of the greatest of the great books. The greatest of them are inexhaustible. They are always over our heads no matter how many times we have read them, and so they always deserve rereading to lift our heads up to a higher level of understanding.

When the reading of great books is begun by children in the early grades, the books chosen for them should be books that are over their heads, considering their age. As they go on, the great books selected for them should become more and more difficult—always over their heads so that they are challenged to reach higher.

Third, in all fields other than imaginative literature, a great book must be written by a generalist, whether or not the author is also a specialist in some particular field, and it must be written for the curious, intelligent layman, not for the specialist author's peers—other specialists in his field. It is this criterion that makes it so difficult to find great books written in the twentieth century, written after the Second World War, when specialization became so intense in all fields of science and scholarship. Before the twentieth century, with few exceptions—mainly German—the great books were not written by university professors with academic reputations to enhance.

A fourth criterion has already been indicated: that great books are to be drawn from all types of imaginative and narrative literature and from all areas of human learning. They are not to be limited to great epics, novels, or plays.

Finally, there is the negative restriction that the influence of authors is *not* a basis for including what they have written if that does not consist in a great book by the foregoing criteria. This excludes many authors who have not written great books but who have exerted great influence upon Western thought and culture. It should, perhaps, be added, for the benefit of those engaged in the current academic controversies about "great books," that the fact that, in the Western tradition until the nineteenth century, there simply were no great books written by women, blacks, or non-Europeans, does not make those that were written by white males in earlier centuries any less great.

With these criteria or prerequisites to guide the process of selection, I offer the reader a list of great authors from Homer in antiquity down to William James, Ibsen, and Freud at the end of the nineteenth century, giving in each case one or more titles of works written by them.

The list that follows is compiled from the array of great authors and books appended to the two editions of *How to Read a Book* and from other sources. Only a small number of these *completely fulfill* the criteria for judging a book as truly great. Many more than half are at best only approximations, in various degrees, of the criteria stated above.

    1. Homer (9th? century B.C.)
      Iliad
      Odyssey

2. The Old Testament
3. Aeschylus (ca. 525–456 B.C.)
    Tragedies
4. Sophocles (ca. 495–406 B.C.)
    Tragedies
5. Herodotus (ca. 484–425 B.C.)
    History (of the Persian Wars)
6. Euripides (ca. 485–406 B.C.)
    Tragedies
    (esp. *Medea, Hippolytus, The Bacchae*)
7. Thucydides (ca. 460–400 B.C.)
    History of the Peloponnesian War
8. Hippocrates (ca. 460–377? B.C.)
    Medical writings
9. Aristophanes (ca. 448–380 B.C.)
    Comedies
    (esp. *The Clouds, The Birds, The Frogs*)
10. Plato (ca. 427–347 B.C.)
    Dialogues
    (esp. *The Republic, Symposium, Phaedo, Meno, Apology, Phaedrus, Protagoras, Gorgias, Sophist, Theaetetus*)
11. Aristotle (384–322 B.C.)
    Works
    (esp. *Organon, Physics, Metaphysics, On the Soul, Nicomachean Ethics, Politics, Rhetoric, Poetics*)
12. Epicurus (ca. 341–270 B.C.)
    Letter to Herodotus
    Letter to Menoeceus
13. Euclid (fl. ca. 300 B.C.)
    Elements (of geometry)
14. Archimedes (ca. 287–212 B.C.)
    Works
    (esp. *On the Equilibrium of Planes, On Floating Bodies, The Sand-Reckoner*)
15. Apollonius of Perga (fl. ca. 240 B.C.)
    On Conic Sections
16. Cicero (106–43 B.C.)
    Works
    (esp. *Orations, On Friendship, On Old Age*)

17. Lucretius (ca. 95–55 B.C.)
    On the Nature of Things
18. Virgil (70–19 B.C.)
    Works
19. Plutarch (ca. 45–120)
    Lives of the Noble Grecians and Romans, Moralia
20. Tacitus (ca. 55–117)
    Histories
    Annals
    Agricola
    Germania
21. Nicomachus of Gerasa (fl. ca. A.D. 100)
    Introduction to Arithmetic
22. Epictetus (ca. 60–120)
    Discourses
    Encheiridion (Handbook)
23. Ptolemy (ca. 100–178, fl. 127–151)
    Almagest
24. Marcus Aurelius (121–180)
    Meditations
25. Galen (ca. 130–200)
    On the Natural Faculties
26. The New Testament
27. St. Augustine (354–430)
    Works
    (esp. *On the Teacher, Confessions, The City of God, On Christian Doctrine*)
28. St. Thomas Aquinas (ca. 1225–1274)
    Summa Theologica
29. Dante Alighieri (1265–1321)
    Works
    (esp. *The New Life, On Monarchy, The Divine Comedy*)
30. Geoffrey Chaucer (ca. 1340–1400)
    Works
    (esp. *Troilus and Criseyde, Canterbury Tales*)
31. Niccolò Machiavelli (1469–1527)
    The Prince
    Discourses on the First Ten Books of Livy

32. Desiderius Erasmus (ca. 1466–1536)
    The Praise of Folly
33. Nicolaus Copernicus (1473–1543)
    On the Revolutions of the Heavenly Bodies
34. Sir Thomas More (ca. 1478–1535)
    Utopia
35. Martin Luther (1483–1546)
    Three Treatises
    Table-Talk
36. François Rabelais (ca. 1495–1553)
    Gargantua and Pantagruel
37. John Calvin (1509–1564)
    Institutes of the Christian Religion
38. Michel de Montaigne (1533–1592)
    Essays
39. William Gilbert (1540–1603)
    On the Loadstone and Magnetic Bodies
40. Miguel de Cervantes (1547–1616)
    Don Quixote
41. Francis Bacon (1561–1626)
    Essays
    The Advancement of Learning
    Novum Organum
    New Atlantis
42. William Shakespeare (1564–1616)
    Works
43. Galileo Galilei (1564–1642)
    The Starry Messenger
    Dialogues Concerning Two New Sciences
44. Johannes Kepler (1571–1630)
    Epitome of Copernican Astronomy
    Concerning the Harmonies of the World
45. William Harvey (1578–1657)
    On the Motion of the Heart and Blood in Animals
    On the Circulation of the Blood
    On the Generation of Animals
46. Thomas Hobbes (1588–1679)
    Leviathan

58. Jonathan Swift (1667–1745)
    A Tale of a Tub
    Journal to Stella
    Gulliver's Travels
    A Modest Proposal
59. William Congreve (1670–1729)
    The Way of the World
60. George Berkeley (1685–1753)
    The Principles of Human Knowledge
61. Charles de Secondat, Baron de Montesquieu (1689–1755)
    Persian Letters
    The Spirit of Laws
62. Voltaire (1694–1778)
    Letters on the English
    Candide
    Micromégas
63. Henry Fielding (1707–1754)
    Joseph Andrews
    Tom Jones
64. Samuel Johnson (1709–1784)
    The Vanity of Human Wishes
    Rasselas
    The Lives of the Poets
65. David Hume (1711–1776)
    A Treatise of Human Nature
    Essays, Moral and Political
    An Enquiry Concerning Human Understanding
66. Jean-Jacques Rousseau (1712–1778)
    On the Origin of Inequality
    On Political Economy
    Émile
    The Social Contract
67. Laurence Sterne (1713–1768)
    Tristram Shandy
    A Sentimental Journey Through France and Italy
68. Adam Smith (1723–1790)
    The Theory of the Moral Sentiments
    Inquiry into the Nature and Causes of the Wealth of Nations

69. Immanuel Kant (1724–1804)
    The Critique of Pure Reason
    Fundamental Principles of the Metaphysic of Morals
    The Critique of Practical Reason
    The Science of Right
    The Critique of Judgement
    On Perpetual Peace
70. Edward Gibbon (1737–1794)
    The Decline and Fall of the Roman Empire
    Autobiography
71. James Boswell (1740–1795)
    Journals
    The Life of Samuel Johnson, LL.D.
72. Antoine Laurent Lavoisier (1743–1794)
    Elements of Chemistry
73. John Jay (1745–1829), James Madison (1751–1836), and Alexander
    Hamilton (1757–1804)
    The Federalist Papers
    (together with the Articles of Confederation, the Constitution
    of the United States, and the Declaration of Independence)
74. Johann Wolfgang von Goethe (1749–1832)
    Faust
    Poetry and Truth
75. John Dalton (1766–1844)
    A New System of Chemical Philosophy
76. Georg Wilhelm Friedrich Hegel (1770–1831)
    The Phenomenology of Spirit
    The Philosophy of Right
    Lectures on the Philosophy of History
77. Jane Austen (1775–1817)
    Pride and Prejudice
    Emma
78. Karl von Clausewitz (1780–1831)
    On War
79. Stendhal (1783–1842)
    The Red and the Black
    The Charterhouse of Parma
    On Love

80. Arthur Schopenhauer (1788–1860)
    The World as Will and Idea
    On the Fourfold Root of the Principle of Sufficient Reason
81. Michael Faraday (1791–1867)
    Experimental Researches in Electricity
82. Charles Lyell (1797–1875)
    Principles of Geology
83. Auguste Comte (1798–1857)
    The Positive Philosophy
84. Honoré de Balzac (1799–1850)
    Le Père Goriot
    Eugénie Grandet
85. Alexis de Tocqueville (1805–1873)
    Democracy in America
86. John Stuart Mill (1806–1873)
    On Liberty
    Representative Government
    Utilitarianism
    Principles of Political Economy
    The Subjection of Women
    Autobiography
87. Charles Darwin (1809–1882)
    Origin of Species
    The Descent of Man
88. Charles Dickens (1812–1870)
    Works
    (esp. *Pickwick Papers, David Copperfield, Bleak House, Little Dorrit*)
89. Claude Bernard (1813–1878)
    An Introduction to the Study of Experimental Medicine
90. Søren Kierkegaard (1813–1855)
    Either/Or
    Fear and Trembling
    The Sickness Unto Death
    The Concluding Unscientific Postscript
91. Karl Marx (1818–1883)
    Capital
    (together with the *Communist Manifesto*)

104. David Hilbert (1862–1914)
  The Foundations of Geometry

3. 1900 to the Present

As we move into the fourth quarter of the twentieth century, it seems fitting to ask ourselves about books of lasting humanistic significance that have left their mark on the development of thought and culture in the first half of this century.

The term "great books" should not be a stumbling block. We used that term rather than the word "classics," for the latter has the unfortunate connotation of an enduring cultural monument rather than a perennially contemporary work. If we say that a good book is a book that is worth reading carefully once, and that a better book than that —a great book—is one that is worth reading carefully a second or third time, then the greatest books are those worth reading over and over again—endlessly. The last 2,500 years of Western civilization have produced few books that can measure up to that standard. I cannot think of more than fifteen at the most.

But that is too high a standard for judging the major contributions or seminal works of the twentieth century. It would require us to assess them as having the perennial humanistic significance of the writings of Homer, Plato, Aristotle, Dante, Montaigne, Shakespeare, Goethe, and Kant. Let us instead ask ourselves what twentieth-century authors and works we would nominate as joining the larger company of important books of lasting significance, even if they are not inexhaustibly rereadable.

I acknowledge the cultural parochialism of confining ourselves to Western culture in drawing up a list of nominees. No one has yet compiled a list of the world's great books, adequately representing its five or six major cultural streams; nor has anyone yet tried to determine the books that would belong to the common cultural heritage of mankind when those five or six cultural streams become confluent to constitute a unified world cultural community. So, for the moment at least, let us limit ourselves to asking about the significant contributions to Western culture made during this century.

It is also necessary to recognize that this century is not yet completed, and that its first eighty-eight years are far from being homogeneous or all of one piece. As one considers the contributions to literature since

1900, to philosophy, science, and history, one becomes acutely aware that the century breaks sharply into two culturally heterogeneous periods—the first being the period from 1900 until the end of World War II; the second being the period between 1945 and the present. Whether the years from 1989 until the dawn of the twenty-first century will be homogeneous with the second of these periods or will constitute a differing third segment, is anybody's guess. When I come to nominating my own candidates for selection as outstanding twentieth-century works, it will become immediately obvious that it is much easier for me to name authors and works from the first than from the second period. That may be due in part to the fact that we are further removed from them in time and so have a better perspective on them; but I also tend to think that there is another reason for it.

The major works that appeared between 1900 and 1945 were written by authors whose own education and cultural inspiration still drew heavily on the literary and intellectual achievements of the nineteenth century. Consequently, the important books of this first period are much more akin in their general character to the outstanding works of the preceding century. That is not as true of the authors and works since 1945. In fact, the difficulty in suggesting as many names and titles for this second period may be due not only to its recency, as compared with the first period, but also to the basic cultural rift between the first and the second period, resulting in a radical change in the criteria for judging what is of lasting humanistic significance.

For another thing, while the production of major works in literature and in philosophy has the same general character during the first period of the twentieth century that it had in the nineteenth century, a remarkable change seems to have occurred in the natural and social sciences. The great scientific contributions have tended to take the form of highly technical and specialized monographs not intended for the average, curious, intelligent layman. Lavoisier's *Elements of Chemistry*, Faraday's *Experimental Researches in Electricity*, Darwin's *Origin of Species* and his *Descent of Man* can be read by the nonspecialist layman with pleasure and profit. There are few, if any, works in the natural sciences of that character in the twentieth century; nor are there many in the behavioral sciences comparable to William James's *Principles of Psychology* and Freud's *General Introduction to Psychoanalysis*.

Thus, when we come to name the scientific works of the present century, we must employ an additional criterion over and above that of intrinsic worth. That additional criterion is their intelligibility to and readability by the intelligent but nonspecialist layman.

Finally, one other preliminary consideration deserves attention. It concerns the number of works we might reasonably expect as the products of the twentieth century that will endure because of their lasting humanistic significance. Here we are somewhat helped by the count derived from the preceding twenty-five centuries. We can take *Great Books of the Western World* as providing one fairly good indication of that count. In that set, thirty-eight authors represent the two thousand years or more from Homer to the dawn of modern times, and thirty-six represent the last three hundred years. Of these, twelve belong to the seventeenth century (often called "the century of genius"), thirteen to the eighteenth century, and eleven to the nineteenth century. In view of the fact that many more books have been written and published in the twentieth century than in all preceding centuries put together, one might expect that, out of such a vast production, there would be more eminent and outstanding works in this century than in any preceding one.

In considering the candidates to be nominated, let us, therefore, aim at selecting at least twenty authors from the twentieth century. However, in doing so, let us remember that the names we are considering are drawn only from the first forty-five years since 1900. We must leave room for the last forty-three years or so; to do that, we should perhaps limit ourselves to selecting not more than fifteen from those nominated.

Having laid down these conditions, I am willing to stick my neck out by nominating the authors and works from which a selection should be made. I hasten to confess that my nominations are likely to be biased by the fact that I am myself a product of the first period of the twentieth century and that my own intellectual and cultural formation probably has more affinities with the nineteenth century than it does with the currents of thought and the winds of doctrine that have been prevalent since the end of World War II. Nevertheless, for whatever it is worth, here are my candidates, proceeding from easy to hard: that is, naming, first, authors and works from the period between 1900 and 1945, and, second, authors and works since 1945; also in each of the two periods, naming, first, the outstanding contributions to literature (plays, novels, and poems), then, outstanding contributions to philosophy and theology, and finally, outstanding contributions in the field of the natural and the social or behavioral sciences and in the field of history.

FROM 1900 TO 1945

Literature (plays, novels and poems)

GEORGE BERNARD SHAW
>   *Man and Superman*
>   *Major Barbara*
>   *Heartbreak House*
>   *Saint Joan*

JAMES JOYCE
>   *Portrait of the Artist as a Young Man*
>   *Ulysses*

MARCEL PROUST
>   *Remembrance of Things Past*

THOMAS MANN
>   *The Magic Mountain*
>   *Joseph and His Brothers*

JOSEPH CONRAD
>   *Nostromo*
>   "The Secret Sharer"
>   *Heart of Darkness*

WILLIAM FAULKNER
>   *Sartoris*
>   *The Sound and the Fury*
>   *Light in August*

D. H. LAWRENCE
>   *Sons and Lovers*
>   *Women in Love*

T. S. ELIOT
>   *Murder in the Cathedral*
>   *The Cocktail Party*
>   *The Wasteland*

FRANZ KAFKA
>   *The Trial*
>   *The Castle*

Natural Science

MAX PLANCK

Where Is Science Going?
The Philosophy of Physics
Scientific Autobiography

ALBERT EINSTEIN

Sidelights on Relativity
The Meaning of Relativity
The Method of Theoretical Physics

NIELS BOHR

Atomic Physics and Human Knowledge

ERWIN SCHRÖDINGER

What Is Life?

JOSEPH H. WOODGER

Biological Principles

JULES-HENRI POINCARÉ

Science and Hypothesis

THEODOSIUS DOBZHANSKY

Genetics and the Origin of Species

Social or Behavioral Science and History

GEORGES SOREL

Reflections on Violence

LEON TROTSKY

The History of the Russian Revolution

NICOLAI LENIN

The State and Revolution

WILLIAM SUMNER

Folkways

MAX WEBER

Essays in Sociology

R. H. TAWNEY

The Acquisitive Society

THORSTEIN VEBLEN

The Theory of the Leisure Class

JOHN MAYNARD KEYNES

The General Theory of Employment, Interest, and Money

So much for the first period of the twentieth century. Before I turn
to the second period perhaps I should report my list of also-rans, from

1900 to 1945. They include: Henri Bergson (*Creative Evolution; The Two Sources of Morality and Religion*); André Malraux (*Man's Fate; Man's Hope*); André Gide (*The Counterfeiters*); Heinrich Böll (*The Clown*); Ernest Hemingway (*The Sun Also Rises; The Old Man and the Sea; For Whom the Bell Tolls*); Virginia Woolf (*Mrs. Dalloway*); Reinhold Niebuhr (*The Nature and Destiny of Man*); Michael Rostovtzeff (*The Social and Economic History of the Roman Empire*); Karl Polanyi (*The Great Transformation*).

Now let us consider the much sparser list of names and works drawn from the second period of the twentieth century—from 1945 to the present.

FROM 1945 TO THE PRESENT

Literature (plays, novels, poems)

ALBERT CAMUS
   The Plague
   The Fall
   The Stranger

GEORGE ORWELL
   Animal Farm

THOMAS PYNCHON
   Gravity's Rainbow

ALEXANDER SOLZHENITSYN
   Cancer Ward
   The First Circle

SAUL BELLOW
   Mr. Sammler's Planet
   Herzog

SAMUEL BECKETT
   Waiting for Godot
   Endgame

Philosophy, Theology, and Religion

LUDWIG WITTGENSTEIN
   Philosophical Investigations

MARTIN HEIDEGGER
   Being and Time

MARTIN BUBER
  I and Thou

Natural Science
WERNER HEISENBERG
  Philosophical Problems of Nuclear Science
  Physics and Philosophy
  Physics and Beyond
JACQUES MONOD
  Chance and Necessity
RICHARD PHILLIPS FEYNMAN
  Q.E.D.
STEPHEN HAWKING
  A Brief History of Time

Social or Behavioral Science and History
ARNOLD TOYNBEE
  A Study of History
  Civilization on Trial
TEILHARD DE CHARDIN
  The Phenomenon of Man
CLAUDE LÉVI-STRAUSS
  The Savage Mind
  The Raw and the Cooked
FERNAND BRAUDEL
  On History
  Civilization and Capitalism
E. LE ROY LADURIE
  The Territory of the Historian

My nominations of authors and titles from 1945 to the present seem to me woefully inadequate. Could it be that my nineteenth-century mentality enables me to discern appraisingly the literary and intellectual productions of the first forty-five years of this century while, at the same time, blinding me to the merit of works that represent the artistic and intellectual culture of the last forty or so years, with which obviously I am not as much in sympathy? If that is the case, as I suspect, then I need help from others, especially from those younger than I who are more in tune with turns of mind and imagination that have dominated the more recent period.

NOTES

Tradition and Progress in Education

1. See *What Man Has Made of Man* (New York, 1937). Reviews by Hook in *The Nation*, Ayres in *The New Republic*, Leighton in *The Christian Century*, etc., indicate not only the failure of communication but also the reasons for it. I have discussed these reasons in a recent monograph on *St. Thomas and the Gentiles* (Milwaukee, 1938).

2. See J. Maritain, *Theonas* (New York, 1933), chaps. 7–11.

3. To say that human nature is constant, that man's *specific* nature remains the same through the generations, is not to deny the kind of variations within the human group which are rightly called *individual* differences. There are, of course, definite limits even to this individual variability. There is relative constancy in the range of these differences and an invariance in their distribution, from generation to generation.

4. See *What Man Has Made of Man*, lect. 1, notes 6, 7, 16a, 47.

5. "The safest general characterization of the European philosophical tradition is that it consists of a series of footnotes to Plato" (*Process and Reality* [New York, 1929], p. 63).

6. New York, 1937. See especially chaps. 4, 8, 11, 12.

7. "To expatiate upon the importance of thought would be absurd. The traditional definition of man as 'the thinking animal' fixes thought as the essential difference between man and the brutes—surely an important matter" (Dewey, *How We Think*, 1st ed. [1910], p. 14). Cf. ibid., 2nd ed. (1953), p. 17: "We all acknowledge, in words at least, that ability to think is highly important; it is regarded as the distinguishing power that marks man off from other animals."

8. See *The Higher Learning in America* (New Haven, 1936). For a description of what is going on at St. John's, see the program bulletin, obtainable from the college upon request.

9. When neither the teacher nor the student is a liberal artist, trained in the art of giving or receiving communication critically, teaching must degenerate into *indoctrination* in that vicious sense in which the student is a sponge passively absorbing doctrines which, however true or excellent they may be in themselves, cannot be more than prejudices or opinions as they are received.

Two Essays on Docility

1. St. Thomas does not discuss docility in connection with the life of learning and as a companion virtue to *studiositas*. He considers it *only* as an integral part of prudence, as a willingness to take counsel concerning practical matters. "In matters of prudence, man stands in very great need of being taught by others, especially by old folk who have acquired a sane understanding of the ends in practical matters" (S.T., II-II, 49, 3). And he goes on to say: "Even the learned should be docile in some respects, since no man is altogether self-sufficient in matters of prudence" (ibid., *Reply to Objection* 3). I am

here considering docility differently, not as a part of prudence, but as a virtue indispensable in the theoretic life. I have generalized St. Thomas's conception of docility as "readiness to be taught" *anything*. St. Thomas agrees with an objection which says "docility is requisite for every intellectual virtue," though he maintains in opposition that "it belongs chiefly to prudence." On this point, I side with the objector, distinguishing two meanings of docility. Docility toward counsel in practical matters belongs chiefly to prudence. But the docility requisite for every intellectual virtue, docility in the life of learning, is a moral virtue which seems to me most properly associated with justice. The only other alternative is that there is a kind of "artistic prudence" needed for the exercise of the liberal arts, and that docility in theoretic matters is a part thereof.

INDEX

353

natural, 177
Nock's theory of, 130
organized, 78
in philosophy, 204–208
philosophy of, 56–58
problems of, 40–41, 115, 139
professional, 106
public, 121–27
reforming, 311–27
religious, 177
scheme of, 183
beyond schooling, 210–24
self-education, 136
society and, 79
specialized, 95
views of, 234
vocational, 95–96, 105–106, 216–17,
    287
Educational objectives, xxxi
Educational principles, 57
Educational system, 76
Elective courses, 145
Elementary education, 77–78
Eliot, Charles William, 124–25
Elitism, xiv, 280
Encyclopaedia Britannica, xvii
English, schooling in, 150–64
English departments, 151
Entertainment vs. education, 236
Equality, 129
    philosophical doctrine of, 130
Erskine, John, xiv, 161, 332
Eternal happiness, 252
Ethical happiness, 85, 243–44
Ethics, xxix–xxx, 240
    noncognitive, 255
    views on, 265–74
    youth and, 246
Examinations
    oral, 112, 146, 174
    written, 146
Excellence, 102
Exegesis, 206
Exercise, 97
Expository method, 190
Extremism, 66

Facts, 226
Faith, 52
Fallacies in reasoning, 63–64
False liberalism, 47–52
Fascism, 19–20, 44
Fatigue, 99
Formal lectures, 146, 307–308
Fortune and virtue, 246–47
Free time, 97
Freedom, 50
    idea of, 230
Friendship, 252

Garden of Eden, 100
General education, 95
General liberal schooling, 141–42
Global civilization, xxxii–xxxiii
God, 252
Good
    defined, 241
    senses of word, 258
Good habits, 60–61
Goodlad, John, 173
Goods, 85–86
    consumable, 99–100
    economic, 86
    intellectual, 110
    political, 86
    social, 86
Government, 43
    idea of, 277
Graduates, high school, 148
Grammar, 153, 154, 157–58
    kinds of, 156
    separating logic and, 158–62
Great books, xvi, xix–xxxiii, 75, 147,
    162–63, 223
    800 B.C. to A.D. 1900, 332–43
    1900 to present, 343–50
    1945 to present, 349–50
    defined, 195, 333
    "junior," xxx
    past and present, 318–50
    teachers and, 201–203
Great books educational program, xix–xx
Great Books Foundation, xxi, xxii, 304